NASA Monographs in
Systems and Software Engineering

The **NASA Monographs in Systems and Software Engineering** series addresses cutting-edge and groundbreaking research in the fields of systems and software engineering. This includes in-depth descriptions of technologies currently being applied, as well as research areas of likely applicability to future NASA missions. Emphasis is placed on relevance to NASA missions and projects.

Christopher A. Rouff, Michael Hinchey,
James Rash, Walter Truszkowski, and
Diana Gordon-Spears (Eds)

Agent Technology from a Formal Perspective

With 83 Figures

 Springer

Christopher A. Rouff, PhD, MS, BA
Science Applications International Corporation, USA

Michael Hinchey, PhD, MSc, BSc, CMath, CEng, CPEng, CITP, FBCS, FIEE, FIMA,
   FIEAust, SMIEEE
James Rash, MA, BA
Walter Truszkowski, MA, BA
NASA Goddard Space Flight Center, USA

Diana Gordon-Spears, PhD
Computer Science Department, University of Wyoming, USA

Series Editor
Professor Michael Hinchey

British Library Cataloguing in Publication Data
Agent technology from a formal perspective. — (NASA
   monographs in systems and software engineering)
   1. Intelligent agents (Computer software)   2. Intelligent
   agents (Computer software) — Design
   I. Rouff, Chris, 1960–   II. Hinchey, Michael G. (Michael
   Gerard), 1969–
   006.3

NASA Monographs in Systems and Software Engineering ISSN 1860-0131
ISBN-13: 978-1-84996-969-7
e-ISBN-13: 978-1-84628-271-3

Printed on acid-free paper.

Printed in the United States of America.   (SBA)

9 8 7 6 5 4 3 2 1

Springer Science+Business Media
springeronline.com

Preface

During the last several years, the field of agent and multi-agent systems has experienced tremendous growth, i.e., the topic has gained unprecedented popularity. Meanwhile, the field of formal methods has also blossomed and has proven its importance in substantial industrial and government applications. Thus, in 2000 it was quite timely to pursue a workshop to merge the concerns of the two fields. The need for such a workshop was particularly compelling given the growing concerns of agent-based systems users that their systems should be accompanied by behavioral assurances. The Formal Approaches to Agent-Based Systems (FAABS'00) workshop was the first step in trying to address this need. The overwhelming response to FAABS'00 motivated subsequent FAABS ('02 and '04) workshops, as well as this book, which is designed to provide a more in-depth treatment of the topic.

This book is organized into four parts. Part I provides introductory background material on the two central topics of the book, namely, agents and formal methods.

Chapter 1, by Truszkowski, is an overview of agents. The chapter begins by introducing the basic concept of an agent from a very simple, abstract perspective. It then gradually refines this notion into a detailed agent architecture, using the Goddard agent architecture as an example model. First, the major architectural components (e.g., percepts, effectors, communications, reasoning, planning, execution) are defined and described. Then, agent behaviors are defined and related to the architectural components that generate them. The chapter concludes with an intriguing discussion of multi-agent communities.

Chapter 2, by Hinchey et al., provides an introduction to formal methods, and, in particular, formal methods for agent-based systems. A definition of the term "formal methods" is presented along with overview of the field of formal methods, as well as examples of several formal methods and how they have been used. It begins by describing different classes of formal specification languages and provides an overview of modelling systems and tools. Next, technology transfer and research issues are discussed, describing some of the hurdles that have prevented formal methods from being more fully utilized in industry. The chapter then discusses formal methods that have been used on, or are good candidates for use on, agent-based systems. The chapter concludes with sources of information on formal methods, a list of important terms that are used in the formal methods community, and a wide range of references to related formal methods work.

Chapter 3, by Luck and d'Inverno, gives an introduction to formally specifying agent-based systems. Specifically, it provides a conceptual framework for modeling, analyzing, implementing, and deploying multi-agent systems. The formal specification language used for modeling, Z, facilitates the transition to implementation. The power of this framework is demonstrated in the context of a paradigm consisting of agents that are autonomous (i.e., generate their own goals and motivations), and in which sociological behavior occurs as a result of enabling agents to discover, evaluate, and revise theories about their environment and the other agents within it.

Part II, on formal methods in agent design, focuses on using formal methods to facilitate the task of transitioning from the conceptualization of an agent-based system to its implementation. The organization of this part progresses from more conventional to less conventional techniques.

Chapter 4, by Esterline et al., describes the PI-calculus process algebra for modeling multi-agent systems in which the emphasis is on communication. In this framework, agents are considered to be processes, and the modeling of communication protocols is straightforward. The effectiveness of such an approach is demonstrated by modeling the NASA LOGOS multi-agent system. LOGOS is a prototype automated grounds operation center for flight control, which is described in greater detail in Chapter 10 of this book. The latter portion of Chapter 4 describes the applicability of process algebraic models to multi-agent systems in which one or more agents are human. The agent architecture is assumed to be BDI, and the viewpoint adopted is that of the intentional stance. Again, the emphasis is on communication—in this case, mixed-initiative.

In Chapter 5, Fisher et al. present METATEM, one of the few high-level agent-based programming languages. METATEM is an executable formal specification, based on linear temporal and modal logic. Furthermore, it allows resource-bounded reasoning about belief contexts (e.g., agent A believes that agent B believes that z will eventually occur). Using broadcast message communication, concurrent METATEM can be used for asynchronous executing agents to dynamically form a team to achieve a joint goal.

Part II concludes with Chapter 6. In this chapter, Whittle and Schumann present a method for using "scenarios" as a basis for (semi)automatically synthesizing and explaining agent-based systems. Scenarios are execution traces of interactions between a system's components or its users. The chapter's primary focus is on forward engineering, i.e., using the scenarios for system design. Agent-based systems are represented as statecharts, which are a generalization of finite-state machines that includes models of hierarchy and concurrency. A secondary focus of this chapter is on reverse engineering of agent communication protocols. This novel application of the synthesis algorithm enables (semi)automatic construction of an explanatory model from cryptic code via traces of the code's execution.

Part III is about formal agent verification and re-design. As in Part II, the organization of this section progresses from more conventional to less conventional techniques. The verification techniques include theorem proving, model checking, and average case analyses.

Part III begins with Chapter 7, by Hustadt et al. Research on practical proof methods for expressive theories of rational agency has been sparse. This chapter helps to fill this gap by focusing on how to apply formal verification, in particular, theorem proving, within the exceptionally expressive KARO agent framework. Two proof methods are presented in this chapter. The first consists of translating KARO modal formulae to first-order logic and then using conventional first-order theorem proving techniques. This translation morphism has the advantage of being an elegant treatment of the informational component of KARO. The second method first translates the dynamic component of KARO into a branching time temporal logic, but leaves the epistemic component unchanged. Then, clausal resolution-based theorem proving is applied to the branching time temporal logic. An advantage of this latter method is its potential to provide a complete calculus for the dynamic component of KARO.

Chapter 8, by Spears, addresses the issue of formally verifying multiagent systems in which the agents can adapt. Agent plans/strategies are represented with finite-state automata, and they are adapted using evolutionary learning. Verification is performed using model checking. Two approaches are presented for behavioral assurance following adaptation. The first consists of a priori results that certain learning operators are guaranteed to be property-preserving. For these operators, no reverification is needed. Second, incremental reverification algorithms are presented, along with time complexity results demonstrating that they can produce substantial speedups over nonincremental reverification (i.e., reapplication of traditional model checking).

In the concluding chapter of Part III, Chapter 9, Menzies and Hu present a nonstandard formal analysis that makes a nondeterminism assumption. Given a group of agents working in a highly dynamic environment, it is important to verify whether their behavior is correct, despite "wild" influences (e.g., random perturbations). Menzies and Hu address this issue by defending two claims. The first claim is that in the average case, it is possible to learn effective and efficient control strategies despite the wild variables. Using an average case analysis involving the combinatorics of possible worlds of belief, Menzies and Hu present a case that supports the first claim, e.g., they show that in most circumstances only a small number of different behaviors are possible, despite the wild inputs. Their second claim is that it is possible to redesign particular devices in order to increase their immunity to wild variables. This second claim is supported by a sensitivity analysis.

Part IV, on significant applications, presents two substantial and exciting NASA applications. The chapters in this section demonstrate the power of using formal methods for agent-based systems for solving important, real-world problems.

Chapter 10, by Rouff et al., describes a successful NASA Goddard Space Flight Center (GSFC) application of formal methods to a multi-agent system called "Lights-Out Ground Operations Systems" (LOGOS). In LOGOS, a community of software agents cooperates to perform satellite ground system operations normally done by human operators. Due to the asynchronous, parallel nature of both the agents and their communications, debugging LOGOS using traditional techniques is difficult or impossible. On the other hand, by specifying LOGOS within the Communicating Sequential Processes (CSP) formalism, the GSFC team has found debugging to be straightforward. The effectiveness of this formal specification is demonstrated in the context of errors involving race conditions.

In Chapter 11, Pecheur et al. present two important applications of formal verification to Livingstone, a model-based health monitoring and diagnosis system developed at NASA Ames. Prior to verification, an automatic translation method, described in the chapter, converts Livingstone models into specifications that can be verified with the Carnegie Mellon SMV model checker. Symbolic model checking is then performed with SMV. As a last step, diagnostic error traces are converted from SMV back to Livingstone. The two applications that are explored are the use of Livingstone for an In-Situ Propellant Production (ISPP) plant, a system intended to produce spacecraft propellant using the Martian atmosphere, and the Remote Agent architecture on the Deep Space One spacecraft. In both cases, application of the verification methodology described in the chapter resulted in identification of modeling errors. This proves the effectiveness of verification for highly complex real-world applications.

Finally, Appendix A discusses a linear time algorithm for walking and-or graphs that was referenced in Chapter 9.

The objective of this book is to provide an in-depth view of some of the key issues related to agent technology from a formal perspective. However, since this is a relatively new interdisciplinary field, there is enormous room for further growth. We hope that this book will not only create an initial foundation for some of the key issues, but will also point out many of the gaps in the field, thus indicating open problems to be addressed by future researchers and students.

Christopher A. Rouff
Michael Hinchey
James Rash
Walter Truszkowski
Diana F. Spears

Acknowledgements

Chapter 1 – The author wishes to thank James Rash, Tom Grubb, Troy Ames, Carl Hostetter, Jeff Hosler, Matt Brandt (all at Goddard), Chris Rouff (SAIC), Dave Kocur, Kevinb Stewart, Dave Zoch (all formerly of Lockheed-Martin), Jay Karlin (Viable Systems, Inc.), and Victoria Yoon (UMBC). These very talented people are or have been members of the Goddard Agent Group and have made major contributions to the Goddard agent technology program. A special thanks is due to James Rash, who provided a critical review of this chapter.

This chapter is based on work sponsored by the NASA Office of Aerospace Technology and the Advanced Architectures and Automation Branch at NASA Goddard Space Flight Center.

Chapter 2 – The section on formal methods for agent-based systems was based on work supported by the NASA Office of Safety and Mission Assurance (OSMA) Software Assurance Research Program (SARP) and managed by the NASA Independent Verification and Validation (IV&V) Facility.

Chapter 3 – The authors are especially grateful to the three anonymous reviewers of this paper whose many corrections and suggestions for improvement have been included.

Chapter 4 – This research was supported by Grant NAG 5-4102, "Formal Foundations of Agents," from NASA Goddard Space Flight Center and by Grant NAG 2-1213, "Motion Planning in a Society of Mobile Intelligent Agents," from NASA Ames Research Center. Special thanks are due to the Goddard personnel, especially Walter Truszkowski. Thanks are also due to Oliver Hinds, Department of Computer Science, North Carolina A&T State University, for help with LaTeX.

Chapter 6 – This work was supported by the NASA Grant 749–10–11, Thinking Systems/Program Synthesis. We also want to thank the anonymous referees for their helpful suggestions.

Chapter 7 – This research was supported by a grant of the Netherlands Organization for Scientific Research (NWO) and the British Council under the UK–Dutch Joint Scientific Research Programme JRP 442, and EPSRC Grant GR/M88761.

Chapter 8 – This research was supported by ONR Contract N0001499-WR20010 and performed while the author was employed at the Naval Research Laboratory. The author is grateful to the anonymous reviewers for their helpful comments and especially grateful to Bill Spears for numerous constructive suggestions. The presentation of this material was improved enormously thanks to Bill's advice.

The figures and tables in this chapter are reprinted from an earlier article entitled "Asimovian adaptive agents," in the *Journal of Artificial Intelligence Research*, Volume 13, copyright 2000, pages 95–153, with permission from the publisher Elsevier.

Chapter 10 – The authors would like to thank the LOGOS development team for helping us to understand the inner workings of LOGOS. The development team includes Tom Grubb, Troy Ames, Carl Hostetter, Jeff Hosler, Matt Brandt, Dave Kocur, Kevin Stewart, Jay Karlin, Victoria Yoon, Chariya Peterson, and Dave Zock, who are or have been members of the Goddard Agent Group.

This chapter is based on work sponsored by the NASA Office of Aerospace Technology and the Advanced Architectures and Automation Branch at NASA Goddard Space Flight Center.

The editors would also like to thank Adriane Donkers for her many hours of work converting figures to native LaTeX, work on the bibliographies, the index, and editing of the manuscript.

Contents

List of Contributors

Jonathan P. Bowen
Business, Computing and
 Information Management
London South Bank University
London, UK
jonathan.bowen@lsbu.ac.uk

Mark d'Inverno
Cavendish School of
 Computer Science
University of Westminster
London, UK
dinverm@wmin.ac.uk

Clare Dixon
Department of Computer Science
University of Liverpool
Liverpool, UK
C.Dixon@csc.liv.ac.uk

Peter Engrand
NASA/KSC
Kennedy Space Center, FL, USA
peter.engrand-1@ksc.nasa.gov

Albert Esterline
Department of Computer Science
North Carolina A&T
State University
Greensboro, NC, USA
esterlin@ncat.edu

Michael Fisher
Department of Computer Science
University of Liverpool
Liverpool, UK
M.Fisher@csc.liv.ac.uk

Chiara Ghidini
Automated Reasoning
Systems Division
ITC-IRST
Povo, Trento, Italy
ghidini@itc.it

Michael Hinchey
Goddard Space Flight Center
NASA
Greenbelt, MD, USA
Mike.Hinchey@gsfc.nasa.gov

Abdollah Homaifar
Department of Electrical
 Engineering/NASA ACEIT
North Carolina A&T
State University
Greensboro, NC, USA
homaifar@ncat.edu

Ying Hu
Department of Electrical and
 Computer Engineering
University of British Columbia
Vancouver, BC, Canada
huying_ca@yahoo.com

Ullrich Hustadt
Department of Computer Science
University of Liverpool
Liverpool, UK
U.Hustadt@csc.liv.ac.uk

Antony Kakoudakis
Sapient Limited
London, UK
Akakoudakis@sapient.com

Michael Luck
Department of Electronics and
  Computer Science
University of Southampton
Southampton, UK
mml@ecs.soton.ac.uk

Tim Menzies
Department of Computer Science
Portland State University
Portland, OR, USA
tim@menzies.us

John-Jules Charles Meyer
Institute of Information and
  Computing Sciences
Utrecht University
Utrecht, The Netherlands
jj@cs.uu.nl

Charles Pecheur
Department of Computing Science
  and Engineering
Université Catholique de Louvain
Louvain-la-Neuve, Belgium
pecheur@info.ucl.ac.be

James Rash
Goddard Space Flight Center
NASA
Greenbelt, MD, USA
James.Rash@gsfc.nasa.gov

Toinette Rorie
Lucent Technologies
Cary, NC, USA
rorie@lucent.com

Christopher A. Rouff
Intelligent Systems Division
SAIC
McLean, VA, USA
rouffc@saic.com

Renate A. Schmidt
School of Computer Science
University of Manchester
Manchester, UK
Renate.Schmidt@manchester.ac.u

Johann Schumann
RIACS/NASA Ames
Moffett Field, CA, USA
schumann@email.arc.nasa.gov

Reid Simmons
School of Computer Science
Carnegie Mellon University
Pittsburgh, PA, USA
reids@cs.cmu.edu

Diana F. Spears
Computer Science Department
University of Wyoming
Laramie, WY, USA
dspears@cs.uwyo.edu

Walt Truszkowski
Goddard Space Flight Center
NASA
Greenbelt, MD, USA
Walt.F.Truszkowski@nasa.gov

Wiebe van der Hoek
Department of Computer Science
University of Liverpool
Liverpool, UK
wiebe@csc.liv.ac.uk

Jon Whittle
QSS/NASA Ames
Moffett Field, CA, USA
jonathw@email.arc.nasa.gov

Part I

Background

1

What Is an Agent?
And What Is an Agent Community?

Walter F. Truszkowski

1.1 Introduction

This chapter provides a brief, intuitive introduction to the concept of "agent" as it is used in the artificial intelligence community. There have been many attempts to define the term "agent." One needs only to look at the burgeoning agent literature to see the variety of definitions from which to choose. Some authors rely on the reader's intuition and bypass the definition process altogether. Some authors feel strongly that the concept of agent cannot be completely defined at all. The reader is directed to the selected references [1-5] for more formal definitions of the terms "agent" and "multi-agent systems."

In this chapter we take a somewhat constructionist approach to the definition. We postulate a functional architecture (leaving out implementation details that may vary from implementation to implementation), discuss the major components of the architecture, build up an incremental understanding of the dynamic behaviors of the components, and finally arrive at an understanding of the higher-level behavioral dynamics of the agent resulting from the proper composition of the constituent components. A few comments about agent communities ensues.

We first consider the concept of "agent" from a fairly abstract point-of-view. We then proceed by considering a complete agent architecture and begin to look at the individual pieces (components) that compose it. This architecture was developed by the agent-group at the Goddard Space Flight Center as a centerpiece for some of its initial research in applied agent technology. The application domain was ground-based and space-based satellite operations. The examples that will be cited will reflect this domain of interest.

1.2 The Abstract Agent

Let us begin with a very abstract view of the agent concept. Consider Figure 1.1.

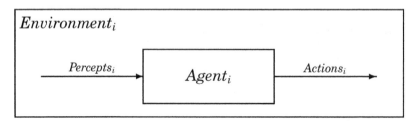

Fig. 1.1. Abstract view of an agent.

An agent exists in an environment and, in some cases, may itself be considered to be a contributing part of the environment. Generally speaking, the environment is the aggregate of surrounding things, conditions, or influences with which the agent is interacting. Data/information is "sensed" by the agent. This data/information is typically called "percepts". The agent operates on the percepts in some fashion and generates "actions" that could affect the environment. This general flow of activities, i.e., sensing the environment, processing the sensed data/information and generating actions that can affect the environment, characterizes the general behavior of all agents.

Every agent has the basic structure as shown in figure 1.2.

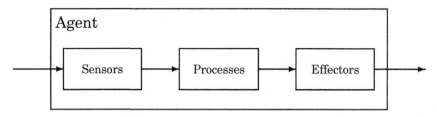

Fig. 1.2. Basic structure of an agent.

Sensors are the agent's means of probing the environment in which it exists and interacting with the environment for the purpose of gaining data/information about the state of the environment. The agent may have several differing sensors, each capable of different environmental observations and receiving different types of data/information from the environment. As noted above, the data/information accessed by the agent are commonly called percepts. Sensors may be considered to be environmental probes.

"Processes" refers to the systematic handling of the percepts that the agent receives from the environment. It is in the function of processing of the percepts that the "intelligence" of the agent usually resides. The spectrum of possible degrees of intelligence for agents is quite broad. An agent may act in a stimulus-response mode, automatically performing some activity. This is the type of behavior normally associated with simple expert systems that may be considered as simple agents. Other levels of processing may require more deliberation. Accessing environmental models and self models, utilizing these models in understanding the percepts, utilizing planning and scheduling processes in the development of appropriate reactions to the percepts, verifying and executing of plans, re-planning as required, monitoring of plan execution and updating of environmental and self models are all components of the reasoning processes that are associated with more complex, more "intelligent" agents.

"Effectors" refers to the mechanisms used by the agent to carry out the results of the "Processes" handling of the percepts received by the agent. The Effectors are the agent's means of directly interfacing with and influencing the environment.

1.3 The Goddard Agent Architecture Overview

In this section we introduce the agent architecture that will be the basis for the detailed discussion of the agent concept in this chapter. The Goddard agent architecture is a highly component-based (modular) architecture. Before we look closely at the components in our agent architecture we will briefly consider "What is a component?".

A component is a software module that performs a defined task. Components, when combined with other software components, can constitute a more robust piece of software that is easily maintained and upgraded. Components interact with one another through various communication mechanisms. Each component in our agent architecture can communicate information to/from all other components as needed through, for example, a publish/subscribe communication mechanism. Components may be implemented with a degree of intelligence through the addition of, for example, reasoning and learning functions. The use of components is intended to facilitate maintaining and upgrading agent systems.

A component needs to implement certain interfaces and embody certain properties. In our case, components must implement functionality to publish information and subscribe to information, and must be able to accept queries for information from other components or objects. In order to function properly, components need to keep a status of their state, know what types of information they possess, and know what types of information they need from external components and objects.

Components can communicate through different mechanisms. Components can communicate by sending messages in some language, by calling methods of other components, by using TCP/IP socket communication, by using a blackboard communications model, or by using a publish and subscribe model. Our initial investigations favored the publish/subscribe approach.

The use of components gives a great deal of flexibility to the designer of agents. A simple agent can be designed using a minimum number of simple components that would receive percepts from the environment and react to those percepts. A robust agent may be designed to use many components that allow the agent to do what a simple agent does and, in addition, reason, plan, schedule, model the environment, and learn. The following architecture (Figure 1.3) focuses on an agent that is on the highly robust side of the scale; it contains components for reasoning, modeling, and planning. These components give the agent a higher degree of intelligence when interacting with its environment, i.e., they allow the agent to interact with its environment in a smarter fashion.

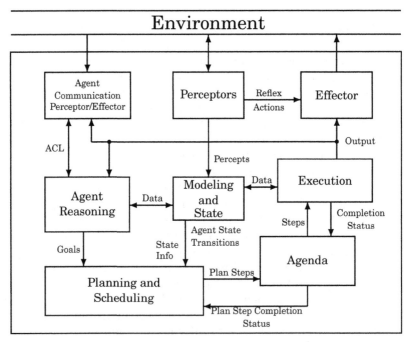

Fig. 1.3. A robust agent with planning, modeling, and reasoning capabilities.

Here is a brief overview of the architecture. The Perceptor component receives percepts through sensors and communication with external software/systems and agents. These percepts are passed from the perceptor to the Modeling and State component where a model's state is updated as needed. A special perceptor (the Agent Communication Perceptor/Effector) sends messages to and receives messages from other agents. Incoming Agent Communication Language (ACL) messages are formatted and passed to the Agent Reasoning component. The Agent Reasoning component reasons with respect to received ACL messages, knowledge that it contains, and information that is acquired from the Modeling and State component to formulate goals for the agent when necessary. Goals are then acquired by the Planning component along with state and state transition information. The Planning component formulates a plan for the agent to achieve the desired goals. When a plan has been developed, the Agenda keeps track of the execution of the plan's steps. Steps are marked when they are ready for execution and the completion status of each step is also tracked by the Agenda. The Execution component manages the execution of steps and determines the success or failure of each step's execution. Output produced during a step's execution can be passed to an Effector or the Reasoning component. State changes will be recorded by the Modeling and State component. When a plan is finished executing, a completion status is passed to the Planning component for evaluation of the plan for future use.

The architecture under discussion incorporates a distributed knowledge-base. Each component that creates or stores a kind of information is responsible for keeping that information current. Distributing responsibility for knowledge is advantageous when compared to a central, shared knowledge-base. With a central, shared knowledge-base, the knowledge-base component needs to understand the content of all data it keeps in order to allow it to update data appropriately and keep data current. Centralizing responsibility for knowledge, on the other hand, results in a complex component that needs to be very intelligent, as well as efficient. By keeping the data distributed to the components that create and store it, the data can be updated more efficiently, accurately, and in an overall simpler fashion. In the architecture under discussion, the Modeling and State component is the closest thing to a centralized knowledge base for the agent.

What follows is a closer look at each component in the agent architecture.

1.3.1 Environment

The Environment is defined as everything that is accessible to the agent but external to the agent itself. The agent may receive percepts from systems, the operating environment, or sensors and, in turn, affect systems or the operating environment. The agent may also communicate with other agents located in its Environment.

In the Goddard domain the Environment consists of a spacecraft and its subsystems/experiments, a communication system for commanding the spacecraft and receiving telemetry from the spacecraft, and a ground system that includes human operators for overall command/control/monitoring of the spacecraft and supporting systems.

1.3.2 Perceptor

The Perceptor component (Figure 1.4) is responsible for monitoring all or parts of the environment for the agent and for acting as an input port for receiving data/information for the agent from the environment. In the above-described overall architecture, any data received by the agent from the environment, other than agent-to-agent messages, enters through Perceptors. An agent may have zero or more Perceptors, where each Perceptor receives data/information from specific parts of the agent's environment. A purely social agent (see Sections 3.6, 3.7) will have zero Perceptors.

Perceptors may be more than just a data/information input mechanism. Perceptors may have varying levels of "intelligence." A Perceptor may just receive data and pass it on to another component in the agent. In this case the filtering and conversion functions act as identity mappings. Or the Perceptor may perform varying levels of filtering/conversion before passing data to another component in the agent. A Perceptor may also act intelligently through the use of reasoning systems if it is desired. The end of this section gives examples.

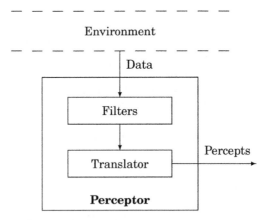

Fig. 1.4. Agent perceptor component.

In the Goddard domain, which is ground-based, and space systems for the command and control of scientific near-Earth satellites, an agent in the ground-based system may receive telemetry for the spacecraft. The spacecraft, in this event, is the environment for the agent. The telemetry may need to be converted from its "raw" form (zeros and ones) to engineering units. This would be the role of the Perceptor's filter and translator. This information can then be used by the Modeling and State component to update its models and knowledge bases (see section 2.6).

The Perceptor can be given the capability to "look at" the incoming telemetry with respect to data limits that are used to determine if a value is in a critical state. It could then immediately inform the Effector to respond with a canned response in reaction to the out-of-limits condition. This capability gives the perceptor some reasoning and decision-making capabilities and would be an example of a simple intelligent perceptor.

1.3.3 Effector

The Effector component (Figure 1.5) is responsible for effecting changes to and/or sending output to the agent's environment. Any agent output data, other than agent-to-agent messages, is handled through Effectors. There may be one or more Effectors, where each Effector sends data/information to specific parts of the agent's environment. An Effector may perform data conversions when necessary and may even act intelligently through the use of reasoning systems if it is desired.

In the Goddard domain, the Effectors could support a range of activities from sending commands to the spacecraft to sending messages to an operator in the control center associated with the spacecraft.

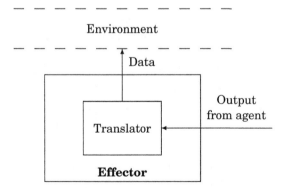

Fig. 1.5. Agent effector component.

The Effector's data usually comes from the Executor component (see architecture figure). However, it could receive data directly from the Perceptor if, for example, the Perceptor is smart enough to detect a highly anomalous situation that requires immediate reaction. This reaction, handled by the Effector, could be an emergency command to the spacecraft and/or an alert to ground-based personnel. The Translator portion of the Effector maps internal agent data into something more understandable by the environment. Translation to an emergency spacecraft command is an example.

1.3.4 Agent-to-Agent Communications (ATAC)

This communications component (Figure 1.6) is designed specifically to support agent-to-agent message passing, thus facilitating the sharing of data/information among agents in the environment. The component takes an agent data object that needs to be transmitted to another agent and converts it to a message format understood by the receiving agent. The message format that is used can be KQML, FIPA, or some other Agent Communication Language (ACL). The message is then transmitted to the appropriate agent through the use of an agent messaging protocol/software. This protocol/messaging software could be simple TCP/IP sockets or other communications software. The reverse process is performed for an incoming agent message.

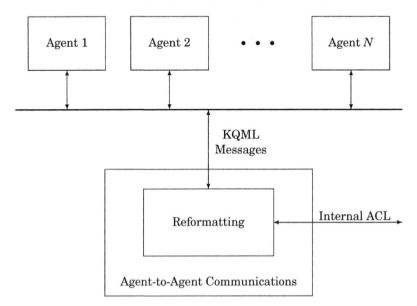

Fig. 1.6. Agent-to-agent communications component.

1.3.5 Agent Reasoning (AR)

The Agent Reasoning component (Figure 1.7) works with information in its local knowledge-base as well as model and state information to make decisions and formulate goals for the agent. This component reasons with state and model data to determine whether any actions need to be performed by the agent to change its state, perform housekeeping tasks, or other general activities. The AR will also interpret and reason with ACL messages that are received by the agent. When action is necessary for the agent, the AR will produce goals for the agent to achieve.

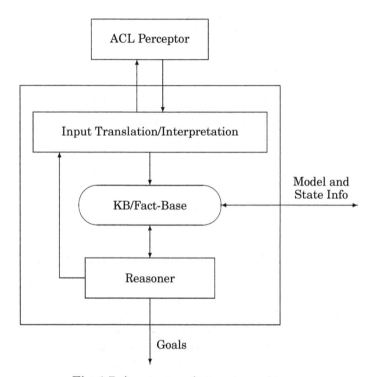

Fig. 1.7. Agent reasoning component.

The diagram shows ACL messages as well as model and state information being input to the component. The component reasons with the input data as well as existing information in its knowledge-base to formulate any goals for the agent.

1.3.6 Modeling and State (M&S)

The Modeling and State component (Figure 1.8) is the model and state manager for the agent. This component manages models of the environment as well as the agent's internal model. The state information associated with each model will be updated as necessary based upon the percepts received by the component. The modeler is also responsible for reasoning with the models to act proactively and reactively with the environment and events that affect the model's state. The M&S component can also handle what-if questions for each model.

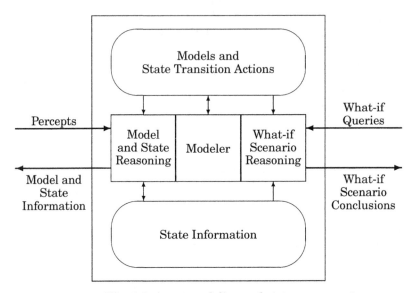

Fig. 1.8. Agent modeling and state component.

The diagram shows percepts entering the component. The state information is updated appropriately based upon the input percepts. Model and state information is then published. The component can be queried for what-if scenario information. The component will reason with state information and models to develop answers for the what-if queries. In the future the component will be able to learn by updating its models based on percepts of changes in the item being modeled.

1.3.7 Planning and Scheduling (P&S)

The Planning and Scheduling component (Figure 1.9) is responsible for any agent-level planning and scheduling. This component is given a goal or set of goals to fulfill. These typically come from the Agent Reasoning component but may be generated by any component in the agent. At the time that the goals are given, a state of the agent, usually the current state, as well as the actions that can be performed are acquired by the P&S component. This information will typically be acquired from the

Modeling and State component. The P&S component then generates a plan as a directed graph of "steps". A step is composed of preconditions to check, the action to perform and the expected results from the action. When each step is created, it is passed to any Domain Expert components for verification of correctness. If a step is deemed incorrect or dangerous, the Domain Expert may provide an alternative step, solution or data to be considered by the P&S.

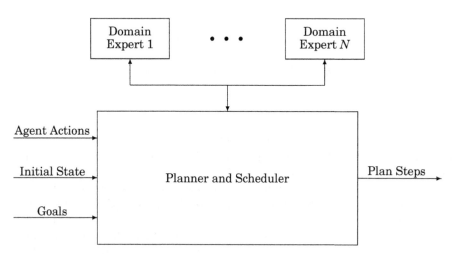

Fig. 1.9. Agent planning and scheduling component.

1.3.8 Agenda

The Agenda component (Figure 1.10) receives a plan from the Planner. It interacts with the Execution component to send the plan's steps in order, for execution. The Agenda keeps track of which steps are finished, idle, or waiting for execution. It will update the status of each step appropriately as the step moves through the execution cycle. The Agenda reports the plan's final completion status to the Planner and Agent Reasoner when the plan is complete.

The possible states of steps on the agenda are:

- Pending—not ready for execution
- Ready—can be sent for execution
- Executing—currently being executed
- Completed Fail—finished executing, failed
- Completed Success—finished executing, success

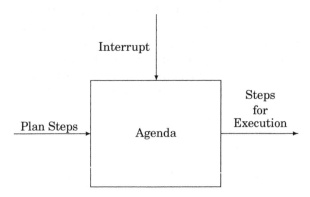

Fig. 1.10. Agent agenda component.

1.3.9 Execution

The Execution component (Figure 1.11) operates by executing the steps of the plan developed by the Planning and Scheduling component and laid out into executable steps by the Agenda component. An executable step contains preconditions, an action and possible post-conditions. If the preconditions are met, the action is executed. When execution is finished, the post-conditions are evaluated, and a completion status is generated for that step. The completion status is returned, which allows for overall plan evaluation. The Execution component will interact with the Agenda in the following way.

The Agenda sends the first step to the Execution component. This wakes the component up. The component then begins executing that step. The component then checks to see whether another step is ready for execution. If not, the component will go back to sleep until it receives another step from the Agenda, once all executing steps are completed.

This completes the intuitive overview of the major components in our sample agent architecture. Next we consider the types of "behaviors" that can be supported by the architecture.

1.4 Agent Behaviors

What is a "behavior"? In our context a behavior is the sequence of actions or steps that are taken in response to some sort of stimulus. In our case this stimulus can be either internal or external to the agent. Though the agent architecture discussed in the previous section is fairly simple, it is capable of supporting several major types of agent behaviors. Basically, agent "behavior" refers to the manner in which an agent responds to some sort of stimulus, either from the environment or from the agent itself.

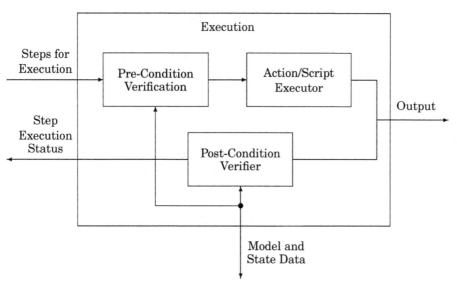

Fig. 1.11. Agent execution component.

Four basic types of behaviors for our agent to realize have been identified. These are:

- Reactive,
- Deliberative,
- Proactive (self-motivating, reflective), and
- Social.

These are further broken down by the source of the stimulus. The current list of behavior types is:

- Reactive—triggered by another agent
- Reactive—triggered by a percept
- Deliberative—triggered by another agent
- Deliberative—triggered by a percept
- Proactive
- Social—triggered by another agent
- Social—triggered by the agent itself

What follows is a brief discussion of the identified agent behavior types. Each type of behavior is illustrated by showing the major agent architecture components involved in realizing the behavior (solid black line) and optional components involved in the behavior (dashed black line). These lines are superimposed over the agent architecture diagram. Not all components are required for all behavioral types.

1.4.1 Reactive—Triggered by another agent

An agent in the environment might trigger a reactive behavior in another agent. This type of behavior involves the Agent Communications Perceptor/Effector, Agent Reasoning, Modeling and State, Execution and Effector components. Once a message is received from another agent, the Reasoning component, informed with information from the Modeling and State component, can decide that a real-time reaction is required. The appropriate reaction is communicated to the Execution component, which then causes the Effector to appropriately act. There is no need for (or usually time for) detailed planning and scheduling. The reaction is "predefined" and stored in the agent's knowledge base for use in circumstances that warrant it.

As depicted in Figure 1.12, the agent may communicate back to the agent originating the reaction to, for example, let that agent know that a message was received and for which an immediate response is being activated.

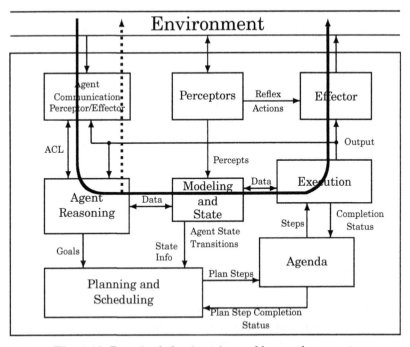

Fig. 1.12. Reactive behavior triggered by another agent.

1.4.2 Reactive—Triggered by a percept

This Reactive type of behavior is triggered by a percept from the environment detected by the agent. The Model component is updated to reflect the percept. The Reasoner is informed of the event and reacts with some pre-defined response that is sent to the Execution component. The Effector carries out the response (Figure 1.13).

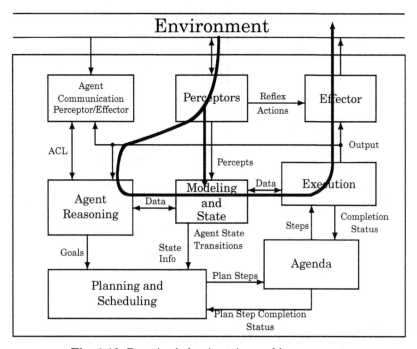

Fig. 1.13. Reactive behavior triggered by a percept.

As in the case with the previous behavior (Reactive - triggered by another agent), this behavior involves the Agent Reasoning, Modeling and State, Execution and Effector components in addition to the Perceptor.

There is a second type of reaction behavior—that pictured in Figure 1.14. In this case the Perceptor acts in a more "intelligent fashion" and is capable of activating a reflex action. The modeler is informed of the percept and the Perceptor immediately informs the Effector of which actions to take. As an example, in our context this is the type of quick response that would be associated with the detection of a critical anomalous situation on-board a spacecraft. Usually this type of anomaly requires immediate action like sending up a command to turn something off or going into a safe-hold mode-of-operation while a more deliberative action is planned.

Note that the Reasoner gets informed of the action through its access to the Modeling and State component.

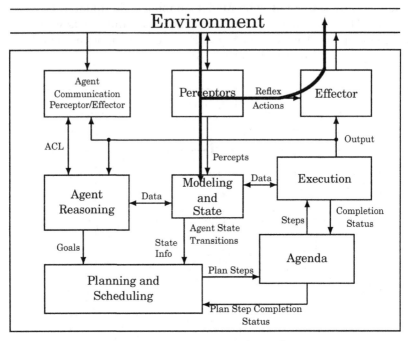

Fig. 1.14. Reactive behavior with a reflex action.

1.4.3 Deliberative—Triggered by another agent

This type of behavior (along with the following) is the most complex type of behavior that the agent architecture can support. All components (except the Perceptor) of the agent architecture are involved in one way or another in realizing this behavior. It is initiated or triggered by a message from another agent in the environment. The Agent Communication Perceptor/Effector is the component used to relay the message to the Reasoner component.

The reception of this message by the Reasoner triggers the most complicated sequence of activities possible for the agent. All components, except the Perceptors, are utilized to some extent (Figure 1.15).

1.4.4 Deliberative—Triggered by a percept

This type of behavior is very similar to the previous behavior—the only difference being the source of the triggering message or event (Figure 1.16).

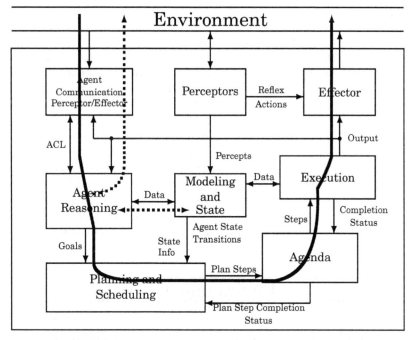

Fig. 1.15. Deliberative behavior triggered by another agent.

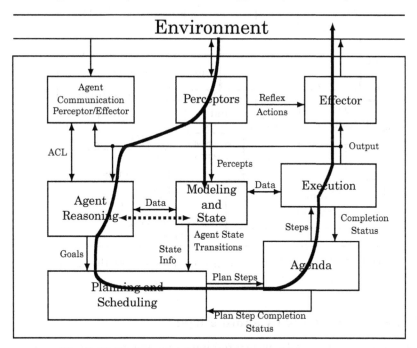

Fig. 1.16. Deliberative behavior triggered by a percept.

1.4.5 Proactive

Proactive behavior originates from within the agent itself. There can be many differing sources of proactive behavior. The Reasoning component of the agent may be "programmed" to go into a reflective mode and evaluate its performance for some time period. It may have an established sequence of high-level goals that causes the Reasoner to track the status of a problem under consideration. Proactive behavior like this might trigger communication with other agents involved in the problem solution.

The agent may have "built-in" goals that periodically trigger the Reasoner to initiate and/or accomplish some task. This type of behavior will most likely lead to a behavior of another type. This type of behavior is stimulated in some way by the agent itself. For our agents there is one type of proactive behavior that will be supported, i.e., self-motivating. Self-motivating behaviors are triggered by built-in or intrinsic goals (Figure 1.17).

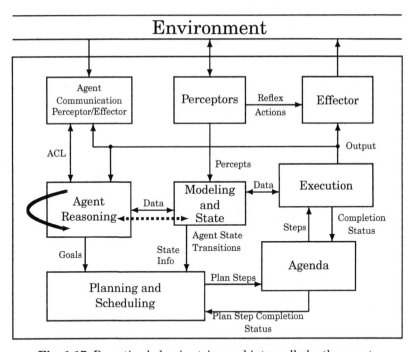

Fig. 1.17. Proactive behavior triggered internally by the agent.

1.4.6 Social—Triggered by another agent

Social behavior is typically associated with one agent dialoging with another. This type of behavior is triggered by another agent in the environment. Figure 1.18 indicates the flow through the agent components that are brought into play by a social behavior triggered by another agent in the environment. The Agent Communications Perceptor and the Reasoner are needed to respond to a message of the type that does not require any sort of reaction or deliberation. Access to the Modeling and State component's information might be required. Knowledge of the agents in the environment along with models of the agents is assumed for this type of behavior as well as the following type of social behavior.

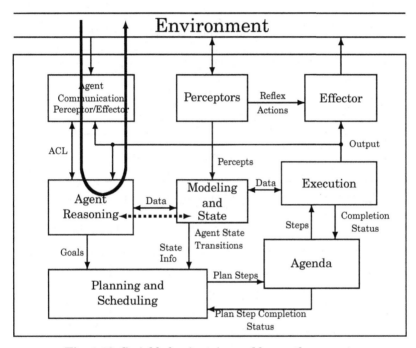

Fig. 1.18. Social behavior triggered by another agent.

1.4.7 Social—Triggered by the agent itself

The motivations for this type of social activity may be a need that cannot be satisfied by the agent itself or an activity triggered by goals built into the agent itself (Figure 1.19). This type of behavior may eventually require access to the Modeling and State component. For accomplishing complex goals, planning information may be required by the Reasoner.

Table 1.1 summarizes the behavior/component relationships. This table clearly indicates that both the Reasoner and the Modeler are involved

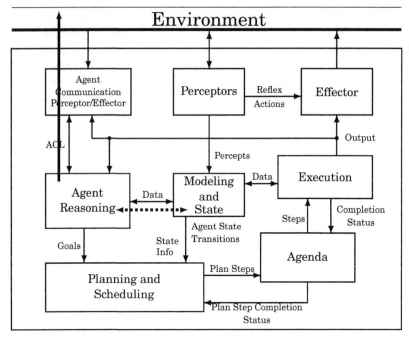

Fig. 1.19. Social behavior triggered by the agent internally.

Table 1.1. Summary of the behavior/component relationships.

	Per-ceptor	Commun-ication	Rea-soner	Modeler	Planner/ Scheduler	Agenda	Exec-ution	Ef-fector
Reactive-Agent		X	X	X			X	X
Reactive-Percept	X		X	X			X	X
Deliberative-Agent		X	X	X	X	X	X	X
Deliberative-Percept	X		X	X	X	X	X	X
Proactive-Agent			X	X				
Social-Agent		X	X	X				
Social-Itself		X	X	X				

in all agent behaviors. The proactive behavior is the one behavior that initially involves the fewest components.

This section has advanced the idea that even with a simple agent architecture a complete gamut of agent behaviors can be realized by using selective components of the architecture. Again, the details have been suppressed in favor of giving an intuitive overview.

1.5 Agent Communities (Very Briefly)

Even with this very intuitive introduction to the concept of an agent, the reader has probably noticed that the components of the sample agent architecture used as the infrastructure for the discussion of agents in this chapter could themselves be considered as agents. Thus, the agent architecture could be legitimately considered to be a "community" of smaller agents. From our perspective an "agent community" is a collection of two or more agents that act in concert with one another to achieve some goal (or goals) in either a collaborative or coordinated fashion. Collaboration arises when the agents act as peers with one another. Coordination requires that one of the agents acts as the leader and gives direction to the other agent(s) involved in the community. Thus a community has multiple members, some structure and a purpose and goal(s) that establish a boundary for the community. This boundary means that the community can be considered to be a system.

One important quality of a community of agents is the property of emergent behaviors and intelligence. In Section 3 of this chapter four major and seven distinguished behaviors were identified as being associated with the specific agent architecture studied. Not one of the components, considered individually, was capable of any of the identified behaviors. The behaviors emerged from an interaction of two or more components within the agent architecture. If we consider the architecture as an example of a community, then the extremely important concept of "emergence" becomes apparent. The behavior of a community can be greater than the behavior of any one agent in the community. From fairly simple functional capabilities of the components in our sample agent architecture emerge the somewhat sophisticated behaviors that we have addressed above.

A community of agents may be viewed as a "knowledge community." This concept is related to that of "emergence". Each agent in the community has a level of knowledge that is appropriate to its capability. In our sample architecture, for example, the Reasoner knows how to reason, the Planner knows how to plan, etc. However, the knowledge level of the community as a whole may exceed the individual levels of knowledge of the constituent agents as reflected in the emergent behaviors exhibited by the community.

1.6 Conclusions

This chapter has attempted to explicate the concept of agent from an intuitive constructionist point-of-view. The agent architecture developed by the Goddard Agent-Group was used as a sample architecture on which to base discussion of the major constituents of current agent architectures. Based on these constituent functionalities, the spectrum of agent behaviors was introduced and discussed. The concept of agent-community was briefly presented. The important concepts of "emergence" and "knowledge community" were briefly introduced. It is hoped that with this informal and intuitive background, more formal approaches to agents and agent-communities may be read with a greater understanding.

References

1. Ferber, J. *Multi-Agent Systems*. Addison-Wesley. 1999.
2. Russell, S. and Norvig, P. *Artificial Intelligence: A Modern Approach*. Prentice Hall. 1995.
3. d'Inverno, M. and Luck, M. *Understanding Agent Systems*. Springer. 2001.
4. Wooldridge, M. *Reasoning About Rational Agents*. The MIT Press, Cambridge, MA. 2000.
5. Wooldridge, M. *An Introduction to Multiagent Systems*. John Wiley and Sons, Ltd. 2002.

2

Introduction to Formal Methods

Michael Hinchey, Jonathan P. Bowen, and Christopher A. Rouff

2.1 Introduction

Computers do not make mistakes, or so we are told. However, computer software is written by, and hardware systems are designed and assembled by, humans, who certainly *do* make mistakes.

Errors in a computer system may be the result of misunderstood or contradictory requirements, unfamiliarity with the problem, or simply human error during design or coding of the system. Alarmingly, the costs of maintaining software—the costs of rectifying errors and adapting the system to meet changing requirements or changes in the environment of the system—greatly exceed the original implementation costs.

As computer systems are being used increasingly in safety-critical applications—that is, systems where a failure could result in the loss of human life, mass destruction of property, or significant financial loss—both the media (e.g., [84]) and various regulatory bodies involved with standards, especially covering safety-critical and security applications (e.g., see [39]) have considered formal methods and their role in the specification and design phases of system development.

2.2 Underlying Principles

There can be some confusion over what is meant by a "specification" and a "model." David Parnas differentiates between specification and descriptions or models as follows [155]:

- A **description** is a statement of some of the actual attributes of a product, or a set of products.
- A **specification** is a statement of properties required of a product, or a set of products.

- A **model** is a product, neither a description nor a specification. Often it is a product that has some, but not all, of the properties of some "real product."

Others use the terms *specification* and *model* more loosely; a model may sometimes be used as a specification. The process of developing a specification into a final product is one in which a model may be used along the way or even as a starting point.

2.2.1 Formal Methods

Over the last 50 years, computer systems have increased rapidly in terms of both size and complexity. As a result, it is both naive and dangerous to expect a development team to undertake a project without stating clearly and precisely what is required of the system. This is done as part of the **requirements specification** phase of the software life cycle, the aim of which is to describe *what* the system is to do, rather than *how* it will do it.

The use of natural language for the specification of system requirements tends to result in ambiguity and requirements that may be mutually exclusive. Formal methods have evolved as an attempt to overcome such problems, by employing discrete mathematics to describe the function and architecture of a hardware or software system, and various forms of **logic** to reason about requirements, their interactions, and validity.

The term **formal methods** is itself misleading; it originates from formal logic but is now used in computing to refer to a plethora of mathematically based activities. For our purposes, a formal method consists of notations and tools with a mathematical basis that are used to unambiguously specify the requirements of a computer system and that support the **proof** of properties of this specification and proofs of correctness of an eventual implementation with respect to the specification.

Indeed, it is true to say that so-called "formal methods" are not so much methods as formal systems. Although the popular formal methods provide a **formal notation**, or formal specification language, they do not adequately incorporate many of the methodological aspects of traditional development methods.

Even the term **formal specification** is open to misinterpretation by different groups of people. Two alternative definitions for "formal specification" are given in a glossary issued by the IEEE [120]:

1. A specification written and approved in accordance with established standards.
2. A specification written in a formal notation, often for use in proof of correctness.

In this chapter we adopt the latter definition, which is the meaning assumed by most formal methods users.

The notation employed as part of a formal method is "formal" in that it has a mathematical semantics so that it can be used to express specifications in a clear and unambiguous manner and allow us to abstract from actual implementations to consider only the salient issues. This is something that many programmers find difficult to do because they are used to thinking about implementation issues in a very concrete manner.

While programming languages are formal languages, they are generally not used in formal specification, as most languages do not have a full formal semantics, and they force us to address implementation issues before we have a clear description of what we want the system to do. Instead, we use the language of mathematics, which is universally understood, well established in notation, and, most importantly, enables the generalization of a problem so that it can apply to an unlimited number of different cases [58]. Here we have the key to the success of formal specification—one must *abstract* away from the details of the implementation and consider only the essential relationships of the data, and we can model even the most complex systems using simple mathematical objects: e.g., **sets**, **relations**, functions, etc.

At the specification phase, the emphasis is on clarity and precision, rather than efficiency. Eventually, however, one must consider how a system can be implemented in a programming language that, in general, will not support abstract mathematical objects (functional programming languages are an exception) and will be efficient enough to meet agreed requirements and concrete enough to run on the available hardware configuration.

As in structured design methods, the formal specification must be translated to a design—a clear plan for implementation of the system specification—and eventually into its equivalent in a programming language. This approach is known as **refinement** [14], [179].

The process of **data refinement** involves the transition from abstract data types such as sets, sequences, and mappings to more concrete data types such as arrays, pointers, and record structures, and the subsequent verification that the concrete representation can adequately capture all of the data in the formal specification. Then, in a process known as **operation refinement**, each **operation** must be translated so that it operates on the concrete data types. In addition, a number of **proof obligations** must be satisfied, demonstrating that each concrete operation is indeed a "refinement" of the abstract operation—that is, performing at least the same functions as the abstract equivalent, but more concretely, more efficiently, involving less nondeterminism, etc.

Many specification languages have relatively simple underlying mathematical concepts involved. For example, the Z (pronounced "zed") notation [123], [188] is based on (typed) set theory and first-order predicate logic, both of which *could* be taught at the university level. The problem is that many software developers do not currently have the necessary education and training to understand these basic principles, although there have been attempts to integrate suitable courses into university curricula [8], [28], [35], [80].

It is important for students who intend to become software developers to learn how to abstract away from implementation detail when producing a system specification. Many find this process of **abstraction** a difficult skill to master. It can be useful for reverse engineering, as part of the software maintenance process, to produce a specification of an existing system that requires restructuring. Equally important is the skill of refining an abstract specification towards a concrete implementation, in the form of a program for development purposes [150].

The process of refinement is often carried out informally because of the potentially high cost of fully formal refinement. Given an implementation, it is theoretically possible, although often intractable, to *verify* that it is correct with respect to a specification, if both are mathematically defined. More usefully, it is possible to *validate* a formal specification by formulating required or expected properties and formally proving, or at least informally demonstrating, that these hold. This can reveal omissions or unexpected consequences of a specification. **Verification** and **validation** are complementary techniques, both of which can expose errors.

2.3 Best Practices

Technology transfer (e.g., see [45], [51]) has always been an issue with formal methods, largely because of the significant training and expertise that is necessary for their use. Most engineering disciplines accept mathematics as the underpinning foundations, to allow calculation of design parameters before the implementation of a product [109]. However, software engineers have been somewhat slow to accept such principles in practice, despite the very mathematical nature of all software. This is partly because it *is* possible to produce remarkably reliable systems without using formal methods [108]. In any case, the use of mathematics for software engineering is a matter of continuing debate [192].

However, there are now well-documented examples of cases in which a formal approach has been taken to develop significant systems in a beneficial manner, examples which are easily accessible by professionals (e.g., see [91], [103], [104], [135]). Formal methods, including formal specification and modeling, should be considered as one of the possible techniques to improve software quality, where it can be shown to do this cost-effectively.

In fact, just using a formal specification within the software development process has been shown to have benefits in reducing the overall development cost [39]. Costs tend to be increased early in the life cycle, but reduced later on at the programming, testing, and maintenance stages, where correction of errors is far more expensive. An early and widely publicized example was the IBM CICS (Customer Information Control System) project, where Z was used to specify a portion of this large transaction processing system with an estimated 9% reduction in development costs [117]. There were approximately half the usual number of errors discovered in the software, leading to increased software quality.

Writing a good specification is something that comes only with practice, despite the existence of guidelines. However, there are some good reasons why a mathematical approach may be beneficial in producing a specification:

1. **Precision:** Natural language and diagrams can be very ambiguous. A mathematical notation allows the specifier to be very exact about what is specified. It also allows the reader of a specification to identify properties, problems, etc., which may not be obvious otherwise.
2. **Conciseness:** A formal specification, although precise, is also very concise compared with an equivalent high-level language program, which is often the first formalization of a system produced if formal methods are not used. Such a specification can be an order of magnitude smaller than the program that implements it, and hence is that much easier to comprehend.
3. **Abstraction:** It is all too easy to become bogged down in detail when producing a specification, making it very confusing and obscure to the reader. A formal notation allows the writer to concentrate on the essential features of a system, ignoring those that are implementation details. However, this is perhaps one of the most difficult skills in producing a specification.
4. **Reasoning:** Once a formal specification is available, mathematical reasoning is possible to aid in its validation. This is also useful for discussing implications of features, especially within a team of designers.

A design team that understands a particular formal specification notation can benefit from the above improvements in the specification process. It should be noted that much of the benefit of a formal specification derives from the process of producing the specification, as well as the existence of the formal specification after this [90].

2.3.1 Specification Languages

The choice of a specification language is likely to be influenced by many factors: previous experience, availability of tools, standards imposed by various regulatory bodies, and the particular aspects that must be addressed by the system in question. Another consideration is the degree to which a specification language is executable. This is the subject of some dispute, and the reader is directed elsewhere for a discussion of this topic [38], [76], [97].

Indeed, the development of any complex system is likely to require the use of multiple notations at different stages in the process and to describe different aspects of a system at various levels of abstraction [107]. As a result, over the last 25 years, the vast majority of the mainstream formal methods have been extended and reinterpreted to address issues of concurrency [106], [148], real-time behavior [129], and object orientation [62], [184].

There is always, necessarily, a certain degree of trade-off between the expressiveness of a specification language and the levels of abstraction that it supports [205]. While certain languages may have wider "vocabularies" and constructs to support the particular situations with which we wish to deal, they are likely to force us towards particular implementations; while they will shorten a specification, they will make it less abstract and more difficult for reasoning [36].

Formal specification languages can be divided into essentially three classes:

1. **Model-oriented approaches** as exemplified by ASM (Abstract State Machines) [32], B-Method [2], [27], [177], RAISE (Rigorous Approach to Industrial Software Engineering) [53],[166], VDM (Vienna Development Method) [122], [127] and the Z notation [123], [188]. These approaches involve the derivation of an explicit model of the system's desired behavior in terms of abstract mathematical objects.

2. **Property-oriented approaches** using **axiomatic semantics** (such as Larch [89]), which use first-order predicate logic to express **preconditions** and **postconditions** of operations over abstract data types, and **algebraic semantics** (such as the OBJ family of languages including CafeOBJ [57], [77]), which are based on multisorted algebras and relate properties of the system in question to equations over the entities of the system.

3. **Process algebras** such as CSP (Communicating Sequential Processes) [106], [176] and CCS (Calculus of Communicating Systems) [42], [148], which have evolved to meet the needs of concurrent, distributed, and real-time systems, and which describe the behavior of such systems by describing their algebras of communicating processes.

Unfortunately, it is not always possible to classify a formal specification language in just one of the categories above. LOTOS (Language Of Temporal Ordering Specifications) [121], [194], for example, is a combination of ACT ONE and CCS; while it can be classified as an algebraic approach, it exhibits many properties of a process algebra too. Similarly, the RAISE development method is based on extending a model-based specification language (specifically, VDM-SL) with concurrent and temporal aspects.

As well as the basic mathematics, a specification language should also include facilities for structuring large specifications. Mathematics alone is all very well in the small, but if a specification is a thousand pages long (and formal specifications of this length exist), there must be aids to organize the inevitable complexity. Z provides the **schema notation** for this purpose, which packages up the mathematics so that it can be reused subsequently in the specification. A number of schema operators, many matching logical connectives, allow recombination in a flexible manner.

A formal specification should also include an informal explanation to put the mathematical description into context and help the reader understand the mathematics. Ideally, the natural language description should be understandable on its own, although the formal text is the final arbiter as to the meaning of the specification. As a rough guide, the formal and informal descriptions should normally be of approximately the same length. The use of mathematical terms should be minimized, unless explanations are being included for didactic purposes.

Formal methods have proved useful in embedded systems and control systems (e.g., see [190], [193]). Synchronous languages, such as Esterel, Lustre and Signal, have also been developed for **reactive systems** requiring continuous interaction with their environment [22]. Specialist and combined languages may be needed for some systems. More recently, **hybrid systems** [54], [136] extend the concept of **real-time systems** [71]. In the latter, time must be considered, possibly as a continuous variable. In hybrid systems, the number of continuous variables may be increased. This is useful in control systems where a digital computer is responding to real-world analog signals.

More visual formalisms, such as Statecharts [93], are available and are appealing for industrial use, with associated STATEMENT tool support [96] that is now part of the widely used Unified Modeling Language (UML). However, the reasoning aspects and the exact semantics are less well defined. Some specification languages, such as SDL (Specification and Design Language) [194], provide particularly good commercial tool support, which is very important for industrial use.

There have been many attempts to improve the formality of the various structural design notations in widespread use [38], [180]. UML includes the Object Constraint Language (OCL) developed by IBM [202], an expression language that allows constraints to be formalized, but this part of UML is under-utilized with no tool support in most major commercial UML tools and is only a small part of UML in any case.

Object orientation is an important development in programming languages that is also reflected in specification languages. For example, Object-Z is an object-oriented version of the Z notation that has gained some acceptance [62], [55], [184]. More recently, the Perfect Developer tool has been developed by Escher Technologies Limited to refine formal specifications to object-oriented programming languages such as Java.

2.3.2 Modeling Systems

As previously discussed, the difference between specification and modeling is open to some debate. Different specification languages emphasize and allow modeling to different extents. Algebraic specification eschews the modeling approach, but other specification languages such as Z and VDM actively encourage it.

Some styles of modeling have been formulated for specific purposes. For example, Petri nets may be applied in the modeling of concurrent systems using a specific diagrammatic notation that is quite easily formalizable. The approach is appealing, but the complexity can become overwhelming. Features such as deadlock are detectable, but full analysis can be intractable in practice, since the problem of scaling is not well addressed.

Mathematical modeling allows reasoning about (some parts of) a system of interest. Here, aspects of the system are defined mathematically, allowing the behavior of the system to be predicted. If the prediction is correct this reinforces confidence in the model. This approach is familiar to many scientists and engineers.

Executable models allow rapid prototyping of systems [76]. A very high-level programming language such as a functional program or a logic program (which have mathematical foundations) may be used to check the behavior of the system. Rapid prototyping can be useful in demonstrating a system to a customer before the expensive business of building the actual system is undertaken. Again, scientists and engineers are used to carrying out experiments by using such models.

A branch of formal methods known as **model checking** allows systems to be tested exhaustively [23], [88]. Most computer-based systems are far too complicated to test completely because the number of ways the system could be used is far too large. However, a number of techniques, **Binary Decision Diagrams** (BDDs), for example, allow relatively efficient checking of significant systems, especially for hardware [134]. An extension of this technique, known as **symbolic model checking**, allows even more generality to be introduced.

Mechanical tools exist to handle BDDs and other model-checking approaches efficiently. SPIN is one of the leading general model-checking tools that is widely used [116]. A more specialist tool based on CSP [106], known as FDR (Failure Divergence Refinement), from Formal Systems (Europe) Ltd., allows model checking to be applied to concurrent systems that can be specified in CSP.

2.3.3 Summary

Driving forces for best practice include standards, education, training, tools, available staff, certification, accreditation, legal issues, etc. [39]. A full discussion of these is beyond the scope of this chapter. Aspects of best practice for specification and modeling depend significantly on the selected specification notation.

2.4 Technology Transfer and Research Issues

Claims that formal methods can guarantee correct hardware and software, eliminate the need for testing, etc., have led some to believe that formal methods are something almost magical [90]. More significantly, beliefs that formal methods are difficult to use, delay the development process, and raise development costs [37] have led many to believe that formal methods offer few advantages over traditional development methods. Formal methods are not a panacea; they are just one of a range of techniques that, when correctly applied, have proven themselves to result in systems of the highest integrity [36].

Hitherto, the uptake of formal methods has been hindered, at least in part, by a lack of tools. Many of the successful projects discussed in [103] and [104] required significant investment in tool support. Just as the advent of compiler technology was necessary for the uptake of high-level programming languages, and CASE (Computer Aided Software Engineering) technology provided the impetus for the emergence of structural design methodologies in the 1970s, a significant investment in formal methods tools is required for formal methods to be practical at the level of industrial application.

In the future, we envisage greater emphasis on IFDSEs (Integrated Formal Development Support Environments) that will support formal specification and development, based on an emerging range of high-quality stand-alone tools. The framework for this could well be based around the Extended Markup Language (XML) that has emerged from the World Wide Web community. For example, ZML provides an XML-based markup for the Z notation that could be useful in the communication of specifications between tools [197].

Method integration is one approach that may aid in the acceptance of formal methods and may help in the technology transfer from academic theory to industrial practice. This has the advantage of providing multiple views of a system, for example, incorporating a graphical representation that is likely to be more acceptable to nonspecialists, while retaining the ability to propose and prove system properties and to demonstrate that requirements are not contradictory before rather than after implementation.

The Unified Modeling Language (UML) provides a popular software development framework which could benefit from the formal methods approach. For example, amid concerns over the lack of formality (or even uniform interpretation) in UML, the OMG (Object Management Group) has issued a request for proposals on re-architecting UML version 2.0. A number of groups are interested in making the notation more formal, understandable and unambiguous including the 2U Consortium (Unambiguous UML) and the pUML group (precise UML).

Cleanroom is a method that provides a middle road between correctness proofs and informal development by stipulating significant checking of programs before they are first run [165]. The testing phase then becomes more like a certification phase since the number of errors should be much reduced. **Static analysis** involved rigorous checking of programs without actually executing them. SPARK Ada [19] is a restricted version of the Ada programming language that includes additional comments that facilitate formal tool-assisted analysis, especially worthwhile in high-integrity system development. Such approaches may be more cost-effective than full formal development using refinement techniques.

In any case, formal development is typically not appropriate in most software systems. However, many systems could benefit from some use of formal methods at some level (perhaps just specification) in their most critical parts. This approach has been dubbed "lightweight" formal methods [69], [175]. In particular, many errors are introduced at the requirements stage and some formality at this level could have very beneficial results because the system description is still relatively simple [63].

Formal methods are complementary to testing in that they aim to avoid the introduction of errors whereas testing aims to remove errors that have been introduced during development. The best balance of effort between these two approaches is a matter for debate [133]. In any case, the existence of a formal specification can benefit the testing process by providing an objective and exact description of the system against which to perform subsequent program testing. It can also guide the engineer in deciding which tests are worthwhile (for example, by considering disjunctive preconditions in operations and ensuring that there is full test coverage of these).

In practical industrial use, formal methods have proved to have a niche in high integrity systems such as safety-critical applications where standards may encourage or mandate their use in software at the highest levels of criticality. Formal methods are also being successfully used in security applications such as smart cards, where the technology is simple enough to allow fully formal development. They are also useful in discovering errors during cryptographic protocol analysis [145].

Formal methods have largely been used for software development, but they are arguably even more successful in hardware design where engineers may be more open to the use of rigorous approaches because of their background and training. Formal methods can be used for the design of microprocessors, where errors can be costly because of the large numbers involved and also because of there possible use in critical applications [128]. Fully formal verification of significant hardware systems is possible even within the limits of existing proof technology (e.g., see [119]).

Full formal refinement is the ideal but is expensive and can sometimes be impossible to achieve in practice. Retrenchment [16] is a suggested liberalization of refinement designed for formal description of applications too demanding for true refinement. Examples are the use of infinite or continuous types or models from classical physics and applications including inconsistent requirements. In retrenchment, the abstraction relation between the models is weakened in the operation postcondition by a *concession* predicate. This weakened relationship allows approximating, inconsistent, or exceptional behaviors to be described in which a *false* concession denotes a refinement.

There are many different formal methods for different purposes, including specification (e.g., the Z notation) and refinement (e.g., the B-Method). There are some moves to produce more general formal approaches (e.g., see B$^{\#}$, combining ideas from B with some concepts from Z [3]). There have also been moves to relate different semantic theories like algebraic, denotational and operational approaches [111]. In any case, it is clear that there are still many research and technology transfer challenges ahead in the field of formal methods (e.g., see [110]).

2.5 Formal Methods for Agent-Based Systems

As software becomes more complex, it also becomes more difficult to test and find errors. This is especially true of parallel processes and distributed computing such as agent-based systems. Errors in these systems can rarely be found by inputting sample data into the system and checking if the results are correct. These types of errors are time-based and only occur when processes send or receive data at particular times or in a particular sequence. To find these errors, the software processes involved have to be executed in all possible combinations of states (state space) that the processes could collectively be in. Because the state space is exponential to the number of states, the state space grows extremely fast with the number of states in the processes, and becomes untestable with a relatively small number of processes. Traditionally, to get around the state explosion problem, testers have artificially reduced the number of states and approximated the underlying software using models.

The following is a list of potential formal approaches that could be used for formally specifying agent-based systems. This list gives the name of each of the formal approaches, a brief summary, history, applications that it has been used on, a list of its strengths, weaknesses and any

tool support. This list of approaches was determined through a literature search. A high emphasis was given to those approaches that have
been used in agent technologies or other highly distributed, concurrent
environments.

2.5.1 Process Algebras

Process algebras generally are made up of the following: a language for
describing systems, a behavioral equivalence or inequivalence that allows comparison of system behaviors, and axioms that allow for proofs of
equivalence between systems. Some algebras include a refinement ordering to determine whether one system is a refinement of another. Process
algebras usually use a handshake mechanism (rendezvous) between processes via a port or channel. One process may wait for data at a channel
until another process sends data over the channel (or vice versa). Once
the data is exchanged, both processes continue. The receiving process
then may then execute different processes based on the data received.
Process algebras are often used to determine if deadlock and livelock exist in communicating systems. Internal, noncommunications aspects of
processes are not reflected by process algebras.

Communicating Sequential Processes (CSP)

Communicating Sequential Processes (CSP) was designed by C.A.R.
Hoare [105, 106] to specify and model concurrent systems. CSP specified
systems consist of independently executing processes that communicate
over unbuffered, unidirectional channels and use events for synchronization. Processes in CSP are recursively defined as the occurrence of an
event followed by a process. The events guard the processes so that the
process does not execute until the event occurs. When a process needs
to synchronize with another process or send it data, data is sent over
a channel and then blocks until the other process reads the data from
the channel. If the reading process tries to read data from a channel and
there is no data on the channel, it also blocks until data arrives. There
are also standard processes, such as STOP, SKIP, RUN and bottom ($\perp$).
Choice operators and conditionals also exist that allow for choosing one of
many processes to execute depending on a condition. Several people have
used CSP to model and specify agent-based systems. Rouff, et al. [173]
(Chapter 10) used CSP to specify a multi-agent system.

CSP has a proof system associated with it so that properties of CSP
specifications can be proven correct or not correct. Proofs are based on
traces of events that can be produced by a specification. Every time an
event occurs, the event is listed as part of a trace for the process. A specification has a set of acceptable traces that can occur. By applying the laws
of CSP traces to a set of traces, it can be determined whether the given set

of traces can be produced by a given specification. It can also determine the set of possible traces that a specification can produce. Correctness of a specification can then be determined by proving that a sequence of traces can never be produced by the specification and/or that a set of traces can be produced by the specification. In addition, properties such as deadlock and liveness can also be proven as properties of a specification. CSP has also been updated several times with several variations such as Timed CSP [170], CSP-i [212] and Receptive Process Theory [130].

Some model checkers have used CSP as a basis for their model checking languages, such as the Promela model checking language for SPIN [115]. Many programming languages and other modeling languages are using CSP as a model when adding concurrency features, such as Communicating Java Threads (CJT) [102] and Modula-P [199]. This means that doing specifications in CSP can transfer to other implementation languages or model checkers, or automatically produce code or code fragments based on CSP specifications.

Calculus of Communicating Systems (CCS)

The Calculus of Communicating Systems (CCS) [148] was developed by Robin Milner for reasoning about concurrent systems and was one of the first process algegras. CCS defines concurrent systems as a set of processes using actions (or events) and operators on the actions. Actions represent external inputs and outputs on ports from the environment or internal computation steps. Operators on actions consist of an action prefix operator, a nil operator, a choice operator (+), a parallel composition operator (|), a restriction operation (\) that permits actions to be localized within a system, a renaming operator [f] that maps actions to other actions, and an invocation function that allows systems to be defined recursively. Similar to CSP, processes in CCS are defined recursively and communicate with other processes through ports. CCS also has a set of axioms that can be used to reason about the processes and prove properties of systems. CCS has had several extensions made to it, including CCS with Broadcast (CCS+b) and Temporal CCS (TCCS).

CCS has been used to specify agents, where instead of a process that is defined by a set of equations, an agent is substituted. CCS can also be used to represent systems at different levels of abstraction to give a high-level overview of a system as well as a detailed view. With its refinement ability, CCS can also maintain equivalences between higher level and lower level specifications. In addition, there is the ability to test that two specifications are bisimulations of each other (to specifications simulate each other). CCS also allows for proof of correctness as well as deadlock and livelock.

π-Calculus

π-Calculus [149] is a process algebra based on CCS that differs from some of the other process algebras in that it supports mobility of processes. It does this by being able to pass a link (channel) as data in a handshake. This allows data links to be passed to other processes and links can then be represented by variable names and compared for equality or inequality, and reasoned about.

There are two versions of the π-calculus: monadic calculus and polyadic calculus. The monadic calculus communicates one name at each handshake and the polyadic calculus can communicate zero or more names at each handshake. The two are equivalent (multiple single name communications can be used to represent one polyadic communication). π-Calculus contains constructs for input and output on links, a silent (empty) prefix, sum operator, parallel composition operator, match and mismatch link comparison, restricted links, and parameterized process names which can be used for invocation. The π-calculus was first extended to pass link names by Astesiano and Zucca [12] and Engberg and Nielson [66]. These early versions were viewed by some as overly complicated, and were later refined by Milner, Parrow and Walker [149].

π-Calculus has been used by several people to model agent-based systems. Esterline et al. [68] (Chapter 4) have used π-calculus to specify the LOGOS multi-agent system and Kawabe et al. [131] have developed a π-calculus-based system called $Nepi^2$ to specify communicating software or agents.

Input/Output Automata (IOA)

Input/output automata (IOA) are nondeterministic state machines. They can be described as a labeled transition system for modeling asynchronous concurrent systems [142]. An IOA consists of a set of states with a transition function. IOA may have an infinite number of states, an infinite alphabet with strings of infinite length in the language that are accepted by the automata. Actions are classified as input, output or internal. The inputs to the automata are generated by its environment. The outputs and internal actions are generated by the automata with the outputs being sent to the environment. Actions can also have preconditions for them to fire.

An I/O automaton has "tasks"; in a fair execution of an I/O automaton, all tasks are required to get turns infinitely often. The behavior of an I/O automaton is describable in terms of traces, or alternatively in terms of fair traces. Both types of behavior notions are compositional.

The input/output automaton model was developed by Lynch and Tuttle [142]. Variants of IOA have been developed that include Hybrid Automata [143] for modeling systems that are a combination of continuous and discrete systems, Timed Automata [87] for reasoning about real-time systems, probabilistic versions (PIOA) [213] for specifying systems with a combination of probabilistic and nondeterministic behavior, and dynamic IOA (DIOA) [13] for describing systems with run-time process creation, termination and mobility.

IOA has been used to verify a number of types of systems, including various communication protocols (e.g., TCP) [185] and performance analysis of networks (upper and lower bounds and failures). It has also been used for specification and reasoning about agent-based systems [10].

A strength of I/O Automata is that inputs from the environment can not be blocked. This enforces an environment-driven model of the system. Additional strengths are that IOA can model multiple levels of abstractions of a system, from high-level specifications to detailed algorithms, they are executable or can be simulated, and are highly nondeterministic. It is a calculus, so I/O automata can be used to generate code, and IOA has constructs for proving correctness of a specification.

2.5.2 Model-Oriented Approaches

Z

Z is based on set theory and is used to describe the behavior of sequential processes. In general, concurrency and timing cannot be described in Z. Z is strongly typed, with types being associated with sets and operators of equality and membership defined for all types. The main construct of Z to describe the functionality of a system is the schema, which is a visual construct that includes a declaration part and an optional predicate part. The declaration part contains named and typed schema components with constraining information. The predicate part contains pre- and post-conditions of the components in the declaration as well as invariants and operations on the components. The schema calculus of Z allows schemas to be combined to form new schemas and describe the functionality of a system as a whole.

Z was originally developed by Jean-Raymond Abrial at the Programming Research Group at the Oxford University Computing Laboratory (OUCL) and elsewhere since the late 1970s. There have also been several object-oriented extensions to Z that include Hall, ZERO, MooZ, Object-Z, OOZE, Schuman & Pitt, Z++, ZEST and Fresco, with currently Object-Z being the leading version. Z has also been combined with other formal methods, such as CSP, to give it the ability to handle concurrency and timing. An example is Timed Communicating Object Z (TCOZ), which has Object Z's strength in modeling algorithms and data and CSP's strength in modeling process control and real-time interactions [144].

For agent-based systems, d'Inverno and Luck [59, 60] (Chapter 3) used Z to specify an agent framework. In their framework they have specified a four-tiered hierarchy that consists of entities, objects, agents and autonomous agents. As part of the agent framework specification they specify engagement, cooperation, inter-agent relationships, sociological agent, plans and goals.

B

The B method uses the Abstract Machine Notation (AMN), which is based on set theory and predicate logic. The AMN uses a finite state machine model (FSM) that supports states (variables of an abstract machine), invariants (constraints/relations between variables) and operations on the environment. Expressions in B can also have guards on them. Development of a specification in B is done by first specifying the system behavior in AMN, refining the specification and then implementing the specification. B specifications describe the state variables, invariants between the variables and operations on the variables. The specification is developed iteratively through refinements of the model until the specification is completed. Verifications and simulations during the development of the specification can also be done using the B toolkit, a set of tools that support the methodology, to prove that invariants are preserved after operations are performed.

The B method was developed by Abrial [2], who also developed the Z specification language. B is a relatively new formal method, but has already found a large amount of use in complex systems specifications. The B method has also been modified for specifying distributed cooperative algorithms by adding temporal logic aspects to it [30].

An advantage of the B method is the iterative refinements, so specifications are developed in a top-down fashion. Another advantage is the component-based approach to developing the specifications, which maps well to component-based architectures and development methodologies. An additional strength of the B method is its tool support. From a B specification code can be generated, it can be analyzed for correctness, and an animator and proof of correctness can be performed. The ability to easily reuse specifications has also been cited as a plus to the B method and tools.

Finite State Machines (FSMs)

Finite State Machines (FSMs) model behavior using states and transitions between the states. Transitions contain events and conditions needed for the FSM to change states. The conditions act as guards on the transitions and the events are matches to inputs. State changes can occur when a transition from the current state has an event that matches the current input and the condition on the transition evaluates to true. For

AI systems, FSMs often represent knowledge systems where the states represent knowledge and the transitions represent rules. Finite state machines have been used in specifying AI-related systems for a long time. Since FSMs are inherently sequential, they have been modified over time to work in a concurrent environment. Concurrent systems are often described using concurrent FSMs with the ability of the FSMs to communicate with each other either at checkpoints or through buffers. Extensions of FSMs include statecharts, fuzzy state machines (FuSM) and others.

FSMs have been used to specify a wide range of applications and have been very popular in specifying AI-related applications. FSMs have also been used to specify multi-agent systems. They are usually modified so that concurrency and communication between the agents can be specified. An example is the Java-based Agent Framework for Multi-Agent Systems (JAFMAS) that uses FSMs to specify multi-agent conversations [78].

Statecharts

Statecharts extend finite state machines by adding hierarchy, concurrency and communication and were designed to specify complex discrete-event systems. The main advantage of statecharts over FSMs is that statecharts have built in the means to represent concurrency. The specifications can be developed in a hierarchical fashion, which aids in abstraction and top-down or bottom-up development.

Statecharts were developed by David Harel [93, 94, 95]. Statecharts have been widely used on many projects for specification and design of many types of systems. Coleman, Hayes and Bear [50] introduced a variant of statecharts called Objectcharts for object-oriented design. Several hybrid versions of statecharts that in conjunction use formal methods have been introduced. Uselton and Smolka combine statecharts with a process algebra [195] and also added the Labeled Transition Systems algebra [196] in order to establish formal semantics for statecharts. Andrews, Day and Joyce [9] have used statecharts embedded with a typed predicate logic. Other hybrid approaches have been introduced for real-time systems that embed the concept of time, such as Sowmya and Ramesh who extended statecharts with temporal logic [186]. Statecharts have been used to specify agent-based systems by a number of people. A few of them include Kimiaghalam, et al. [132], who have used a statechart-based approach for specifying agents, Hilaire et al. [101], who used a combination of Object-Z and statecharts to specify agent-based systems, and Griss et al. [86] who used statecharts for defining agent behavior.

Petri Nets

Petri nets are a graph-based system for specifying asynchronous processes in concurrent systems. Petri nets are represented by the 5-tupple (P, T, I, O, M), where P is a set of places, T is a set of transitions, I is a set of inputs, O is a set of outputs, and M is a set of initial markings. Petri nets were developed in 1962 by Carl Adam Petri [160] and were one of the first theories to address concurrency issues [158, 159]. Several variants of Petri nets have been developed over the years. Some of the variants include colored Petri nets, hierarchical Petri nets, object-oriented Petri nets, temporal Petri nets, and G-Nets.

Petri nets have been used extensively to model concurrent systems. Petri nets have been used by several people to specify multi-agent systems [70]. Examples of using Petri nets for specifying multi-agent systems include: Brown [41], who used hierarchical colored Petri nets to specify the NASA Lights-Out Ground Operations Systems (LOGOS); Bakam et al. [15], who used colored Petri nets to study a multi-agent model of hunting activity in Cameroon; Shen [182], who used Petri nets to model mobile agents; Xu and Shatz [214], who used a variant of Petri nets called G-Nets to model buyer and seller agents in electronic commerce; and Weyns and Holvoet [203] used colored Petri nets to study the social behavior of agents.

X-Machines (XM)

X-machines are based on finite state machines (FSM) except they have an internal memory state and transitions between states are labeled as functions which accept input symbols and output symbols based on the action of the action of the function with reference to the internal memory state. X-machines can be thought of as typed FSMs with the set X acting as a memory and also having input and output tapes.

X-machines were developed by the mathematician Samuel Eilenberg in 1974 [64]. In 1986, Mike Holcome started using X-machines for biological specification purposes [112, 113] and then for system specifications [114]. X-machines have undergone modifications to specify a wider range of systems, such as Stream X-Machines [83] that are used to control a family of distributed grammars, Communicating Stream X-Machines to better model concurrent systems [18], and Object Communicating X-Machines [17].

2.5.3 Logics

There are several types of logics that have been used and they are used for different applications. Propositional and predicate logics are used to represent factual information. For agents this may be a knowledge base or the agent's environment. These logics use and, or, not, implication, universal and existential operators. Modal logics are used for different modes of truth, such as possibly true and necessarily true. Denotic logic describes what is obliged to be done. Dynamic logic is like modal logic but is action based. Temporal logic is the logic of time.

Temporal Logic

Temporal logic is used to express time-related aspects of systems. There are both modal and predicate approaches to temporal logic. In the original modal temporal logic created by Prior [164] there were four additional operators to the standard logic operators: P, which stands for "It has at some time been the case that ...," F, which stands for "It will at some time be the case that ...," H, which stands for "It has always been the case that ...," and G, which stands for "It will always be the case that ...." P and F are called weak tense operators, and H and G are called strong tense operators.

In temporal logic, an expression is always true or will be true at some time in the future. There are two types of semantic models used: timed specifications based on linear time and branching time. With linear time a specification is a set of linear states with each state being part of a possible execution sequence (used in CSP traces). With branching time, states are a specification described as a tree structure of states, with each path in the tree a possible execution sequence (used in CCS). Other differences in temporal logics include discrete vs. dense, and moment-based vs. period-based times.

Temporal logic has gone through several modifications by different people for application to different fields. The idea of temporal logic has also been added to other formal methods to give them the basis of time in those methods. Also, a wide variety of temporal logics have been developed. Bellini, Mattolini and Nesi give a good survey of temporal logics in [21]. The differences in the different temporal logics range from expressiveness, availability of support tools for executability, and verifiability.

Temporal logic has been widely used for adding timing constraints and sequencing formation in real-time and artificial intelligence applications. In AI, it has been used to find a general framework for temporal representations [7]. In specification and verification of concurrent programs, modal temporal logic has been successfully used to specify the timing of concurrent programs running on separate processors [163]. Temporal logic has also been widely used to add timing to other formal specification languages like Z, Petri nets, statecharts and process algebras.

Real-Time Logic (RTL)

Real-time logic (RTL) is a predicate logic that relates the events of a system to their time of occurrence. RTL uses a discrete model of time that allows for reasoning about absolute timing (wall clock) properties in a system. RTL differs from modal temporal logic in that modal temporal logic uses relative timing of events for specifying time, which is qualitative. Since RTL uses a discrete model of time, it uses integers in RTL formulas. RTL uses an occurrence relation that assigns a time value to each occurrence of an event. The occurrence relation is denoted as R(e, i, t), which means that the i-th occurrence of event e happens at time t.

RTL was developed by Jahanian and Mok [126] in 1986. RTL has been extended by other researchers and combined with other logics. It has been combined with Z for specifying real-time systems, temporal linear logic for specifying event-based logical systems, and Presburger arithmetic. The University of Texas Real-Time Systems Group (headed by Mok) supports RTL with ongoing research and the development of supporting tools, such as Modechart and Timetool.

BDI Logics

Belief, Desires and Intentions (BDI) is an agent architecture for describing agent behaviors [82] based on the theory of action in humans by the philosopher M. Bratman [40]. To give formal semantics to BDI architectures, BDI logics were developed [168, 169] that are multi-modal and extensions to the branching time logic CTL* [65]. The BDI logics allow the BDI architectures to be formally modeled and then proofs of correctness on BDI-based agents can be done. The BDI logics tend to be modal type logics and describe beliefs, desires, intentions and the plans (or plan library) that an agent can follow to achieve its intentions.

Rao and Georgeff [168] initially introduced the idea of a logic for BDI architectures and since there has been much work on evolving it, such as Wooldridge [209, 210, 211] for plans, Padgham and Lambrix [152] for capabilities in plans, and Singh and Asher [183] for intentions. Different people have added on or concentrated on one aspect of the BDI logic to give it more formalism or extend it to cover specific aspects of a BDI agent specification.

BDI logic has been applied to a programming language called AgentSpeak(L) [167], which is based on a restricted first-order language with events and actions. An AgentSpeak(L) interpreter is available free for downloading [5]. The interpreter will run AgentSpeak(L) and AgentSpeak(XL) programs. This allows agent specifications written in BDI logic to be executed. A restricted version of AgentSpeak(L) is AgentSpeak(F), which can be model checked. The restricted nature of AgentSpeak(F) allows it to be converted to Promela and then run on the model checker Spin [115]. Other BDI-based agent architectures based on BDI logic include the Java Agent Compiler and Kernel (JACK) [124] and dMARS (Distributed Multi-Agent Reasoning System) [189].

BDI logics tend to be very expressive and formal so a large number of specifications can be written with a formal foundation and properties of the systems it specifies can be proven to be correct. Since BDI logics are based on BDI architectures, agent specifications can be easily mapped into it.

KARO Logic

The KARO (Knowledge, Abilities, Results and Opportunities) logic [118, 198] (Chapter 7) is a formal system based on modal logic for reasoning about and specifying the behavior of intelligent multi-agent systems. KARO formalizes the notion of knowledge contained within agents and the agents' possible execution of actions. The KARO framework allows agents to reason about their own and other agent's abilities to perform actions, the possible results of those actions, and the availability of the opportunities to take those actions. KARO combines both dynamic and epistemic logic into a single modal logic with additional modal operators, and adds the notion of abilities.

KARO was proposed by van Linder, van der Hoek and Meyer in 1998 [198]. So it is a relatively new logic and framework. Additional work is also being done on KARO that includes Hustadt, et al., who are developing automated proof methods for KARO [118]; Meyer, et al., who are working on linking KARO to agent programming languages [147]; Aldewereld [6], who has worked on extending KARO from single-agent to multi-agent; and Dixon et al. [61], who have applied Computational Tree Logic (CTL) instead of dynamic logic.

KARO is based on modal logic, which has historically been used to describe knowledge, belief, time, obligation, desire and other attributes that apply to agent-based systems. The use of modal logic can be more concise than first-order logics. In addition, modal logic lends itself to logical proofs of correctness and it tends to be more intuitive than first-order logic representations, while at the same time being able to be reducible to first-order logic and those first-order methods and techniques can still be applied.

2.5.4 Other Approaches

The following is a list of other approaches that are being used to specify and verify agent-based or swarm-based systems.

Artificial Physics

Artificial physics (AP) is based on using properties from physics to model constraints and interaction between agents [187]. Control of agents in an

AP framework is mapped to one of minimizing potential energy (PE). If constraints are violated or performance degrades, PE increases, triggering a reactive response. Global behaviors are automatically computed via local interactions between agents. Given a set of initial conditions and desired global behavior, sensors, effectors, and local force laws can be determined for the desired global behavior to emerge.

As an example of artificial physics, suppose a set of agents are treated as physical particles. Particles move in response to the virtual forces that are exerted upon them by their neighbors – in essence the particles act as if they were part of a molecular dynamics simulation. Particles have a position, mass, velocity, and momentum. Friction is included, for self-stabilization. The net action of the system of particles is to reduce potential energy in a continuously changing virtual potential field.

The work that is most related to artificial physics is referred to as "swarm intelligence" [100] and "social potential field" [171]. In swarm intelligence, the swarm distribution is determined via a system of linear equations describing difference equations with periodic boundary conditions. The social potential fields method relies on a force-law simulation that is similar to that found in molecular dynamics.

Artificial physics has been used to generate a variety of vehicle formations in simulation and it has demonstrated the capability of clustering agents into subgroups [187]. Others have used physicomimetics for physical simulations of self-assembly. Schwartz, et al. [178] investigated the self-assembly of viral capsids in a 3D solution. Winfree [204] has investigated the self-assembly of DNA double-crossover molecules on a 2D lattice. Shehory, et al. [181] used physics-based systems for modeling emergent behavior.

Software Cost Reduction (SCR)

SCR is a formal method based on tables for specification and analysis of black-box behavior of complex safety-critical systems [25]. A toolset called SCR* is available to help automate as much of the method as possible. SCR describes both the system's environment (which is usually nondeterministic) and the system's behavior (usually deterministic). The system is represented as a state machine and the environment is represented as a nondeterministic event generator. An SCR specification represents the state machine's transitions as a set of tables.

The system environment specification monitors variables (environmental quantities that the system monitors) and controlled variables (environmental quantities that the system controls) [26]. The system behavior is represented by two relations, NAT and REQ. NAT represents the natural constraints on the system behavior (such as physical laws and the system environment constraints). REQ represents the relationships between the monitored and the controlled quantities that the system must maintain. Tables are used to describe transitions, events, and conditions of a state machine for the system.

Mathematical Analysis

Mathematical analysis uses mathematical formulas to model or specify a system and then uses mathematical techniques for analyzing the resulting system specification. From the mathematical specification system properties can be proven correct or that they remain in bounds. Some techniques use physics-based approaches (see artificial physics) and others use stochastic approaches [138]. Mathematical analysis can be used to study the dynamics of swarms and predict long-term behavior as well as such things as efficiency and steady state characteristics without having to do simulations. It also allows parameters to be found that determine swarm behavior and how the actions of a single member of the swarm affect the entire swarm.

Mathematical analysis has been used in many different fields. It has been used in biology to study insects and model their macroscopic and microscopic behavior, molecular dynamics, cellular automata and particle hopping. Due to its wide use in a number of fields, there are many reference materials and mathematicians who are experienced in this type of modeling and analysis. The strengths of a mathematical approach are that a precise model of the system is obtained and there is a wide range of analytical methods to analyze the system. In addition, there are a large number of tools and techniques available in which to perform the analysis as well as a long history of these types of analysis being done, so they are also well-understood methods.

Mathematical analysis has been used for multi-agent systems by Lerman [137, 138], who used a stochastic-based method for modeling a multi-agent system that formed coalitions. Sheory, et al. [181] used a physics based systems and applied physics-based mathematical techniques to the analysis of multi-agent systems.

Game Theory

Game theory uses mathematical analysis to analyze decision making in conflict situations. It provides for the study of human behavior and optimizing choices. It uses probability and other mathematical techniques for analyzing situations and coming up with the best choice. It has been used extensively in economics, politics, management, biology, social sciences and other sciences to describe interacting entities. It has recently been applied to agent-based and swarm-based systems as a way of modeling and analyzing agents and their societies.

There have been a number of researchers who have used game theory to analyze and verify agent-based systems; a sampling can be found in

[156]. Rudnianski and Bestougeff [174] have used games of deterrence to analyze and simulate agent-based systems. Others [141, 191] have used game theory as a way to model agent-based systems as a noncooperative, zero-sum dynamic game with self-interested agents where the actions of agents are modeled as disturbances to the other agents. Some of these are modeled as 2-player games and others as n-player games. These models have been applied to sharing limited resources (such as airport runways or automated highways) or for collision avoidance. Once a model for a system is developed, properties of the system can be proven correct by showing the model maintains those properties. Game theory has also been used to study biological [172] and swarm-based systems [47].

UML

The Unified Modeling Language (UML) is a language for specifying, visualizing and documenting models of software systems [31]. UML has twelve different diagram types divided into three classes: structural diagrams, behavior diagrams, and model management diagrams. UML does not specify a particular methodology for using the language, so it is methodology independent, though many of the UML tools use a particular methodology.

It has also been used to specify agent-based systems. One of the main thrusts for using UML for agents is Agent UML (AUML) [20], which a standard is now being worked on by the Foundation for Intelligent Physical Agents (FIPA) [3] Modeling Technical Committee (Modeling TC). The FIPA AUML standard is currently working on class diagrams for specifying the internal behavior of agents and the external environment, and interaction diagrams. The Modeling TC has also identified modeling areas for multi- vs. single agent, use cases, social aspects, temporal constraints, deployment and mobility, and workflow/planning, as well as other areas. One of the main challenges of AUML is adding semantics to UML that reflect the autonomy, social structures, and asynchronous communication aspects of agents.

Other work on extending UML for agent specification includes the Agent-Object-Relationship Modeling Language (AORML) [200], which enhances UML sequence diagrams for specifying agent interactions; MAS-SIF [146], which uses standard UML sequence diagrams for describing interactions; Oechslein, et al. [151] uses UML Object Constraint Language (OCL) to extend UML to formally specify agents using UML; Role-Based Modeling Method for Multi-Agent Systems (RoMAS) [215], which uses UML use cases for defining system events and interactions; extension of use cases for specifying agent behavior [98]; and extensions to UML [154] to support the Java Agent Compiler and Kernel (JACK) [124] agents.

Hybrid Approaches

The majority of formal notations currently available were developed in the 1970s and 1980s and reflect the types of distributed systems being developed at that time. Current distributed systems are evolving and may not be able to be specified the same way past systems have been developed. Because of this, it appears that many people are combining formal methods into hybrid (integrated) approaches to address some of the new features of distributed systems (e.g., mobile agents, swarms, emergent behavior).

Hybrid approaches have been very popular in specifying concurrent and agent-based systems. Hybrid approaches often combine a process algebra or logic-based approach with a model-based approach. The process algebra or logic-based approach allows for easy specification of concurrent systems, while the model-based approach provides strength in specifying the algorithmic part of a system. The following is a partial list of hybrid approaches that have been used for specifying concurrent and agent-based systems: Communicating X-Machines [18], CSP-OZ – a combination of CSP and Object-Z [73], Object-Z and Statecharts [43], Timed Communicating Object Z [144], Temporal B [30], Timed CSP [170], Temporal Petri Nets (Temporal Logic and Petri Nets) [15], and ZCCS – a combination of Z and CCS [79].

2.6 Sources of Information on Formal Methods

A number of organizations have been established to meet the needs of formal methods practitioners; for example:

- Formal Methods Europe (FME) organizes a regular conference (e.g., [67], [207]), formerly the VDM symposia, and other activities for users of various formal methods.
- The British Computer Society Specialist Group on Formal Aspects of Computing Science (BCS-FACS) organizes workshops and meetings on various aspects of formal methods, as well as a series of Refinement Workshops (e.g., see [56]).
- The Z User Group (ZUG) has organized a regular international conference, historically known as the Z User Meeting (ZUM), attracting users of the Z notation from all over the world. The International B Conference Steering Committee (Association de Pilotage des Conférences B, APCB) has organized a similar International B Conference series. Since 2000 these have been combined as a single conference (e.g., see [24]).

There are now a number of journals devoted specifically to formal methods. These include *Formal Methods in System Design* and *Formal*

Aspects of Computing. The FAC journal is published by Springer-Verlag in association with BCS-FACS. Other European-based journals, such as *The Computer Journal, IEE Proceedings – Software* (formerly the *Software Engineering Journal*) and *Information and Software Technology*, publish articles on, or closely related to, formal methods, and they have run special issues on the subject.

While there are no U.S.-based journals that deal specifically with formal methods, they regularly are featured in popular periodicals such as *IEEE Computer* (e.g., [36], [107], [161], [175], [205]), and *IEEE Software* (e.g., [37], [90], [91], [135], [140], [153]) as well as in journals such as the *Annals of Software Engineering* (e.g., [28], [29]), *IEEE Transactions on Software Engineering* (e.g., [51], [63], [69], [92], [99], [206]), *ACM Transactions on Software Engineering and Methodology* [52], and the *Journal of the ACM*. A classic paper on the state of the art in formal methods has also appeared in the *ACM Computing Surveys* [49].

In addition to the conferences mentioned earlier, the IFIP (International Federation of Information Processing) FORTE international conference concentrates on **Formal Description Techniques** (FDTs, e.g., see [157]). The International Conference on Formal Engineering Methods series (ICFEM) has also been established more recently (e.g., see [81]). A number of more specialist conferences on formal methods have been established. For example, the Integrated Formal Methods (IFM) International Conference concentrates on the use of formal methods with other approaches (e.g., see [44]). The International Workshop on Formal Methods for Industrial Critical Systems (FMICS) concentrates on industrial applications, especially using tools [11].

Some more wide-ranging conferences give particular attention to formal methods; primary among these are the ICSE (International Conference on Software Engineering) and ICECCS (International Conference on Engineering of Complex Computer Systems) series of conferences. Other specialist conferences in the safety-critical sector, such as SAFECOMP, and SSS (the Safety-critical Systems Symposium) also regularly cover formal methods.

There have been some collections of case studies on formal methods with various aims and themes. For some industrial applications, see [39] and [38]. Solutions to a control specification problem using a number of different formal approaches are presented in [4]. [75] collected together a number of formal specification methods applied to an invoicing case study where the presentations concentrate on the *process* of producing a formal description, including the questions raised along the way.

A number of electronic forums are available as online newsgroups:

```
comp.specification.misc     Formal specification
comp.specification.larch    Larch
comp.specification.z        Z notation
```

In addition, the following electronic mailing lists are available, among others:

`formal-methods-request@` `cs.uidaho.edu`	Formal Methods
`fmnet-request@jiscmail.ac.uk`	Formal Methods Network
`procos-request@jiscmail.ac.uk`	Provably Correct Systems
`vdm-forum-request@jiscmail.ac.uk`	VDM
`zforum-request@comlab.ox.ac.uk`	Z (gatewayed to comp.specification.z)

For up-to-date online information on formal methods in general, readers are directed to the following World Wide Web URL (Uniform Resource Locator) that provides formal methods links as part of the WWW Virtual Library:

http://vl.fmnet.info/

2.7 Summary of Important Terms

Formal methods: Techniques, notations, and tools with a mathematical basis, used for specification and reasoning in software or hardware system development.

Formal notation: A language with a mathematical semantics, used for formal specification, reasoning, and proof.

Logic: A scheme for reasoning, proof, inference, etc. Two common schemes are **propositional logic** and **predicate logic**, which is propositional logic generalized with quantifiers. Other logics, such as modal logics, including **temporal logics** which handle time are also available. Examples include TLA (Temporal Logic of Actions), ITL (Interval Temporal Logic), and more recently Duration Calculus. Schemes may use **first-order logic** or **higher-order logic**. In the former, functions are not allowed on predicates, simplifying matters somewhat, but in the latter they are, providing greater power. Logics include a calculus which allows reasoning in the logic.

Operation: The performance of some desired action. This may involve the change of a state of a system, together with inputs to the operation and outputs resulting from the operation. To specify such an operation, the **before state** (and inputs) and the **after state** (and outputs) must be related with constraining predicates.

Precondition: The predicate which must hold before an operation for it to be successful. Compare **postcondition**, which is the predicate which must hold after an operation.

Predicate: A constraint between a number of variables which produces a truth value (e.g., *true* of *false*).

Proof: A series of mathematical steps forming an argument of the correctness of a mathematical statement or theorem. For example, the **validation** of a desirable property for a formal specification could be undertaken by proving it correct. Proof may also be used to perform a formal **verification** that an implementation meets a specification. A less formal style of reasoning is **rigorous argument**, where a proof outline is sketched informally, which may be done if the effort of undertaking a fully formal proof is not considered cost-effective.

Refinement: The stepwise transformation of a specification towards an implementation (e.g., as a program). Compare **abstraction**, where unnecessary implementation detail is ignored in a specification.

Relation: A connection or mapping between elements in a number of sets. Often two sets (a **domain** and a **range**) are related in a **binary relation**. A special case of a relation is a **function** where individual elements in the domain can only be mapped to at most one element in the range of the function. Functions may be further categorized. For example, a **partial function** may not map all possible elements that could be in the domain of the function, whereas a **total function** maps all such elements.

Set: A collection of distinct objects or **elements**, which are also known as **members** of the set. In a typed language, types may consist of maximal sets, as in the Z notation.

Specification: A description of *what* a system is intended to do, as opposed to *how* it does it. A specification may be *formal* (mathematical) or *informal* (natural language, diagrams, etc.). Compare an **implementation** of a specification, such as a program, which actually performs and executes the actions required by a specification.

State: A representation of the possible values which a system may have. In an abstract specification, this may be modeled as a number of sets. By contrast, in a concrete program implementation, the state typically consists of a number of data structures, such as arrays, files, etc. When modeling sequential systems, each operation may include a **before state** and an **after state** which are related by some constraining predicates. The system will also have an **initial state**, normally with some additional constraints, from which the system starts at initialization.

References

1. Abadi, M. and Gordon, A. D. A calculus for cryptographic protocols: The Spi calculus. *Journal of Information and Computation*, **143**:1-70, 1999.
2. Abrial, J. R. *The B-Book*. Cambridge University Press, Cambridge, U.K. 1996.
3. Abrial, J. R. $B^{\#}$: *Towards a synthesis between Z and B*. In Bert et al. 2003, pp. 168–177.

4. Abrial, J. R., Börger, E. and Langmaack, H., eds. *The Steam Boiler Control Specification Problem (LNCS 1165)*. Springer-Verlag. 1996.
5. *AgentSpeak(L)*. http://protem.inf.ufrgs.br/cucla/
6. Aldewereld, H. *Rational Teams: Logical Aspects of Multi-Agent Systems*, Master's Thesis, Utrecht University, May 2002.
7. Allen, J. F. Towards a general theory of action and time. *Artificial Intelligence* **23**:123-154, 1984.
8. Almstrum, V. L., Dean, C. N., Goelman, D., Hilburn, T. B. and Smith, J. Working group reports from ITiCSE on innovation and technology in computer science education. In *Annual Joint Conference Integrating Technology into Computer Science Education*, ACM Press, New York, 2001, pp. 71–88.
9. Andrews, J. H., Day, N. A. and Joyce, J. J. Using Formal Description Technique to Model Aspects of a Global Air Traffic Telecommunications Network. In *1997 IFIP TC6/WG6.1 Joint International Conference on Formal Description Techniques for Distributed Systems and Communication Protocols, and Protocol Specification, Testing, and Verification (FORTE/PSTV)*. T. Higashino and A. Togashi, editors. Chapman and Hall, November 1997, pp 417-432.
10. Araragi, T., Attie, P., Keidar, I., Kogure, K., Luchangco, V., Lynch, N. and Mano K.. On Formal Modeling of Agent Computations. In *Proceedings of First International Workshop on Formal Approaches to Agent-Based Systems, (LNAI 1871)*, Greenbelt, MD, Springer, 2001.
11. Arts, T. and Fokkink, W. *Eighth International Workshop on Formal Methods for Industrial Critical Systems*, Roros, Norway, June 5–7, 2003. European Research Consortium for Informatics and Mathematics (ERCIM).
12. Astesiano, E. and Zucca, E. Parametric channels via label expressions in CCS. *Theoretical Computer Science*, **33**:45-64, 1984.
13. Attie, P. C. and Lynch, N. A. Dynamic Input/Output Automata: A Formal Model for Dynamic Systems. In *Proceedings of International Conference on Concurrency Theory*, 2001, pp 137-151.
14. Back, R. J. and von Wright, J. *Refinement Calculus: A Systematic Introduction*. Graduate Texts in Computer Science, Springer-Verlag. 1998.
15. Bakam, I., Kordon, F., Le Page, C. and Bousquet, F. Formalization of a Spatialized Multiagent Model Using Coloured Petri Nets for the Study of an Hunting Management System. In *Proceedings of First International Workshop on Formal Approaches to Agent-Based Systems* (LNAI 1871), Greenbelt, MD, Springer, 2001.
16. Banach, R. and Poppleton, M. 1999. Sharp Retrenchment, Modulated Refinement and Simulation, *Formal Aspects of Computing*, **11**(5):498–540, 1999.
17. Barnard, J. Object COMX: Methodology Using Communicating X-Machine Objects. *Journal of Object-Oriented Programming (JOOP)*, Nov-Dec 1999.
18. Barnard, J., Whitworth, J. and Woodward, M. Communicating X-machines. *Journal of Information and Software Technology*, **38**(6), 1996.
19. Barnes, J. *High Integrity Software: The* SPARK *Approach to Safety and Security*. Addison-Wesley. 2003.
20. Bauer B., Muller J. P. and Odell J. Agent UML: A Formalism for Specifying Multiagent Software Systems. In *Proceedings of ICSE 2000 Workshop on Agent-Oriented Software Engineering AOSE 2000*, Limerick, 2000.
21. Bellini, P., Mattolini, R. and Nesi, P. Temporal Logics for Real-Time System Specification. *ACM Computing Surveys*, **32**(1):12-42, March 2000.

22. Benveniste, A., Caspi, P., Edwards, S. A., Halbwachs, N., Le Guernic, P. and de Simone, R. The synchronous languages 12 years later. *Proc. of the IEEE*, **91**(1):64–83, 2003.
23. Bérard, B., Bidoit M., Finkel, A., Laroussinie, F., Petit, A., Petrucci, L., Schnoebelen, Ph. and McKenzie, P. *Systems and Software Verification: Model-Checking Techniques and Tools*. Springer-Verlag. 2001.
24. Bert, D., Bowen, J. P., King, S. and Waldén, M., eds. *ZB2003: Formal Specification and Development in Z and B (LNCS 2651)*. Springer-Verlag. 2003.
25. Bharadwaj, R. and Heitmeyer, C. Hardware/Software Co-Design and Co-Validation Using the SCR Method. In *Proceedings of the IEEE International High Level Design Validation and Test Workshop (HLDVT'99)*, November 1999.
26. Bharadwaj, R. and Heitmeyer, C. Model Checking Complete Requirements Specifications Using Abstraction. *Automated Software Engineering*, **6**:37-68, 1999.
27. Bicarregui, J. C., Clutterbuck, D. L., Finnie, G., Haughton, H., Lano, K., Lesan, H., Marsh, D. W. R. M., Matthews, B. M., Moulding, M. R., Newton, A. R., Ritchie, B., Rushton, T. G. A. and Scharbach, P. N. Formal methods into practice: Case studies in the application of the B method. *IEE Proceedings – Software*, **144**(2):119–133, 1997.
28. Bjørner, D. and Cuéllar, J. R. Software engineering education: Roles of formal specification and design calculi. *Annals of Software Eng*, **6**(1–4):365–409, 1999.
29. Bjørner, D. Pinnacles of software engineering: 25 years of formal methods. *Annals of Software Eng*, **10**(1–4):11–66, 2000.
30. Bonnet, L., Florin, G., Duchien, L. and Seinturier, L. A Method for Specifying and Proving Distributed Cooperative Algorithms. *Workshop on Decentralized Intelligent and Multi-Agent Systems (DIMAS'95)*, November 1995.
31. Booch, G., Rumbaugh, J. and Jacobson, I. *The Unified Modeling Language User Guide*. The Addison-Wesley Object Technology Series, Addison-Wesley, Reading, MA. 1999.
32. Börger, E. and Stärk, R. *Abstract State Machines: A Method for High-Level System Design and Analysis*. Springer-Verlag. 2003.
33. Borgia, R., Degano, P., Priami, C., Leth, L. and Thomsen, B. Understanding mobile agents via a non-interleaving semantics for Facile. In *Proceedings of SAS'96, (LNCS 1145)*, R. Cousot and D. A. Schmidt, eds. Springer, 1996, pp 98-112.
34. Bowen, J. P. *Formal Specification and Documentation using Z: A Case Study Approach*. International Thomson Computer Press, London. 1996.
35. Bowen, J. P. Experience teaching Z with tool and web support. *ACM SIGSOFT Software Eng. Notes*, **26**(2):69–75, 2001.
36. Bowen, J. P. and Hinchey, M. G. Ten commandments of formal methods. *IEEE Comput*, **28**(4):56–63, 1995(a).
37. Bowen, J. P. and Hinchey, M. G. Seven more myths of formal methods. *IEEE Software*, **12**(4):34–41, 1995(b).
38. Bowen, J. P. and Hinchey, M. G. *High-Integrity System Specification and Design*. FACIT Series, Springer-Verlag, London. 1999.
39. Bowen, J. P. and Stavridou, V. Safety-critical systems, formal methods and standards. *IEE/BCS Software Eng. J*, **8**(4):189–209, 1993.

40. Bratman, M. *Intentions, Plans, and Practical Reason*. Harvard University Press, Cambridge. 1987.
41. Brown, B. *High-Level Petri Nets for Modeling Multi-Agent Systems*. MS project report, Dept. of Computer Science, North Carolina A&T State University, Greensboro, NC, 1998.
42. Bruns, G. *Distributed System Analysis with CCS*. Prentice Hall International Series in Computer Science, Hemel Hempstead, U.K. 1996.
43. Bussow, R., Geisler, R. and Klar, M. Specifying Safety-critical Embedded Systems with Statecharts and Z: A Case Study. In *Proceedings of the International Conference on Fundamental Approaches to Software Engineering, (LNCS 1382)*. Astesiano, E., editor. Springer-Verlag, Berlin, 1998, pp 71–87.
44. Butler, M., Petre, L. and Sere, K., eds. *Integrated Formal Methods (LNCS 2335)*. Springer-Verlag. 2002.
45. Caldwell, J. L. Formal methods technology transfer: A view from NASA. *Formal Methods in System Design*, **12**(2):125–137, 1998.
46. Cardelli, L. and Gordon, A.D. Mobile ambients. In *Proceedings of FoSSaCS'98, (LNCS 1378)*. M. Nivat, editor. Springer, 1998, pp 140-155.
47. Challet, D. and Zhang, Y. C. Emergence of Cooperation and Organization in an Evolutionary Game. *Physica A* **246**, 407, 1997.
48. Clarke, E. M. , Grumberg, O. and Peled, D. *Model Checking*. MIT Press. 1999.
49. Clarke, E. M. and Wing, J. M. *et al.* Formal methods: State of the art and future directions. *ACM Computing Surveys*, **28**(4):626–643, 1996.
50. Coleman, D., Hayes, F. and Bear, S. Introducing Objectcharts, or How to Use Statecharts in Object Oriented Design. *IEEE Transactions on Software Engineering*, January 1992, pp 9-18.
51. Craigen, D., Gerhart, S. L. and Ralston, T. J. Formal methods reality check: Industrial usage. *IEEE Trans. Software Eng*, **21**(2):90–98, 1995.
52. Crow, J. and Di Vito, B. Formalizing space shuttle software requirements: Four case studies. *ACM Trans. Software Eng. and Methodology*, **7**(3):296–332, 1998.
53. Dang Van, H., George, C., Janowski, T. and Moore, R., eds. *Specification Case Studies in RAISE*. FACIT Series, Springer-Verlag, London. 2002.
54. Davoren, J. M. and Nerode, A. Logics for hybrid systems. *Proc. of the IEEE*, **88**(7):985–1010, 2000.
55. Derrick, J. and Boiten, E. A. *Refinement in Z and Object-Z*. FACIT Series, Springer-Verlag, London. 2001.
56. Derrick, J., Boiten, E. A., Woodcock, J. and von Wright, J. *REFINE 2002: The BCS FACS Refinement Workshop*. Electronic Notes in Theoretical Computer Science, **70**(3), Elsevier Science Publishers. 2002.
57. Diaconescu, R. and Futatsugi, K. *CafeOBJ Report: The Language, Proof Techniques, and Methodologies for Object-Oriented Algebraic Specification*. AMAST Series in Computing, **6**, World Scientific Publishing Co. 1998.
58. Dijkstra, E. W. Why correctness must be a mathematical concern. In *The Correctness Problem in Computer Science*, R. S. Boyer and J. S. Moore, eds. Academic Press, London, 1981, pp. 1–6.
59. d'Inverno, M. and Luck, M. Formal Agent Development: Framework to System. *Proceedings of First International Workshop on Formal Approaches to Agent-Based Systems, (LNAI 1871)*, Greenbelt, MD, Springer, 2001.
60. d'Inverno, M. and Luck, M. *Understanding Agent Systems*. Springer-Verlag, 2001.

61. Dixon, C., Fisher, M. and Bolotov, A. Resolution in a Logic of Rational Agency. *Proceedings of the 14th European Conference on Artificial Intelligence (ECAI 2000)*. IO Press. 2000.
62. Duke, R. and Rose, G. *Formal Object-Oriented Specification Using Object-Z*. Cornerstones of Computing Series, MacMillan. 2000.
63. Easterbrook, S., Lutz, R., Covington, R., Kelly, J., Ampo, Y. and Hamilton, D. Experiences using lightweight formal methods for requirements modeling. *IEEE Trans. Software Eng*, **24**(1):4–14, 1998.
64. Eilenberg, S. *Automat, Languages and Machines*, Vol. A. Academic Press. 1974.
65. Emerson, E. A. and Halpern, J. Y. 'Sometimes' and 'not never' revisted: on branching time versus linear time temporal logic. *Journal of the ACM*, **33**(1):151-178, 1986.
66. Engberg, U. and Nielsen, M. *A calculus of communicating systems with label-passing*. Technical Report DAIMI PB-208, Computer Science Department, University of Aarhus, Denmark, 1986.
67. Eriksson, L. H. and Lindsay, P. A., eds. *FME 2002: Formal Methods – Getting IT Right (LNCS 2391)*. Springer-Verlag. 2002.
68. Esterline, A., Rorie, T. Using the π-Calculus to Model Multiagent Systems. In *Proceedings of First International Workshop on Formal Approaches to Agent-Based Systems, (LNAI 1871)*, Greenbelt, MD, Springer, 2001.
69. Feather, M. S. Rapid application of lightweight formal methods for consistency analyses. *IEEE Trans. Software Eng*, **24**(11):949–959, 1998.
70. Ferber, J. *Multi-Agent Systems: An Introduction to Distributed Artificial Intelligence*. Addison-Wesley. 1999.
71. Fidge, C., Kearney, P. and Utting, M. A formal method for building concurrent real-time software. *IEEE Software*, 14(2):99–106, 1997.
72. *FIPA. Foundation for Intelligent Physical Agents.* http://www.fipa.org
73. Fischer, C. *Combination and Implementation of Processes and Data: from CSP-OZ to Java*. Ph.D. Dissertation, Fachbereich Informatik, Universitat Oldenburg.
74. Fournet, C. and Gonthier, G. The reflexive chemical abstract machine and the join-calculus. In *Proceedings of POPL'96*, J.G. Steel, ed. ACM, January 1996, pp 372-385.
75. Frappier, M. and Habrias, H., eds. *Software Specification Methods: An Overview Using a Case Study*. FACIT Series, Springer-Verlag, London. 2001.
76. Fuchs, N. E. Specifications are (preferably) executable. *Software Engineering Journal*, 7(5):323–334, 1992.
77. Futatsugi, K., Nakagawa, A. T. and Tamai, T., eds. *CAFE: An Industrial-Strength Algebraic Formal Method*. Elsevier Health Sciences. 2000.
78. Gala, A. K. and Baker, A. D. Multi-Agent Communication in JAFMAS. In *Workshop on Specifying and Implementing Conversation Policies, Third International Conference on Autonomous Agents, (Agents '99)*, Seattle, Washington, 1999.
79. Galloway, A. J. and Stoddart, W. J. An operational semantics for ZCCS. In *IEEE International Conference on Formal Engineering Methods (ICFEM'97)*, Hiroshima, Japan, November 1997, M. Hinchey and S. Liu, editors. IEEE Computer Society Press, 1997, pp 272-282.
80. Garlan, D. Making formal methods effective for professional software engineers. *Inf. Software Tech*, **37**(5/6):261–268, 1995.

81. George, C. and Miao, H., eds. *Formal Methods and Software Engineering (LNCS 2495)*. Springer-Verlag. 2002.

82. Georgeff, M. P. and Lansky, A. L. Reactive reasoning and planning. In *Proceedings of the Sixth National Conference on Artificial Intelligence (AAAI-87)*, Seattle, WA, 1987, pp 677-682.

83. Gheorghe, M. *Stream X-Machines and Grammar Systems*. Department of Computer Science, Faculty of Mathematics, Bucharest University, Bucharest, Romania.

84. Gibbs, W. W. Software's chronic crisis. *Sci. Am*, **271**(3):86–95, 1994.

85. Goguen, J. and Winkler, T. *Introducing OBJ3*. SRI International, Menlo Park, CA. Tech. Rep. SRI-CSL-88-9. 1988.

86. Griss, M. L., Fonseca, S., Cowan, D. and Kessler, R. *SmartAgent: Extending the JADE Agent Behavior Bodel*. HP Laboratories Technical Report HPL-2002-18, Palo Alto, CA, 2002.

87. Grobauer, B. and Muller, O. From I/O Automata to Timed I/O Automata. In *Proceedings of the 12th International Conference on Theorem Proving in Higher Order Logics, TPHOLs'99 (LNCS 1690)*, Nice, France, 1999. Y. Bertot, G. Dowek, Ch. Paulin-Mohring and L. Thry, editors. Springer-Verlag, 1999, pp 273-290.

88. Grumberg, O., Peled, D. and Clarke, E. M. *Model Checking*. MIT Press. 2000.

89. Guttag, J. V. *Larch: Languages and Tools for Formal Specification*. Springer-Verlag. 1993.

90. Hall, J. A. Seven myths of formal methods. *IEEE Software*, **7**(5):11–19, 1990.

91. Hall, J. A. Using formal methods to develop an ATC information system. *IEEE Software*, **13**(2):66–76, 1996.

92. Hansen, K. M., Ravn, A. P. and Stavridou, V. From safety analysis to software requirements. *IEEE Trans. Software Eng*, **24**(7):573–584, 1998.

93. Harel, D. Statecharts: A visual formalism for complex systems. *Science of Computer Programming*, **8**:231–274, 1987.

94. Harel, D. On Visual Formalisms. *Communications of the ACM*, **31**(5):514-530, May 1988.

95. Harel, D. Pnueli, A., Schmidt, J. P. and Sherman, R. On the formal semantics of statecharts. In *Procedings of the 2nd IEEE Symposium on Logic in Computer Science*, Ithaca, N.Y., June 22-24. IEEE Press, New York, 1987, pp 54-64.

96. Harel, D. and Politi, M. *Modeling Reactive Systems with Statecharts: The Statemate Approach*. McGraw-Hill, New York. 1998.

97. Hayes, I. J. and Jones, C. B. Specifications are not (necessarily) executable. *Software Engineering Journal*, **4**(6):330–338, 1989.

98. Heinze, C., Papasimeon, M. and Goss, S. Specifying agent behavior with use cases. In *Proceedings of Pacific Rim Workshop on Multi-Agents, PRIMA2000*, 2000.

99. Heitmeyer, C., Kirby, J., Jr, Labaw, B., Archer, M. and Bharadwaj, R. Using abstraction and model checking to detect safety violations in requirements specifications. *IEEE Trans. Software Eng*, **24**(11):927–948, 1998.

100. Hiebeler, D. The Swarm Simulation System and Individual-based Modeling. In Proceedings of Decision Support 2001: Advanced Technology for Natural Resource Management, Toronto, Ontario, Canada, Sept 1994.

101. Hilaire, V., Koukam, A., Gruer, P. and Muller, J. P. Formal Specification and Prototyping of Multi-Agent Systems. In *Proceedings of Engineering Societies in the Agents World (LNAI 1972)*, Springer-Verlag, 2000.
102. Hilderink, G., Broenink, J. and Bakkers, A. A new Java Thread model for Concurrent Programming of Real-time Systems. *Real-Time Magazine*, January 1998, pp 30-35.
103. Hinchey, M. G. and Bowen, J. P., eds. *Applications of Formal Methods*. Prentice Hall International Series in Computer Science, Hemel Hempstead, U.K. 1995.
104. Hinchey, M. G. and Bowen, J. P., eds. *Industrial-Strength Formal Methods in Practice*. FACIT Series, Springer-Verlag, London. 1999.
105. Hoare, C. A. R. Communicating Sequential Processes. In *Communications of the ACM*, **21**(8):666–677, August 1978.
106. Hoare, C. A. R. *Communicating Sequential Processes*. Prentice Hall International Series in Computer Science, Hemel Hempstead, U.K. 1985.
107. Hoare, C. A. R. An overview of some formal methods for program design. *IEEE Comput*, **20**(9):85–91, 1987.
108. Hoare, C. A. R. How did software get so reliable without proof? In *FME '96: Industrial Benefit and Advances in Formal Methods (LNCS 1051)*. M.-C. Gaudel and J. Woodcock, eds. Springer-Verlag. 1996(a), pp 1–17.
109. Hoare, C. A. R. The logic of engineering design. *Microprocessing Microprogramming*, **41**(8/9):525–539, 1996(b).
110. Hoare, C. A. R. The verifying compiler: A grand challenge for computing research. *Journal of the ACM*, **50**(1):63–69, 2003.
111. Hoare, C. A. R. and He, J. *Unified Theories of Programming*. Prentice Hall International Series in Computer Science, Hemel Hempstead, U.K. 1998.
112. Holcombe, M. *Mathematical models of cell biochemistry*. Technical Report CS-86-4. Dept. of Computer Science, Sheffield University, United Kingdom. 1986.
113. Holcombe, M. *Towards a formal description of intracellular biochemical organization*. Technical Report CS-86-1, Dept. of Computer Science, Sheffield University, U.K. 1986.
114. Holcombe, W.M.L. X-machines as a Basis for System Specification. *Software Engineering Journal*, **3**(2):69-76, 1988.
115. Holzmann, G. *Design and Validation of Computer Protocols*, Prentice Hall Software Series, Englewood Cliffs, NJ, 1991.
116. Holzmann, G. J. *The Spin Model Checker – Primer and Reference Manual*. Addison-Wesley. 2003.
117. Houston, I. S. C. and King, S. CICS project report: Experiences and results from the use of Z in IBM. In *VDM '91: Formal Software Development Methods (LNCS 551)*, Vol. 1, S. Prehn and W. Toetenel, eds. Springer-Verlag. 1991, pp 588–596.
118. Hustadt, U., Dixon, C., Schmidt, R., Fisher, M., Meyer, J. and van Wiebe, H. Verification within the KARO Agent Thery. In *Proceedings of First International Workshop on Formal Approaches to Agent-Based Systems(LNAI 1871)*, Greenbelt, MD, Springer, 2001.
119. Hunt, W. A., Jr. and Sawada, J. Verifying the FM9801 microarchitecture. *IEEE Micro*, **19**(3):47–55, 1999.

120. IEEE. IEEE standard glossary of software engineering terminology. In *IEEE Software Engineering Standards Collection*. Elsevier Applied Science, Amsterdam. 1991.

121. ISO. *Information Processing Systems – Open Systems Interconnection – LOTOS – A formal description technique based on the temporal ordering of observational behaviour*. International Standard ISO 8807:1989, International Organization for Standardization, Switzerland. 1989.

122. ISO. *Information Technology – Programming languages, their environments and system software interfaces – Vienna Development Method – Specification Language – Part 1: Base language*. International Standard ISO/IEC 13817-1:1996, International Organization for Standardization, Switzerland. 1996.

123. ISO. *Information Technology – Z Formal Specification Notation – Syntax, Type System and Semantics*. International Standard ISO/IEC 13568:2002. International Organization for Standardization, Switzerland. 2002.

124. *JACK Intelligent Agents User Guide*. http://www.agent-software.com.au

125. Jacky, J. *The Way of Z: Practical Programming with Formal Methods*. Cambridge University Press, U.K. 1997.

126. Jahanian, F. and Mok, A. K. Safety Analysis of Timing Properties in Real-Time Systems. *IEEE Transactions on Software Engineering*, **SE-12**(9):890–904, 1986.

127. Jones, C. B. *Software Development Using VDM*, 2nd ed. Prentice Hall International Series in Computer Science, Hemel Hempstead, U.K. 1991.

128. Jones, R. B., O'Leary, J. W., Seger, C. J. H., Aagaard, M. D. and Melham, T. F. Practical formal verification in microprocessor design. *IEEE Design & Test of Computers*, **18**(4):16–25, 2001.

129. Joseph, M., ed. *Real-Time Systems: Specification, Verification and Analysis*. Prentice Hall International Series in Computer Science, Hemel Hempstead, U.K. 1996. http://www.tcs.com/techbytes/htdocs/book_mj.htm (2001).

130. Josephs, M. B. Receptive Process Theory. *Acta Informatica*, **29**(1):17-31, 1992.

131. Kawabe, Y., Mano, K. and Kogure, K. The $Nepi^2$ Programming System: A π-Calculus-Based Approach to Agent-Based Programming. In *Proceedings of First International Workshop on Formal Approaches to Agent-Based Systems, (LNAI 1871)*, Greenbelt, MD, Springer, 2001.

132. Kimiaghalam, B., Homaifar, A. and Esterline, A. A Statechart Framework for Agent Roles that Captures Expertise and Learns Improved Behavior. In *Proceedings of Second International Workshop on Formal Approaches to Agent-Based Systems (FAABS II)(LNCS 2699)*. Springer, 2003.

133. King, S., Hammond, J., Chapman, R. and Pryor, A. Is proof more cost-effective than testing? *IEEE Trans. Software Eng*, **26**(8):675–686, 2000.

134. Kropf, T. *Introduction to Formal Hardware Verification*. Springer-Verlag. 2000.

135. Larsen, P. G., Fitzgerald, J. and Brookes, T. Applying formal specification in industry. *IEEE Software*, **13**(7):48–56, 1996.

136. Lee, J. S. and Cha, S. D. Qualitative formal method for requirements specification and validation of hybrid real-time safety systems. *IEE Proceedings – Software*, **147**(1):1–11, 2000.

137. Lerman, K. Design and Mathematical Analysis of Agent-Based Systems. In *Proceedings of First International Workshop on Formal Approaches to Agent-Based Systems, (LNAI 1871)*, Greenbelt, MD, Springer, 2001.

138. Lerman, K. and Galstyan, A. *A General Methodology for Mathematical Analysis of Multi-Agent Systems*. USC Information Sciences Technical Report ISI-TR-529, 2001.

139. Lightfoot, D. *Formal Specification Using Z*. 2nd ed. Grassroots Series, Palgrave. 2001.

140. Luqi and Goguen, J. A. Formal methods: Promises and problems. *IEEE Software*, **14**(1):73–85, 1997.

141. Lygeros, J., Godbole, D. N. and Sastry, S. Verified Hybrid Controllers for Automated Vehicles. *IEEE Transactions on Automatic Control*, **43**(4):522–539, April 1998.

142. Lynch, N. A. and Tuttle, M. R. Hierarchical Correctness Proofs for Distributed Algorithms. In *Proceedings of the 6th Annual ACM Symposium on Principles of Distributed Computing*, ACM, August 1987, pp 137-151.

143. Lynch, N. A., Segala, R. and Vaandrager, F. W. Hybrid I/O automata. *Information and Computation*, **185**(1):105-157, August 2003.

144. Mahony, B. and Dong, J. S. Timed Communicating Object Z. *IEEE Transactions on Software Engineering*, **26**(2):150-177, Feb 2000.

145. Meadows, C. Formal methods for cryptographic protocol analysis: Emerging issues and trends. *IEEE Journal on Selected Areas in Communications*, **21**(1):44–54, 2003.

146. Mentges, E. Concepts for an agent-based framework for interdisciplinary social science simulation. *Journal of Artificial Societies and Social Simulation*, **2**(2), 1999.

147. Meyer, J.J., de Boer, F., van Eijk, R., Hindriks, K. and van der Hoek, W. On Programming KARO Agents. In *Proc. Int. Conf. on Formal and Applied Practical Reasoning (FAPR2000)*, Imperial College, London, J. Cunningham and D. Gabbay, editors. 2000.

148. Milner, R. *Communication and Concurrency*. Prentice Hall International Series in Computer Science, Hemel Hempstead, U.K. 1989.

149. Milner, R., Parrow, J. and Walker, D. A Calculus of Mobile Processes, Parts I and II. *Journal of Information and Computation*, **100**:1-77, 1992.

150. Morgan, C. *Programming from Specifications*, 2nd ed. Prentice Hall International Series in Computer Science, Hemel Hempstead, U.K. 1994. http://web.comlab.ox.ac.uk/oucl/publications/books/PfS/ (1998).

151. Oechslein, C., Klugl, F., Herrler, R. and Puppe, F. UML for Behavior-Oriented Multi-Agent Simulations. In *From Theory to Practice in Multi-Agent Systems. Second International Workshop of Central and Eastern Europe on Multi-Agent Systems, CEEMAS 2001, (LNCS 2296)*, Cracow, Poland, September 26-29, 2001, B. Dunin-Keplicz, E. Nawarecki, editors. Springer, 2002, pp 217-226.

152. Padgham, L. and Lambrix, P. Agent Capabilities: Extending BDI Theory. In *Proceedings of Seventeenth National Conference on Artificial Intelligence – AAAI 2000*, Aug 2000, pp 68-73.

153. Palshikar, G. K. Applying formal specifications to real-world software development. *IEEE Software*, **18**(6):89–97, 2001.

154. Papasimeon, M. and Heinze, C. Extending the UML for Designing JACK Agents. In *Proceedings of the Australian Software Engineering Conference (ASWEC 01)*, Canberra, Australia, August 26-27, 2001.

155. Parnas, D. Using mathematical models in the inspection of critical software. In *Applications of Formal Methods*, M. G. Hinchey and J. P. Bowen, eds. Prentice Hall International Series in Computer Science, Hemel Hempstead, U.K. 1995, pp 17–31.

156. Parsons, S. Gymtrasiewicsz, P. and Wooldridge, M. *Game Theory and Decision Theory in Agent-Based Systems*. Kluwer. 2002.

157. Peled, D. and Vardi, M. Y., eds. *Formal Techniques for Networked and Distributed Systems – FORTE 2002 (LNCS 2529)*. Springer-Verlag. 2002.

158. Peterson, J. L. Petri Nets. *ACM Computing Surveys (CSUR)*, **9**(3):223-252, Sept. 1977.

159. Peterson, J. L. *Petri Net Theory and the Modeling of Systems*. Prentice Hall, Englewood Cliffs, N.J. 1981.

160. Petri, C. A. *Kommunikation mit Automaten. Bonn: Institut fr Instrumentelle Mathematik, Schriften des IIM Nr.* 2, 1962. Also in New York: Griffiss Air Force Base, Technical Report RADC-TR-65–377, Vol.1, 1966, Pages: 1-Suppl. 1, English translation.

161. Pfleeger, S. L. and Hatton, L. Investigating the influence of formal methods. *IEEE Comput*, **30**(2):33–43, 1997.

162. Pierce, B. C. and Turner, D. N. Pict: A programming language based on the pi-calculus. In *Proof, Language and Internacion: Essays in Honour of Robin Milner*, G. Plotkin, C. Stirling and M. Tofte, eds. 1999.

163. Pnueli, A. The Temporal Logic of Programs. *Proceedings of the 18th IEEE Symposium on Foundations of Computer Science*. 1977, pp 46-67.

164. Prior, A. N. *Time and Modality*. Oxford University Press. 1957.

165. Prowell, S. J., Trammell, C. J., Linger, R. C. and Poore, J. H. *Cleanroom Software Engineering: Technology and Process*. Addison-Wesley. 1999.

166. RAISE Language group. *The RAISE Specification Language*. BCS Practitioner Series, Prentice-Hall, Hemel Hempstead, U.K. 1992.

167. Rao, A. S. AgentSpeak(L): BDI Agents speak out in a logical computable language. In *Proceedings of the Seventh European Workshop on Modelling Autonomous Agents in a Multi-Agent World, (LNAI 1038)*. W. Van de Velde and J. W. Perram, editors. Springer-Verlag, 1996.

168. Rao, A. S. and Georgeff, M. P. Modeling Rational Agents within a BDI-Architecture. *Proceedings of the 2nd International Conference on Principles of Knowledge Representation and Reasoning (KR'91)*, J. Allen, R. Fikes and E. Sandewall, editors. Morgan Kaufmann, 1991.

169. Rao, A. S. and Georgeff, M. P. BDI Agents: From Theory to Practice. *Proceedings of the First International Conference on Multi-Agent Systems (ICMAS-95)*, San Francisco, CA, June 1995.

170. Reed, G. M. and Roscoe, A. W. Metric Spaces as Models for Real-Time Concurrency. In *Proceedings, Workshop on the Mathematical Foundations of Programming Language Semantics, (LNCS 298)*. Springer-Verlag, 1987, pp 331-343.

171. Reif, J. and Wang, H. Social Potential Fields: A Distributed Behavioral Control for Autonomous Robots. In Proceedings of WAFR'94, San Francisco, California, February 1994.

172. Rowe, G. W. Game Theory in Biology. In *Physical Theory in Biology: Foundations and Explorations*, C. J. Lumsden, L. E. H. Trainor and W. A. Brandts. World Scientific. 1997.

173. Rouff, C., Rash, J. and Hinchey, M. Experience Using Formal Methods for Specifying a Multi-Agent System. In *Proceedings of the Sixth IEEE International Conference on Engineering of Complex Computer Systems (ICECCS 2000)*, 2000.

174. Rudnianski, M. and Bestougeff, H. Modeling Task and Teams through Game Theoretical Agents. In *Proceedings of First International Workshop on Formal Approaches to Agent-Based Systems, (LNAI 1871)*, Greenbelt, MD, Springer, 2001.

175. Saiedian, H., ed. An invitation to formal methods. *IEEE Comput*, **29**(4):16–30, 1996.

176. Schneider, S. *Concurrent and Real-time Systems: The CSP Approach*. John Wiley & Sons. 1999.

177. Schneider, S. *The B-Method: An Introduction*. Cornerstones of Computing Series, MacMillan. 2001.

178. Schwartz, R., Shor, P., Prevelige, P. and Berger, B. Local Rules Simulation of the Kinetics of Virus Capsid Self-Assembly. *Biophysics*, **75**:2626-2636, 1998.

179. Sekerinski, E. and Sere, K., eds. *Program Development by Refinement*. FACIT Series, Springer-Verlag, London. 1999.

180. Semmens, L. T., France, R. B. and Docker, T. W. G. Integrated structural analysis and formal specification techniques. *The Computer Journal*, **35**(6):600–610, 1992.

181. Shehory, O., Sarit, K. and Yadgar, O. Emergent cooperative goal-satisfaction in large-scale automated-agent systems. *Artificial Intelligence*, **110**(1):1-55, 1999.

182. Shen, C.Y.L. Behavior Modeling for Mobile Agents. *UCI Undergraduate Research Journal*, 1998.

183. Singh, M. and Asher, N. Towards a formal theory of intentions. In *Logics in AI, (LNAI 478)*, J. van Eijck, editor. Springer-Verlag, 1990, pp 472-486.

184. Smith, G. *The Object-Z Specification Language*. Advances in Formal Methods Series, Kluwer Academic Publishers. 2000.

185. Smith, M. *Formal verification of TCP and T/TCP*. Ph.D. Thesis, MIT, Department of Electrical Engineering and Computer Science, September 1997.

186. Sowmya, A. and Ramesh, S. Extending Statecharts with Temporal Logic. *IEEE Transactions on Software Engineering*, **24**(3):216-229, 1998.

187. Spears, W. and Gordon, D., Using artificial physics to control agents. In *Proceedings of the IEEE International Conference on Information, Intelligence, and Systems*, Charlotte, NC. November 1999.

188. Spivey, J. M. *The Z Notation: A Reference Manual*, 2nd ed. Prentice Hall International Series in Computer Science, Hemel Hempstead, U.K. 1992.

189. *The dMARS V1.6.11 System Overview*. Technical Report, Australian Artificial Intelligence Institute (AAII), 1996.

190. Tiwari, A., Shankar, N. and Rushby, J. Invisible formal methods for embedded control systems. *Proc. of the IEEE*, **91**(1):29–39, 2003.

191. Tomlin, C., Pappas, G. and Sastry, S. Conflict Resolution for Air Traffic Management: A Case Study in Multi-Agent Hybrid Systems. *IEEE Transactions on Automatic Control*, **43**(4):509–521, April 1998.

192. Tremblay, G. Formal methods: Mathematics, computer science or software engineering? *IEEE Trans. on Education*, **43**(4):377–382, 2000.
193. Tretmans, J., Wijbrans, K. and Chaudron, M. Software engineering with formal methods: The development of a storm surge barrier control system revisiting seven myths of formal methods. *Formal Methods in System Design*, **19**(2):195–215, 2001.
194. Turner, K. J., ed. *Using Formal Description Techniques: An Introduction to Estelle, LOTOS and SDL*. John Wiley & Sons, Chichester, U.K. 1993.
195. Uselton, A. C. and Smolka, S. A. A Process Algebraic Semantics for Statecharts via State Refinement. In *Proceedings of IFIP Working Conference on Programming Concepts, Methods and Calculi (PROCOMET)*, June 1994.
196. Uselton, A. C. and Smolka, S. A. A Compositional Semantics for Statecharts using Labeled Transition Systems. In *Proceedings of CONCUR'94 - Fifth International Conference on Concurrency Theory*, Uppsala, Sweden, August 1994.
197. Utting, M., Toyn, I., Sun, J., Martin, A., Dong, J. S., Daley, D. and Currie, D. ZML: XML support for standard Z. In *Proceeding of ZB2003: Formal Specification and Development in Z and B, (LNCS 2651)*, Third International Conference of B and Z Users, Turku, Finland, June 4-6, 2003, D. Bert, J. Bowen, S. King and M. Waldén, eds. Springer, 2003, pp 437–456.
198. van Linder, B., van der Hoek, W. and Meyer, J.-J. Ch. Formalizing abilities and opportunities of agents. *Fundamenta Informaticae*, **34**(1,2):53-101, 1998.
199. Vollmer, J. and Hoffart, R. Modula-P, a language for parallel programming: Definition and implementation on a transputer network. In *Proceedings of the 1992 International Conference on Computer Languages ICCL'92*, Oakland, California, IEEE Computer Society Press, April 1992, pp 54-65.
200. Wagner, G. The Agent-Object-Relationship Meta-Model: Towards a Unified Conceptual View of State and Behavior. *Information Systems* **28**(5):475-504, 2003.
201. Walker, D. Objects in the pi-calculus. *Journal of Information and Computation*, **116**(2):253-271, 1995.
202. Warmer, J. and Kleppe, A. *The Object Constraint Language: Precise Modeling with UML*. Addison-Wesley. 1998.
203. Weyns, D., Holvoet, T. A Colored Petri Net for a Multi-Agent Application. In Proceedings of Second Workshop on Modeling of Objects, Components, and Agents, Aarhus, Denmark, August 2002, pp 121-140.
204. Winfree, E. *Simulations of Computing by Self Assembly*. Presented at DIMACS: DNA-Based Computers, June 1998. Technical Report 1998.22, California Institute of Technology. 1998.
205. Wing, J. M. A specifier's introduction to formal methods. *IEEE Comput*, **23**(9):8–24, 1990.
206. Wing, J. M. and Woodcock, J. Special issues for FM '99: The first World Congress on formal methods in the development of computing systems. *IEEE Trans. Software Eng*, **26**(8):673–674, 2000.
207. Wing, J. M., Woodcock, J. and Davies, J., eds. *FM'99 – Formal Methods (LNCS 1708, LNCS 1709)*. Springer-Verlag. 1999.
208. Woodcock, J. and Davies, J. *Using Z: Specification, Refinement, and Proof*. Prentice Hall International Series in Computer Science, Hemel Hempstead, U.K. 1996.

209. Wooldridge, M. A Logic of BDI Agents with Procedural Knowledge. *Working Notes of 3rd ModelAge Workshop: Formal Models of Agents*, Sesimbra, Portugal, P. Schobbens, editor. 1996.

210. Wooldridge, M. Practical reasoning with procedural knowledge: A logic of BDI agents with know-how, Practical Reasoning. *Proceedings of FAPR'96, (LNAI 1085)*, D. Gabbay and H-J. Ohlbach, eds. Springer Verlag, 1996, pp 202–213.

211. Wooldridge, M. *Reasoning about Rational Agents. Intelligent Robot and Autonomous Agents Series*. MIT Press, Cambridge, MA. 2000.

212. Wrench, K. L. CSP-I: An implementation of communicating sequential processes. *Software-Practice and Experience*, **18**(6):545-560, June 1988.

213. Wu, S. H, Smolka, S. A. and Stark, E. W. Composition and behaviors of probabilistic I/O automata. *Theoretical Computer Science*, **176**(1-2):1-38, 1997.

214. Xu, H. and Shatz, S.M. An Agent-based Petri Net Model with Application to Seller/Buyer Design in Electronic Commerce. In Proceedings of Fifth International Symposium on Autonomous Decentralized Systems, Dallas, Texas, March 2001.

215. Yan, Q., Shan, L., Mao, X. and Qi, Z. RoMAS: a role-based modeling method for multi-agent system. In *Proceedings of Second International Conference on Active Media Technology*, May, 2003.

3

Formal Methods and Agent-Based Systems

Michael Luck and Mark d'Inverno

3.1 Introduction

As has been discussed elsewhere [17], much agent-related work has tended to focus on either the development of practical applications or the development of sophisticated logics for reasoning about agents. Our own view is that work on formal models of agent-based systems is valuable inasmuch as they contribute to a fundamental goal of computing to build real agent systems. This is not to trivialize or denigrate the effort of formal approaches, but to direct them towards integration in a broader research program. In an ongoing project that has been running for several years, we have sought to do exactly that through the development of a formal framework, known as SMART, that provides a conceptual infrastructure for the analysis and modeling of agents and multi-agent systems on the one hand, and enables implemented and deployed systems to be evaluated and compared on the other. In this chapter, we describe our research program, review its achievements to date, and suggest directions for the future.

In particular, we consider the role of autonomy in interaction. *Autonomy* is independence; it is a state that does not rely on any external entity for purposeful existence. In this chapter, we use our existing agent framework to address the issues that arise in a consideration of autonomous interaction. We begin by considering several problems that are prevalent in existing models of interaction, and which must be addressed in attempting to construct a model of autonomous interaction. Then we introduce a previously developed agent framework on which the remainder of the chapter is based. The next sections describe and specify an autonomous social agent that acts in an environment, the way in which it generates its goals, and finally how it interacts with others in its environment. We discuss how this can be viewed as a process of discovery, and what such a view usefully brings to the problem.

3.1.1 Theory and Practice

Though the fragmentation into theoretical and practical aspects has been noted, and several efforts made in attempting to address this fragmentation in related areas of agent-oriented systems by, for example, [14], [22], and [32], much remains to be done in bringing together the two strands of work.

This section draws on Luck's outline [17] of the ways in which some progress has been made with BDI agents, a well-known and effective agent architecture. Rao, in particular, has attempted to unite BDI theory and practice in two ways. First, he provided an abstract agent architecture that serves as an idealization of an implemented system and as a means for investigating theoretical properties [28]. Second, he took an alternative approach by starting with an implemented system and then formalizing the operational semantics in an agent language, AgentSpeak(L), which can be viewed as an abstraction of the implemented system, and which allows agent programs to be written and interpreted [27].

In contrast to this approach, some work aims at constructing directly executable formal models. For example, Fisher's work on Concurrent MetateM [11] has attempted to use temporal logic to represent individual agent behaviors where the representations can either be executed directly, verified with respect to a logical requirement, or transformed into a more refined representation. Further work aims to use this to produce a full development framework from a single high-level agent to a cooperating multi-agent system. In a similar vein, [25] aims to address the gap between specification and implementation of agent architectures by viewing an agent as a multi-context system in which each architectural component is represented as a separate unit, an encapsulated set of axioms, and an associated deductive mechanism whose interrelationships are specified using bridge rules. Since theorem-provers already exist for multi-context systems, agents specified in this way can also be directly executed.

As yet, the body of work aimed at bridging the gap between theory and practice is small. Fortunately, though, there seems to be a general recognition that one of the key roles of theoretical and practical work is to inform the other [8], and while this is made difficult by the almost breakneck pace of progress in the agent field, that recognition bodes well for the future. Some skeptics remain, however, such as Nwana, who followed Russell in warning against *premature mathematization*, and the danger that lies in wait for agent research [4].

3.1.2 General Approach

As stated above, we view our enterprise as that of building programs. In order to do so, however, we need to consider issues at different points along what we call the *agent development line*, identifying the various foci of research in agent-based systems in support of final deployment, as shown in Figure 3.1. To date, our work has concentrated on the first three of the stages identified.

- We have provided a formal agent framework within which we can explore some fundamental questions relating to agent architectures, configurations of multi-agent systems, inter-agent relationships, and so on, independent of any particular model. The framework continues to be extended to cover a broader range of issues, and to provide a more complete and coherent conceptual infrastructure.
- In contrast to starting with an abstract framework and refining it down to particular system implementations, we have also attempted to start with specific deployed systems and provide formal analyses of them. In this way, we seek to move backwards to link the system specifications to the conceptual formal framework, and also to provide a means of comparing and evaluating competing agent systems.
- The third strand aims to investigate the process of moving from the abstract to the concrete, through the construction of agent development methodology, an area that has begun to receive increasing attention. In this way, we hope to marry the value of formal analysis with the imperative of systems development in a coherent fashion, leading naturally to the final stage of the development line, to *agent deployment*.

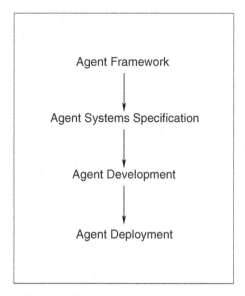

Fig. 3.1. The agent development line.

This chapter can be seen as an extension of the work contained in [21], which describes the results of the research program in providing a foundation for the exploration of more advanced issues in agent-based systems. That work introduced requirements for formal frameworks, and showed how our agent framework satisfied those requirements in relation to, for example, some initial inter-agent relationships, and their application to the Contract Net Protocol. In this chapter, we build on that work, showing further levels of analysis of agent relationships, and also describe further work on formal agent specification.

In what follows, we use the Z specification language [31], for reasons of accessibility, clarity and existing use in software development. The arguments are well-rehearsed and can be found in many of the references given at the end of the chapter. Here, we present a brief introduction to the language but more details can be found in an array of text books such as [31]. The specification in this chapter is not intended to be complete, nor to provide the most coherent exposition of a particular piece of work, but to show how a broad research program in support of the aims above is progressing. Details of the different threads of work may be found in the references in each of the relevant sections. In particular, this chapter is concerned with the design of *autonomous* agents: what it means for an agent to be autonomous and what that entails for any adequate model of interaction between such agents. Complex environments admit an inherent uncertainty that must be considered if we are to cope with more than just toy problems. In such uncertain environments, an agent must be autonomous; an agent cannot know in advance the exact effects of its or others' actions. This is of paramount importance, and an agent must therefore be designed with a flexibility that enables it to cope with this uncertainty by evaluating it and responding to it in adequate ways.

3.1.3 Introduction to Z

The formal specification language, Z, is based on set theory and first-order predicate calculus. It extends the use of these languages by allowing an additional mathematical type known as the *schema type*. Z schemas have two parts: the upper declarative part, which declares variables and their types, and the lower predicate part, which relates and constrains those variables. The type of any schema can be considered as the Cartesian product of the types of each of its variables, without any notion of order, but constrained by the schema's predicates.

It is therefore appropriate to liken the semantics of a schema to that of Cartesian products. For example, suppose we define a schema as follows:

$$
\begin{array}{|l}
\hline
\_Pair _____ \\
\hline
first : \mathbb{N} \\
second : \mathbb{N} \\
\hline
\end{array}
$$

This is very similar to the following Cartesian product type:

$$Pair == \mathbb{N} \times \mathbb{N}$$

The difference between these forms is that there is no notion of order in the variables of the schema type. In addition, a schema may have a predicate part that can be used to constrain the state variables. Thus, we can state that the variable *first* can never be greater than *second*.

```
__Pair_____
  first : ℕ
  second : ℕ
_____
  first ≤ second
_____
```

Modularity is facilitated in Z by allowing schemas to be included within other schemas. We can select a state variable, *var*, of a schema, *schema*, by writing *schema.var*. For example, it should be clear that *Pair.first* refers to the variable *first* in the schema *Pair*.

Now, operations in a state-based specification language are defined in terms of *changes to the state*. Specifically, an operation relates variables of the state after the operation (denoted by dashed variables) to the value of the variables before the operation (denoted by undashed variables). Operations may also have inputs (denoted by variables with question marks), outputs (exclamation marks) and preconditions. In the *GettingCloser* schema below, there is an operation with an input variable, *new?*; if *new?* lies between the variables *first* and *second*, then the value of *first* is replaced with the value of *new?*. The value of *second* does not change, and the output *old!* is equal to the value of the variable *first* as it was before the operation occurs. The $\Delta Pair$ symbol, is an abbreviation for *Pair* $\land$ *Pair'* and, as such, includes in the operation schema all the variables and predicates of the state of *Pair* before and after the operation.

```
__GettingCloser_____
  new? : ℕ
  ΔPair
  old! : ℕ
_____
  first ≤ new?
  new? ≤ second
  first' = new?
  second' = second
  old! = first
_____
```

To introduce a type in Z, where we wish to abstract away from the actual content of elements of the type, we use the notion of a *given set*.

For example, we write $[NODE]$ to represent the set of all nodes. If we wish to state that a variable takes on some set of values or an ordered pair of values we write $x : \mathbb{P}\,NODE$ and $x : NODE \times NODE$, respectively. A *relation* type expresses some relationship between two existing types, known as the *source* and *target* types. The type of a relation with source X and target Y is $\mathbb{P}(X \times Y)$. A relation is therefore a set of ordered pairs. When no element from the source type can be related to two or more elements from the target type, the relation is a *function*. A *total* function $(\rightarrow)$ is one for which every element in the source set is related, while a *partial* function $(\nrightarrow)$ is one for which not every element in the source is related. A sequence (seq) is a special type of function where the domain is the contiguous set of numbers from 1 up to the number of elements in the sequence. For example, the first relation below defines a *function* between nodes, while the second defines a *sequence* of nodes.

$$Rel1 = \{(n1, n2), (n2, n3), (n3, n2)\}$$
$$Rel2 = \{(2, n3), (3, n2), (1, n4)\}$$

In Z, a sequence is more usually written as $\langle n4, n3, n2 \rangle$. The *domain* (dom) of a relation or function comprises those elements in the source set that are related, and the *range* (ran) comprises those elements in the target set that are related. In the examples above, $\mathrm{dom}\,Rel1 = \{n1, n2, n3\}$, $\mathrm{ran}\,Rel1 = \{n2, n3\}$, $\mathrm{dom}\,Rel2 = \{1, 2, 3\}$ and $\mathrm{ran}\,Rel2 = \{n2, n3, n4\}$. Sets of elements can be defined using set comprehension. For example, the following expression denotes the set of squares of natural numbers greater than 10 : $\{x : \mathbb{N} \mid x > 10 \bullet x * x\}$.

For a more complete treatment of the Z language, the interested reader is referred to one of the numerous texts, such as [31].

3.2 Autonomous Interaction

Autonomy allows the design of agents to be flexible enough to function effectively and efficiently in a sophisticated world [5]. Typically, real autonomy has been neglected in most research. We hear of benevolent, altruistic, trusting, sympathetic or cooperative agents, yet a truly autonomous agent will behave only in a selfish way. Cooperation, for example, should occur only as a consequence of an agent's selfish motivations (which might of course include motivations relating to social acceptance that would drive what appears at face value to be "social" or "altruistic" behavior). Autonomy allows for no artificially imposed rules of behavior; all behavior must be a consequence of the understanding and processing capabilities of that agent. Modeling this fundamental notion of selfish behavior and the generation of goals by such a selfish autonomous agent is of vital importance in the design of autonomous agents.

In multi-agent systems, the interactions between agents are the basis for usefully exploiting the capabilities of others. However, such a pragmatic approach has not been the concern of many researchers who instead often focus on small areas of interaction and communication, and in particular on specialized forms of intention recognition and interpretation.

In many existing models of interaction, agents are not autonomous. In considering these models, we can identify problem-issues in autonomous interaction. Our intention is simply to show why these models are not adequate for autonomous interaction, and so isolate problems which contribute to the nonautonomous nature of these models.

Predetermined Agenda: Problem-solving can be considered to be the task of finding actions that achieve current goals. Typically, goals have been presented to systems without regard to the problem-solving agent so that the process is divorced from the reality of an agent in the world. This is inadequate for models of autonomy which require an understanding of how such goals are generated and adopted. Surprisingly, however, this is an issue which has received very little attention with only a few notable exceptions (e.g., [24]).

Benevolence: In traditional models of goal adoption, goals are broadcast by one agent, and adopted by other agents according to their own relevant competence [30]. This assumes that agents are already designed with common or nonconflicting goals that facilitate the possibility of helping each other satisfy additional goals. Negotiation as to how these additional goals are satisfied typically takes the form of mere goal-node allocation. Thus an agent simply has to communicate its goal to another agent for cooperation in the form of joint planning to ensue. The concept of benevolence—that agents will cooperate with other agents whenever and wherever possible—has no place in modeling autonomous agents [7, 12]. Cooperation will occur between two parties only when it is considered advantageous to each party to do so. Autonomous agents are thus selfish agents. A goal (whether traditionally viewed as 'selfish' or 'altruistic') will always be adopted so as to satisfy a 'selfish' motivation.

Guaranteed Effects: Speech Act Theory (SAT) [3, 29] underlies much existing work in AI [6], typically because as Appelt points out, speech acts are categorizable and can be modeled as action operators in a planning environment [2]. However, this work admits a serious flaw. Although the preconditions of these operators are formulated in terms of the understanding of the planning agent, the post-conditions or effects of these operators do not update the understanding of the planning agent, but of the agent at whom the action is directed [1]. No agent can ever actually *know* with any certainty anything about the effects of an action, whether communicative or otherwise. It is only through an understanding of the *target* agent and through observing the future behavior of that agent that the agent can discover the actual effects of the interaction. This uncertainty is inherent in communication between autonomous agents and must be a feature of any model of interaction which hopes to reflect this reality.

Automatic Intention Recognition: A related though distinct problem with using SAT in the design of *communication* models involves the notion that the meaning of an utterance is a function of the linguistic content of that utterance. SAT is unable (even when one tries to force rather undistinguished ad-hoc rules [15]) to model any kind of utterance where the linguistic content is not very close to the speaker's intended meaning. That is to say that the operators themselves are context independent, and information about how context affects the interpretation of utterances is not explicitly captured. Communication varies from utterances with a meaning identical to linguistic content through utterances which have a meaning opposite to the linguistic content to utterances where the meaning does not seem to be categorized at all by the linguistic content. In short, Speech Act Theory cannot lead to a model of autonomous interaction. It merely serves to describe a very limiting case of linguistic communication at a suitable level for planning operators. A more flexible account of how intention is recovered from a multitude of different utterances is required.

Multi-agent Modeling: This is also a related but more subtle problem. Much work has modeled communicative actions in terms of mutual beliefs about the operator and its known effects [26]. This proposes to show not only how certain mental states lead to speech actions, but how speech actions affect mental states. We argue that any account of autonomous interaction should only model the effects of an action upon the mental state of the agent initiating the interaction (or another single agent).

In summary, there are several important claims here: first, an agent cannot be truly autonomous if its goals are provided by external sources; second, an agent will only adopt a goal and thus engage in an interaction if it is to its advantage to do so; third, the effects of an interaction cannot be guaranteed; fourth, the intentions of others cannot always be recognized; fifth, an agent can only know about itself.

Note that the first claim requires goals to be generated from within. It is this internal goal generation that demands an explicit model of the motivations of the agent. The second claim requires a notion of advantage that can only be determined in relation to the motivations of the agent. The third and fourth claims demand that the uncertain nature of autonomous interaction be explicitly addressed. We argue that viewing autonomous interaction as motivated discovery provides us with a means for doing this. Finally, the fifth claim imposes constraints on the problem we are considering, and provides a strong justification for our concern with constructing a model of autonomous interaction from the perspective of an individual agent.

3.3 The Formal Agent Framework

We begin by briefly reviewing earlier work. In short, we propose a four-tiered hierarchy comprising *entities*, *objects*, *agents* and *autonomous agents* [18]. The basic idea underlying this hierarchy is that all components of the world are entities. Of these entities, some are objects, of which some, in turn, are agents and of these, some are autonomous agents, as shown in Figure 3.2.

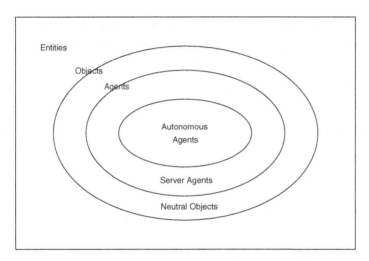

Fig. 3.2. The entity hierarchy.

Before it is possible to construct agent models it is necessary to define the building blocks or *primitives* from which these models are created. We start by defining three primitives: *attributes*, *actions* and *motivations*, which are used as the basis for development of the SMART agent framework. Formally, these primitives are specified as given sets which means that we say nothing about how they might be represented for any particular system. In addition, two secondary concepts, *goals* and *environments*, are specified in terms of attributes.

Attributes are simply features of the world, and are the only characteristics that are manifest. They need not be perceived by any particular entity, but must be potentially perceivable in an omniscient sense. This notion of a feature allows anything to be included, such as, the fact that a tree is green, or is in a park, or is twenty feet tall. An environment is then simply a set of attributes that describes *all* the features within that environment. Thus a type, *Environment*, is defined to be a (nonempty) set of attributes. The second primitive that needs defining is an *action*. Actions can change environments by adding or removing attributes. For example, the action of a robot, responsible for attaching tires to cars in a factory, moving from one wheel to the next, will delete the attribute that the robot is at the first wheel and add the attribute that the agent is at the second. A goal defines a state of affairs that is desirable in some way. For example, a robot may have the goal of attaching a tire to a car. A goal can therefore be very simply defined as a nonempty set of attributes that describes a state of affairs in the world. Lastly, *motivations* can be introduced. A motivation is any desire or preference that can lead to the generation and adoption of goals and that affects the outcome of the reasoning or behavioral task intended to satisfy those goals.

In summary we have the following definitions, from which we can construct an *entity* that has a nonempty set of attributes, and is therefore perceivable. For example, a goal is defined as a nonempty set of attributes.

$$[Attribute, Action, Motivation]$$

$$Environment == \mathbb{P}_1 Attribute$$

$$Goal == \mathbb{P}_1 Attribute$$

─── *Entity* ────────────────────────────────
$attributes : \mathbb{P} Attribute$
$capabilities : \mathbb{P} Action$
$goals : \mathbb{P} Goal$
$motivations : \mathbb{P} Motivation$
──────────────────────────────────────
$attributes \neq \{\ \}$
──────────────────────────────────────

3.3.1 Objects

Entities able to affect their environment through action lead to the concept of *objects*. An object in our model is an entity with *capabilities*. The *Object* schema below has a declarative part that simply includes the previously defined schema, *Entity*. The predicate part of the schema specifies that an object must have a nonempty set of actions as well as attributes. Objects are therefore defined by their ability in terms of their actions, and their characteristics in terms of their attributes.

```
┌─ Object ─────────────────────────────────────────────────
│ Entity
├──────────────
│ capabilities ≠ { }
└──────────────────────────────────────────────────────────
```

Since an object has actions, these may be performed in certain environments that will be determined by the state of that environment. The behavior of an object can therefore be modeled as a mapping from the environment to a set of actions that are a subset of its capabilities. This mapping is known as the *action-selection* function. The variable, *willdo*, specifies the next actions that the object will perform. Its value is found by applying the *objectactions* function to the current environment, in which it is situated.

```
┌─ ObjectState ────────────────────────────────────────────
│ Object
│ objectactions : Environment → ℙ Action
│ willdo : ℙ Action
│ environment : Environment
├──────────────────────────────────────
│ willdo = objectactions environment
└──────────────────────────────────────────────────────────
```

An *interaction* with the environment occurs as a result of performing actions in it. Its effects on the environment are determined by applying the *effectinteract* function in the axiom definition below to the current environment and the actions taken.

$$effectinteract : Environment \rightarrow \mathbb{P}\,Action \nrightarrow Environment$$

3.3.2 Agents and Autonomy

An agent is then just an object either that is useful to another agent where this usefulness is defined in terms of satisfying that agent's goals, or that exhibits independent purposeful behavior. In other words, an agent is an object with an associated set of goals. This definition of agents relies on the existence of other agents that provide the goals that are adopted in order to instantiate an agent. In order to escape an infinite regress of goal adoption, we define *autonomous agents*, which are agents that generate their own goals from motivations.

```
┌─ Agent ──────────────────────────────────────────────────
│ Object
├──────────────
│ goals ≠ { }
└──────────────────────────────────────────────────────────
```

AutonomousAgent _____
Agent
_____
motivations $\neq$ { }

For completeness we also define neutral objects as those objects that are not agents, and server agents as those agents that are not autonomous.

NeutralObject _____
Object
_____
goals = {}

ServerAgent _____
Object
_____
motivations = {}

3.3.3 Autonomous Perception

An agent in an environment can perceive certain attributes subject to its capabilities and current state but, due to limited resources, may not be able to perceive all attributes. The action of an agent is based on a subset of attributes of the environment, the agent's *actual* percepts.

To distinguish between representations of mental models and representations of the *actual* environment, a type, *View*, is defined to be the perception of an environment by an agent. This has an equivalent type to that of *Environment*, but now physical and mental components of the same type can be distinguished.

$$View == \mathbb{P}_1 \, Attribute$$

An autonomous agent has a (possibly empty) set of actions that enable it to perceive its world, which we call its *perceiving actions*. The set of percepts that an autonomous agent is potentially capable of perceiving is a function of the current environment, which includes the agent's situation and its perceiving actions. Since the agent is resource-bounded, it may not be able to perceive the entire set of attributes and selects a subset based on its current goals. For example, the distributed Multi-Agent Reasoning System (dMARS) [10], may have a set of events to process, where events correspond to environmental change. Each of these percepts (or events) is available to the agent but because of its limited resources it may only be able to process one event, and must make a selection based on its goals.

The perception capabilities of an agent are defined in the schema below, *AutonomousAgentPerception*, which includes the *AutonomousAgent* schema and refines it by introducing three variables. First, the set of perceiving actions is denoted by *perceivingactions*, a subset of the capabilities of an autonomous agent. The *canperceive* function determines the attributes that are potentially available to an agent through its perception capabilities. Notice that this function is applied to a physical environment (in which it is situated) and returns a mental environment. The second argument of this schema is constrained to be equal to *perceivingactions*. Finally, the function, *willperceive*, describes those attributes actually perceived by an agent. This function is always applied to the motivations and goals of the agent and, in contrast to the previous function, takes a mental environment and returns another mental environment.

$$\begin{array}{l} \underline{\;AutonomousAgentPerception\;}\underline{\qquad\qquad\qquad\qquad\qquad} \\ AutonomousAgent \\ perceivingactions : \mathbb{P}\,Action \\ canperceive : Environment \rightarrow \mathbb{P}\,Action \nrightarrow View \\ willperceive : \mathbb{P}\,Motivation \rightarrow \mathbb{P}\,Goal \rightarrow View \rightarrow View \\ \hline perceivingactions \subseteq capabilities \\ \forall\,e : Environment;\ as : \mathbb{P}\,Action \bullet \\ \qquad as \in \mathrm{dom}(canperceive\ e) \Rightarrow as = perceivingactions \end{array}$$

To specify the actions of an autonomous agent, the next schema includes the *AutonomousAgent* schema and then defines an action-selection function that is determined in relation to the motivations, goals, perceived environment and actual environment of the agent. This function gives the set of actions the agent will perform, in order to achieve some goal. The physical environment is important here as it determines the action that is actually performed by the agent as opposed to the action which is intended (or selected) by the agent. These will not be the same in all cases as the agent may, for example, have incomplete or incorrect perceptions of its environment.

$$\begin{array}{l} \underline{\;AutonomousAgentAct\;}\underline{\qquad\qquad\qquad\qquad\qquad} \\ AutonomousAgent \\ autoactions : \mathbb{P}\,Motivation \rightarrow \mathbb{P}\,Goal \rightarrow View \\ \qquad\qquad\qquad\qquad \rightarrow Environment \rightarrow \mathbb{P}\,Action \end{array}$$

Now, we need to define the state of an agent as follows by including the previous schemas and the current environment, and introducing variables for possible percepts, *posspercepts*, actual percepts, *actualpercepts*, and the actions performed, *willdo*.

```
┌─ AutonomousAgentState ─────────────────────────────────
│  ObjectState
│  AutonomousAgentPerception
│  AutonomousAgentAct
│  env : Environment
│  posspercepts, actualpercepts : View
│  willdo : ℙ Action
├────────────────────────────────────────────────────────
│  actualpercepts ⊆ posspercepts
│  posspercepts = canperceive env perceivingactions
│  actualpercepts = willperceive motivations goals posspercepts
│  willdo = autoactions motivations goals actualpercepts env
└────────────────────────────────────────────────────────
```

3.3.4 Goal Generation

As stated above, in order for an agent to be autonomous, it must generate *goals* from *motivations*. The initial point in any interaction is when this goal generation process occurs. In this section, we describe how an autonomous agent, *defined* in terms of its somewhat abstract *motivations*, can construct goals or concrete states of affairs to be achieved in the environment. Our model requires a repository of known goals which capture knowledge of limited and well-defined aspects of the world. These goals describe particular *states* or *sub-states* of the world with each autonomous agent having its own such repository. An agent tries to find a way to mitigate motivations by selecting an action to achieve an existing goal or by retrieving a goal from a repository of known goals, as considered below.

In order to retrieve goals to mitigate motivations, an autonomous agent must have some way of assessing the effects of competing or alternative goals. Clearly, the goals that make the greatest positive contribution to the motivations of the agent should be selected. The *GenerateGoal* schema below describes at a high level an autonomous agent monitoring its motivations for goal generation. First, as indicated by *ΔAutonomousAgent*, the sociological agent changes, and a new variable representing the repository of available known goals, *goalbase*, is declared. Then, the motivational effect on an autonomous agent of satisfying a set of new goals is given. The *motiveffect* function returns a numeric value representing the motivational effect of satisfying a set of goals with a particular configuration of motivations and a set of existing goals. The predicate part specifies all goals currently being pursued must be known goals that already exist in the goalbase. Finally, there is a set of goals in the goalbase that has a greater motivational effect than any other set of goals, and the current goals of the agent are updated to include the new goals.

GenerateGoal

$\Delta AutonomousAgent$
$goalbase : \mathbb{P}\,Goal$
$motiveffect : \mathbb{P}\,Motivation \rightarrow \mathbb{P}\,Goal \rightarrow \mathbb{P}\,Goal \rightarrow \mathbb{Z}$

$goals \subseteq goalbase \;\wedge\; goals' \subseteq goalbase$
$\exists gs : \mathbb{P}\,Goal \mid gs \subseteq goalbase \;\bullet$
$\quad (\forall os : \mathbb{P}\,Goal \mid os \in (\mathbb{P}\,goalbase) \;\bullet$
$\qquad (motiveffect\ motivations\ goals\ gs \geq$
$\qquad\qquad motiveffect\ motivations\ goals\ os) \wedge$
$\quad goals' = goals \cup gs)$

3.4 Inter-agent Relationships

Agents and autonomous agents are thus defined in terms of goals. Agents *satisfy* goals, while autonomous agents may, additionally, generate them. Goals may be adopted by either autonomous agents, nonautonomous agents or objects without goals. Since nonautonomous agents satisfy goals for others they *rely* on other agents for purposeful existence, indicating that goal adoption creates critical inter-agent relationships.

A direct engagement takes place whenever a neutral-object or a server-agent adopts the goals of another. Thus, an agent with some goals, called the *client*, uses another agent, called the *server*, to assist them in the achievement of those goals.

DirectEngagement

$client : Agent$
$server : ServerAgent$
$goal : Goal$

$client \neq server$
$goal \in (client.goals \cap server.goals)$

Once autonomous agents have generated goals and engaged other server-agents, these server-agents may, in turn, engage other nonautonomous entities with the purpose of achieving or pursuing the original goal. This process can then, in principle, continue indefinitely. An *engagement chain* thus represents the goal and all the agents involved in the sequence of direct engagements. Since goals are grounded by motivations, the agent at the head of the chain must be autonomous.

```
┌─ EngagementChain ──────────────────────────────────────────┐
│ goal : Goal                                                 │
│ autonomousagent : AutonomousAgent                           │
│ agentchain : seq ServerAgent                                │
├─────────────────────────────────────────────────────────────┤
│ #agentchain > 0                                             │
│ goal ∈ autonomousagent.goals                                │
│ goal ∈ ⋂{s : ServerAgent | s ∈ ran agentchain • s.goals}    │
└─────────────────────────────────────────────────────────────┘
```

A *cooperation* describes a goal, the autonomous agent that generated the goal, and those autonomous agents that have adopted that goal from the generating agent. In addition, all the agents involved have the goal of the cooperation, an agent cannot cooperate with itself, and the set of co-operating agents must be nonempty. Cooperation cannot, therefore, occur unwittingly between agents, but must arise as a result of the motivations of an agent and the agent recognising that goal in another. (The definition below does not capture the notion of this recognition and adoption but simply provides an abstract template which could be further elaborated as required.)

```
┌─ Cooperation ──────────────────────────────────────────────┐
│ goal : Goal; generatingagent : AutonomousAgent              │
│ cooperatingagents : ℙ AutonomousAgent                       │
├─────────────────────────────────────────────────────────────┤
│ goal ∈ generatingagent.goals                                │
│ ∀ aa : cooperatingagents • goal ∈ aa.goals                  │
│ generatingagent ∉ cooperatingagents                         │
│ cooperatingagents ≠ { }                                     │
└─────────────────────────────────────────────────────────────┘
```

The key relationships in a multi-agent system are direct engagements, engagement chains and cooperations [19]. The combined total of direct engagements, engagement chains and cooperations (represented as *dengagements*, *engchains* and *cooperations*) defines a social organization that is not artificially or externally imposed but arises as a natural and elegant consequence of our definitions of agents and autonomous agents. This organization is defined in the *AgentSociety* schema below.

```
┌─ AgentSociety ─────────────────────────────────────────────┐
│ entities : ℙ Entity                                         │
│ objects : ℙ Object                                          │
│ agents : ℙ Agent                                            │
│ autonomousagents : ℙ AutonomousAgent                        │
│ dengagements : ℙ DirectEngagement                           │
│ engchains : ℙ EngagementChain                               │
│ cooperations : ℙ Cooperation                                │
```

By considering the entire set of engagements, engagement chains and cooperations, a map of the relationships between individual agents can be constructed for a better understanding of their current social interdependence. The direct engagement relationship specifies the situation in which there is a direct engagement for which the first agent is the client and the second agent is the server. In general, however, any agent involved in an engagement chain engages all those agents that appear subsequently in the chain. To distinguish engagements involving an intermediate agent we introduce the indirect engagement relation *indengages*; an agent *indirectly* engages another if it engages it, but does not *directly* engage it. If many agents directly engage the same entity, then no single agent has complete control over it. It is important to understand *when* the behavior of an engaged entity can be modified without any deleterious effect (such as when no other agent uses the entity for a *different* purpose). In this case we say that the agent *owns* the entity. An agent, c, owns another agent, s, if, for every sequence of server-agents in an engagement chain, ec, in which s appears, c precedes it, or c is the autonomous client-agent that initiated the chain. An agent *directly owns* another if it owns it and directly engages it. We can further distinguish the *uniquely owns* relation, which holds when an agent *directly* and *solely* owns another, and *specifically owns*, which holds when it owns it, and has only one goal. These definitions are presented below.

directly engages

$\forall c : Agent;\ s : ServerAgent \bullet (c, s) \in dengages \Leftrightarrow$
$\qquad \exists d : dengagements \bullet d.client = c \wedge d.server = s$

engages

$\forall c : Agent, s : ServerAgent \bullet (c, s) \in engages \Leftrightarrow$
$\qquad \exists ec : engchains \bullet (s \in (\text{ran} \, ec.agentchain) \wedge$
$\qquad\qquad c = ec.AutonomousAgent) \vee$
$\qquad\qquad (((c, s), ec.agentchain) \in before)$

indirectly engages

$indengages = engages \setminus dengages$

owns

$\forall c : Agent;\ s : ServerAgent \bullet (c, s) \in owns \Leftrightarrow$
$\qquad (\forall ec : engchains \mid s \in \text{ran} \, ec.agentchain \bullet$
$\qquad\qquad ec.AutonomousAgent = c \vee$
$\qquad\qquad ((c, s), ec.agentchain) \in before)$

directly owns

$downs = owns \cap dengages$

uniquely owns

$\forall c : Agent;\ s : ServerAgent \bullet (c, s) \in uowns \Leftrightarrow$
$\qquad (c, s) \in downs \wedge \neg\ (\exists a : Agent \mid a \neq c \bullet (a, s) \in engages)$

specifically owns

$\forall c : Agent;\ s : ServerAgent \bullet (c, s) \in sowns \Leftrightarrow$
$\qquad (c, s) \in owns \wedge \#(s.goals) = 1$

Thus, the agent framework allows an explicit and precise analysis of multi-agent systems with no more conceptual primitives than were introduced for the initial framework to describe individual agents. Using these fundamental forms of interaction, we can proceed to define a more detailed taxonomy of inter-agent relationships that allows a richer understanding of the social configuration of agents, suggesting different possibilities for interaction, as shown by the relationships below, taken from [20]. Importantly, the relationships identified are not imposed on multi-agent systems, but arise naturally from agents interacting, and therefore underlie all multi-agent systems.

3.5 Sociological Behavior

Now, social behavior involves an agent interacting with others; sociological behavior requires more, that an agent understand its relationships with others. In order to do so, it must model them, their relationships, and their plans.

3.5.1 Models and Plans

To model their environment, agents require an *internal store*, without which their past experience could not influence direct behavior, resulting in reflexive action alone. A store exists as part of an agent's state in an environment but it must also have existed *prior* to that state. We call this feature an *internal store* or *memory*, and define *store agents* as those with memories. Unlike *social* agents that engage in interaction with others, *sociological* agents model relationships as well as agents. It is a simple matter to define the model an agent has of another agent (*AgentModel*), by re-using the agent framework components as shown below. Even though the types of these constructs are equivalent to those presented earlier, it is useful to distinguish physical constructs from mental constructs such as models, as it provides a conceptual aid. We can similarly define models of other components and relationships so that specifying a sociological agent amounts to a refinement of the *Agent* schema as outlined below.

$EntityModel == Entity$
$AgentModel == Agent$
$AutonomousAgentModel == AutonomousAgent$
$CoopModel == Cooperation$
$EngModel == DirectEngagement$
$ChainModel == EngagementChain$

A sociological agent therefore views its environment as containing a collection of entities with engagements, engagement chains and cooperations between them. There are many consistency checks that need to be specified at this level, such as if a sociological agent has a model of a direct engagement (say) then it must model both those entities involved as having the goal of the direct engagement. However, there are many details, and we omit then in our definition below.

$$
\begin{array}{lll}
ModelAgent & ::= & ent\langle\!\langle Entity\rangle\!\rangle \\
& | & obj\langle\!\langle Object\rangle\!\rangle \\
& | & agn\langle\!\langle Agent\rangle\!\rangle \\
& | & aag\langle\!\langle AutonomousAgent\rangle\!\rangle \\
ModelRelationship & ::= & chain\langle\!\langle ChainModel\rangle\!\rangle \\
& | & eng\langle\!\langle EngModel\rangle\!\rangle \\
& | & coop\langle\!\langle CoopModel\rangle\!\rangle \\
Model & ::= & relmodel\langle\!\langle ModelRelationship\rangle\!\rangle \\
& | & agentmodel\langle\!\langle ModelRelationship\rangle\!\rangle
\end{array}
$$

─── $SociologicalAgent$ ──────────────────────
$AutonomousAgentState$
$models : \mathbb{P}\, Model$
──────────────────────────────────────

Now, in order to consider sociological agents with planning capabilities, we can construct a high-level model of *plan-agents* that applies equally well to reactive or deliberative, single-agent or multi-agent planners. It represents a high-level of abstraction without committing to the nature of an agent, the plan representation, or the agent's environment; we simply distinguish *categories* of plan and possible relationships between an agent's plans and goals. Specifically, we define *active* plans as those identified as candidate plans not yet selected for execution; and *executable* plans as those active plans that have been selected for execution.

Formally, we initially define the set of all agent plans to be a given set ([*Plan*]), so that at this stage we abstract out any information about the nature of plans themselves. Our highest-level description of a *plan-agent* can then be formalized in the *PlanAgent* schema below.

__PlanAgent_____

Agent
$goallibrary : \mathbb{P}\, Goal$
$planlibrary, activeplans, executableplans : \mathbb{P}\, Plan$
$activeplangoal, plangoallibrary : Goal \nrightarrow \mathbb{P}\, Plan$

_____

$\mathrm{dom}\, activeplangoal \subseteq goals \;\wedge$
$\qquad \bigcup(\mathrm{ran}\, activeplangoal) = activeplans$
$\mathrm{dom}\, plangoallibrary \subseteq goallibrary \;\wedge$
$\qquad \bigcup(\mathrm{ran}\, plangoallibrary) \subseteq planlibrary$
$goals \subseteq goallibrary \;\wedge$
$\qquad executableplans \subseteq activeplans \subseteq planlibrary$
_____

__SociologicalPlanAgent_____

SociologicalAgent
PlanAgent
_____

The variables *goallibrary*, *planlibrary*, *activeplans* and *executable-
plans* represent the agent's repository of goals, repository of plans, active plans and executable plans, respectively. Each active plan is necessarily associated with one or more of the agent's current goals as specified by *activeplangoal*. For example, if the function contains the pair
$(g, \{p_1, p_2, p_3\})$, it indicates that p_1, p_2 and p_3 are competing active plans
for g. While active plans must be associated with at least one active goal,
the converse is not true, since agents may have goals for which no plans
have been considered. Analogously the *plangoallibrary* function relates
the repository of goals, *goallibrary*, to the repository of plans, *planlibrary*.
However, not necessarily all library plans and goals are related by this
function.

3.5.2 Plan and Agent Categories

Now, using these notions, we can describe some example categories of
goals, agents and plans (with respect to the models of the sociological
plan-agent), that may be relevant to an agent's understanding of its environment. Each of the categories is formally defined below, where the
sociological plan-agent is denoted as *spa*. Any variable preceded by *model*
denotes the models that *spa* has of some specific type of entity or relationship. For example, *spa.modelneutralobjects* and *spa.modelowns* are the
neutral objects and ownership relations the sociological agent models.

self-suff plan

$$\forall p \in spa.planlibrary \bullet selfsuff(p) \Leftrightarrow spa.planentities(p) \subseteq$$
$$spa.modelneutralobjects \cup spa.modelself \cup$$
$$spa.modelowns(\!|\, spa.modelself\, |\!)$$

self-suff goal

$\forall g \in spa.goallibrary \bullet selfsuffgoal(g) \Leftrightarrow$
$\qquad (\exists p \in spa.plangoallibrary(g) \bullet p \in selfsuff)$

reliant goal

$\forall g \in spa.goallibrary \bullet reliantgoal(g) \Leftrightarrow$
$\qquad spa.plangoallibrary\ g \neq \{\ \} \ \wedge$
$\qquad\qquad \neg\ (\exists p : spa.plangoallibrary\ g \bullet p \in selfsuff)$

A *self-sufficient plan* is any plan that involves only neutral-objects, server-agents the plan-agent owns, and the plan-agent itself. Self-sufficient plans can therefore be executed without regard to other agents and exploit current agent relationships. (The formal definition uses the relational image operator: in general, the relational image $R(\!|\ S\ |\!)$ of a set S through a relation R is the set of all objects y to which R relates to some member x of S.) A *self-sufficient goal* is any goal in the goal library that has an associated self-sufficient plan. These goals can then, according to the agent's model, be achieved independently of the existing social configuration. A *reliant-goal* is any goal that has a nonempty set of associated plans that is not self-sufficient.

For each plan that is not self-sufficient, a sociological plan-agent can establish the autonomous agents that may be affected by its execution, which is an important criterion in selecting a plan from competing active plans. An autonomous agent A may be affected by a plan in one of two ways: either it is required to perform an action directly, or it is engaging a server-agent S required by the plan. In this latter case, a sociological plan-agent can reason about either persuading A to share or release S, taking S without permission, or finding an alternative server-agent or plan. To facilitate such an analysis, we can define further categories of agents and plans, as described in [20], but we do not consider them further here.

3.6 Autonomous Interaction as Motivated Discovery

Many traditional models of interaction have assumed an ideal world in which unfounded assumptions have given rise to inadequate characterizations of interaction amongst autonomous agents. If we consider autonomous interaction to be a process of uncertain outcome (which it must be), then we can characterize it in a more general way as a process of *discovery* in terms of the effects of actions. This allows us to deal effectively with the inherent uncertainty in interaction. In this section, we show how the ideas of discovery can be used to approach autonomous interaction. We begin with an introduction to the ideas of discovery, and then show how they may be applied and formalized in the multi-agent domain.

3.6.1 Motivated Discovery

Scientific discovery is a process that occurs in the real world. Many examples of actual discovery have been observed and recorded, providing a basis for analyses of the reasoning methods used by real scientists. This has led to the identification of temporally and physically distinct elements in the discovery process which strongly support the notion of discovery as a methodology for reasoning rather than a single 'magical' process. Moreover, the underlying motivation behind scientific reasoning (and discovery) is one of increasing knowledge, understanding and awareness of a natural external environment in order to be able to explain, predict and possibly manipulate that environment. The second of these provides us with a large part of what we want to achieve in AI — to explain, predict and manipulate our environment. The first, if the notion of a methodology for discovery is even partly correct, provides us with a suitable means (in AI) for achieving it.

In the context of autonomous interaction, agents behave according to a certain understanding or *theory* of their environment and the agents within it, that we might in a different context consider to be the models we have just described. In this section, we will refer to a *theory* for the sake of adopting the *discovery* stance, but we might equally be referring to these models of others, and of interaction itself.

We adopt Luck's simple but encompassing model for discovery [16] that entails six stages, as follows:

1. **Prediction:** deductively generating predictions from a theory of interaction and a scenario;
2. **Experimentation:** testing the predictions (and hence the theory of interaction) by constructing appropriate experiments;
3. **Observation:** observing the results of experiments;
4. **Evaluation:** comparing and evaluating observations and predictions to determine if the theory has been refuted;
5. **Revision:** revising the theory to account for anomalies; and
6. **Selection:** choosing the best resulting revised theory.

The framework is a cyclical one, repeating until stability is achieved with a consistent theory. It begins with *prediction* which entails generating predictions for a given scenario, and then subjecting these to some kind of *experimentation*. Through *observation* and *evaluation*, the results of the experiment are compared with the predictions and, in the event that they are consistent with each other, no action is necessary. If the observations and predictions are anomalous, however, the theory must be *revised*, and a suitable revision *selected* to be passed through to the beginning of the cycle for use in generating new predictions. Even when no failure occurs, the theory is still liable to provide anomalies at a later stage.

Prediction

Perhaps the least troublesome part of the cycle is prediction. This is a simple deductive procedure that draws logical inferences from a theory and background knowledge given a description of a particular scenario. In order to make sense of our environment, we continually anticipate the effects of our actions, and of external factors—we make predictions about what will happen next. Usually, our predictions are correct and we anticipate well, but there are instances when the predictions fail, and we must deal with these failures later on in the cycle.

Generating predictions can be an expensive procedure, however, demanding time and resources which may not be available. We might for example be able to predict first, second and third places in an election, yet if we are only interested in who wins, only one of the predictions needs to be generated. This is related to the motivations of the reasoning agent, in the context of which the relevance of predictions can be assessed.

Experimentation

Once predictions have been generated, they may be empirically tested, and the results of these experiments can be compared with the predictions to determine if the theory (or indeed background knowledge) is, as much as possible, correct and consistent. This implies a certain requirement on theories that has not yet been mentioned—that they be refutable, or *falsifiable*.

We can think of experimentation as being one of two kinds. First, there are *active* experiments in which the experimenter carefully constructs apparatus, or forces controlled environmental conditions with the aim of testing a particular characteristic or condition of a theory. Included in these are typical laboratory experiments. Alternatively, and more commonly, there are *passive* experiments which include any situation for which an expectation is generated, but for which there is no explicit theory. For example, squeezing a tube of toothpaste when brushing teeth is a passive experiment which has no controlled conditions, but which will determine if the expectation of producing toothpaste is correct or not. Both of these are important. When concerned with the problem of specifically acquiring knowledge in narrow domains, active experiments are prevalent. In normal everyday affairs, passive experiments are the norm unless they meet with a prediction failure. In this case, it is typical to switch to active experiments to find the reason for the failure, if necessary. In the case of autonomous interaction, any kind of act designed to elicit a response can be regarded as an experiment.

Thus, experimentation is responsible for designing and constructing experiments in order that imperfections in the theory may be detected and corrected.

Observation

We intend this to be a complete and encompassing framework. Were we to exclude observation, it would not be so. Although observation immediately appears transparently simple, requiring merely that changes in the environment be observed and recorded for future reference, it is a little more complicated. (It should be noted that observations may be forced by the use of controlled experiments, or may occur independently.) Observations are compared with predictions and used to decide whether the theory is acceptable, or whether it needs to be revised.

Ideally, we would want an independent observer, a system capable of perceiving the external world, filtering out irrelevant information, and providing observations as input to the reasoning system.

Evaluation

At this point, the experiment has been carried out, the observations have been recorded, but it remains to decide whether or not the theory has been falsified, whether or not it is acceptable. To make this decision, we need to be aware of a number of influential factors and to evaluate the evidence in this light. Principally, this is concerned with the quality of the evidence. If an agent is to be effective, then it must be able to cope with both experimental and observational error, and must be able to evaluate them in an appropriate context. Little needs to be said about the occurrence of errors, for it is undeniable that they are always present to some degree. It is, however, unacceptable to pretend to cope with them by introducing simple tolerance levels. Experimental evidence must be evaluated relative to the current motivations of a system, taking into account the implications of success or failure. In medical domains, for example, even a small degree of error may be unacceptable if it would lead to the loss of a patient's life, while weather prediction systems may, in certain circumstances, allow a far greater error tolerance.

Revision

If it is decided that the theory has been falsified, then it must be revised so that it is consistent with the falsifying observations. Alternatively, new theories may be introduced or generated by another reasoning technique such as analogy, case-based reasoning, etc. The problem of creating new theories beyond direct observation is outside of this framework. Yet we do allow for their introduction into the inductive cycle, and in addition we allow for new theories based solely upon direct observation.

Revisions to the theory should include all those possible within the restrictions of the knowledge representation used that are consistent with the observations. This leads to the problem of combinatorial explosion, however, and the revision process should therefore be additionally constrained by heuristic search, the search heuristics being considered in the next and final stage. Allowing all revisions, potentially at least, is important in order that they are not prejudged out of context.

Selection

As mentioned above, this is not really a separate stage, and proceeds in tandem with revision, but the task is distinct. Since the number of possible revisions to a given theory is extremely large, there must be criteria for selecting those theories which are better than others. Many criteria for rating theories have been proposed, such as simplicity, predictive power, modesty, conservatism and corroboration.

However, selection of theories must be in context. This means that the goals and motivations of a system are relevant to the task of judging which criteria are more important in evaluating a theory. The way in which these criteria are applied depends upon the context in which they are used and the need for which they are used. For appropriateness of use in many situations, we may prefer Newton's laws to Einstein's, but in other circumstances, only Einstein's may be acceptable.

3.6.2 Autonomous Interaction

In this subsection, we apply the framework just described to the problem of autonomous interaction, reformulating the discovery concepts, and formalizing the process of interaction.

In order to make sense of our environment and to function effectively in it, we continually anticipate the effects of our actions and utterances — we make predictions (or expectations) about what will happen next. The action-selection function, *autoactions*, of the *AutonomousAgentAct* schema encompasses the deliberation of the agent. The action that is selected is intended to satisfy the goals of the agent through its resulting effects and consequent changes to the environment. In the case of an interaction episode involving two agents, the initiating agent selects an action that is intended to cause the desired response in the responding agent. The uncertainty inherent in such interaction means that the effects cannot be known in advance, but can only be discovered after the event has taken place, or action performed. We describe this by specifying the *predicted* effects of actions selected in the *AutonomousAgentAct* schema by applying the *socialeffectinteract* function to the current view of the environment and those actions. The agent thus predicts that these actions will change the environment to achieve the desired results. Remember that the environment includes all of the entities in it, so that a change to an agent in the environment will in turn cause a change to the environment itself. We also introduce a variable to store an agent's actual percepts prior to an operation, *oldpercepts*, which will be used later in the *Decide* schema.

Last, remember that *willdo*, specifies the actions that are performed and not the actions that the agent *selects* to perform next. In general, this is specified by the variable *todo* which is a function of the agents motivations, goals and current view of the environment (and *not* of the actual environment which dictates what actions are actually performed). In successful operation, *willdo* should equal *todo*. However, when agents have only limited knowledge, perceptual capabilities or habiting dynamic open worlds these variables will not always equate. It is such anomalies that signal to the agent that it must revise its current model of itself and environment.

$$\begin{array}{|l}
\underline{\quad SocialAgentPredict\ }\rule{8cm}{0pt} \\
SociologicalAgent \\
socialeffectinteract : View \rightarrow \mathbb{P}\,Action \nrightarrow View \\
oldpercepts, prediction : View \\
selectaction : \mathbb{P}\,Motivation \rightarrow \mathbb{P}\,Goal \rightarrow View \rightarrow \mathbb{P}\,Action \\
todo : \mathbb{P}\,Action \\
\hline
todo = selectaction\ motivations\ goals\ actualpercepts \\
prediction = socialeffectinteract\ actualpercepts\ todo \\
prediction \cap \bigcup goals \neq \{\} \\
\end{array}$$

In order to achieve the desired result, the relevant actions must be performed. Effectively, this acts as an experiment, testing whether the predictions generated are consistent with the resulting effects. In this sense, experimentation is central to this model, for such interaction with the environment is the only way in which an agent's understanding of its capabilities and its environment can be assessed to bring to light inadequacies, inconsistencies and errors. When an action is performed, it affects the models of other agents and of the agent society which, after the change, are derived from the previous models (of both the agents and inter-agent relationships) and the view of the environment through the function, *updatemodels*. These models of agents and their relationships are critical in determining if the action was successful.

$$\begin{array}{|l}
\underline{\quad SocialAgentInteract\ }\rule{7cm}{0pt} \\
SocialAgentPredict \\
updatemodels : \mathbb{P}\,Model \rightarrow View \rightarrow \mathbb{P}\,Model \\
\end{array}$$

The action also has an effect on the environment, which changes accordingly, and a similar effect on the agent itself whose percepts also change. For example, in the case of an action which issues a request to another agent to tell the current time, the resulting model will either encode the fact that the agent is telling the time, or not. By inspecting this model and its attributes, the requesting agent can determine if its action has been successful. Note that the new value of *oldpercepts* takes the previous value of *actualpercepts* for later use.

$$
\begin{array}{l}
\underline{\quad SocialEnv\ \rule{0pt}{0pt}\hrulefill} \\
\Delta SocialAgentPredict \\
SocialAgentInteract \\
\hline
env' = effectinteract\ env\ willdo \\
posspercepts' = canperceive\ env'\ perceivingactions \\
actualpercepts' = willperceive\ motivations\ goals\ posspercepts' \\
willdo' = autoactions\ motivations\ goals\ actualpercepts'\ env' \\
models' = updatemodels\ models\ actualpercepts' \\
oldpercepts' = actualpercepts \\
prediction' = prediction
\end{array}
$$

Evaluating the results of the actions appears simple. At the most basic level, it involves the comparison of predictions with observations. Thus, if the intended effects of the actions and the actual effects match, then the actions have achieved the desired result and the episode is successful. If they are anomalous, then it reveals an erroneous understanding of the environment and the agents within it, or an inadequate capability for perception of the results. The important point here is that there is no guarantee of success, and failure can be due to any number of reasons.

This analysis assumes that the evidence is perfect, however, which may not always be appropriate. In any real environment this is not so, and error can be introduced into evidence in a variety of ways, reducing the quality of the observed evidence accordingly. Not only may there be inaccuracy due to the inherent uncertainty in both performing the actions and perception of the results (experimentation and observation respectively), but also, if the actions taken by the agent are communicative actions intended to elicit a response from another autonomous agent, then there may be inaccuracy due to malicious intent on the part of the responding agent by providing misleading information, for example [23]. Thus, the response may itself be the vessel for the error.

In addition to assessing the fit of observations with predictions, therefore, the quality of the observations themselves must also be assessed in order to ascertain whether they are acceptable to be used in the comparison at all. Simple tolerance levels for assessing the acceptability of perceived evidence are inadequate, for they do not consider the need for the interaction episode, and the importance of achieving the desired result. The quality demanded of the observations can thus only be assessed in relation to the motivations of the agent which provide a measure of the importance of the situation, and take into account the implications of success and failure. In medical domains, for example, where the agents are highly motivated, even a small degree of error in interaction of relevant patient details may be unacceptable if it would lead to the loss of a patient's life, while neighbourly discussion of the weather with low motivations and little importance may allow a far greater error tolerance.

The schemas below describe evaluation with two predicates. The predicate *accept*, holds between the capabilities of the agent, its perceived environment before and after the actions were performed, and the agent models, if the evidence is acceptable. The capabilities of the agent capture the uncertainty information that arises from the agent itself, while the perceived environment and agent models include details of difficulties arising through the environment, or other agents. The *consider* predicate compares predictions and observations once evidence is accepted. Note that the potentially difficult question of when observations match predictions is bound up in the function itself which may be interpreted either as a simple equality test or as something more sophisticated.

The *Decide* schema also states at the beginning that though the agent changes as a result of this evaluation ($\Delta SocialAgent$), the state of the agent remains the same ($\Xi AutonomousAgentState$). Finally, if the evidence is accepted, and the observations do not match the predictions, then the agent models must be revised as specified by *revisemodels*.

$$bool ::= True \mid False$$

$$
\begin{array}{|l}
\hline
\;SocialAgentEvaluate \underline{\hspace{5cm}} \\
\hline
\;accept\_ : (\mathbb{P}\,Action \times View \times View \times \mathbb{P}\,Model) \\
\;consider\_ : \mathbb{P}(View \times View) \\
\hline
\end{array}
$$

$$
\begin{array}{|l}
\hline
\;Decide \underline{\hspace{5cm}} \\
\hline
\;\Delta SociologicalAgent \\
\;\Xi AutonomousAgentState \\
\;SocialAgentPredict \\
\;SocialAgentEvaluate \\
\;revisemodels : View \rightarrow \mathbb{P}\,Model \rightarrow \mathbb{P}\,Model \\
\hline
\;accept\,(capabilities, actualpercepts, oldpercepts, models) \wedge \\
\;\neg\; consider\,(prediction, actualpercepts) \Rightarrow \\
\;\quad models' = revisemodels\ actualpercepts\ models \\
\hline
\end{array}
$$

3.7 Discussion

Our efforts with BDI agents [10, 9] have shown that formal computational models of implemented systems and idealized systems, using the Z specification language [31], a standard (and commonly used) formal method of software engineering, can result in implementations that are much more strongly related. In particular, they can be checked for type-correctness, they can be animated to provide prototype systems, and they can be formally and systematically refined to produce provably correct implementations. In this vein, related work has sought to contribute to the conceptual and theoretical foundations of agent-based systems through the use of such specification languages (used in traditional software engineering) that enable formal modeling yet provide a basis for implementation of practical systems.

Indeed, as the fields of intelligent agents and multi-agent systems move relentlessly forwards, it is becoming increasingly more important to maintain a coherent world view that both structures existing work and provides a base on which to keep pace with the latest advances. Our framework has allowed us to do just that. By elaborating the agent hierarchy in different ways, we have been able to detail both individual agent functionality and develop models of evolving social relationships between agents with, for example, our analyses of goal generation and adoption, and our treatment of engagement and cooperation. Not only does this provide a clear conceptual foundation, it also allows us to refine our level of description to particular systems and theories.

The problems with existing notions of agency and autonomy are now well-understood, but the importance of these notions remains high, nevertheless. In previous work we have addressed this by constructing a formal specification to identify and characterise those entities called agents and autonomous agents, in a precise yet accessible way. Our taxonomy provides clear definitions for objects, agents and autonomous agents that allow a better understanding of the functionality of different systems. It explicates those factors that are necessary for agency and autonomy, and is sufficiently abstract to cover the gamut of agents, both hardware and software, intelligent and unintelligent.

Then, by taking autonomous interaction to be a process of discovery within the framework, we can avoid the problems identified earlier of *guaranteed effects* and *automatic intention recognition*. In discovery, no effects are known for certain in advance, but instead, (tentative) predictions or expectations of future states of the world can be generated. It is only possible to be certain about effects once the actions have been carried out. This can lead to a re-evaluation of existing models.

Additionally, we assert that the process of autonomous communication must be motivated, and consequently a motivated agent does not have a *predetermined agenda*, nor is it *benevolent*. Motivations provide a means by which an agent can set its own agenda, or set its own goals and determine which actions to perform in achieving them. The effects of benevolent behavior are possible, but only through self-serving motivations. Moreover, because effects are not guaranteed, failure is always possible, but the combination of discovery and motivations allow effective exploitation of these failures and also recovery from them whenever possible.

Our aim in constructing the model for autonomous interaction is ambitious. We are attempting to provide a common unifying framework within which different levels of abstraction of reasoning, behavioral and interaction tasks can be related and considered. We have necessarily concentrated on a high-level specification so that the key principles can be explicated, but without sacrificing the need for preciseness through formality. By explicitly introducing motivated reasoning as part of the agent framework, and providing the capacity for effectively dealing with dynamic worlds through discovery, we provide a way in which the inadequacies in existing models may be addressed.

A significant claim of this work is that it can provide a general mathematical framework within which different models, and particular systems, can be defined and contrasted. Z is particularly suitable in squaring the demands of formal modeling with the need for implementation by allowing transition between specification and program. There are many well-developed strategies and tools to aid this transformation. Programs can also be *verified* with respect to a specification; it is possible to prove that a program behaves precisely as set out in the Z specification. This is not possible when specifications are written in modal logics since they have the computationally ungrounded possible-worlds model as their semantics. Thus our approach to formal specification is pragmatic; we need to be formal to be precise about the concepts we discuss, yet we want to remain directly connected to issues of implementation. We have also found the Z language is sufficiently expressive to allow a consistent, unified and structured account of a computer system and its associated operations.

References

1. Allen, J. *A plan-based approach to speech act recognition*. Technical Report 131, Department of Computer Science, University of Toronto, 1979.
2. Appelt, D. E. *Planning English Sentences*. Cambridge University Press. 1985.
3. Austin, J. L. *How to Do Things with Words*. Oxford University Press. 1962.
4. Aylett, R., Brazier, F., Jennings, N., Luck, M., Preist, C. and Nwana, H. Agent systems and applications. *Knowledge Engineering Review*, **13**(3):303–308, 1998.
5. Boissier, O. and Demazeau., Y. A distributed artificial intelligence view on general purpose vision systems. In *Decentralized AI 3: Proceedings of the Third European Workshop on Modeling Autonomous Agents in a Multi-Agent World*, E. Werner and Y. Demazeau, editors. Elsevier, 1992, pp 311–330.
6. Campbell, J. A. and d'Inverno, M. Knowledge interchange protocols. In *Decentralized AI: Proceedings of the First European Workshop on Modeling Autonomous Agents in a Multi-Agent World*, Y. Demazeau and J. P. Müller, editors. Elsevier, 1990, pp 63–80.

7. Castelfranchi, C. Social power. In *Decentralized AI: Proceedings of the First European Workshop on Modeling Autonomous Agents in a Multi-Agent World*, Y. Demazeau and J. P. Müller, editors. Elsevier, 1990, pp 49–62.

8. d'Inverno, M., Fisher, M., Lomuscio, A., Luck, M., de Rijke, M., Ryan, M. and Wooldridge, M. Formalisms for multi-agent systems. *Knowledge Engineering Review*, **12**(3):315–321, 1997.

9. d'Inverno, M., Kinny, D. and Luck, M. Interaction protocols in agents. In *ICMAS'98, Third International Conference on Multi-Agent Systems*, Paris, France, IEEE Computer Society, 1998a, pp 112–119.

10. d'Inverno, M., Kinny, D., Luck, M. and Wooldridge M. A formal specification of dMARS. In *Intelligent Agents IV: Proceedings of the Fourth International Workshop on Agent Theories, Architectures and Languages, (LNAI 1365)*, M. P. Singh, A. Rao and M. J. Wooldridge, editors. Springer-Verlag, 1998b, pp 155–176.

11. Fisher, M. Representing and executing agent-based systems. In *Intelligent Agents: Theories, Architectures, and Languages, (LNAI 890)*, M. Wooldridge and N. R. Jennings, editors. Springer-Verlag. 1995, pp 307–323.

12. Galliers. J. R. The positive role of conflicts in cooperative multi-agent systems. In *Decentralized AI: Proceedings of the First European Workshop on Modeling Autonomous Agents in a Multi-Agent World*, Y. Demazeau and J. P. Müller, editors. Elsevier, 1990.

13. Galliers, J. R. Modeling autonomous belief revision in dialogue. In *Decentralized AI 2: Proceedings of the Third European Workshop on Modeling Autonomous Agents in a Multi-Agent World*, Y. Demazeau and J. P. Müller, editors. Elsevier, 1991, pp 231–245.

14. Goodwin, R. A formal specification of agent properties. *Journal of Logic and Computation*, **5**(6):763–781, 1995.

15. Grice, H. P. Logic and conversation. In *Syntax and Semantics, Volume 3: Speech Acts*, P. Cole and J. L. Morgan, editors. Academic Press. 1975, pp 41–58.

16. Luck, M. Evaluating evidence for motivated discovery. In *Progress in Artificial Intelligence, (LNAI 727)*, M. Filgueiras and L. Damas, editors. Springer-Verlag. 1993, pp 324–339.

17. Luck, M. From definition to deployment: What next for agent-based systems? *The Knowledge Engineering Review*, **14**(2):119–124, 1999.

18. Luck, M. and d'Inverno, M. A formal framework for agency and autonomy. In *Proceedings of the First International Conference on Multi-Agent Systems*, AAAI Press / MIT Press, 1995, pp 254–260.

19. Luck, M. and d'Inverno, M. Engagement and cooperation in motivated agent modeling. In *Proceedings of the First Australian DAI Workshop, (LNAI 1087)*, Springer-Verlag, 1996, pp 70–84.

20. Luck, M. and d'Inverno, M. Plan analysis for autonomous sociological agents. In *Intelligent Agents VII, Proceedings of the Seventh International Workshop on Agent Theories, Architectures and Languages, (LNAI 1986)*, Springer-Verlag, 2001a, pp 182–197.

21. Luck, M. and d'Inverno, M. A conceptual framework for agent definition and development. *The Computer Journal*, **44**(1):1–20, 2001b.

22. Luck, M., Griffiths, N. and d'Inverno, M. From agent theory to agent construction: A case study. In *Intelligent Agents III: Proceedings of the Third*

International Workshop on Agent Theories, Architectures, and Languages, (LNAI 1193), J. Müller, M. Wooldridge and N. R. Jennings, editors. Springer-Verlag, 1997, pp 49–63.

23. Marsh, S. Trust in distributed artificial intelligence. In *Artificial Social Systems: Selected Papers from the Fourth European Workshop on Modeling Autonomous Agents in a Multi-Agent World, (LNAI 830)*, C. Castelfranchi and E. Werner, editors. Springer-Verlag. 1994, pp 94–114.

24. Norman, T. J. and Long, D. Goal creation in motivated agents. In *Intelligent Agents: Proceedings of the First International Workshop on Agent Theories, Architectures, and Languages, (LNAI 890)*, M. Wooldridge and N. R. Jennings, editors. Springer-Verlag, 1995, pp 277–290.

25. Parsons, S., Sierra, C. and Jennings, N. Agents that reason and negotiate by arguing. *Journal of Logic and Computation*, 8(3):261–292, 1998.

26. Perrault, C. R. An application of default logic to speech act theory. In *Intentions in Communication*, P. R. Cohen, J. Morgan and M. E. Pollack, editors. MIT Press. 1990, pp 161–186.

27. Rao, A. S. Agentspeak(l): BDI agents speak out in a logical computable language. In *Agents Breaking Away: Proceedings of the Seventh European Workshop on Modeling Autonomous Agents in a Multi-Agent World, (LNAI 1038)*, W. Van de Velde and J. W. Perram, editors. Springer-Verlag, 1996, pp 42–55.

28. Rao, A. S. and Georgeff, M. P. An abstract architecture for rational agents. In *Proceedings of Knowledge Representation and Reasoning*, C. Rich, W. Swartout, and B. Nebel, editors. 1992, pp 439–449.

29. Searle, J. R. *Speech Acts*. Cambridge University Press. 1969.

30. Smith, R. G. The contract net protocol: High-level communication and control in a distributed problem solver. *IEEE Transactions on Computers*, 29(12):1104–1113, 1980.

31. Spivey, J. M. *The Z Notation: A Reference Manual*. Prentice Hall, Hemel Hempstead, 2nd edition. 1992.

32. Wooldridge, M. J. and Jennings, N. R. Formalizing the cooperative problem solving process. In *Proceedings of the Thirteenth International Workshop on Distributed Artificial Intelligence*, 1994.

Part II

Formal Methods in Agent Design

A Process-Algebraic Agent Abstraction

Albert Esterline, Toinette Rorie, and Abdollah Homaifar

4.1 Introduction

Wooldridge [47] defines an agent as a computer system capable of autonomous action that meets its design objective in the environment in which it is situated. An *intelligent* agent in particular is capable of flexible autonomous action, where flexibility involves two somewhat opposing attributes: reactivity (the ability to perceive its environment and to respond to changes in it) and proactiveness (aiming at goals by taking the initiative). In addition, since agents are autonomous, to achieve goals they must cooperate with other agents, so a third aspect of flexibility is social ability. Wooldridge notes that an object is superficially like an agent: it is a computational entity encapsulating a state in which it can perform actions (method execution) and communicate (message passing). However, the decision whether to execute an action lies with the object invoking the method in an object system but with the agent receiving the request in an agent system. This chapter focuses on multi-agent systems rather than individual agents. One characteristic of multi-agent environments identified by Huhns and Stephens [22] is that they "provide an infrastructure specifying communication and interaction protocols." Indeed, one feature of multi-agent systems that we ensure that we capture is the patterns of communication acts. (These acts of agents are generally taken to be speech acts.) The other characteristics of multi-agent environments identified by Huhns and Stephens are that they are typically open (with no "centralized designer") and (echoing Wooldridge) the agents are autonomous and distributed. Abstractly, the open nature of these environments entails that smaller systems (agents) can be *composed* to form larger systems (multi-agent systems), where composition involves coordinated concurrent activity. We also ensure that we capture composition in this sense. Huhns and Stephens also see coordination as critical and, in the case of self-interested agents (where negotiation is involved), as a major challenge.

In considering models (formal or not) of multi-agent systems, we use what we call the *agent abstraction*: the notion of an autonomous, flexible computational entity in an open environment that specifies communication protocols. This notion is useful even though there is little agreement on details and even though this is not a formal notion: any particular model of a multi-agent system would have to explicate with its own concepts the characteristics mentioned above. Singh *et al.* [40] maintain that this abstraction is valuable because it provides higher-level abstractions for complex systems, which lead to design and development techniques that are simpler since they avoid the complexity inherent in such systems. A model as understood here is expressed by a set of well-formed (formal or informal) expressions. A model is (partially) expressed by a specification when our goal is system development, where we wish ultimately to realize the model in an implementation. In the opposite direction, when we analyze an existing implementation, we generally construct a model, expressed in a notation different from that of the implementation. General (for example, abstract) models may subsume more specific (for example, more concrete) models. We take a (modeling) *framework* to be a notation along with directions on using it to express (and hence to construct) models.

We advocate formally modeling multi-agent systems, that is, using rigorous formalisms in expressing models of multi-agent systems. This chapter suggests some aspects of a formal framework for modeling such systems (without actually developing the framework). In particular, we formally explicate the agent abstraction. Formal modeling naturally lags quick-and-dirty approaches to system design, but once a field has been defined in practice, formal modeling offers rigor, eliminates ambiguity, and allows one to abstract away inessential details. This improved understanding allows one to debug specifications before extensive effort is committed to design and implementation, and it allows us to prescribe rigorously system behavior against which an implementation is tested. A formalism rigorously defines how well-formed expressions may be manipulated, so it allows us to construct tools that facilitate reasoning about and animating specifications.

An agent is a *reactive* system in the sense of Manna and Pnueli [28] (different from the above sense of "reactive" in which it is contrasted with "proactive"). In this sense, a reactive program is contrasted with a transformational program, which produces a final result at the end of a terminating computation so is conceptualized as a function from an initial state to a final state or result. The role of a reactive program is not to produce a final result but to maintain some ongoing interaction with the environment. Since many reactive programs (such as those controlling robotic agents) are tightly coupled with the hardware they control, we should generally address *reactive systems*. Reactivity and concurrency are closely related since, in the reactive case, the program and its environment act concurrently whereas, in the transformational case, they act sequentially.

This suggests that we focus on the concurrency aspect of the agent abstraction. Many systems have several components that not only work independently or concurrently but also interact or communicate. Conceptually, Olderog [35] treats such systems and their components uniformly as *concurrent processes*. Here a *process* is an object designed for a possibly continuous interaction with its user (possibly another process) and an interaction (such as an input or an output of a value) is regarded abstractly as a *communication*. Generalizing somewhat on Olderog's classification of concurrency formalisms, we recognize three levels of abstractness. The most abstract concurrency formalisms are (temporal and modal) logics, used to describe or specify the communication behavior of processes. More concrete are process algebras, which are term algebras used as abstract concurrent programming languages that stress the composition of processes by a small set of process operators. The most concrete level is occupied by concurrency automata (paradigmatically Petri nets, but also, for example, Statecharts), which describe processes as concurrent and interacting machines with all the details of their operational behavior.

There are several reasons to consider agents as processes and to model multi-agent systems with a process-algebraic framework. Compositionality allows process terms for agents to be combined simply to form a term for a multi-agent system. A process algebra encourages one to think of a process as capable of certain interactions with its environment that could be discovered by experimenting with it. When convenient, the environment itself may be modeled as a (system of) process(es) and compositionality allows the process-cum-environment to be viewed as a single process (system). Communication protocols required of a multi-agent environment can be formulated straightforwardly in process algebras, which are often used for formalizing protocols. The basic action in a process algebra is communication across an interface with a *handshake*. Two processes performing a handshake must be prepared at the time to perform complementary actions (usually thought of as output and input on a given channel, hence communication), hence a handshake synchronizes the processes. Handshakes are remarkably like speech acts in face-to-face communication. (Suchman claims on p. 71 of [41] that "... analyses of face-to-face communication indicate that conversation ... is a joint action accomplished through the participants' continuing engagement in speaking and listening.") The symmetry of a handshake distributes control between the participating processes/agents hence respects their autonomy. Since there are handshakes with the environment, the reactive (in the sense opposed to proactive) nature of agents can be accommodated.

A process-algebraic framework for modeling multi-agent systems does not so directly capture aspects of the agent abstraction that are not directly related to communication. The proactive aspect involves (internal)

planning, and negotiation involves (internal) computation by the nego-
tiators in addition to their communication. Process algebras, however,
typically allow "silent" actions (handshakes not observable outside the
process making them) among components that have had their communication ports in some sense internalized within a single process. Sequences
of silent actions offer hope for modeling computations internal to agents.

But not all processes are agents. Generally, a process P can perform
a communication action, or *transition*, then behave like the process resulting from reducing P in a certain way. Some of the operators (and the
syntactic patterns they govern) persist through transitions; an example is
the (parallel) composition operator. Others, such as the alternative operator, do not thus persist—once one alternative is selected, the others are
no longer available. Think of a system as an encompassing process whose
several component processes—agents—persist (perhaps in reduced form)
through transitions. We picture a pair of agents P and Q as connected by
a link—a possibility for a handshake—when P contains a name denoting an action and Q contains a name denoting the complementary action.
This framework, then, gives a picture of the communication linkage of a
multi-agent system.

In interesting multi-agent systems, however, this linkage generally
changes dynamically—consider delegation of tasks or subtasks and the
changing relations a mobile agent has to stationary agents as it moves
from one region to another. Thus, the process algebra we use in our framework is the π-calculus, which allows *mobility*, the communication of a
link as data in a handshake. The π-calculus has the advantage over other
process algebras supporting mobility that it allows us to simulate higher-
order features (passing processes as data) by simply passing links. In particular, link passing can model a system whose agent population changes
since an agent that is not yet or no longer part of the system is one that
has no links to agents currently in the system. Also, it has been shown
that the π-calculus is a universal model for computation, so we can *in
principle* model with it any computational aspect of agents.

One principal task of this chapter is to show how the π-calculus can
be used to model certain aspects that have already been specified for a
major multi-agent system, the LOGOS agent community being designed
at NASA Goddard Space Flight Center. We capture aspects sufficient to
support a scenario that has been supplied by NASA/GSFC; we are concerned with the branch of the scenario that requires dynamic change
in the communication structure. Section 4.3 of this chapter outlines the
LOGOS agent community; Section 4.4 presents the scenario. Section 4.5
gives a π-calculus specification for supporting the scenario; the π-calculus
is presented in Section 4.2. Section 4.6 suggests how a π-calculus framework supports development activities in this context. Building on the experience gained in this exercise, Section 4.7 briefly addresses aspects of
multi-agent systems from the point of view of our framework.

Our notion of an agent—an autonomous, flexible computational entity in an open environment—intentionally includes human-like features. This view, which unifies agent research, is justified by *adopting the intentional stance*, that is, by treating systems as though they are rational agents (with beliefs, attitudes, and so on), because this allows us to predict their behavior. If our agent abstraction is indeed a good explication of the general notion of an agent, then this abstraction should be useful in modeling humans, at least those aspects of humans significant for interaction with computing systems. The two most salient features of modeling intentional behavior with a process-algebraic agent abstraction are handshake communication and plans expressed in process-algebraic terms.

The second, shorter part of this chapter looks at our agent abstraction from this point of view. Section 4.8 picks up the intentional stance and summarizes our research in applying our agent abstraction to agents collaborating with humans and to the humans themselves. Section 9 begins by reviewing criticism of the notion of plans as formal structures generating actions coming from the perspective of ethnomethodology and conversation analysis. These criticisms have fostered a view of plans as merely resources for orienting and recording coordinated activity. We, however, must maintain that plans in some sense control coordinated action—otherwise, the description in a process algebra of the sequence of actions an agent or human can perform is disengaged from the agent or human that realizes the model. We argue that specifications introduce obligations and that handshakes create obligations among the parties involved. We further argue that an agent must normally intend to meet its obligations and it must normally do what it intends. Thus, our use of the intentional stance emphasizes obligations, and imposing, being subject to, and discharging obligations are significant features that must be included in our agent abstraction.

4.2 The π-Calculus

The π-calculus [31, 32, 38] can be used to model a system that consists of processes that interact with each other, and whose environment is constantly changing. The π-calculus is available in two basic styles: the monadic calculus [32], where exactly one name is communicated at each synchronization, and the polyadic calculus [30], where zero or more names are communicated. This presentation mainly follows the monadic π-calculus. The basic concept behind the π-calculus is naming or reference. Names are the primary entities, and they may refer to links or channels (or any other kind of basic entity). Processes, sometimes referred to as agents, are the only other kind of entities. We shall use the term "p-agent" instead of "agent" in this context to avoid confusion. We let lowercase letters from the end of the alphabet (e.g., x, y) range over the names and uppercase letters from the beginning of the alphabet (e.g., A) range over process identifiers. Also, uppercase letters from the middle of the alphabet (e.g., P, Q) range over p-agents or process expressions, of which there are six kinds (corresponding to the six kinds of combinators or operators).

1. A *summation* has the form $\sum_{i \in I} P_i$, where the set I is a finite index set. The p-agent behaves like one or another of the P_i. The empty summation or inaction, represented by 0, is the p-agent that can do nothing. The binary summation is written as $P_1 + P_2$.
2. A *prefix* is of the form $\bar{y}x.P$, $y(x).P$, or $\tau.P$. $\bar{y}x.P$ is a *negative prefix*; $\bar{y}$ can be thought of as an output port of a p-agent which contains it. $\bar{y}x.P$ outputs x on port $\bar{y}$ then behaves like P. $y(x).P$ is a *positive prefix*, where y is the input port of a p-agent; it binds the variable x. At port y the arbitrary name z is input by $y(x).P$, which behaves like $P\{z/x\}$, where $P\{z/x\}$ is the result of substituting z for all free (unbound) occurrences of x in P. We think of the two complementary ports y and $\bar{y}$ as connected by a channel (link), also called y. τ is the *silent action*; $\tau.P$ first performs the silent action and then acts like P.
3. A *composition*, $P_1 \mid P_2$, is a p-agent consisting of P_1 and P_2 acting in parallel.
4. A *restriction* $(x)P$ acts like P and prohibits actions at ports x and $\bar{x}$, with the exception of communication between components of P along the link x. Restriction, like positive prefix, binds variables.
5. $[x = y]P$ is a match, where a p-agent behaves like P if the names x and y are identical.
6. A *defined p-agent* (with arity n), $A(y_1 \ldots, y_n)$, has a unique defining equation, $A(x_1 \ldots, x_n) =_{def} P$, where $x_1 \ldots, x_n$ are distinct names and the only names that may occur free in P. $A(y_1 \ldots, y_n)$ behaves like $P\{y_1/x_1 \ldots, y_n/x_n\}$ for the simultaneous substitution of y_i for all free occurrences of $x_i (1 \leq i \leq n)$ in P.

A p-agent P may perform a communication action (or transition) α, corresponding to a prefix, and evolve into another p-agent P'. This is indicated by the notation $P \xrightarrow{\alpha} P'$. The meanings of the combinators are formally defined by transition rules. Each rule has a conclusion (stated below a line) and premises (above the line). The following rule is of particular interest.

$$\frac{P \xrightarrow{\bar{x}y} P', \; Q \xrightarrow{x(z)} Q'}{P \mid Q \xrightarrow{\tau} P' \mid Q' \{y/z\}}$$

This indicates communication between P and Q, resulting in a silent action, τ, whereby a name, y, is communicated between P (now P') and Q (now Q'). For example,

$$\bar{y}x.P \mid y(z).Q \xrightarrow{\tau} P \mid Q\{x/z\}$$

so that after this communication all free occurrences of z in Q are replaced by whatever value x had in $\bar{y}x.P$. Of particular interest are those cases where we use restriction to internalize ports so that they cannot be observed from the outside, forcing communication actions to match their complements. For example, $(y)\,(\bar{y}(x).P \mid y(z).Q)$ can perform only a τ action where x is communicated along channel y to become the value of z in Q.

Consider next a simple case of restructuring a system of p-agents. We begin with

$$(y)(m)\,(y(x).\bar{x}z.0 \mid \bar{y}m.0 \mid m(u).P)$$

with three parallel components. Because of the restrictions on channels y and m, the only action that can occur in this system is a τ action by which the second p-agent sends m on channel y to the first p-agent. We then have $(m)(\bar{m}z.0 \mid m(u).P)$. The second p-agent has disappeared, being reduced to the do-nothing process 0. Also, the restriction (y) has been dropped since y no longer occurs in the expression. The second p-agent communicated to the first a channel, m, and the only action the resulting system can perform is a τ action by which z is communicated along this channel, resulting in $P\{z/u\}$.

In Section 4.6, we discuss concepts that have been developed in the theory of the π-calculus that facilitate refinement and reasoning about correctness. These include notions of equivalence and a modal logic. We also discuss a software tool that automates the techniques that go with these concepts.

4.3 The LOGOS Multi-agent System

The Lights Out Ground Operations System (LOGOS) [43, 44] is a multi-agent system in its initial stages of development at the Advanced Architecture and Automation Branch of the NASA Goddard Space Flight center (NASA/GSFC) . This system is intended to be a prototype for an unattended grounds operation-center. The main objectives of the system are to demonstrate the integration of existing technologies, to deploy and evaluate evolving agent concepts in the context of lights-out operations, to support the evaluation of data visualization ideas and cognitive studies, and to establish an environment that supports the development of multi-agent systems.

The LOGOS system provides an infrastructure for extending the capabilities of legacy Goddard Space Flight Center control center systems via the use of intelligent agents. A LOGOS agent acts as a "substitute controller" in order to link together ground control center technologies. These technologies include the control center's software system, Genie/GenSAA,

VisAGE, MOPSS and WorkPlace. The control center's software system interfaces with and controls the spacecraft. See Figure 4.1 for a depiction of the LOGOS community.

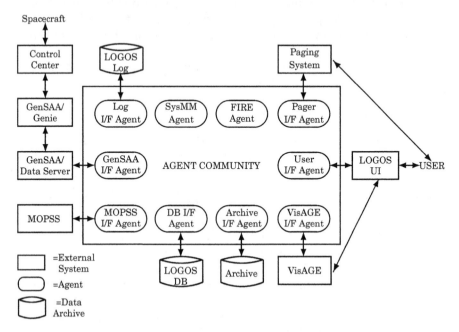

Fig. 4.1. LOGOS agent architecture.

GenSAA and Genie are products that graphically build expert systems to monitor and command spacecraft operations. VisAGE allows an analyst to flexibly construct dynamic three-dimensional visualizations. MOPSS generates spacecraft activity plans and binary loads that are uplinked to the spacecraft. WorkPlace is an environment that provides a simple and efficient device for integrating distributed processes. The agents of the LOGOS system perform many activities that are similar to those currently being performed by human flight controllers. They accomplish this via autonomy, proactivity, reactivity, communication and collaboration with other agents, and goal orientation.

We only model the communication that takes place between agents that make up a subpart of the LOGOS system. This subsystem involves five agents that are responsible for resolving detected mission faults within LogosSAT, a simulated spacecraft. These agents effectively resolve faults by coordinating analysis activities and tracking the progress of fault resolution activities. The following are the agents that make up this subsystem. The FIRE (Fault Isolation and Resolution Expert) [36] agent is an internal agent. It is responsible for providing procedures for resolving mission faults reported by the GenSAA agent or requesting the direct intervention of a human expert to isolate and resolve them. The FIRE agent is also responsible for supporting the human expert by contributing as much resolving information as possible. It contains no knowledge for anomaly resolutions. Resolutions and recognition of faults are hardcoded. The DBIFA is another internal agent. It is responsible for storing and retrieving information into and from databases, such as mnemonic metadata, anomaly information, and anomaly resolution procedures. The GIFA (GenSAA/IF Agent) [15] agent is a reactive agent that perceives its environment, which in this case is other agents within the LOGOS community. It responds in a reasonable amount of time to any changes that occur. This agent is responsible for broadcasting anomaly alerts and providing real-time telemetry. The UIFA (User Interface Agent) [37] agent is responsible for responding to an agent request or any other type of data that it receives from the user interface, informing the user of anomalies and schedule changes. When the UIFA agent receives an anomaly and a user is not logged on, a message is sent to the PAGER agent to page the appropriate user. The PAGER agent [21] is responsible for contacting system personnel or a mission engineer when a situation arises within the LOGOS community that requires human intervention.

The agents in this subsystem collaborate as follows. The FIRE agent receives a message from the GIFA informing it of a detected mission fault within LogosSAT. Upon receipt of the message, the FIRE agent checks to see whether it needs any mnemonic values or inferred variable values associated with a fault. Mnemonic values are used to determine whether any TMONS are outside their limits. For example, the Star Tracker anomaly is an anomaly that occurs in the LogosSAT spacecraft and is represented by the inferred variable value 1240000. If such values are needed, the FIRE agent will send a message to the GIFA requesting this information. The FIRE agent will then request matching fault resolution procedures from the DBIFA. Upon receipt of these procedures, the FIRE agent will attempt to resolve the mission fault. If, however, the FIRE agent is unable to do so, it sends a message to the UIFA agent requesting human intervention in resolving the fault. If a human is not present at the UIFA, the FIRE agent will send a message to the PAGER agent commanding it to locate the human expert by sending a page or email message. Once the human expert agent has received the page or email message requesting that it resolve a fault, it analyzes the fault and determines whether it will handle the fault alone or request that the FIRE agent aid it.

We focus primarily on the FIRE agent since it is responsible for resolving the detected mission faults. The FIRE agent cannot resolve groups of faults; it can only resolve one fault at a time. The relationship that the FIRE agent has with the GIFA, the DBIFA, the UIFA, the PAGER and the external agents is represented by the contextual diagram in Figure 4.2. This diagram shows the information that will be passed between the FIRE agent and the other agents mentioned above.

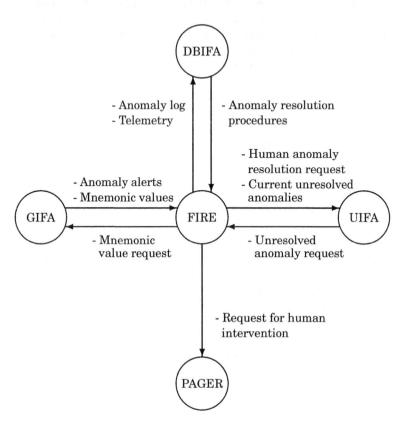

Fig. 4.2. FIRE Contextual Diagram

4.4 A LOGOS Fault-Resolution Scenario

We shall give a π-calculus specification that models behaviors of a part of the LOGOS agent community. The specific behavior we take as an example is a fault resolution scenario. There are two branches to the scenario. In the first branch of the scenario, the FIRE agent is able to resolve the fault. In the second branch of the scenario, the FIRE agent is not able to resolve the fault and requests the direct intervention of a human. In this example, we look only at the second branch. The scenario proceeds as follows:

A. GIFA to FIRE Alerts FIRE that a fault has occurred.

B. FIRE to GIFA Requests GIFA for the mnemonic values associated with the fault.
C. GIFA to FIRE Informs FIRE of the mnemonic values associated with the fault.
D. FIRE to DBIFA Requests DBIFA for fault resolution procedures for resolving the fault.
E. DBIFA to FIRE Sends FIRE matching fault resolution procedures or informs it that no procedures were found.

In this branch of the scenario, FIRE is unable to resolve the fault and requests UIFA for human assistance.

F. FIRE to UIFA Requests UIFA for human intervention in resolving the fault.
G. UIFA to FIRE Responds to FIRE that a user will resolve the fault or that no user is present.
H. FIRE to PAGER Requests PAGER to locate a user.
I. PAGER to UIFA Signals UIFA to resolve a fault.
J. UIFA to PAGER Commands PAGER to stop paging.
K. UIFA to FIRE Responds to FIRE that it will resolve the fault.

4.5 The π-Calculus Specification for the Scenario

As a first step for modeling a system that may support the above scenario, we identify communication links required to support the communication behavior exhibited in this scenario. Table 4.1 gives, for each link, its mnemonic name, the agent ("Sender") at the output port of the link, the agent ("Receiver") at the input port, and the kind of message passed by a handshake on the link.

Table 4.1. The links for the anomaly system.

Name	Sender	Receiver	Message Type
mvreq	FIRE	GIFA	mnemonic value request
amsg	GIFA	FIRE	advisory message
areq	FIRE	DBIFA	request for resolution procedures
matproc	DBIFA	FIRE	matching resolution procedures
humreq	FIRE	UIFA	request for a human to resolve the fault
humres	UIFA	FIRE	response from the human
reqhum	FIRE	PAGER	request for a human to resolve the fault
sighum	PAGER	UIFA	signal to contact the human
respsig	UIFA	PAGER	response to request for human intervention

Next, we develop a *flowgraph* of the system being modeled. A flow-graph depicts the structure of a system, that is, the linkage among its components, not its dynamic properties. A node in a flowgraph is a black box with "buttons," that is, ports that appear in the process expressions. A complementary pair $(x, \bar{x})$ of ports represents a means of interaction between black boxes. Such a pair of ports is connected in the flowgraph by an edge representing the corresponding link or channel. In a flowgraph that corresponds to (part of) a multi-agent system, it is natural to have exactly one node for each agent. Thus, at this point, we have identified five agents/nodes for our flowgraph (*FIRE, GIFA, DBIFA, UIFA*, and *PAGER*), and Table 4.1 gives the links between these nodes. Figure 4.3 is the resulting flowgraph. To reduce the amount of text in the figure, we have modified the representation so that, given two nodes with a complementary pair $(x, \bar{x})$ of ports, we write the name x next to the edge representing the link connecting these ports; the edge is shown directed (as an arrow) from the output port, $\bar{x}$, to the input port, x.

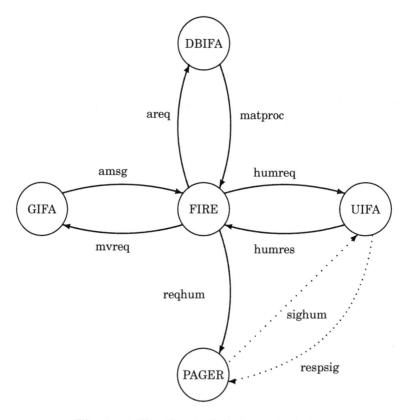

Fig. 4.3. A Flow Graph of the Anomaly System

In Figure 4.3, the links *sighum* and *respsig* are shown dashed. This indicates that these links are established as the system evolves. In general, we would not know in advance whether the system would evolve so that the links connecting *UIFA* and *PAGER* are indeed *sighum* and *respsig*. Indeed, we would not generally know in advance that there would be a linkage between *UIFA* and *PAGER* since there are generally several ways in which the linkage of a system may evolve. Here, however, we are modeling a system only to the extent that it supports one branch in a scenario (where linkage is established). Furthermore, we have simplified the situation by assuming that only the link *sighum* is available for *PAGER*-to-*UIFA* communication and only the link *respsig* is available for *UIFA*-to-*PAGER* communication. A more complex setting would admit several pager agents and several user interface agents. It might also admit several links in both directions. Summation captures straightforwardly any indifference in the model to choices among the resources.

Since the anomaly system encompasses the five processes shown in the flowchart of Figure 4.3 operating in parallel, the process expression for the entire system should include the composition

$$FIRE \mid GIFA \mid DBIFA \mid UIFA \mid PAGER$$

All we need add to this are restrictions that bind the nine links (see Table 4.1) that will appear in the process expressions that elaborate the five processes shown in the flowgraph.

At this point, we have addressed the anomaly system in its full generality; there is nothing in our model specific to the scenario branch on which we are focusing. Of course, the anomaly system is part of the LOGOS community, and eventually one would like to model this entire community. Since the agents operate in parallel, the process expression for the entire community would be a composition like the expression above but containing considerably more process identifiers. The scope of a given restriction in this expression would not necessarily include the entire composition. Firstly, we may not want certain ports to be visible to certain agents. Secondly, we may want to conceptualize the community as partitioned into subcommunities or subsystems. A link local to a given subsystem would be bound by a restriction whose scope is the composition representing the subsystem. Since the current analysis has not addressed the extent to which the anomaly system is self-contained, we have no suggestions on how the scopes of the restrictions in the above expression for this system would be extended when this expression is viewed as part of the larger community.

In using the π-calculus to model a system that supports the scenario in question, we have defined most processes without parameters since the only names being substituted for are generally bound by positive prefixes (that is, intuitively, they receive input values). A typical, if simple, example of a process definition of this form is

$$A =_{def} x(y).A1$$

(Note that neither A nor $A1$ has parameters.) Here, after y is bound to a value, A behaves like $A1$, which apparently makes no use of the value just input on link x. In fact, at the level of abstraction appropriate for our model, this value is not essential to the communication behavior of $A1$. We assume, however, that any input values are available for internal processing. In the π-calculus definitions given below, heavy use is made of the match operator to choose between alternative ways for an agent to proceed. This allows us to forego describing internal processing that relates input to output at the expense, however, of defining more processes.

In the definitions given below, a description (e.g., "anomaly resolution procedures") is sometimes given in the position of an output value in a negative prefix. This avoids the need for additional commentary. Again, only a small number of representative values of the parameters of the system are accommodated. For example, the alert sent from $GIFA$ to $FIRE$ in our model admits only two values (124000 and 246000). This is for simplicity's sake; more values could be accommodated in the obvious way with more complex summations for output and more process definitions for input but with little gain in understanding. As another simplification, we occasionally use a negative prefix without an output value (e.g., $\bar{y}$ instead of $\bar{y}x$) and a corresponding positive prefix without a bound variable (e.g., y instead of $y(x)$). It is trivial to make the cases conform to strict π-calculus syntax; doing so here would introduce names with no obvious purpose. Finally, the definitions overspecify the system in that, given two values to be communicated in any order, the linear order of nested prefixes in a process expression requires us to settle on one order or the other. This rather minor nuisance (like the previous inconvenience) could be avoided by using the polyadic version of the π-calculus (which allows zero or more values to be communicated in one handshake).

The following, then, are the π-calculus definitions for modeling a system that supports the scenario in question. See Table 4.2 for the correspondence between the steps in the scenario and the definitions that support those steps in the model.

$$GIFA =_{def} \overline{amsg}(124000).GIFA1$$
(4.1)
$$+ \overline{amsg}(246000).GIFA1$$
$$FIRE =_{def} amsg(x).$$
$$([x = 124000].FIRE1$$
(4.2)
$$+ [x = 246].FIRE2)$$
(4.3) $$FIRE1 =_{def} \overline{mvreq}(tm12st).\overline{mvreq}(tm13st).FIRE3$$
(4.4) $$FIRE2 =_{def} \overline{mvreq}(tm14st).\overline{mvreq}(tm15st).FIRE3$$
$$GIFA1 =_{def} mvreq(x).mvreq(y).$$

Table 4.2. Correspondence between scenario steps and π-calculus process definitions

Scenario Steps	Process Definitions
A	1–2
B	3–5
C	6–8
D	9–10
E	11–12
F	13–14
G	15–16
H	17–19
I,J	20–21
K	22-23

$$([x = tm12st][y = tm13st]GIFA2$$

(4.5) $$+ [x = tm14st][y = tm15st]GIFA3)$$

(4.6) $$GIFA2 =_{def} \overline{amsg}(45).\overline{amsg}(47).GIFA$$

(4.7) $$GIFA3 =_{def} \overline{amsg}(50).\overline{amsg}(52).GIFA$$

(4.8) $$FIRE3 =_{def} amsg(x).amsg(y).FIRE4$$

$$FIRE4 =_{def} \overline{areq}(\text{anomaly resolution procedures}).$$

(4.9) $$FIRE5$$

(4.10) $$DBIFA =_{def} areq(x).DBIFA1$$

$$DBIFA1 =_{def} \overline{matproc}(\text{fault resolution procedures}).DBIFA$$

$$+ \overline{matproc}(\text{no fault resolution procedures}).$$

(4.11) $$DBIFA$$

$$FIRE5 =_{def} matproc(x).$$

$$([x = \text{fault resolution procedures}]FIRE$$

$$+ [x = \text{fault resolution procedures}]$$

(4.12) $$FIRE6)$$

(4.13) $$FIRE6 =_{def} \overline{humreq}.FIRE7$$

(4.14) $$UIFA =_{def} humreq.UIFA1$$

$$UIFA1 =_{def} \overline{humres}(\text{no user}).UIFA2$$

$$+ \overline{humres}(\text{user}).\overline{humres}(\text{resolve fault}).$$

(4.15) $$UIFA$$

$$FIRE7 =_{def} humres(resp).$$

$$([resp = \text{user}]humres(\text{resolve fault}).FIRE$$

(4.16) $$+ [resp = \text{no user}]FIRE8)$$

$$FIRE8 =_{def} \overline{humreq}(sighum).\overline{humreq}(respsig).$$
$$\overline{reqhum}(sighum).\overline{reqhum}(respsig).$$

(4.17) $FIRE9$

(4.18) $UIFA2 =_{def} humreq(x).humreq(y).UIFA3(x,y)$

(4.19) $PAGER =_{def} reqhum(x).reqhum(y).PAGER1(x,y)$

(4.20)$PAGER1(x,y) =_{def} \overline{x}.y.PAGER$

(4.21) $UIFA3(x,y) =_{def} x.\overline{y}.UIFA4$

$$UIFA4 =_{def} \overline{humres}(user).\overline{humres}(resolve\ fault).$$

(4.22) $UIFA$

(4.23) $FIRE9 =_{def} humres(resp1).humres(resp2).FIRE$

For process identifiers, we have used the names of agents, possibly followed by a positive integer. The right-hand side of each definition consists of a summation (allowing the case where no '+' combinator occurs to be the trivial, one-summand case) where each summand has at least one prefix preceding a single process identifier. In any given definition, the process identifiers on the right-hand side use the same name as the one of the left but with numbers greater than it in sequence (taking an unadorned agent name to contain a virtual '0'). The set of definitions, therefore, is partitioned into five subsets, one for each agent. (This partition reflects the static structure shown in the flowgraph.) Each subset defines a transition diagram for the corresponding agent.

These are shown in Figure 4.4, where the number of the definition of each process is shown to the left of its identifier. The actions labeling the transitions have been omitted. For the transition from process Xm to process Xn, the action is the string of prefixes preceding Xn in the definition of Xm. (For example, the action labeling the transition from $FIRE3$ to $FIRE4$ is $amsg(x).amsg(y)$.) The mutually recursive nature of these definitions is clear from the transition diagrams. Other branches of the scenario (and other anomaly-system scenarios) would be accommodated by including additional paths in the transition diagrams. Embedding the anomaly system into the entire LOGOS community would require further elaboration of each transition diagram. It is critical to the modeling used here that the transition diagrams are coordinated by handshake communication.

4.6 Analysis and Design

In this section, we briefly discuss concepts that have been developed in the theory of the π-calculus that facilitate refinement of a specification into a design and that support reasoning about the correctness of a specification and the results of refinement. These concepts include notions of

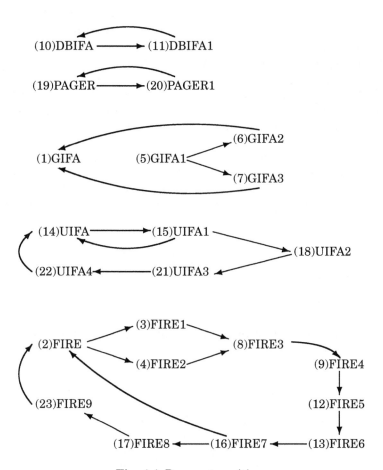

Fig. 4.4. Process transitions.

equivalence, some of which support equational reasoning, and a logic in which one can express properties that should hold of the specified system. We also discuss a software tool that automates the techniques that go with these concepts. The techniques suggested here were applied to the specification given in the last section. Space limitations preclude details of how this was done.

Intuitively, we wish to distinguish between two processes if and only if the distinction can be detected by an external agent interacting with each of them. (This agent may be ourselves or it may be another process.) If two agents cannot be distinguished in some sense, then they are equivalent in that sense. Various equivalence relations are defined in the π-calculus (as in CCS) in terms of various notions of *bisimulation*: two equivalent processes must be able to perform the same actions, and, when they perform the same action, then must yield equivalent processes. There are equational laws that support equational reasoning with process expressions (replacing equals with equals within an expression). These laws are based on congruence relations. A given equivalence relation $\equiv$ is a congruence relation when, if $A \equiv B$, then $C \equiv C[B/A]$ for any term C, where $C[B/A]$ is the result of replacing A in C with B. Not all bisimulation relations define equivalence relations that are congruences. Some define near congruences, which support equational reasoning in all but a few contexts.

The theory of bisimulations in the π-calculus has been developed mostly in the context of the polyadic version, where we must address not only processes but also *abstractions* and *concretions*. An abstraction of arity n has the form $(x_1 \ldots_n)P$. Instead of writing a parametric definition as

$$K(x_1, \ldots, x_n) =_{def} P$$

we now write

$$K =_{def} (x_1 \ldots x_n)P$$

We factor the input prefix into two parts, abstraction and *location* (x in the following):

$$x(y_1 \ldots y_n).P =_{def} x.(y_1 \ldots y_n)P$$

Dually, output prefix is factored into two parts:

$$\overline{x}y_1 \ldots y_n.P =_{def} \overline{x}.[y_1 \ldots y_n]P$$

Here $\overline{x}$ is the *co-location* and $[y_1 \ldots y_n]P$ is the concretion (of arity n). A process is both an abstraction of arity zero and a concretion of arity zero. An *agent* (or *p-agent*, to continue the terminology we introduced to avoid confusion) is either an abstraction or a concretion (possibly a process). Bisumulations in the π-calculus are defined over p-agents in general. As with CCS, bisimulations differ on whether they take silent actions (τ) into account. In addition, some π-calculus bisimulations differ on how they are sensitive to substitutions for parameters. The major bisimulation relations are near congruences, failing to be closed only under abstraction.

The Hennessy-Milner logic $\mathcal{L}$ for the π-calculus is similar to the logic $\mathcal{PL}$ for CCS, but it must accommodate abstractions and concretions in general, not just processes. $\mathcal{L}$ has the usual sentential connectives, the two Boolean constants, and several modal operators. Where A is a p-agent and φ is a formula of $\mathcal{L}$, $A \models \varphi$ means that A *satisfies* φ (or φ is true of A). $\mathcal{L}$ is an alternative to the bisimulation relations since the aim is to define the satisfaction relation so that p-agents A_1 and A_2 are bisimilar exactly when $A_1 \models \varphi$ if and only if $A_2 \models \varphi$ for all formulae φ of $\mathcal{L}$. Where α is an action, $P \models <\alpha> \varphi$ holds if it is possible for P to do α and thereby reach a state satisfying φ. As $<\alpha>$ is a possibility operator (like the diamond operator of dynamic logic), its dual, $[\alpha]$, is a necessity operator (like the box operator of dynamic logic): $P \models [\alpha]\varphi$ means that, if P can perform α, then it must thereby reach a state where φ holds. There are more complex modal operators when satisfaction is defined relative to abstractions and concretions. The logic $\mathcal{L}$ allows us to begin the development cycle, not with a complete specification of a system, but with only certain conditions on its behavior. The set of conditions can be augmented incrementally and applies throughout the refinement process.

The Mobility Workbench (MWB, see [45] and [46]) was developed in the pattern of the Concurrency Workbench (CWB) [9] but addresses the polyaic π-calculus instead of CCS. *Open bisimulation equivalences* are supported to automate equivalence checking. There is a weak version of open bisimulation (which ignores τ) and a strong version. In addition to deciding equivalence, the MWB supports some of the other techniques of the CWB, such as finding deadlocks, and it supports interactive simulation.

To give a realistic feel, we present some examples of the syntax of the MWB. The following is the translation of definition 10 into the MWB notation:

```
agent BFIFA(areq,matproc)=areq(x).DBIFA1(matproc)
```

Process ("agent") definitions in the MWB must contain parameters that include the channel(s) used in these definitions to input or output some message. The parameters also include any arguments of the evolved process.

The MWB can also determine whether an agent satisfies a formula, using the logic $\mathcal{L}$ supplemented (as $\mathcal{PL}$ is supplemented in the CWB) with the greatest fixed-point (ν) and least fixed-point (μ) operators of the μ-calculus [9]. A formula involving the diamond operator, such as $<a> P$, must be written so that a variable occurs within this operator; for example, we write `<x>(a=x & P)`, where '&' is the conjunction operator. Dually, for $[a]P$ we would write `[x](a # x | P)`, where '#' is used for '$\neq$.'

The fixed-point operators allow familiar operators from branching-time temporal logic to be encoded and hence are particularly useful for formulating properties required to hold of particular agents. The μ-calculus formula $\mu x.\varphi$ represents an infinite conjunction. Let φ_0 be the constant T (truth). Define φ_{i+1} ($i \geq 0$) as $\varphi[\varphi_i/x]$, the formula obtained by substituting φ_i for free occurrences of x in φ. (An occurrence of a variable x in a formula φ is *bound* if it occurs within the scope of a νx or μx operator; otherwise it is *free*.) Then

$$\mu x.\varphi \equiv \bigwedge_{i=0}^{\infty} \varphi_i$$

Dually, the formula $\mu x.\varphi$ represents the infinite disjunction$\bigvee_{i=0}^{\infty} \varphi_i$. To define some familiar temporal logic operators, we use the notation of the CWB, which is less involved than that of the MWB. The CWB notation allows a set L of actions (in addition to a single action) to appear within a box $[\,]$ or a diamond $<>$ operator. If Act is the set of all actions (for the application in question) and L is the name of a subset of A, then the expression $-L$ denotes the set $Act - L$, that is, the set of all actions not in L. By extension, $-$ alone denotes $Act - \varnothing$, that is, the set Act. Thus, for example, $[-]\varphi$ holds of a process A if, whenever A performs any action, the result is a p-agent satisfying φ. Similarly, $<->\varphi$ holds of A if A can perform some action that results in a p-agent satisfying φ. In the CWB, "max" is used for "ν" and "Z" is a typical (propositional) variable name. We can define a parameterized proposition named, for example, $\mathtt{Bx(P)}$ as

```
max(Z. P & [-]Z),
```

which, partially translated, comes to $\nu Z.P \wedge [-]Z$. This states of a process (say, A) that P holds of A and recursively continues to hold when A does any action. Therefore, $\mathtt{Bx(P)}$ is $\Box P$ of branching-time temporal logic: P is true all along <u>all</u> branches from the current state (A). Dually, we can define a parameterized proposition named, for example, $\mathtt{Poss(P)}$, as follows, where "min" is used for "μ" and "$|$" is the disjunction operator.

```
min(Z. P | <->Z),
```

Partially translated, this comes to $\mu Z.P \vee <->Z$. This states of a process (say, A) that P holds of A or holds at some state (p-agent) reachable from the current state (A) by a sequence of actions. This is $\Diamond P$ of branching-time temporal logic: P is true somewhere along <u>some</u> branch from the current state.

A version of the anomaly system without the mobility aspect was translated into the notation used by the value-passing CCS translator [6]. The CWB does not support value passing (input and output prefixes cannot take parameters); it thus supports only basic or pure CCS. The value-passing translator translates value-passing CCS expressions into equivalent sets of non-value-passing expressions that can be input to the CWB. (This translation is based on a result in [29]. Briefly, a finite set of values is placed in one-one correspondence with a set of channels used in creating alternative subexpressions for communicating the specific values.) Since the CWB is considerably more mature than the MWB, this allowed us conveniently to explore aspects of the specification (without mobility) and refinements of it before moving to the MWB. This exploration included simulation, checking equivalences, and checking that certain formulas (expressing safety and liveness properties) were satisfied by certain processes. Note that the expressions output by the value-passing translator (hence input by the CWB), rather than the value-passing formulas themselves, must be used when interacting with the CWB. The anomaly system including the mobility aspect was translated into the MWB, which accommodates value passing, and similar properties were explored. Experience from the initial exploration using the CWB and the value-passing translator greatly facilitated exploration with the MWB. One useful trick was to introduce certain actions, not part of the original specification, to facilitate checking safety and liveness properties.

4.7 General Considerations on Modeling Multi-agent Systems

In [32] it is shown how to translate the lazy λ-calculus (which gives all the normal forms achievable without a restriction on the reduction order) into the polyadic π-calculus. Thus, by Church's Thesis, a multi-agent system as a system with computational components can be simulated in the polyadic π-calculus because not only any communication pattern but also any computation can be simulated in the polyadic π-calculus. Imagine the π-calculus supplying the model for programming-language constructs as the λ-calculus has supplied the model for constructs used in functional programming languages. Lists are available using an encoding like that used in the λ-calculus. Action-continuation patterns, like those heavily used in AI programming, are captured by prefix and summation. Link passing, which, among other things, allows us to simulate procedure call, allows modularity. Given these and other constructs that allow us to avoid low-level details, it remains to determine, however, exactly which aspects of agents and multi-agent systems may be fruitfully or reasonably modeled in the π-calculus. We here sketch a few suggestions relative to BDI architectures [16], which we take as the best articulated and motivated architectures for artificial agents and multi-agent systems.

Besides looking at a multi-agent system from the point of view of the architecture of its agents, however, we may look at it from the point of view of the communication actions supported by the agent communication language (ACL) that it uses. The semantics of an ACL must relate the primitives of the language to these communication actions and show how well-formed expressions composed from these primitives relate to action patterns. A process algebra is an appropriate formalism for expressing some of the semantics of an ACL since a process algebra essentially is a means to specify patterns of communication events. Thus, the second part of this section sketches an approach to the semantics of ACLs based on the π-calculus.

4.7.1 Modeling Multi-agent Systems with the π-Calculus

BDI (Beliefs, Desires, and Intentions) architectures address intentional systems, whose behavior can be described by attributing to the system mental (or intentional) attitudes such as belief, preference, and intention. These attitudes, which are represented explicitly, fall into three categories (corresponding to the headings "belief," "desire," and "intention"). (1) Cognitive attitudes include epistemic attitudes such as belief and knowledge. (2) Conative attitudes relate to action and control and include intention, commitment, and having plans. (3) Affective attitudes refer to the motivations of an agent and include desires, goals, and preferences. (While both desires and intentions are pro-attitudes, intentions involve *commitment*, which influences future activity and deliberation and which is lacking with desires.) BDI architectures lie between purely reactive and deliberative planning systems and aim to enable limited computational agents situated in a dynamic environment to behave rationally.

The most influential early, single-agent BDI architecture was IRMA [4]. It introduced stores for beliefs, desires, plans as recipes (a "plan library"), and adopted plans ("intentions structured into plans"). The adopted plans are commitments the agent currently follows, while plans as recipes are beliefs about what plan is applicable for accomplishing which task under what circumstances. Planning here involves filling in the gaps in skeletal plans and composing plans. In broad outline, such plans could be represented in the π-calculus as follows. A sequential plan is represented by a sequence of actions (using prefix), and branches in a conditional plan are captured by the combination of prefix and summation. An action not generally thought of as a communication (e.g., seizing an object or moving to a location) can be represented as a communication with the environment. (Gibson [14] maintained that the stimulus information in the structure of the ambient light is not transmitted like the information we communicate with other people. There is, however, no need to view a handshake as a transmission; all that is required by the formalism is that both parties actively participate, and the medium can be abstracted out.) The composition of plans in the π-calculus is obvious. For filling out skeletal plans, there are at least two options. The position for a subplan could be filled by a process constant defined as a summation. Alternatively, the gap for a subplan could be occupied by an action that passes a link to a process responsible for the subplan.

Updatable stores could be implicitly reflected in the state of a π-calculus process. This, however, destroys modularity since we cannot identify a store with a subexpression. Link passing would appear to be the best hope for modularity. Plans as recipes are alternatives not yet realized, and adopted plans are already selected alternatives. Beliefs and desires could be represented as lists. The IRMA processes that opreate on the stores require considerable flexibility. Suffice it to point out here that implementations of such processes make heavy use of action-continuation patterns, captured in the π-calculus with prefix and summation.

One of the most influential BDI architectures addressing multi-agent systems is GRATE* [23], which is like IRMA but appeals to the concepts of joint intention and joint responsibility in establishing and monitoring collaborative activity. Events may occur locally, in the environment, or elsewhere in the community. If an agent decides to pursue an objective locally, then we proceed much as in IRMA. If, however, it decides to pursue the objective collaboratively, then a social action must be established. Initial team selection results in a skeletal joint intention. A second phase finalizes the outline of the proposal and the assignment of actions to individuals. These results are passed to each group member, which must fit its assigned action in with its existing commitments in a way that satisfies the overall joint intention.

Once a joint intention is finalized and roles are assigned, modeling collecitve activity is similar to modeling individual activity as in the case of IRMA. The challenge here is modeling what goes before. Initial team selection could be modeled with communication patterns that poll agents and action patterns that structure groups of agents. Role assignment could be modeled by communication patterns that culminate in passing links that enable various roles. And finalization of the joint intention, as regards the structure of the intention, could be modeled as we suggested modeling the filling out of skeletal plans in IRMA. What makes filling out a skeletal plan challenging here is that typically several agents are involved. But, again, communication and action patterns could be used to model the negotation and decision.

4.7.2 Semantics for Agent Communication Languages

The approach we suggest for supplying the semantics for an ACL is (1) to characterize the ACL in terms of performatives (bearers of the illocutionary forces of speech acts) and what may be done with them, then (2) to give the semantics of these performatives in the π-calculus and an appropriately enhanced version of the logic $\mathcal{L}$.

Regarding (1), Labrou and Finan [25] present a semantic description for ACLs in general and KQML in particular. This semantics is based on speech act theory and associates cognitive states of the agent with the use of the language's primitives (performatives). KQML is a collection of communication primitives (message types) that express an attitude regarding the expression exchanged. Labrou and Finan's semantics gives the minimum set of preconditions and postconditions for both the sender and the receiver for the use of a performative and the final state of the successful performance of the performative (which may be a step or so beyond the postconditions).

Regarding (2), Singh [39] presents the semantics of speech acts by formally describing the conditions of satisfaction for the different types of speech acts; these conditions generally involve actions other than speech acts. Illocutionary acts are classified into assertives, directives, commissives, permissives, and declaratives. Singh's semantics relies on the notion of whole-hearted satisfaction of a speech act. For example, the whole-hearted satisfaction of a directive requires that an agent to whom it is addressed forces the appropriate state of affairs to come about, which in turn requires that the agent know how to bring about this state and intend to bring it about. The formal language used here is based on the propositional branching-time logic CTL*, which is augmented with an operator for intention and two operators for know-how. Singh's semantics, therefore, relies a great deal on dispositions of the interlocutors, and the logic favors propositions or the states of affairs that make them true over actions. This is acceptable given that this logic is in the tradition of epistemic modal logics, where modal operators relate to propositional attitudes of agents and apply to sentences to produce sentences. This same tradition favors analysis of speech acts as illocutionary force-proposition pairs despite the fact that expressions that denote actions normally are what go along with the verbs for directives, commissives, permissives, and prohibitives.

The modal logic $\mathcal{L}$ (associated with the π-calculus) is from a different tradition: Hennessy-Milner logics. The modalities in these logics are formed from sequences of actions (labels or τ). We suggest that an enhanced Hennessy-Milner logic could be used to represent the semantics of speech acts, complemented with the π-calculus process expressions. This would be advantageous in that it would relate the meanings of performatives to patterns of actions and reduce the reliance on the dispositions of the interlocutors. The enhancements to Hennessy-Milner logics in question are those of the Mobility Workbench: the maximum (ν) and minimum (μ) fixed-point operators, and allowing sets of actions (including the empty and universal sets) in forming modalities.

In distinguishing speech acts, we still need a notion that corresponds to whole-hearted satisfaction. This is because of the nondeterminism that exists in π-calculus expressions. For one thing, there is no limit on when an action needs to be performed. A π-calculus expression generally allows many different transitions (or has a nonsingleton set of commitments) and therefore can evolve in many different ways. We would expect only a few of these ways to correspond to the satisfaction of a given speech act, and we would expect the satisfaction before certain other actions are performed. Therefore, the notion of whole-hearted satisfaction is needed to narrow the set of alternatives.

4.8 Extending the Agent Abstraction to Users

Our original characterization of an agent intentionally includes characteristics that usually distinguish humans from computational entities. Indeed, the key feature that unifies agent research is viewing certain computational entities as human-like. Sometimes this is expressed using a "mentalistic" vocabulary for agents. The theoretical step justifying this use of language is known as *adopting the intentional stance* and receives its classical articulation in the work of the philosopher Dennett [10]. Given the intentional stance, an agent abstraction should be useful for modeling systems where agents and humans collaborate or where human collaboration is computer supported. However, while Dennett is interested in the philosophical problem of the status of beliefs (hence his mentalistic terminology), we are interested in agent coordination, which requires communication acts, which are public, socially situated acts, not mental acts. These acts, interpreted as speech acts, indeed fall under the intentional stance since, for example, they express beliefs and desires.

The aspect of agent architectures whose representation in the π-calculus (or any process algebra) is most obvious is the repertoire of plans. One would expect that, when our agent abstraction is extended to cover human collaborators as well, the nature of plans will be a major issues as will how the handshake communication of process algebras applies to human-human and agent-human communication. In the rest of this section, we summarize some of our research in modeling societies of agents and humans using our agent abstraction, and we briefly describe work where humans collaborate in handshake fashion mediated by distributed software that facilitates negotiation. The following section begins with a review of influential criticism by ethnomethodologists of how the AI and CSCW communities have viewed plans (used by humans or computers). This criticism fosters the view of plans as resources rather than generators of action. If, however, our process-algebraic descriptions of the sequences of actions an agent or human can perform are to capture what these actors endeavor to do, then plans must in some sense control coordinated action. In the rest of that section, we argue that specifications (say, of distributed systems in a process algebra) introduce obligations and that handshakes establish obligations among the communicating parties. Since an agent must normally intend to meet its obligations and must normally do what it intends, we focus the intentional stance on obligations, which are primarily public, not mental. So obligations must be a significant aspect of our agent abstraction.

As computing resources become more readily available, certain tasks now done by groups of humans may be achieved more efficiently and reliably by allowing humans to collaborate with computing systems even as they collaborate among themselves. We have shown how such collaboration can be formally modeled so that human users and computational entities are modeled uniformly [33]. We consider abstractly the communications that systems (users and computing resources) perform. This part of our research addresses an abstract aspect of the topic NASA has termed human-centered computing [34], and it is related to dialogue modeling (see [11], sec. 8.1), which addresses the exchange of information (conversation) between a user and a computer system. We abstract away from the syntax of interfaces by modeling communication events and their content.

We use the agent abstraction described in this chapter—a process-algebraic process that persists through communication actions—in modeling both humans and computational resources. Developing human-centered systems has unique demands since humans must also be modeled. A competence model of a user predicts legal sequences of behavior; a performance model also addresses what is required to produce each sequence (see [11], sec. 6.2). The agent abstraction allows us to formulate a competence model of the participants.

For this part of our research we used the process algebra CSP to express the agent abstraction. We shall later indicate how the π-calculus would allow more features to be modeled, but, for now, we may assume generic process-algebraic resources, without mobility. Alexander [1], addressing the design of software geared toward human-computer interaction, presents a collection of languages, tools, and methods that views dialogue in terms of discrete events. Events are modeled with a functional language. The overall structure of the dialogue is specified with a subset of CSP, which defines the possible sequences of events. We, however, use only CSP as supported by FDR [12], a tool for analyzing CSP models that identifies deadlocks and livelocks and verifies refinement relations. This version of CSP allows data types to be declared and functions to be defined and applied.

As an example for applying the agent abstraction to human-computer integration, we consider an electronic purchasing system composed of human and nonhuman agents [33]. This allows (artificial) agents to negotiate the sale of a car without direct human intervention except to finalize the transaction. Each customer (buyer) is represented by a personal assistant, and each seller is represented by a sales representative. We would generally expect the customers and sellers to be humans and the other agents to be artificial, but this need not be the case. When a customer wants to buy a car, he sends information about the intended purchase to his personal assistant, who notifies the broker. If the broker is notified by a sales representative that its seller wants to sell the kind of car the customer in question is looking for, then the broker initiates a negotiation session between the personal assistant and that sales representative. If no sales representative informs the broker that it has the kind of car in question for sale, then the broker takes the initiative and asks the sales representatives whether they are selling such a car. If one replies positively, then the broker initiates a negotiation session between it and the

personal assistant in question. If the broker cannot find a sales representative selling the kind of car the customer wants, then it waits until something becomes available. In a similar way but with the roles reversed, the
attempted sale can also be initiated at the seller's end. The negotiation is
handled by the personal assistant and the sales representative that the
broker has paired. If they reach an agreed price, the respective customer
and seller may concur and conclude the transaction, or one or both may
cancel the transaction, in which case everyone starts over again.

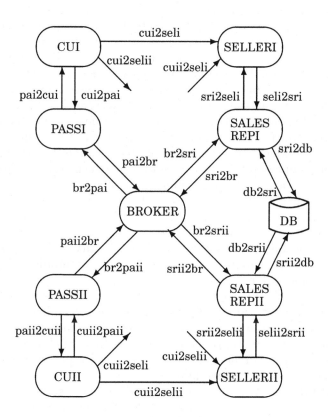

Fig. 4.5. Part of the flowgraph of the electronic purchasing system.

Figure 4.5 is a flow graph representing our system specification with
the exception of the channels used during negotiation between a personal
assistant and a sales representative. In this particular specification, there
are two customers (CU), each with its own personal assistant (PASS), and
there are two sellers (SELLER), each with its own sales representative

(SALESREP). We distinguish the two instances of each kind of agent by appending "I" to the name of the first and "II" to the name of the second. There is a single broker (BROKER) and a single database (DB), which contains information of the particular cars being sold. All channels are simplex, which makes the specification clearer. Where x is an abbreviation for agent X and y is an abbreviation for agent Y, the channel from X to Y is named x2y. The abbreviations for the kinds of agents are sr (SALESREP), cu (CUSTOMER), pa (PASS), sel (SELLER), br (BROKER), and db (DB). The abbreviation for the particular agent is formed by appending "i" or "ii" to the abbreviation for its kind. Thus, for example, the channel from CUI to PASSI is named cui2pai. Figure 4.6 continues the flow graph in Figure 4.5, showing the channels used during the negotiation between a personal assistant and a sales representative. Since only one personal assistant and one sales representative are involved in the negotiation, only one pair of these channels is used in a given session.

The type of a channel is a sequence of more basic types. Any given channel may not use all the data fields available, allowing a single channel to be used for different kinds of communications. Every channel except those from the database begins, in the spirit of KQML, with a performative. On a channel from a customer to a personal assistant or from a seller to a sales representative, we communicate the negotiation parameters. Some channels communicate information about a vehicle, and some communicate economic actions in two fields: buy or sell and the model. When the broker pairs a personal assistant with a sales representative, it must tell the personal assistant the identity of the sales representative (sr1 or sr2) and the sales representative the identity of the personal assistant (pa1 or pa2). Finally, to conclude a deal, communications must include a response yes or no.

It is clear that the modeling afforded by the π-calculus would give a more succinct and natural specification. This is because, instead of having pairs of channels connecting personal assistants and sales representatives in all possible ways, we could have one pair of channels that is passed to the chosen personal assistant and sales representative when the time comes for them to negotiate.

Since the full specification resulted in far too many states for FDR to handle, we scaled the specification down by reducing the range of values allowed for communicating data, by having only one customer, personal assistant, sales representative, and seller, by eliminating BROKER, and by generally simplifying the behavior of the retained agents. The resulting system, called BUYSELL, was formed by first composing the customer and his personal assistant, restricting over the links between them. Then the seller and his sales representative were composed, restricting over the links between them. This gave two subsystems, which themselves were composed. All links between the subsystems were restricted over except for that on which the final result of the transaction is communicated.

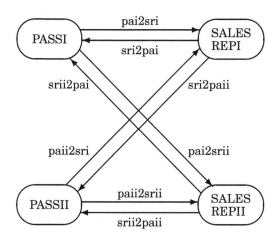

Fig. 4.6. The Remaining Part of the Flow Graph

FDR confirmed that BUYSELL is deadlock free. It is not, however, live-lock free. Investigation using the FDR Debug tool indicated that livelock arises when the CUI process keeps being told that the seller is not willing to sell and evolving back into itself. In fact, this is a possibility we anticipated, and no other source of livelock is present.

We abstracted out a component of the system and refined it so as to capture more focused aspects of human-computer integration. We refined the customer, CUI, expanding it to include an interface that allows humans at the periphery of the system to interact with the agents in the system. Figure 4.7 shows the flow graph for the refinement. PERSON is a human and INT is the interface. INT communicates with the personal assistant, PASS, which is now a dummy. SELLER too is now a dummy; it comes into play only if and when the deal is arranged. The channels are similar to those in the scaled specification except for those between PERSON and INT. Channel int2per generally forwards messages INT receives from PASS except that the messages are broken into their smallest constituents. What is indicated as a channel from PERSON to INT is really just three events, ack, ok, and refuse, thought of as initiated by PERSON. These processes were combined using the parallel operator and hiding, with the overall system named SYSTEM, where only communication on channel seli2cui is not hidden. FDR was used to confirm that indeed SYSTEM failures-divergences refines BUYSELL.

In complementary research, we have experimented with situations where humans collaborate in handshake fashion [19]. The scenarios used here involve participants moving proxy agents around a grid to achieve

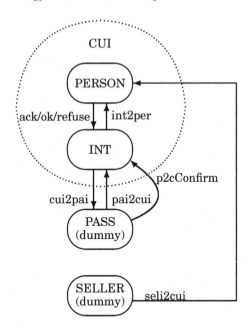

Fig. 4.7. The flowgraph for the refinement.

joint goals. The grid, along with a negotiation interface, is displayed in exactly the same way at each participant's workstation. Proxy agent itineraries are developed incrementally by series of suggestions, each accepted only if all participants handshake on it. A handshake is implemented by each participant moving his or her mouse cursor within a certain time window into a small box in the common display while depressing a given key or button. This is analogous to humans offering their hands and results in an atomic joint action performed only when all parties are prepared to perform it. Handshake communication between computer-supported collaborators forces them to attend concurrently to a sequence of communication actions. This is in the spirit of Clark's position on face-to-face conversation [8], where the addressee is active—consider the nods, expressions, and interjections an addressee normally makes.

4.9 Handshakes, Specifications, Obligations, and Human and Agent Plans

Suchman [41] has criticized the general notion of plans as formal structures generating actions that predominates in the cognitive sciences and classical AI planning. Her particular target is the application of this notion in human-computer interaction. She also finds the notion pervasive in research on natural language understanding, where the concept of a speech act has allowed communication to be subsumed under the traditional planning model. Everyday, face-to-face human conversation is taken as the baseline for assessing the state of human-computer interaction, and such conversation is found to be at odds with the traditional planning model since it is not so much an alternating series of actions as a joint activity continuously engaging the participants. In general, Suchman maintains that a plan is not a generative mechanism for action but an artifact of our reasoning about actions, specifically, an abstraction over actions. As such, a plan is a resource for action. It may be used retrospectively to justify a course of action and before the fact to orient us as we face the contingencies of the environment.

Suchman's work heralded a body of naturalistic research by social scientists into the organization of interaction in technology-supported activities in complex work environments. Ethnomethodology and conversation analysis, which are the main orientations here, "examine the ways in which participants reflexively, and ongoingly, constitute the sense of intelligibility of the 'scene' from within the activities in which they are engaged" [17] (p. 19). Heath and Luff found that, in almost all the settings they studied,

> the accomplishment of complex tasks, which may in principle be the responsibility of a particular individual in a setting, is 'ongoingly' co-ordinated with the actions of others. The 'situated' and contingent character of workplace activities derives from the ways in which the competent accomplishment of those activities is necessarily sensitive to, and thoroughly embedded in, the real-time actions of others ([17], p. 20).

Bardram [2], in response to Suchman's critique, presents the notion of *situated planning*, which is supposed to remove the dichotomy between plans and situated action. He describes a workflow system for coordinating and planning patient care. A workflow system routes information among users and specifies actions to be taken along the route, typically according to a process model. A process model is a computerized (hence formal) representation of work procedures that controls the order in which a sequence of tasks is to be performed. Bardram asserts that a plan does not imply total prehandling and control of work. Rather, a plan is a socially constructed and socially used (shared) resource that lets us anticipate and prehandle recurrent events in working life and reuse experience gained in handling these events. This notion of a plan, he claims, motivates a planning tool that does not emphasize a rigid match between process models and work.

Having looked at plans as resources, we turn to what relates to plans that *is* effective of action. Bratman [3] distinguishes between a plan as a sort of recipe (as in the planning model) and a plan in the sense of having a plan as a mental state, essentially an intention. Bratman distinguishes between two kinds of pro-attitudes. Pro-attitudes that are merely *potential influencers* of conduct include such things as desires and valuations. Intentions, in contrast, are *conduct controlling*. Intentions (plans) provide *consistency constraints* since they must be both internally consistent and consistent with the agent's beliefs. Intentions should also have *means-end coherence*: they must be elaborated enough to do what I now plan. Given the requirement of means-end coherence, intentions pose problems for deliberation and hence determine the relevance of options. Given the need for coherence, prior intentions constrain future intentions hence provide a "filter of admissibility" for options. This requires intentions to be *stable* yet (to maintain rationality) not be irrevocable. So future-directed intentions allow deliberation in advance of conduct. They also support coordination by supporting expectations of their successful execution. A feature of plans/intentions characteristic of limited agents that Bratman notes is that they are partial: details are left for later deliberation. Another feature is that they are hierarchical: plans concerning ends embed plans concerning means and preliminary steps, and more general intentions embed more specific ones.

Roughly, a plan as a resource is a sort of recipe, which, if embraced by intention, becomes a plan effective of action. At least some plans may be chains of anticipations based on experience of recurrent events (Bardram), but the notion of expectations based on intentions comes much closer to the core of multi-agent systems and human group activity. An intention, however, is an attitude, something private. And we are interested in communication acts, which are public. We therefore move the focus from intentions to *obligations*. The terms "obligation" and "commitment" are closely related, but "commitment" can also be used to describe an attribute or quality of a person (a resolve to do something), so we prefer "obligation."

Obligations, like intentions, are normally stable, and they are defeasible (overridable). There is an interesting interplay between the consistency constraint on obligations and their defeasibility. We often have two or more *prima facie* obligations that clash in the sense that they cannot both be discharged (met). For example, I might be obligated to teach at 10:00 AM and also be obligated to appear in court at 10:00 AM. One of the *prima facie* obligations overrides (defeats) the others and becomes the actual obligation. What was once an actual obligation may be defeated by a new obligation (as when I receive the summons after my class schedule has been arranged). Whereas having an intention/plan and its reconsideration is up to the agent, being under an obligation and which *prima facie* obligations defeat others is more objective. For example, I have little say in my obligation to pay my taxes. Again, whether I promise to meet you in the library at 11:00 is up to me, but, once I have made the promise, the obligation is out of my hands. Again, it is odd to say that I intend to do something and the time to do it is at hand yet I do not do it. In contrast, there is nothing odd (just irresponsible) about violating an obligation: obligations relate to ideal cases. Thus, one can have an obligation to A yet not intend to A. It is clear that, conversely, one can have an intention without the corresponding obligation. Yet there is a close relation between intentions and obligations since normally one intends to discharge one's obligations—otherwise, obligations would be pointless.

Thus, obligations serve much the same functions Bratman identifies for intentions. They support coordination by supporting expectations of their successful discharge because they are normally stable and drive means-end reasoning. Obligations are also hierarchical. Imposing an obligation on oneself (by, for example, promising) or another (by, for example, commanding him) allows deliberation in advance of conduct. Obligations, however, have a more meager requirement of means-end coherence. This generally arises only when we spell out a cooperative plan in detail and require explicit commitments from all parties. This is because obligations are generally more abstract (and in this sense more partial) than intentions, being one more step away from conduct. They are also conduct controllers, again one more step away from conduct, although they are not attitudes.

Focusing on obligations, which normally lead to intentions, gives an angle on the intentional stance different from the usual one. It emphasizes ideal behavior. One more way the intentional stance now differs from the design stance (ignoring the details of a system's constitution and predicting that it will behave as it is designed to) is that, while an artifact that behaves abnormally is considered broken and in need of repair, an agent not conforming to an obligation is considered to have violated it and to be subject to sanction. In the physical stance (applying the laws of physics to predict a system's behavior), when a system's behavior contradicts a law-like statement, the statement, not the system, is at fault. The focus on obligations also emphasizes speech acts since they are the normal way of establishing directed obligations, where there is an obligor (subject to the obligation) and an obligee (to whom the obligation is owed). For example, a promise establishes the speaker as the obligor and the addressee as the obligee, while a command establishes the speaker as the obligee and the addressee as the obligor.

Khosla and Maibaum [24] point out that a specification of a software system establishes obligations on the behavior of the specified system. When the system is an agent, critical aspects of the specification that relate to its behavior within a multi-agent system are the constraints on the sequences of communication acts it may perform. These can be seen as sequences of speech acts establishing and discharging obligations. Violation does not indicate need for repair but rather warrants a sanction, such as taking a compensating action. These obligations are effective of action as are, from other points of view, the gates designed for the computer and the computer as an electrical system. A multi-agent system is an open system, and the expectations agents have of the behavior of other agents derives from the specifications of the other agents. Thus, the agent abstraction is at the specification level.

Since a specification can be implemented any number of times, this abstraction is for a *role*. Keeping with the general notion of an agent, this role should allow for autonomous behavior. This is consistent with the view that the agent assuming the role is under obligations, even though they may be seen as delegated by the agent's developers. The role can be seen as a resource since behavior is stated declaratively. Once the role is assumed, however, obligations are assumed, and it becomes effective of action. An agent should also be flexible in filling its role, that is, it should adapt to the contingencies of the situation. A role can introduce *special* obligations, which have an obligor but no obligee. For example, the GIFA agent is responsible for broadcasting anomaly alerts. Special obligations tend to be more abstract than directed obligations. The protocol specified by the environment introduces *general* obligations, with neither an obligor nor an obligee. These are conditions for any agent to be in the multi-agent system.

Our claim is that our process-algebraic agent abstraction allows one to capture a notion of a plan that is effective of action (because of obligations) that applies both to (artificial) agents and to humans. Because the agent abstraction relates to roles, plans in this sense address the division of work. Because the notion of a plan is at the specification level, there is considerable latitude in applying plans in this sense to concrete situations. Plans here are constructed with process-algebraic combinators with the basic actions being handshakes. There are many ways to realize a handshake, and picking out the handshakes is part of characterizing the situation. (See Suchman's quotation, [41], pp. 179-180, of Heritage, [18], p. 302.) The important thing from our point of view is that we can specify that certain handshakes are required and obligate other handshakes no matter how these handshakes are realized.

The specification flavor carries over to how plans followed by humans are characterized. Our position has its most direct application where detail is specified in advance because of the need to operationalize procedures. On the other hand, when achieving a task is embedded in the real-time activity of others, it might be futile to try to identify the handshakes. This could be because the joint activity moves at too fast a pace; or the information has a free form that defies formalization; or the information sources are open-ended. The fact that CSCW systems are often used as mere resources in unintended ways shows that such systems are artifacts whose use as intended for collaboration depends on whether we apply the intentional strategy to them. And this depends, circularly, on our success with them.

To review our models reported earlier, first consider the electronic purchasing system specified in CSP. Here there are expectations about what the humans know about the transaction in which they are engaged since a handshake can have legal implications. The interest is not in the details but in getting the sequence of handshakes right, and this is what the specification captures. This is a very specific activity in a very artificial environment, but it does conform to general practice. There are features of this specification that are formalized sequences of actions but that are not paradigmatic examples of plans—notably, the actions by which the broker assigns roles and the negotiation process. The planning model is usually formulated in a formalism that does not facilitate expression of these patterns. This model is not a good example of a plan as an organizational resource since only part needs to be shared, only part is needed as a (legal) record, and there is not much need for a status overview.

The collaboration system mediating handshakes is an artificial environment where collaborators communicate in a constrained way to meet goals. Humans handshake via a distributed system. The handshake depends little on the situation (just a small part of the interface). This is a small language game where the interlocutors get by with a very small vocabulary and minimal syntax. The rigid negotiation procedure in the whiteboard is a formal structure generating actions but again is not a paradigmatic example of a plan. The collaborators *express* their plans, thus accepting obligations to each other. A possible enhancement would allow them to agree on a previous plan that worked in a similar situation and could be modified for the current situation. This would allow plans to be treated as resources, and then, when agreement is reached, become effective of action.

4.10 Conclusion and Future Work

We first presented a formal framework that uses the π-calculus for modeling multi-agent systems. This framework explicates the agent abstraction as a π-calculus process that persists through communication actions. More generally, we could speak of a process-algebraic (not just a π-calculus) agent abstraction. Our principal task in the first part was to illustrate the use of this framework by modeling certain aspects in the specification of NASA's LOGOS agent community. We have also sketched how a π-calculus framework supports development activities. Generally, we need more experience exploiting formal methods within our framework and in using tools that facilitate the associated activities. These methods must be specialized to multi-agent systems, possibly via notions from particular agent architectures. We have suggested how certain architectural features may be expressed in our framework, but this is just a beginning. A π-calculus semantics for an agent communication language, as discussed here, would help. The strength of a process algebra clearly lies with its handling of communication, but concurrency and communication are some of the most essential features of multi-agent systems, as witness wrapping legacy systems in agent interfaces. The proposed framework perhaps has a bias toward interfaces and communication. This bias, however, is shared by much work over the last few decades in distributed systems, human-computer interaction, linguistics, and philosophy, as witness such notions as those of a speech act, a situation, the flow of information, and common knowledge (perhaps better called shared information).

In the second part, we summarized applications of our process-algebraic abstraction to cases where agents and humans collaborate or human handshakes and negotiation required for collaboration are supported by distributed software. We viewed the agent abstraction from the point of view of the intentional stance, a unifying theme in agent research. From our perspective, obligations and communication acts are the salient concepts that this stance provides. We discussed criticisms of the notion of plans as formal structures effective of action, and we presented the view that plans are resources. We concluded, however, that obligations arise in the use of specifications and from handshakes, and that obligations have a conceptual connection with intentions, which in turn have a conceptual connection with action. In this sense, plans (as might be expressed with a process algebra) are effective of action. We conclude that imposing, being subject to, and discharging obligations are significant features that must be included in our agent abstraction. Experience has shown that it is difficult to get human collaborators to adopt the intentional stance regarding agents or collaboration mediated by software. Research could address, for example, ways to provide natural handshakes and methods to remind users in a context-dependent way of obligations that have not yet been discharged. The notion of a violation (by an agent or a human) of an obligation has been little investigated in CSCW and allied fields. Flexibility and robustness requirements could be addressed by considering compensating actions required by violations.

References

1. Alexander, H. *Formally-Based Tools and Techniques for Human-Computer Dialogues*, E. Horwood, Chichester, U. K. 1987.
2. Bardram, J. E. Plans as Situated Action: An Activity Theory Approach to Workflow Systems. In *Proceedings ECSCW'97 Conference*, Lancaster, U.K., 1997.
3. Bratman, M. What is Intention? In *Intentions in Communication*, P. R. Cohen, J. Morgan, and M. E. Pollack (eds.). The MIT Press, Cambridge, MA. 1990, pp. 15-31.

4. Bratman, M., Israel, D. I. and Pollack, M. E. Plans and Resource-Bounded Practical Reasoning. *Computational Intelligence*, **4**:349–355, 1988.

5. Brown, B. *High-Level Petri Nets for Modeling Multi-Agent Systems.* MS project report, Dept. of Computer Science, North Carolina A&T State University, Greensboro, NC, 1998.

6. Bruns, G. *Distributed Systems Analysis with CCS*, Prentice-Hall, Englewood Cliffs, NJ. 1997.

7. Burge, J. and Esterline, A. C. Using Modal Logics to Model Societies of Agents. In *Proceedings IC-AI'2000*, Las Vegas, NV, 2000.

8. Clark, H. H. *Using Language*, Cambridge University Press, Cambridge. 1996.

9. Cleaveland, R., Parrow, J., and Steffan, B. The Concurrency Workbench: A Semantics-Based Tool for the Verification of Concurrent Systems. *ACM TOPLAS*, **15**(1):36–76, January 1993.

10. Dennet, D. C. True Believers: The Intentional Strategy and Why It Works. In *The Intentional Stance*, D.C. Dennett. The MIT Press, Cambridge, MA. 1987, pp. 13-35.

11. Dix, A., Finlay, J., Abowd, G. and Beale, R. *Human-Computer Interaction* (2nd ed.), Prentice Hall, Hertfordshire, U.K. 1998.

12. *Formal Systems, Failures-Divergences Refinement: FDR2 User Manual.* Formal Systems (Europe) Ltd., 1992-97.

13. Fujinami, T. *A Process Algebraic Approach to Computational Linguisitcs.* Center for Cognitive Science, University of Edinburgh, 1996.

14. Gibson, J. J., *The Ecological Approach to Visual Perception*, Boston: Houghton Mifflin, 1979.

15. Grubb, T. *GenSAA Interface Agent—GIFA.* NASA/Goddard Space Flight Center, Greenbelt, MD, 1997.

16. Haddadi, A. and Sundermeyer, K. Belief-Desire-Intention Agent Architectures. In *Foundations of Distributed Artificial Intelligence*, G. M. P. O'Hare and N. R. Jennings (eds.). Wiley, New York. 1996, pp. 169-185.

17. Heath, C. and Luff, P. *Technology in Action*, Cambridge University Press, Cambridge. 2001.

18. Heritage, J., *Garfinkel and Ethnomethodology*, Polity Press, Cambridge. 1984.

19. Hinds, O. and Esterline, A. Joint Activity Coordination and Common Knowledge in Multi-agent/Multi-person Environments. In *Proc. 5th World Multiconference on Systemics, Cybernetics and Informatics*, Orlando, FL, 2001.

20. Hoare, C. A. R. *Communicating Sequential Processes*. Prentice-Hall, Englewood Cliffs, NJ. 1985.

21. Hosler, J. *LOGOS PAGER Agent.* NASA/Goddard Space Flight Center, Greenbelt, MD, 1997.

22. Huhns, M. N. and Stephens, L. M. Multiagent Systems and Societies of Agents. In *Multiagent Systems: A Modern Approach to Distributed Artificial Intelligence*, G. Weiss (ed.). The MIT Press, Cambridge, MA. 1999, pp. 79-120.

23. Jennings, N. R. Specification and Implementation of a Belief-Desire-Joint-Intention Architecture for Collaborative Probem Solving. *Int. Journal of Cognitive Information Systems*, **2**(3):289–318, 1993.

24. Khosla, S. and Maibaum, T. S. E. The Prescription and Description of State Based Systems. In *Temporal Logic in Specification*, B. Banieqbal, H. Barringer, and A. Pnueli (eds.). Springer-Verlag, Berlin. 1987, pp. 243-294.
25. Labrou, Y. and Finin, T. Semantics and Conversations for an Agent Communication Language. In *Readings in Software Agents*, M. Huhns and M. Singh (eds.). Morgan Kaufmann, San Francisco. 1998, pp. 235-42.
26. Liu, Y. and Esterline A. C. Prima Facie Obligations and a Deontic Transaction Model for Multiagent Systems. In *Proc. IEEE SoutheastCon 2000*, Nashville, TN, April 2000.
27. LOGOS Development Team, Advanced Architectures and Automation Branch. *LOGOS Requirements & Design Document*. NASA/Goddard Space Flight Center, Greenbelt, MD, 1997.
28. Manna, Z. and Pnueli, A. *The Temporal Logic of Reactive and Concurrent Systems: Specification*, Springer-Verlag, New York. 1992.
29. Milner, R. *Communication and Concurrency*, Prentice-Hall, New York. 1989.
30. Milner, R. The Polyadic π-Calculus: a Tutorial. In *Logic and Algebra for Specification*, F. L. Bauer, W. Braueer, and H. Schwichtenberg (eds.). Springer-Verlag, Berlin. 1993, pp. 203-246.
31. Milner, R. *Communicating and Mobile Systems: The π-calculus*, Cambridge University Press, Cambridge. 1999.
32. Milner, R., Parrow, J. and Walker, D. A Calculus of Mobile Processes, Parts I and II. *Journal of Information and Computation*, **100**:1–77, 1992.
33. Mosley, K. and Esterline, A. Modeling Societies of Agents and Users Using CSP. In *Proc. 5th World Multiconference on Systemics, Cybernetics and Informatics*, Orlando, FL, 2001.
34. *NASA Intelligent Systems Program, Intelligent Systems Program Plan*. NASA Ames Research Center, Moffett Field, CA, 2000.
35. Olderog, E. R. *Nets, Terms and Formulas: Three Views of Concurrent Processes and Their Relationship*, Cambridge University Press, Cambridge. 1991.
36. Rash, J. *LOGOS FIRE Agent Concept & Design: Fault Isolation Resolution Expert Agent*. NASA/Goddard Space Flight Center, Greenbelt, MD, 1997.
37. Rouff, C. *User Interface Agent*. NASA/Goddard Space Flight Center, Greenbelt, MD, 1997.
38. Sangiorgi, D. and Walker, D. *The π-Calculus: A Theory of Mobile Processes*, Cambridge University Press, Cambridge. 2001.
39. Singh, M. P. A Semantics for Speech Acts. In *Readings in Software Agents*, M. N. Huhns and M. P. Singh (eds.). Morgan Kaufmann, San Francisco. 1998, pp. 458-470.
40. Singh, M. P., Rao, A. S. and Georgeff, M. P. Formal Methods in DAI: Logic-Based Representation and Reasoning, In *Multiagent Systems: A Modern Approach to Distributed Artificial Intelligence*, G. Weiss (ed.). The MIT Press, Cambridge, MA. 1999, pp. 331-376.
41. Suchman, L. A. *Plans and Situated Actions: The Problem of Human-Machine Communication*, Cambridge University Press, New York. 1987.
42. Tretyakova, Y. and Esterline, A. C. The Logic of Action in the Deontic Transaction Model. In *Proc. IEEE SoutheastCon 2000*, Nashville, TN, April 2000.
43. Truszkowski, W. and Rouff, C. An Overview of the NASA LOGOS and ACT Agent Communities. In *Proc. World Multiconference on Systems, Cybernetics and Informatics*, Orlando, FL, July, 2001.

44. Truszkowski, W. and Hallock, H. Agent Technology from a NASA Perspective. In *CIA-99, Third International Workshop on Cooperative Information Agents*, Uppsala, Springer-Verlag, Berlin, 1999.
45. Victor, B. and Moller, F. *The Mobility Workbench—A Tool for the π-Calculus*. Technical Report DoCS 94/45, Dept. of Computer Sci., Uppsala University, Sweden, 1994.
46. Victor, B. *The Mobility Workbench User's Guide, Polyadic Version 3.122*, University of Uppsala, Sweden. 1995. ftp.docs.uu.se/pub/mwb/guide-3.122.ps.gz.
47. Wooldridge, M. Intelligent Agents. In *Multiagent Systems: A Modern Approach to Distributed Artificial Intelligence*, G. Weiss (ed.). The MIT Press, Cambridge, MA. 1999, pp. 27-77.
48. Wu, X., Cox, B. D. and Esterline, A. C. Representing and Interpreting Multiagent Plans with Statecharts. In *Proc. WAC 2000*, Maui, Hawaii, 2000.

Dynamic Team Formation in Executable Agent-Based Systems

Michael Fisher, Chiara Ghidini, and Antony Kakoudakis

5.1 Introduction

While agent technology has spread rapidly in recent years [20], particularly for applications utilizing the INTERNET, there are still relatively few high-level agent-based programming languages. In addition, the majority of agent applications are developed in Java [19] or its extensions [23], yet such applications rarely have a close link with any of the theories of agency that have been developed in the past, for example [27, 30]. Consequently, any formal development method, involving specification, verification and refinement, becomes difficult to produce.

However, work on *executable specifications* of agent-based systems has shown how high-level logic-based abstractions can be used to represent agents, with their implementation being carried out by direct execution of the corresponding logical formulae. Prominent among this field is work on executable temporal logics [8, 10]. Here, a basic temporal notation is used to represent the dynamic aspects of agents, and then an execution mechanism is used to derive a model from the agent's temporal specification. This core framework has been extended, over a number of years, with deliberation [12] and resource-bounded reasoning [13], in order to provide a logic-based programming language for individual agents. Throughout this research, a key theme has been to achieve many of the high-level elements found within more complex models, such as BDI [26], but using a significantly simpler logical basis.

In parallel, development of the multi-agent aspects of such executable temporal logics has been carried out, providing an open concurrent operational model [7], formal semantics for this concurrent language [9], and mechanisms for *grouping* agents together into more complex computational structures [15]. Briefly, a group is an organizational mechanism that collects and relates some individual agents in a multi-agent system. As we shall see later, groups, in their simplest form, are able to provide appropriate communication patterns between the agents of a multi-agent system. So, consequently, each agent in the system can only send messages within the boundaries of the groups that it is a member of. Additionally, as more and more agents are spawned and evolve new behaviors, such a structuring mechanism is one of the few effective (and formally defined) ways in which emergent multi-agent activity can be controlled.

In this chapter, we review the basic concepts of modeling individual agent behaviors as well as the emergence of simple team structures, where the agents involved have a joint task to achieve while sharing certain simple mental attitudes. Then we consider a recently proposed extension concerning the type of communication that is allowed between agents in this approach. From the original work on Concurrent METATEM [7], agents have only been allowed to communicate positive ground atoms (predicates). In this sense, these agents have a limited communication language, being much less rich than agent communication languages based upon speech acts [5, 6]. While we do not advocate extending communication to such complex languages (since their semantics is not easily describable in the basic logic we use), we show that allowing atoms such as ‘$B_i \Diamond \varphi$’ to be communicated, where ‘B_i’ is a belief operator (meaning “agent i believes”), ‘$\Diamond$’ is a temporal operator (meaning: “at some point in the future”) and ‘φ’ is a ground predicate, is not only natural, but can help the formation of a team helping agent i to achieve either φ or a more complex goal.

The structure of this chapter is as follows. In Section 5.2, we review the key elements of the approach based upon executable temporal logic, drawing on previous descriptions of temporal logic, basic execution, deliberation, and basic belief extensions. In Section 5.3, we review the concurrent operational model for executable temporal logic components, including recent work on grouping. In Section 5.4, we review the idea of agents communicating information about what they *believe* will happen, and describe the semantics and modified operational aspects of this extension. (Note that this aspect is explored much further in [14].) In the following section (Section 5.5) we consider an application of this extended approach in dynamic team construction and, finally, in Section 5.6, we provide concluding remarks.

5.2 Representing Individual Agent Behaviors

The METATEM [1, 8] language has been developed as a high-level mechanism for specifying and executing simple individual agents. It is based upon the principle of specifying an agent using temporal logic, and then *directly executing* [10] this specification in order to provide the agent's behavior. This approach provides a high-level programming notation, maintaining a close link between program and specification.

5.2.1 The Formal Framework

In order to review this approach, we begin by considering a simple temporal logic based on a linear, discrete model of time, and the mechanism for executing specifications given using this logic [25].

The syntax of the temporal logic used here is formally defined as the smallest set of formulae containing: a set, $\mathcal{P}$, of propositional constants, the symbols **true**, **false**, and **start**, and being closed under propositional connectives $\neg$, $\vee$, $\wedge$, $\Rightarrow$ and temporal operators $\bigcirc$, $\Diamond$, $\square$.

As usual, the semantics of this logic is defined via the satisfiability relation on a discrete linear temporal model of time, m, with finite past and infinite future [3]. Thus, m is a sequence of states $s_0, s_1, s_2, s_3, \ldots$ which can be thought of as 'moments' in time. Associated with each of these moments in time, represented by a temporal index $u \in \mathbb{N}$, is a valuation π for the propositional part of the language.

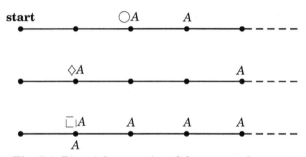

Fig. 5.1. Pictorial semantics of the temporal operators.

Intuitively, the temporal formula '$\bigcirc A$' is satisfied at a given moment in time if A is satisfied at the *next* moment in time, '$\Diamond A$' is satisfied if A is satisfied at *some* future moment in time, '$\square A$' is satisfied if A is satisfied at *all* future moments in time. The graphical representation of the semantics of '$\bigcirc A$','$\Diamond A$', and '$\square A$' is given in the three different sequences of time in Figure 5.1. Notice also the use of the special propositional constant **start**, which is only satisfied at the initial moment in time.

Formally, the semantics of the temporal language used here is defined in Figure 5.2. Satisfiability and validity are defined in the usual way.

5.2.2 Executing Temporal Logic

A close link between theory and implementation is maintained by directly executing the specification of the behavior of an agent, represented by a temporal formula [1]. The execution process attempts to build a model for the formula in a simple forward-chaining fashion. This is extended, in [12], whereby the choice of which formulae to satisfy is provided by user

$$\langle m, 0 \rangle \models \textbf{start}$$

$$\langle m, u \rangle \models \textbf{true}$$

$$\langle m, u \rangle \models p \qquad \text{iff} \quad \pi(u, p) = T \text{ (where } p \in \mathcal{P})$$

$$\langle m, u \rangle \models \neg A \qquad \text{iff} \quad \langle m, u \rangle \not\models A$$

$$\langle m, u \rangle \models A \vee B \qquad \text{iff} \quad \langle m, u \rangle \models A \text{ or } \langle m, u \rangle \models B$$

$$\langle m, u \rangle \models \bigcirc A \qquad \text{iff} \quad \langle m, u+1 \rangle \models A$$

$$\langle m, u \rangle \models \square A \qquad \text{iff} \quad \forall u' \in \mathbb{N}. \text{ if } (u \leq u') \text{ then } \langle m, u' \rangle \models A$$

$$\langle m, u \rangle \models \Diamond A \qquad \text{iff} \quad \exists u' \in \mathbb{N}. (u < u') \text{ and } \langle m, u' \rangle \models A$$

Fig. 5.2. Formal semantics of the temporal language.

defined deliberation functions, rather than by a fixed ordering heuristic. An outline of the basic approach (from [12]) is given below.

1. Specifications of agent behavior are translated into a specific normal form, SNF [11], of the form

$$\textbf{start} \Rightarrow \bigvee_{b=1}^{r} l_b \qquad \text{(an \textit{initial} rule)}$$

$$\bigwedge_{a=1}^{g} k_a \Rightarrow \bigcirc \left[\bigvee_{b=1}^{r} l_b \right] \text{(a \textit{step} rule)}$$

$$\bigwedge_{a=1}^{g} k_a \Rightarrow \Diamond l \qquad \text{(a \textit{sometime} rule)}$$

where each k_i, or l, is a literal. Using SNF the behavior of an agent now (initial rule), in transition to the next moment in time (step rule), and at some time in the future (sometime rule) can be represented. As an example of a simple set of rules which might be part of an agent description, consider the following

$$\textbf{start} \Rightarrow \textit{hungry}$$
$$(\textit{hungry} \wedge \neg \textit{eaten}) \Rightarrow \bigcirc \textit{hungry}$$
$$\textit{has\_food} \Rightarrow \Diamond \textit{eaten}$$

Here, the agent is *hungry* at the beginning of time, and whenever it is *hungry* and has not *eaten*, then *hungry* will be made true at the next moment in time. Similarly, whenever it *has_food*, then a commitment to eventually make *eaten* true is given.

The translation into SNF produces a set, R, of rules.

2. By examining the *initial* rules, constraints on the possible start states for the temporal model can be generated.

We choose one of these possible start states, deriving its valuation from the initial rules.

If all the possible start states have been explored, then we terminate stating that the set of rules, R, is unsatisfiable.

3. Generate constraints on *next* states, C_n, and constraints on *future* states, C_f, by checking applicability in current state of step and sometime rules, respectively.

   C_n represents all the possible choices of valuations for the next state, while C_f provides the set of eventualities that must be satisfied at some time in the future.

4. Make a choice from C_n and check that the chosen valuation is consistent. If there are no unexplored choices, return to a choice point in a previous state.

   The choice mechanism takes into account a combination of C_f, the outstanding eventualities, and the deliberation ordering functions [12].

5. Generate a new state, s, from the choice made in (4). Note that, by default, if propositions are not constrained we choose to leave them unsatisfied.

   Define s as being a successor to the current state and record the eventualities that are still outstanding (i.e. previously generated eventualities that were not satisfied in s); call this set of eventualities Evs.

   If any member of Evs has been continuously outstanding for more than $2^{5|R|}$ states, then return to a previous choice point and select a different alternative.

6. With current state, s, and the set of outstanding eventualities, Evs, go to (3).

The key result here is that, under certain constraints on the choice mechanism within (4), this execution algorithm represents a decision procedure (previously presented in [1]).

Theorem 1 *If a set of SNF rules, R, is executed using the above algorithm, with the proviso that the choice in (4) ensures that the oldest outstanding eventualities are attempted first at each step, then a model for R will be generated if, and only if, R is satisfiable.*

The above proviso ensures that, if an eventuality is outstanding for an infinite number of steps, then it will be attempted an infinite number of times. Once the choice mechanism is extended to include arbitrary ordering functions, as in [12], then a more general version of the above theorem can be given wherein we only require a form of *fairness* on the choice mechanism. While the above proviso effectively means that we *can* potentially explore every possibility, the incorporation in the algorithm of a bound on the number of states that eventualities can remain outstanding, together with the finite model property of the logic, ensures that all of the possible states in the model will be explored if necessary.

In order to illustrate the execution process described above let us consider the following example. Consider the simple set of rules given above, extended as follows:

$$\mathbf{start} \Rightarrow hungry$$
$$(hungry \wedge \neg eaten) \Rightarrow \bigcirc hungry$$
$$has\_food \Rightarrow \Diamond eaten$$
$$\mathbf{start} \Rightarrow \neg has\_food$$
$$\neg has\_food \Rightarrow \bigcirc \neg eaten$$
$$hungry \Rightarrow \bigcirc has\_food$$
$$eaten \Rightarrow \bigcirc \neg hungry$$
$$eaten \Rightarrow \bigcirc \neg eaten$$

If we now begin to execute this set of rules, using the algorithm above, we generate the following sequence of states.

0. state: $hungry, \neg has\_food, \neg eaten$
    eventualities: (none)
1. state: $hungry, has\_food, \neg eaten$
    eventualities: $\Diamond eaten$
2. state: $hungry, has\_food, eaten$
    eventualities: (none)
3. state: $\neg hungry, has\_food, \neg eaten$
    eventualities: $\Diamond eaten$
4. .....

And so on, either infinitely or until a contradiction is generated.

5.2.3 Representing Resource-Bounded Reasoning

An extension of the approach presented above is introduced in [13], where the propositional linear temporal logic introduced above is combined with a multi-context belief logic [18, 16]. While temporal reasoning is essentially infinite, this logic, called TLBB, permits a simple execution mechanism to be employed over a finite structure of belief contexts and so to represent resource-bounded reasoning.

The main idea in defining TLBB, is to add to the language a set of belief predicates, $B_1, \ldots, B_n$, where formulae of the form '$B_i \phi$' mean "agent i believes that ϕ", and to structure the belief of an agent ϵ about a set $I = \{1, \ldots, n\}$ of agents, into a structure of *belief contexts* such as that presented in Figure 5.3. Intuitively, the belief context ϵ represents the beliefs of the external agent ϵ, the belief context 1 represents the beliefs of agent 1 (from the point of view of ϵ), 21 represents the beliefs of agent

2 about the beliefs of agent 1 (from the point of view of ϵ), 212 represents the beliefs of agent 2 about the beliefs of agent 1 about the beliefs of agent 1 (from the point of view of ϵ), and so on. The set of belief contexts that ϵ is able to build is represented by the set, I^k, of the (possibly empty) strings α of the form $i_1 \ldots i_h$ with $\mid i_1 \ldots i_h \mid \leq k$. Depending on the value of k, ϵ is able to consider a smaller/larger set of belief contexts in its reasoning process, and therefore a smaller/larger set of belief about belief.

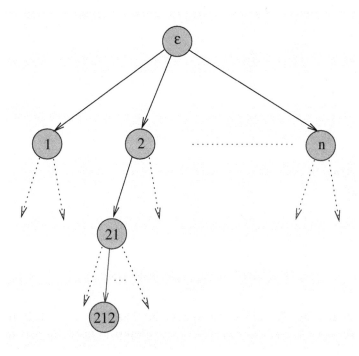

Fig. 5.3. The structure of belief contexts.

The semantics of the TLBB language is based on the semantics for contextual reasoning proposed in [16]. Following this approach, we associate to each belief context α a discrete linear temporal model of time m_α. The propositional and temporal part of the language is interpreted in the usual way, while the semantics of the belief predicates B_i is defined by introducing appropriate constraints among pairs of belief contexts α and αi.

Finally, in order to execute formulae of TLBB, the original temporal normal form, SNF, is extended with a *belief* rule of the form:

$$\bigwedge_{a=1}^{g} k_a \Rightarrow B_i \left[\bigvee_{b=1}^{r} l_b \right] \quad (\text{a } belief \text{ rule})$$

The execution algorithm is also extended to handle the execution of the new normal form. The two main elements of the algorithm affected by this are that the execution process now builds a labelled tree, rather than a sequence, and that once a new belief state is built it must be checked for equivalence with previously generated states. Thus, rather than just generating a set of choices based upon temporal rules, we must now consider both temporal and belief rules. This will (often) lead to the construction of a number of belief contexts and (simulated) temporal sequences in order to derive these choices. For example, in Figure 5.4 the basic temporal se-

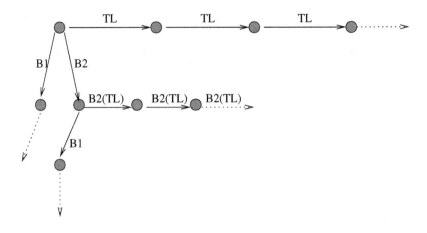

Fig. 5.4. Typical model exploration.

quence (labelled by 'TL') is being constructed. However, at certain points, belief contexts (e.g. B1 and B2) must be explored in order to decide how to proceed. In addition, within these belief contexts, temporal execution itself can be simulated, e.g. B2(TL). Note that exploration of everything within a belief context will be carried out within a finite amount of time. The detailed execution algorithm for TLBB, and theorems concerning the correctness of the execution mechanism are provided in [13].

5.3 The Concurrent Operational Model

Concurrent METATEM [7] is a logic-based programming language comprising two elements: the representation of each individual agent's behavior in the way described above; and an operational framework for agents that provides both asynchronous concurrency and broadcast message-passing. The basic tenets of this approach are that:

(i) all agents are concurrently active;

(ii) the basic mechanism for communication between agents is *broadcast* message-passing;

(iii) each agent defines how it will interact with its environment.

Agents, encapsulating state and behavior, are the basic entities within our framework. By default, the description of each agent's behavior is based on a linear time temporal logic (see Section 5.2). Individual agents only act depending on their state which can be altered through identified messages (modeled as predicates) received from their execution environment. An agent is able to filter out these messages, recognizing those that are of its interest and ignoring all others. The definition of which messages an agent recognizes, together with a definition of the messages that an agent may itself produce, is provided by the *interface definition* of that particular agent. For example, the interface definition for a 'plane' agent, representing an aircraft's navigation controller, may be defined in the following way:

$$plane()$$
$$in : take\_off, land, give\_coordinates...$$
$$out : decr\_speed, incr\_speed...$$

Here, {*take_off*, *land*, *give_coordinates*, ...} represents the set of messages the agent is able to recognize, while {*decr_speed*, *incr_speed*, ...} represents the set of messages the agent itself is able to produce.

As we said before, one of the basic tenets of our approach is that all agents are (potentially) concurrently active; by default they are asynchronously executing. The basic communication mechanism used between agents is broadcast message-passing. Thus, when an agent sends a message, it does not necessarily send it to a specified destination, it merely sends it to its environment, where it can potentially be received by all other agents. Although broadcast is the default communication mechanism, both multicast and point-to-point communication can also be defined.

In this chapter, we emphasize an important aspect of Concurrent ME-TATEM, that is the notion of *grouping* [7]. Briefly, a group is an organizational mechanism that collects and relates a set of individual agents within a multi-agent system. When a particular agent within a group broadcasts a message, the message is distributed only to those other agents within that group. In addition, groups can be overlapping, can have sub-groups, and can even have different environmental conditions within their boundaries (see below). It is important to note that groups were introduced into this approach principally as a way of structuring the agent space, and so reducing the expense of full broadcast communication. However, it is clear from work on complex multi-agent organizations [28, 4] that such simple structuring is not yet sufficient to represent more complex and fluid agent organizations.

Recent work has shown that agent groups can productively be treated in a similar way to agents [15]. Thus, in Concurrent METATEM, groups and agents are basically the same entities, avoiding the need to introduce separate mechanisms and entities dealing with the agent structuring and organization. As a result, the core components of an agent type in Concurrent METATEM can now be defined as:

$$Agent ::= Behavior :\ Logical\_Specification$$
$$Contents : \mathcal{P}(Agent)$$
$$Context : \mathcal{P}(Agent)$$

These three main components define:

- *Behavior*, i.e., this component provides the essential reasoning required for an agent's execution. Here, we follow exactly the approach presented earlier. An agent's behavior is described through a set of rules that are directly executed using the above forward chaining approach.
- *Contents*, i.e., this component is a data structure associated with each agent and holds references to other agents. Roughly speaking, 'Contents' contain references to other agents which are contained in a given agent. Basically, each agent, in addition to its normal execution, concurrently collects and relates a number of other agents which form the agent's contents.
- *Contexts*, i.e., this component, similar to above, is a data structure associated with each agent and holds references to other agents. Each agent, apart from relating a number of individual agents, can itself be collected and related with other agents through its Contexts. In fact, we can describe 'Contexts' as a set of references to other agents which contain our agent. Note that a possible Context for an agent is its environment.

By choosing to represent groups as agents, we are able to model additional properties for a collection of individual agents [15]. These additional properties can be defined and they could, in principle, be of a variety of types, e.g.,

- constraints on execution within the group, e.g. synchronous versus asynchronous [15];
- constraints on communication that can take place within the group, e.g., instantaneous, eventually, 'lossy' [15];
- constraints on common attitudes within the group, e.g., mutual beliefs.

In Figure 5.5, we give examples of such properties, represented as temporal formulae. In contrast, various Java or C++ models for containers (e.g., Java collections) take into account only the relational point of view of the underlying aggregated components. Groups in Concurrent METATEM are, in principle, able to provide more than just the abstract representation of such agent aggregations, they can be used to model common attributes and behavior between the contained agents. Note that the rules characterizing the behavior of *rcv*, *broadcast*, *send*, etc., would occur in the member agents themselves.

Message Passing Properties:

- When an agent receives a message, it may choose to pass this message on to its contents:

$$rcv(\text{self}, Msg) \Rightarrow Msg \wedge (\forall A \in Contents : send(A, Msg))$$

- When an agent broadcasts a message, it sends this message to its context (e.g. environment):

$$broadcast(Msg) \Rightarrow \forall A \in Context : send(A, Msg)$$

Communication Properties:

- A message sent within a group will eventually be received by the group members:

$$send(A, Msg) \Rightarrow \Diamond rcv(A, Msg)$$

- Here, a message sent within a group will be received by the group members at the next moment in time:

$$send(A, Msg) \Rightarrow \bigcirc rcv(A, Msg)$$

- Here, a message sent within a group may be lost:

$$send(A, Msg) \Rightarrow (\Diamond rcv(A, Msg) \vee lost(Msg))$$

Fig. 5.5. Specifying various properties of a group's behavior.

Having reviewed the background concerning both individual agent execution and multi-agent systems, we now introduce a recent extension to the agent communication language. One of the uses of this extension is to facilitate the cooperative formation of multi-agent structures similar to agent teams [29].

5.4 Communicating Beliefs about Eventualities

Instead of restricting communication between agents to be comprised solely of ground predicates, we now extend the language to allow formulae of the form $B_i \Diamond \varphi$, where 'φ' is a ground predicate, to be communicated. The intuition here is that this allows an agent to broadcast information concerning its internal goals, i.e. its beliefs about what *will* happen. Since the "what will happen" here is essentially controlled by the agent itself, then $B_i \Diamond \varphi$ can be seen as representing an internal goal of the agent.

In order to generate messages of this new form, the sending agent (say, agent i) needs only to ensure that '$\Diamond \varphi$' is in its out: list, and either make '$\Diamond \varphi$' true, or make '$B_i \Diamond \varphi$' true explicitly. In either case, '$B_i \Diamond \varphi$' will be broadcast. Thus, in

$$plane()$$
$$in : take\_off, \Diamond land, give\_coordinates...$$
$$out : decr\_speed, incr\_speed, \Diamond cruising...$$

if '$\Diamond cruising$' is to be satisfied, then '$B_{plane} \Diamond cruising$' is broadcast. On the other hand, if '$B_i \Diamond land$' is broadcast by some agent, i, this is recognized by the plane agent.

The semantics of the extended syntax is based on the one given in [9]. In that paper, the basic idea was to rename each predicate, p, occurring in agent, i, as p_i and characterize communication via formulae such as

$$(p_i \wedge (p \in i.out) \wedge (p \in j.in)) \Rightarrow \Diamond p_j.$$

This means that, if p is satisfied in agent i, p is in the set of predicates that agent i can broadcast, and p is in the set of messages that agent j can receive then, at some point in the future, p will be satisfied in agent j.

This semantics can now be extended to incorporate both

$$(\Diamond p_i \wedge (\Diamond p \in i.out) \wedge (\Diamond p \in j.in)) \Rightarrow \Diamond B_i \Diamond p_j$$

and

$$(B_i \Diamond p_i \wedge (\Diamond p \in i.out) \wedge (\Diamond p \in j.in)) \Rightarrow \Diamond B_i \Diamond p_j.$$

It is easy to see that the implementation of an individual agent can easily be modified to handle the above extension. We need simply generate a communication event when either '$\Diamond \varphi$' or '$B_i \Diamond \varphi$' is to be satisfied, and '$\Diamond \varphi$' is in the agent's 'out' list.

Having extended the communication language between agents with such a simple modification, the reader might now ask whether, and in which aspects, this is a useful extension. There is a great deal that can be done with formulae such as '$B_i \Diamond \varphi$' in agent j, and such a simple extension turns out to be very useful within individual agents (for more details, see [14]). In the rest of this chapter, however, we will concentrate on the use of this construct in facilitating multi-agent activities.

5.5 Example of Dynamic Team Formation

In an agent-based system, a single agent suffices as long as the agent has the resources and the capacity to achieve its goals. However, as the complexity and uncertainty of the tasks required in order to achieve these goals increase, the need for collaborative work between a number of individual agents becomes apparent. In this section we provide a novel approach to agent teamwork which enables agent teams to emerge at runtime depending on the beliefs and capabilities of the agents that comprise the underlying multi-agent system. More specifically, we show how the $B_i \Diamond \varphi$ construct is useful within this variety of team building.

5.5.1 Scenario

As an example, let us consider an agent i which receives a request to perform the task *book_holiday*. At the initial moment in time the holiday is not yet booked, but this task must become one of the goals of the agent.

$$(5.1) \qquad \mathbf{start} \Rightarrow \neg done(book\_holiday)$$

$$(5.2) \qquad \mathbf{start} \Rightarrow B_i \Diamond done(book\_holiday)$$

Obviously, agent i must be capable of booking a holiday, that is *capable(i, book_holiday)* has to be true. Therefore, it might try to satisfy $\Diamond do(book\_holiday)$ straight away by using a general rule of the form

$$(5.3) \qquad (B_i \Diamond done(\sigma) \wedge capable(i, \sigma)) \Rightarrow \Diamond done(\sigma)$$

Unfortunately, in this particular scenario, this is not enough. In fact, agent i knows that the action of booking a holiday must be decomposed in three independent (sub)actions *book_hotel*, *rent_car*, and *book_flight*, and that in order to book a holiday it needs first to perform all these three actions

$$(5.4) \qquad \begin{pmatrix} \neg done(book\_hotel) \vee \\ \neg done(rent\_car) \vee \\ \neg done(book\_flight) \end{pmatrix} \Rightarrow \bigcirc \neg done(book\_holiday)$$

Therefore, together with trying to make $\Diamond done(book\_holiday)$ true, i knows it has to decompose the initial goal into the three sub-goals of $B_i \Diamond done(book\_hotel)$, $B_i \Diamond done(rent\_car)$, and $B_i \Diamond done(book\_flight)$. If i is capable of performing all three (sub)actions, then it is able to schedule the initial goal, by using equation (5.3), where σ is instantiated to *book_hotel*, *rent_car*, and *book_flight*, respectively. But what happens if agent i is not capable of booking hotels or renting cars? In other words, what happens if the following is true?

$$(5.5) \qquad \begin{aligned} \neg capable(i, book\_hotel) \;\wedge \\ \neg capable(i, rent\_car) \;\wedge \\ capable(i, book\_flight) \end{aligned}$$

One answer is to collect together a *team* of agents capable of achieving this.

5.5.2 Team Protocol

A team of agents in Concurrent METATEM is a group of agents that have a joint goal to achieve, while sharing some beliefs regarding both the status of the team's goal (whether it is achievable or not) and beliefs regarding each member's contribution to the achievement of that goal. Here we presuppose that communication between the members of the team is essential and, furthermore, we assume that teamwork is achieved through some specific interactions (message exchange) occurring between the agents of the team.

In order to show how we can describe teamwork in this way, we introduce a protocol upon which the coordination of the team members can be based. In order to formally describe this protocol, we introduce certain message predicates (outlined in Table 5.1) that every agent involved will be able to recognize and, additionally, we outline the essential rules that have to be present in the involved agent descriptions that will cause the agents to act in a desirable way.

Table 5.1. Sample message predicates for teamwork in Concurrent METATEM.

Predicate	Meaning
capable?(τ)	Queries whether any agent is capable of achieving τ.
capable(α,τ)	Signals that agent α is capable of achieving task τ.
request(α,τ)	Agent α is delegated to perform task τ.
doing(α,τ)	Agent α is performing taskτ.
done(τ)	Indicates that task τ has been done.
Tbelief(α,ϕ)	Indicates the mutual belief of the members of the team α about ϕ.

5.5.3 Emergence of a Team

A team emerges when an agent recognizes the need for external input with respect to one of its internal goals. In our case, agent i is not capable of renting a car or booking a flight. Thus, although the agent has a conceptual plan indicating what is needed in order to achieve this internal commitment (e.g. the agent believes it has to perform *book_hotel, book_flight*, etc), in our case the agent does not have the appropriate capabilities to carry out this plan alone. In an attempt to achieve its own goals, agent i might choose to broadcast messages to its environment, waiting for other agents x and y (not necessarily disjoint) which have those capabilities of booking a hotel and renting a car, required for the achievement of its goals. The idea here is that agent i will try to form a team with agents x and y to achieve the goal *book_holiday*. We can model the behavior of querying other agents through:

(5.6) $B_i \Diamond done(\sigma) \wedge \neg capable(i, \sigma) \Rightarrow capable?(\sigma)$

where *capable?*(σ) is broadcast.

In our scenario, suppose there is an agent x in the environment, which deals with car rental. Every time agent x receives a message *capable?(rent_car)*, it immediately broadcasts back the message $B_x \Diamond done(rent\_car)$, which indicates its belief that *rent_car* can be achieved. Agent x may therefore be added to the team of agent i, through the next rule (where σ is instantiated to *rent_car*)

(5.7) $B_x \Diamond done(\sigma) \wedge B_i \Diamond done(\sigma) \wedge \neg capable(i, \sigma) \Rightarrow \bigcirc add(x, i)$

and this, together with the next rule, will make agent i believe it (the team) is now capable of achieving this goal.

(5.8) $added(x, i) \wedge B_x \Diamond done(\sigma) \Rightarrow \bigcirc capable(i, \sigma)$.

The same might happen with an agent y capable of booking hotels, as y might broadcast back a similar message $B_y \Diamond done(book\_hotel)$, and then be added to the team of agent i.

The fact that $B_i \Diamond done(rent\_car)$ and $B_i \Diamond done(book\_hotel)$ can be satisfied guarantees that agent i will eventually achieve its initial goal. In fact, agent i is capable of booking a flight (equation (5.5)) and it has a goal $B_i \Diamond done(book\_flight)$. Therefore, it is able to use equation (5.3) in order to force $\Diamond done(book\_flight)$ to be true. Moreover, agents x and y will (sooner or later) make *rent_car* and *book_hotel* true (again by using equation (5.3)). They will broadcast these facts to i which will be able to falsify the premises of equation (5.4), and so make *done(book_holiday)* true.

Note that, here we have chosen to follow a very simple approach to team formation, in the sense that the team agent will add the appropriate team-members into its *Contents* with respect to which agents reply first to its requests. Another, probably more interesting approach would have been to employ some form of negotiation process between x/y and i in this phase of team-formation.

As a final remark note that our approach does not exclude the possibility of prespecified and/or fixed teams of agents. In fact, together with enabling the possibility of team emergence and formation, our approach allows the definition of a specific team, say T, of agents, simply including the required agents $a_1, \ldots, a_n$ into the Contents of T. Moreover, rules can be specified so that no other agents can be added (removed) to the Contents of T.

5.5.4 Generating Shared Team Beliefs

After the team-agent has added into its contents all the agents required for the achievement of its initial commitment, the team-agent may try to build the appropriate mutual beliefs among the team members. The team-agent achieves this by sending appropriate messages to its *Contents*, for example:

$$(5.9) \qquad B_i \begin{pmatrix} \neg doing(i, book\_holiday) \wedge \\ capable(i, book\_hotel) \wedge \\ capable(i, book\_flight) \wedge \\ capable(i, rent\_car) \end{pmatrix}$$

$$\Rightarrow \bigcirc \begin{pmatrix} Tbelief(i, doing(i, book\_holiday)) \wedge \\ Tbelief(i, \Diamond done(book\_holiday)) \end{pmatrix}$$

$$B_i doing(i, book\_holiday)$$

$$(5.10) \qquad \Rightarrow \bigcirc \begin{pmatrix} Tbelief(i, doing(i, book\_hotel)) \wedge \\ Tbelief(i, doing(i, book\_flight)) \wedge \\ Tbelief(i, doing(i, rent\_car)) \end{pmatrix}$$

Now, when an agent receives a *Tbelief* message, it believes that the team is undertaking the activity specified. This allows the agent to act, knowing that certain activities are being performed elsewhere.

5.5.5 Team Computation

The team-members (the team-agent's *Contents*), in order to be able to start the execution of their particular part of the team's joint task, need to accommodate (something like) the following rule:

$$(5.11) \qquad \forall x \in Contexts : \begin{pmatrix} Tbelief(x, doing(\sigma)) \\ \wedge \, capable(i, \sigma) \\ \wedge \, B_i(\neg doing(i, \sigma)) \end{pmatrix}$$

$$\Rightarrow \bigcirc request(i, \sigma) \wedge B_i doing(i, \sigma)$$

The team's execution terminates either when all the individual tasks, required for the achievement of the team-agent's initial goal have been achieved, or when a particular team-member that plays a critical role within the team drops its commitment to carry out the task that the team has delegated to it.

In the first case, the appropriate rules that terminate the team are as follows:

$$(5.12) \quad \left(\begin{array}{c} done(book\_flight) \\ \wedge \, done(book\_hotel) \\ \wedge \, done(rent\_car) \end{array} \right) \wedge B_i \neg done(book\_holiday)$$

$$\Rightarrow \bigcirc Tbelief(i, done(book\_holiday))$$

In the second case we can either incorporate specific rules within the team-agent's description that will try to recover the situation or we can simply terminate the team.

5.6 Summary

In this chapter, we have provided a review of work on executable specifications based upon temporal and modal logics. In particular, we have shown how such an approach might be productively used in the development of simple organizational structures, such as teams.

5.6.1 Related Work

Teams are often viewed as groups of agents requiring their members at least to have a joint goal and, possibly, to share some specific mental properties such as intentions, beliefs and commitments, for example [2, 21, 28]. Typically, an agent team is a group of agents working on a common task having the ability to operate on dynamic environments incorporating *flexible* coordination and communication facilities.

Simple groups of individual agents with prespecified coordination plans in a very dynamic and continuously evolving domain will fail to deliver due to *inflexibility* [28]. This is mainly because of the fact that it is difficult to anticipate, and plan in advance for, all possible coordination failures. Cohen and Levesque developed a framework for constructive agent teamwork, taking into account the fact that teamwork is not just the union of simultaneous actions carried out by the team's members, even if these actions are coordinated [2]. In their framework, they claim that for flexible teamwork in real-time and highly dynamic domains, the teams' members have to share some certain mental features. They argue that the mental notion of *joint intention*, which they formulate as a *joint commitment* to perform a collective action while in a certain mental state, serves as the glue that binds teams members together.

However, joint intention theory assumes that it is always possible to attain mutual belief, and that once an agent comes to think the goal is finished, it never changes its mind. Unfortunately, this may not always be the case.

Another researcher who tried to addresses issues related with agent teamwork is Tambe. Tambe's model of teamwork is based on the notion of hierarchical reactive plans and on a modified version of the joint intentions theory [28] . The framework has been successfully applied in the modeling of a soccer team [22], as well as in the modeling of intelligent pilots in a battlefield simulator [28]. Tambe modifies joint intention theory by: making communication conditional, rather than unconditional; and enhancing mechanisms for dissolution of a joint commitment.

An attempt to model teamwork and, more generally, the cooperation of agents for solving problems, is described by Wooldridge and Jennings in [31]. The model represents the cooperation process from its beginning, with some agent recognizing the potential for cooperation with respect to one of its goals, through to team action that leads to the realization of this goal.

It is important to note that we do not, in this chapter, attempt to model the ideas of joint intentions/goals/beliefs in their full generality, but use a combination of a logic of belief (TLBB), broadcast communication, and the idea of representing groups as agents, in order to enforce common goals.

There is relatively little related work on executable agent specifications. The main alternative approach is that of Golog [24] and Con-Golog [17]. These are both based upon the Situation Calculus, in which the preconditions for, and effects of, actions are specified. These actions can be applied to situations (states) to generate new situations. In this way, a sequence of actions can lead from an initial state to a goal state. The typical way in which this is used in agents is to identify a goal state, and then generate, via a planning process, a sequence of actions that will transform the current/initial state into the goal state. This sequence of actions is then executed by the agent. ConGolog is a multi-agent version of Golog.

5.6.2 Future Work

Our future work in this area includes, representing more complex team building scenarios, for example employing a form of negotiation process between agents during the team formation phase, and development of a more robust implementation whereby dynamic organizations of rational agents can be easily constructed. Finally we intend to look more at complexity results in more depth.

References

1. Barringer, H., Fisher, M., Gabbay, D., Gough, G. and Owens, R. METATEM: An Introduction. *Formal Aspects of Computing*, **7**(5):533–549, 1995.
2. Cohen, P. and Levesque, H. Teamwork. *Nous*, **25**:11–24, 1991.
3. Emerson, E. A. Temporal and Modal Logic. In *Handbook of Theoretical Computer Science*, J. van Leeuwen, editor. Elsevier. 1990, pp 996–1072.
4. Ferber, J. and Gutknecht, O. *Aalaadin: a meta-model for the analysis and design of organizations in multi-agent systems*. Research Report R. R. LIRMM 97189, LIRM, Université Montpelier, France, December 1997.
5. Finin, T. and Fritzson, R. KQML — a language and protocol for knowledge and information exchange. In *Proceedings of the Thirteenth International Workshop on Distributed Artificial Intelligence*, Lake Quinalt, WA, July, 1994, pp 126–136.
6. FIPA. *Agent Communication Language – Spec 2*. Foundation for Intelligent Physical Agents. 1999. http://www.fipa.org/spec/fipa9412.PDF
7. Fisher, M. Concurrent METATEM — A Language for Modeling Reactive Systems. In *Parallel Architectures and Languages, Europe (PARLE), (LNCS 694)*, Munich, Germany, June 1993.
8. Fisher, M. Representing and Executing Agent-Based Systems. In *Intelligent Agents*, M. Wooldridge and N. R. Jennings, editors. Springer-Verlag. 1995.
9. Fisher, M. A Temporal Semantics for Concurrent METATEM. *Journal of Symbolic Computation*, **22**(5/6), November/December 1996.
10. Fisher, M. An Introduction to Executable Temporal Logics. *Knowledge Engineering Review*, **11**(1):43–56, March 1996.
11. Fisher, M. A Normal Form for Temporal Logic and Its Application in Theorem-Proving and Execution. *Journal of Logic and Computation*, **7**(4):429–456, August 1997.
12. Fisher, M. Implementing BDI-like Systems by Direct Execution. In *Proceedings of the Fifteenth International Joint Conference on Artificial Intelligence (IJCAI'97)*, Morgan-Kaufmann, 1997.
13. Fisher, M. and Ghidini, C. Programming Resource-Bounded Deliberative Agents. In *Proceedings of the Sixteenth International Joint Conference on Artificial Intelligence (IJCAI'99)*, Morgan Kaufmann Publ., Inc., 1999, pp 200–206.
14. Fisher, M. and Ghidini, C. A Simplified Model for Rational Agents. 2001.
15. Fisher, M. and Kakoudakis, T. Flexible Agent Grouping in Executable Temporal Logic. In *Proceedings of Twelfth International Symposium on Languages for Intensional Programming (ISLIP)*, World Scientific Press, 1999.
16. Ghidini, C. and Giunchiglia, F. Local Models Semantics, or Contextual Reasoning = Locality + Compatibility. *Artificial Intelligence*, **127**(4):221–259, 2001. A short version appeared in the proceedings of the Sixth International Conference on Principles of Knowledge Representation and Reasoning (KR'98).
17. De Giacomo, G., Lespérance, Y. and Levesque, H. Congolog, a concurrent programming language based on the situation calculus. *Artificial Intelligence*, **121**(1-2):109–169, 2000.
18. Giunchiglia, F. and Serafini, L. Multilanguage hierarchical logics (or: how we can do without modal logics). *Artificial Intelligence*, **65**:29–70, 1994. Also IRST-Technical Report 9110-07, IRST, Trento, Italy.

19. Gosling, J., Joy, B. and Steele, G. *The Java Language Specification*, Addison-Wesley. 1996.
20. Jennings, N. R. and Wooldridge, M. Applications of agent technology. In *Agent Technology: Foundations, Applications, and Markets*, Springer-Verlag, Heidelberg. 1998.
21. Kinny, D., Ljungberg, M., Rao, A. S., Sonenberg, E., Tidhar, G. and Werner, E. Planned team activity. In *Artificial Social Systems — Selected Papers from the Fourth European Workshop on Modelling Autonomous Agents in a Multi-Agent World, MAAMAW-92, (LNAI 830)*, C. Castelfranchi and E. Werner, editors. Springer-Verlag. 1992, pp 226–256.
22. Kitano, H., Tambe, M., Stone, P. and Veloso, M. The robocup synthetic agent challenge. In *Proceedings of the International Joint Conference on Artificial Intelligence (IJCAI97)*, 1997.
23. Lange, D. and Oshima, M. *Programming and Deploying Java Mobile Agents with Aglets*. Addison-Wesley, Reading, MA. 1998.
24. Levesque, H., Reiter, R., Lespérance, Y., Lin, F. and Scherl, R. GOLOG: A Logic Programming Language for Dynamic Domains. *Journal of Logic Programming*, **31**:59–84, 1997.
25. Pnueli, A. The Temporal Logic of Programs. In *Proceedings of the Eighteenth Symposium on the Foundations of Computer Science*, Providence, RI, November 1977.
26. Rao, A. S. and Georgeff, M. P. Modeling Agents within a BDI-Architecture. In *International Conference on Principles of Knowledge Representation and Reasoning (KR)*, R. Fikes and E. Sandewall, editors. Morgan Kaufmann, Cambridge, MA, April 1991.
27. Shoham, Y. Agent-oriented programming. *Artificial Intelligence*, **60**(1):51–92, 1993.
28. Tambe, M. Teamwork in real-world dynamic environments. In *Proceedings of the First International Conference on Multi–Agent Systems*, V. Lesser, editor. MIT Press, 1995.
29. Tambe, M. Towards flexible teamwork. *Journal of Artificial Intelligence Research*, **7**:83–124, 1997.
30. Wooldridge, M. and Rao, A., editors. *Foundations of Rational Agency*. Applied Logic Series, Kluwer Academic Publishers. March 1999.
31. Wooldridge, M. and Jennings, N. The Cooperative Problem Solving Process. *Journal of Logic and Computation*, 1999.

Scenario-Based Engineering of Multi-Agent Systems

Jon Whittle and Johann Schumann

6.1 Introduction

A recent development in software engineering is the paradigm of agent-oriented software engineering (AOSE) – see [35] for a survey of the state of the art. Roughly speaking, AOSE is the engineering of systems that are built from distributed, coordinating sets of agents. Most work in AOSE has been extensions of object-oriented analysis and design methodologies with emphasis placed on features that are particular to agent-based systems, such as complex coordination protocols, a high degree of concurrency and autonomy. An independent area that has also received a lot of interest is that of scenario-based software engineering (SBSE) – see [31]. Scenarios are traces of interactions between system components or its users. They are usually represented as abstract execution traces and serve as an interlingua between customers, system developers and test engineers. SBSE explores the ways in which scenarios can be used in the software development process and has primarily been associated with object-oriented software methodologies.

The use of scenarios is particularly suited to the development of agent-oriented systems. Such systems typically involve complex interactions between multiple coordinating agents. The interaction protocols for these systems can be very tricky to engineer. This chapter will show how some new techniques for utilizing scenarios in software engineering, reported in [34] and extended here, can be applied to AOSE. The focus is on modeling and analyzing agent interaction protocols and excludes discussion of how to model agents' beliefs, desires and intentions. Our methodology thus aims toward applications with weak agency where agent behavior can be much more predetermined during design time (cf. [36]; for a definition of strong agency, see [24]).

Two principal ways of extending the current use of scenarios will be presented. Firstly, scenarios can be used in forward engineering, i.e., using the scenarios as a guide in developing system design models or code.

Although many commercial software development environments provide forward engineering support in the form of stub code generation from design models, there is currently no available technology that can provide automated support in forward engineering design models from scenarios. In this chapter, an algorithm will be presented that can semi-automatically generate initial design models from a collection of scenarios. Secondly, scenarios can be used in reverse engineering, i.e., extracting a design model from existing code. The purpose of reverse engineering is to recover a faithful, high-level design of a piece of software in the case that the software source code is not available or is poorly documented. Execution scenarios can be obtained by executing an instrumented version of the code that outputs trace information to a log file. These scenarios can then be used as the basis for developing a design model.

In the context of agent-based systems, scenarios can be used to develop the following kinds of design models:

- agent interaction protocols, describing the complex interactions between agents when they are placed in the same environment;
- agent skeletons [27] or abstract local descriptions of agents in terms of events that are significant for coordination with other agents;
- detailed models of the internal behavior of an agent.

In this chapter, we focus on the use of statecharts [16] to represent the design models. A statechart is a finite state machine extended by notions of hierarchy and orthogonality (for concurrent behavior). Their event-driven nature make statecharts interesting for agent-based systems. The use of scenarios in forward-engineering is already quite common in the development of object-oriented systems and forms part of many OO methodologies, namely those that are based on use cases [25]. The idea is that use cases (which can be considered as a collection of scenarios) are used in the early stages of software design to map out the behavioral requirements of a software artifact. Scenarios, however, give a global view of a system in terms of the interactions between subcomponents. For implementation, a model of the individual components is required, so the scenarios are used as a guide in developing the local model of each subcomponent. Unfortunately, this transition from global scenarios to local models is currently left grossly underspecified in state of the art methodologies.

We have developed a technique for translating scenarios into behavioral models (semi-)automatically. Given a collection of scenarios, plus additional constraints that may be specified by the user, our algorithm synthesizes a behavioral model for each agent involved in the interaction. These generated models will be either interaction protocols, skeletons or detailed models, depending on the information represented in the input scenarios.

A number of other approaches have been developed for translating from scenarios to behavioral models (e.g., [17, 19, 20, 29]), but our approach has a number of advantages, namely:

- Scenarios will in general overlap. Most other approaches cannot recognize intersections between scenarios. Our approach, however, performs a *justified merging of scenarios* based on logical descriptions of the communications between agents. The communication scenarios are augmented using a constraint language and identical states in different scenarios are identified automatically based on these constraints. This leads to models both vastly reduced in size, and also corresponding more to what a human designer might produce.
- Scenarios will in general conflict with each other. Our algorithm *detects and reports any conflicts* in the specification of the communications.
- The models generated by our algorithm are *highly structured*. Much of this structure is detected automatically from the communication specifications. Additional structure can be deduced from user-specified abstractions. This leads to generated models that are human-readable, reusable and maintainable, not just flat, structureless models.

The model synthesis algorithm introduced in the preceding paragraphs can also be used in a reverse engineering context. Reverse engineering a model from an existing system or prototype is often a necessary process for understanding the operation of the system and how it interacts with other components. This is particularly true for agent-based systems in which agent components may exhibit emergent behaviors not explicitly called out in the software. Reverse engineering using scenarios can be undertaken as follows. Simulations of a working prototype can be instrumented to output event traces, or traces of communication events between agents. These traces, possibly abstracted to remove low-level implementation details, can be considered as scenarios. By running a series of simulations, a collection of scenarios are obtained which can then be used as input to the synthesis algorithm described in the previous paragraph. The result is a model of the interaction protocol in the existing prototype. Such a process could be used to derive abstract models of an existing system so that it could be analyzed for conformance to certain properties.

In order to present these ideas in a concrete context, the Unified Modeling Language (UML) [23], will be used as a language in which to express the scenarios and design models. UML is a widely used industry-standard modeling language consisting of a number of graphical notations as well as a textual constraint language, the Object Constraint Language (OCL) [33]. Recent extensions have been made to UML to better support the design of agent-based systems. UML sequence diagrams will be used to represent scenarios, statecharts will be used as design models, and class diagrams with OCL constraints will be used to give the static structure of a system. These notations will be introduced in the next section.

Section 6.2 introduces the basics of AOSE and SBSE. It also gives background information on UML, including an example that will be used to illustrate the algorithms in the rest of this chapter. Section 6.3 describes the methodology for using the automatic synthesis algorithm which is itself described in Section 6.4. Section 6.5 discusses the reverse engineering aspect and conclusions are drawn in Section 6.6.

6.2 Background

This section briefly describes existing work in Agent-Oriented Software Engineering (AOSE) and Scenario-Based Software Engineering (SBSE). Sections 6.2.1 and 6.2.2 describe AOSE. Previous work on synthesis in SBSE is presented in section 6.2.3.

AOSE is concerned with the development of methodologies for engineering systems that are made up of a collection of agents. Most work in AOSE has grown out of work on object-oriented methodologies. This is due to the fact that the development of large-scale agent-based software requires modeling methods and tools that support the entire development lifecycle. Agent-based systems are highly concurrent and distributed and hence it makes sense to employ methodologies that have already been widely accepted for distributed object-oriented systems. Indeed, agents can be viewed as "objects with attitude" [6] and can themselves be composed out of objects. On the other hand, agents have certain features not possessed by objects — such as autonomy, the ability to act without direct external intervention; and cooperation, the ability to independently coordinate with other agents to achieve a common purpose. The precise nature of the relationship between objects and agents is as yet unclear. However, we anticipate that the use of AOSE (perhaps with further extensions) for modeling agent-based systems will increase.

For a full description of the state of the art in AOSE, see [35]. The discussion here is limited to a small number of examples.

6.2.1 UML and AOSE

Agent UML [2] is an attempt to extend the Unified Modeling Language [23] with agent-specific concepts and notations. The premise of Agent UML is that agents are an "extension of active objects, exhibiting both dynamic autonomy (the ability to initiate action without external invocation) and deterministic autonomy (the ability to refuse or modify an external request)" [22]. Agent UML attempts to augment UML to support these extensions.

In order to give an introduction to UML, an example is now presented. This example will also serve as an ongoing example to illustrate the model synthesis algorithm. The example is that of an automated loading dock in which forklift agents move colored boxes between a central ramp and colored shelves such that boxes are placed on shelves of the same color. The example is presented as a case study in [21] of a three-layered architecture for agent-based systems, in which each agent consists of a reactive, a local planning and a coordination layer. Each layer has responsibility for certain actions: the reactive layer reacts to the environment and carries out plans sent from the planning layer; the planning layer forms plans for individual agent goals; and the coordination layer forms joint plans that require coordination between agents. We have translated part of this example into UML as a case study for our algorithm. Figure 6.1 gives the static structure of part of the system, represented as a UML class diagram. Each class can be annotated with attributes or associations with other classes. coordWith describes whether an agent is currently coordinating its actions with another agent (0..1 is standard UML notation for multiplicity meaning 0 or 1), and coordGoal gives the current goal of this other agent. Agent interaction is based on a leader election protocol which selects an agent to delegate roles in the interaction. leader describes whether an agent is currently a leader. The filled diamonds in the class diagram represent aggregation (the 'part-of' relationship).

Figures 6.2, 6.3 and 6.4 are sample UML sequence diagrams (SDs) for interaction between two agents. SD1 is a failed coordination. Agent[i] attempts to establish a connection with Agent[j], but receives no response.[1] So it moves around Agent[j]. In SD2, the move is coordinated, and SD3 shows part of a protocol for Agent[j] to clear a space on a shelf for Agent[i]. Note that these are actually *extended* sequence diagrams. 'boxShelfToRamp' is a subsequence diagram previously defined and 'waiting' is a state explicitly given by the user. More will be said about extended SDs in Section 6.4.4.

Agent UML (AUML) extends UML by making recommendations as to how to use UML to model agents and by offering agent-specific extensions. Work so far has concentrated on modeling agent interaction protocols. AUML suggests the use of UML sequence diagrams for modeling interactions among agents. The main difference between AUML and UML sequence diagrams is that in UML the arrows in a sequence diagram represent messages passed between objects. In AUML, the arrows are *communication acts* between agents playing a particular role. In addition, AUML introduces additional constructs for supporting concurrent threads of execution in sequence diagrams.

---

[1] tm is a timeout

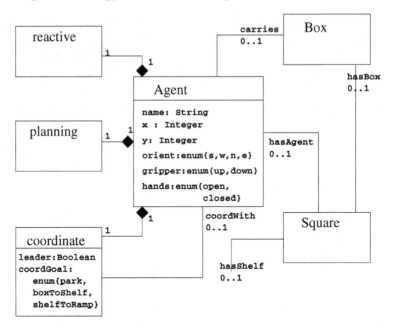

Fig. 6.1. The loading dock domain.

Design models in UML are often expressed as UML statecharts (see Figure 6.14). A statechart is an ideal graphical notation for expressing event-driven behavior as typically found in agent-based systems. Statecharts are finite state machines (FSMs) augmented with notations for expressing hierarchy (multiple levels of states with composite states containing collections of other states) and orthogonality (composite states separated into independent modules which may run concurrently). Transitions in a statechart describe the links between different states and are labeled in the form e/a where e is an event that triggers the transition to fire and a is an action that is executed upon firing. Guards are also allowed on transitions but will not be discussed in this chapter. Statecharts are a good way of presenting large, complex finite state machines since the structuring mechanisms allow information to be hidden as necessary.

In the description of the synthesis algorithm in Section 6.4, interaction scenarios will be expressed as sequence diagrams, behavioral models as statecharts—hence, the synthesis algorithm translates sequence diagrams to statecharts.

6.2.2 AOSE Methodologies

AUML (and similar approaches such as MESSAGE/UML [8]) describe extensions to UML and also suggest methodologies for developing agent-

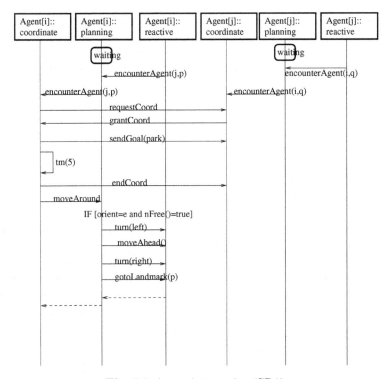

Fig. 6.2. Agent interaction (SD1).

based systems. Other approaches also exist, however. The Gaia methodology [37] advocates a process of refinement of high-level requirements into concrete implementations, and is based on the FUSION model for OO systems [11]. Gaia also includes agent-specific concepts such as *roles* that an agent may play. Each role is defined by four attributes: responsibilities, permissions, activities and protocols. Protocols are interaction patterns (with particular implementation details abstracted away) and are similar to FUSION scenarios. A protocol definition consists of a purpose, an initiator (role responsible for starting the interaction), a responder (roles with which the initiator interacts), inputs (information used by the initiator), outputs (information supplied by/to the responder during the interaction) and processing (a textual description of processing the initiator performs). Gaia has its own diagrammatic notation for expressing interaction protocols.

The final methodology we will mention is Interaction Oriented Programming (IOP) [28] . IOP is mainly concerned with designing and analyzing the interactions between autonomous agents. It consists of three main layers: coordination, commitments and collaboration. Coordination deals with how agents synchronize their activities. IOP specifies agents by *agent skeletons* which are abstract descriptions of agents stating only aspects that are relevant to coordination with other agents. [28] describes a manual procedure for deriving agent skeletons from conversation instances between agents. Conversations are represented as Dooley graphs which are analyzed by the developer to separate out the different roles in the conversation. From this information, agent skeletons can be derived that are consistent with the conversation instances. In many ways, this approach is similar to ours of generating behavioral models from scenarios. However, our procedure is automated and has the advantages already stated in the Introduction.

6.2.3 From Scenarios to Behavioral Models

There have been a number of recent attempts at generating specifications from scenarios. Our work stresses the importance of obtaining a specification which can be read, understood and modified by a designer.

Many approaches make no attempt to interleave different scenarios. [32] gives a learning algorithm for generating a temporal logic specification from a set of examples/counterexamples expressed as scenarios. Each

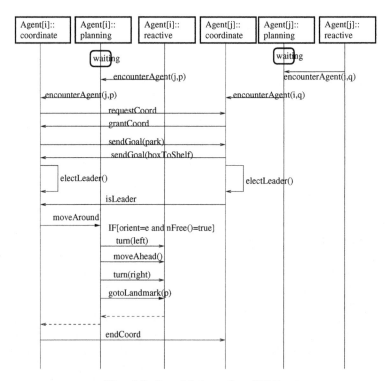

Fig. 6.3. Agent interaction (SD2).

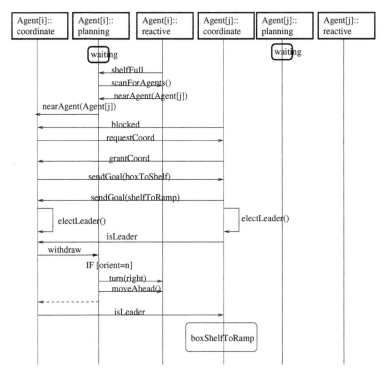

Fig. 6.4. Agent interaction (SD3).

scenario gives rise to a temporal logic formula G_i and scenario integration is merely $\bigcup_i G_i$ augmented with rules for identifying longest common prefixes. However, this does not correspond well to what a human designer would do, as it does not merge states lying beyond the common prefix.

A more effective integration of scenarios necessitates some way of identifying identical states in different scenarios. The solution to this in [17] is to ask the user to explicitly name each state in the finite state machine (FSM) model generated from a scenario. Different states are then merged if they have been given the same name. This approach requires a good deal of effort from the user, however. The SCED tool [20] generates FSMs from traces using the Biermann-Krishnaswamy algorithm [5]. This algorithm uses backtracking to identify identical states in such a way that the final output FSM will be deterministic. As a result, there is no use of semantic information about the states and the algorithm ultimately may produce incorrect results by identifying two states that are in fact not the same. In addition, designers will often introduce nondeterminism into their designs which will only be resolved at a later implementation stage. Hence, the insistence on determinism is overly restrictive. A successor of SCED, the MAS system [30], applies a highly interactive approach to the problem of identifying same states. During synthesis, MAS queries the user whether certain proposed scenarios should be integrated into the generated FSM. MAS chooses generalizations of the set of input scenarios to present to the user in this way. In practice, however, it is likely that the user will be overwhelmed by the large number of interactive queries.

Leue et al. [19] tackles the problem of integration by requiring that the user gives an explicit diagram (a high-level Message Sequence Chart) showing the transitions from one scenario to the next. This merely shows, however, how the start and end points of different scenarios relate. There is no way to examine the contents of scenarios to, for example, detect interleavings or loops. [15] follows a similar approach, essentially using an AND/OR tree instead of a high-level Message Sequence Chart.

The work closest to our own is described in [29] where timed automata are generated from scenarios. The user must provide message specifications with ADD and DELETE lists which maintain a set of currently valid predicates in a STRIPS-like fashion. States are then identified if the set of valid predicates is the same.

The ability to introduce structure and hierarchy into the generated FSM is crucial if user modifications must be made. [17] allows the limited introduction of hierarchy if the structure is explicitly represented in the scenarios (e.g., concurrent threads expressed in a collaboration diagram lead to a statechart node with two orthogonal subnodes). However, structure beyond that present in the scenarios must be introduced manually. Our work extends this approach by introducing hierarchy where the structure is deduced from other UML notations, such as a class diagram or from a domain model.

6.3 Forward Engineering UML Statecharts from Sequence Diagrams

An increasingly popular methodology for developing object-oriented systems is that of use case modeling [25], in which use cases, or descriptions of the intended use of a system, are produced initially and are used as a basis for detailed design. Each use case represents a particular piece of functionality from a user perspective, and can be described by a collection of sequence diagrams. [25] advocates developing the static model of a system (i.e., class diagram) at the same time as developing the sequence diagrams. Once this requirements phase has been completed, more detailed design can be undertaken, e.g., by producing statecharts.

This approach easily fits into popular iterative lifecycles. In contrast to the classical waterfall model where each individual design phase (requirements, design, coding, testing) is only carried out once, the phases in the iterative model are executed multiple times, until the final product is reached. Because of the focus on the final product, one can consider the software phases spiraling down to the product, hence such a process is also called a spiral model. A typical process as it might be used for an object-oriented design of agents usually has a number of phases as shown in Figure 6.5. After the inception phase where the first project ideas (and scenarios) are born, requirements are refined during the elaboration phase. In a highly iterative loop, the software is designed and implemented in this and the construction phase. Finally, efforts to finalize, test, and maintain the software are undertaken in the transition phase. Figure 6.5 also depicts which UML notations are typically used during which phase.

We leverage off this iterative approach and focus on the transition between requirements and design (elaboration and early implementation phase). From a collection of sequence diagrams, plus information from a class diagram and user-specified constraints, a collection of statecharts is generated, one for each class (Figure 6.6). Support for iteration is extremely important—it is not expected that the designer gets the class diagram, sequence diagrams, or constraints correct the first time. On the contrary, sequence diagrams will in general conflict with each other or with the constraints. The sequence diagrams can also miss important information or be ambiguous. Our methodology supports refinements, debugging, and modification of the synthesized artifacts and automatically updates the requirements accordingly. This "upwards" process (Figure 6.6) then facilitates stepwise design, refinement, and debugging of agent designs.

Although we will be focusing mainly on the synthesis part of this process, we will briefly describe how the automatic update of requirements is accomplished. Furthermore, we will demonstrate how specific parts of our approach (e.g., consistency checking and introduction of hierarchy) can be used to support this iterative design process.

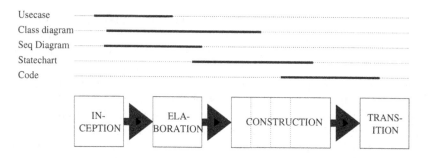

Fig. 6.5. Phases of a software lifecycle and UML notations typically used during each phase.

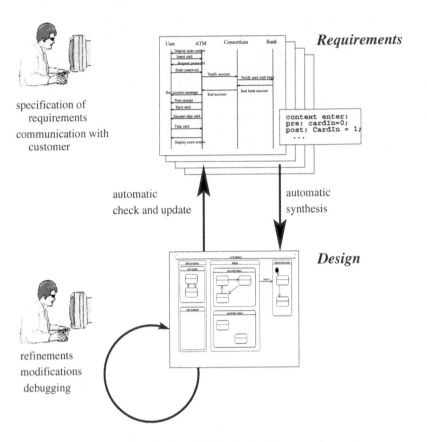

Fig. 6.6. Iterative design of statecharts from requirements.

6.3.1 OCL specification

The lack of semantic content in sequence diagrams makes them ambiguous and difficult to interpret, either automatically or between different stakeholders. In current practice, ambiguities are often resolved by examining the informal documentation but, in some cases, ambiguities may go undetected leading to costly software errors. To alleviate this problem, we encourage the user to give pre/post-condition style OCL specifications of the messages passed between objects. OCL [33] is part of the UML standard and is a side-effect free set-based constraint language. These OCL specifications include the declaration of *state variables*, where a state variable represents some important aspect of the system, e.g., whether or not an agent is coordinating with another agent. The OCL specifications allow the detection of conflicts between different scenarios and allow scenarios to be merged in a *justified* way. Note that not every message needs to be given a specification, although, clearly, the more semantic information that is supplied, the better the quality of the conflict detection. Currently, our algorithm only exploits constraints of the form $var = value$, but there may be something to be gained from reasoning about other constraints using an automated theorem prover or model checker.

Figure 6.7 gives specifications for selected messages in our agents example. Agent.coordWith has type Agent (it is the agent which is coordinating with Agent), and Agent.coordNum, the number of agents Agent is coordinating with, is a new variable introduced as syntactic sugar.

The state variables, in the form of a *state vector*, are used to characterize states in the generated statechart. The state vector is a vector of values of the state variables. In our example, the state vector for the class coordinate has the form:

$$\langle\, \text{coordNum}\hat{}, \text{leader}\hat{}, \text{coordGoal}\hat{}\,\rangle$$

where $var\hat{} \in Dom(var) \cup \{?\}$, and ? represents an unknown value. Note that since each class has a statechart, each class has its own state vector.

```
coordNum : enum {0,1}
leader : Boolean
coordGoal : enum {park, boxToShelf, shelfToRamp}

context Agent.coordinate::grantCoord
    pre:   coordNum = 0 and coordWith.coordinate.coordNum = 0
    post:  coordNum = 1 and coordWith.coordinate.coordNum = 1

context sendGoal(x : enum {park, boxToShelf, shelfToRamp})
    post:  coordWith.coordinate.coordGoal = x

context electLeader
    pre:   leader = false

context isLeader
    post:  coordWith.coordinate.leader = true

context endCoord
    pre:   coordNum = 1 and coordWith.coordinate.coordNum = 1
    post:  coordNum = 0 and coordWith.coordinate.coordNum = 0
           and leader = false
```

Fig. 6.7. Domain knowledge for the loading dock example.

Our algorithm is designed to be fully automatic. The choice of the state vector, however, is a crucial design task that must be carried out by the user. The choice of state variables will affect the generated statechart, and the user should choose state variables to reflect the parts of the system functionality that is of most interest. In this way, the choice of the state vector can be seen as a powerful abstraction mechanism—indeed, the algorithm could be used in a way that allows the user to analyze the system from a number of different perspectives, each corresponding to a particular choice of state vector.

The state variables can be chosen from information present in the class diagram. For instance, in our example, the state variables are either attributes of a particular class or based on associations. The choice is still a user activity, however, as not all attributes/associations are relevant.

6.4 Generating Statecharts

Synthesis of statecharts is performed in four steps: first, each SD is annotated with state vectors and conflicts with respect to the OCL specification are detected. In the second step, each annotated SD is converted into flat statecharts, one for each class in the SD. The statecharts for each class, derived from different SDs, are then merged into a single statechart for each class. Finally, hierarchy is introduced in order to enhance readability of the synthesized statecharts.

6.4.1 Step I: Annotating Sequence Diagrams with State Vectors

The process to convert an individual SD into a statechart starts by detecting conflicts between the SD and the OCL specification (and, hence, other SDs). There are two kinds of constraints imposed on a SD: constraints on the state vector given by the OCL specification, and constraints on the ordering of messages given by the SD itself. These constraints must be solved and conflicts be reported to the user. Conflicts mean that either the scenario does not follow the user's intended semantics or the OCL specification is incorrect.

More formally, the process of conflict detection can be written as follows. An annotated sequence diagram is a sequence of messages $m_1, \ldots, m_n$, with

$$(6.1) \qquad s_1^{\text{pre}} \xrightarrow{m_1} s_1^{\text{post}}, s_2^{\text{pre}} \xrightarrow{m_2} \ldots \xrightarrow{m_{r-1}} s_{r-1}^{\text{post}}, s_r^{\text{pre}} \xrightarrow{m_r} s_r^{\text{post}}$$

where the s_i^{pre}, s_i^{post} are the state vectors immediately before and after message m_i is executed. S_i will be used to denote either s_i^{pre} or s_i^{post}; $s_i^{\text{pre}}[j]$ denotes the element at position j in s_i^{pre} (similarly for s_i^{post}).

In the first step of the synthesis process, we assign values to the variables in the state vectors as shown in Figure 6.8. The variable instantiations of the initial state vectors are obtained directly from the message specifications (lines 1-5): if message m_i assigns a value y to a variable of the state vector in its pre- or post-condition, then this variable assignment is used. Otherwise, the variable in the state vector is set to an undetermined value, ?. Since each message is specified independently, the initial state vectors will contain a lot of unknown values. Most (but not all) of these can be given a value in one of two ways: two state vectors, S_i and S_j ($i \neq j$), are considered the same if they are unifiable (lines 7-8). This means that there exists a variable assignment ϕ such that $\phi(S_i) = \phi(S_j)$. This situation indicates a potential loop within a SD. The second means for assigning values to variables is the application of the frame axiom (lines 9-12), i.e., we can assign unknown variables of a pre-condition with the value from the preceding post-condition, and vice versa. This assumes that there are no hidden side-effects between messages.

A conflict (line 14) is detected and reported if the state vector immediately following a message and the state vector immediately preceding the next message differ.

Input. An annotated SD
Output. A SD with extended annotations

1 **for** each message m_i **do**
2   **if** m_i has a precondition $v_j = y$
3   **then** $s_i^{\text{pre}}[j] := y$ **else** $s_i^{\text{pre}}[j] := ?$ **fi**
4   **if** m_i has a postcondition $v_j = y$
5   **then** $s_i^{\text{post}}[j] := y$ **else** $s_i^{\text{post}}[j] := ?$ **fi**
6 **for** each state vector S **do**
7   **if** $\exists S'$ $S' \neq S$ and some unifier ϕ with $\phi(S) = \phi(S')$ **then**
8   unify S_i and S_j;
9   propagate instantiations with frame axiom:
10   **for each** j and $i > 0$:
11   **if** $s_i^{\text{pre}}[j] = ?$ **then** $s_i^{\text{pre}}[j] := s_{i-1}^{\text{post}}[j]$ **fi**
12   **if** $s_i^{\text{post}}[j] = ?$ **then** $s_i^{\text{post}}[j] := s_i^{\text{pre}}[j]$ **fi**
13   **if** there is some k, l with $s_k^{\text{post}}[l] \neq s_{k+1}^{\text{pre}}[l]$ **then**
14   Report Conflict;
15   **break**;

Fig. 6.8. Extending the state vector annotations.

Example 1 *Figure 6.9 shows SD2 from Figure 6.3 annotated with state vectors for* Agent[i]::coordinate. *Figure 6.10 shows how the state vectors are propagated.*

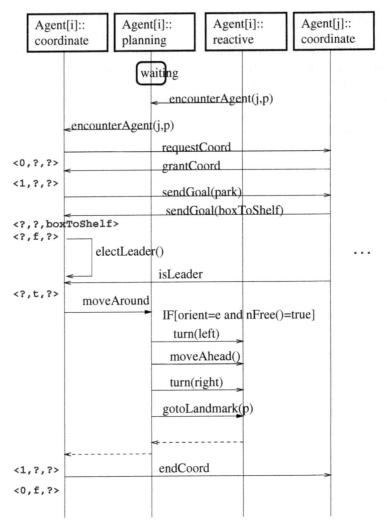

Fig. 6.9. SD2 (parts) with state vectors ⟨ coordNum^, leader^, coordGoal^ ⟩.

6.4.2 Step II: Translation into a Finite State Machine

Once the variables in the state vectors have been instantiated as far as possible, a flat statechart (in fact, a finite state machine) is generated for each class (or agent) in each SD (Figure 6.11). The finite state machine for agent A is denoted by Φ_A; its set of nodes by N_A; its transitions by $\langle n_1, \langle type, label \rangle, n_2 \rangle$ for nodes n_1, n_2 where $type$ is either $event$ or $action$[2];

---

[2] In statecharts, a transition is labeled by e/a which means that this transition can be active only if event e occurs. Then, the state changes and action a is carried out. We use a similar notion in our definition of FSMs.

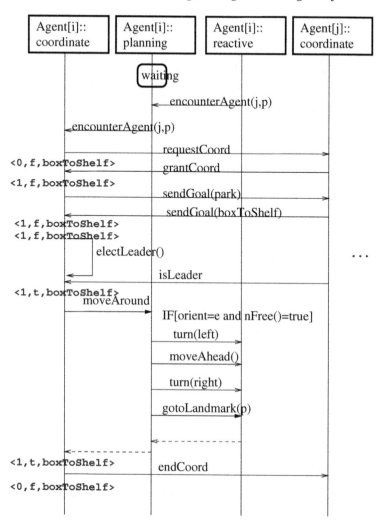

Fig. 6.10. SD2 after extension of state vector annotations with state vectors for Agent[i]::coordinate.

and μ_A is a function mapping a node to its state vector. C_A denotes the currently processed node during the run of the algorithm. Messages directed towards a particular agent, A (i.e., $m_i^{to} = A$) are considered events in the FSM for A. Messages directed away from A (i.e., $m_i^{from} = A$) are considered actions.

The algorithm for this synthesis is depicted in Figure 6.11. Given a SD, the algorithm constructs one FSM for each agent (or for each class, in case we consider agents consisting of objects) mentioned in the sequence diagram. We start by generating a single starting node $n_{A_i}^0$ for each FSM (line 2). Then we successively add outgoing and incoming messages to the FSMs, creating new nodes as we proceed (lines 4–5).

An important step during FSM creation is the identification of loops (lines 10-13): a loop is detected if the state vector immediately after the current message has been executed is the same as an existing state vector *and* if this message is state-changing, i.e., $s_i^{pre} \neq s_i^{post}$. Note that some messages may not have a specification, hence they will not affect the state vector. To identify states based solely on the state vector would result in incorrect loop detection.

Input. A SD, S, with agents $A_1, \ldots, A_k$ and messages $m_1, \ldots, m_r$
Output. A FSM Φ_{A_i} for each agent, $1 \leq i \leq k$.

```
 1  for i = 1, ..., k do
 2      Create a FSM, Φ_{A_i}, with an initial node, n⁰_{A_i}; C_{A_i} := n⁰_{A_i};
 3  for i = 1, ..., r do
 4      ADD(m_i, action, m_i^{from});
 5      ADD(m_i, event, m_i^{to});
 6  where ADD(mess m_i, type t, agent A)
 7      if there is a node n ∈ N_A, a transition ⟨C_A, ⟨t, m_i⟩, n⟩
 8          and s_i^{post} = μ_A(n) then
 9          C_A := n;
10      else if there is n ∈ N_A with s_i^{post} = μ_A(n)
11          and m_i is state-changing then
12          add new transition ⟨C_A, ⟨t, m_i⟩, n⟩;
13          C_A := n;
14      else
15          add a new node n and let μ_A(n) := s_i^{post};
16          add transition ⟨C_A, ⟨t, m_i⟩, n⟩;
17          C_A := n;
```

Fig. 6.11. Translating a sequence diagram into FSMs.

6.4.3 Step III: Merging Multiple Sequence Diagrams

The previous steps concerned the translation of a single SD into a number of statecharts, one for each class. Once this is done for each SD, there exists a collection of flat statecharts for each class. We now show how the statecharts for a particular class can be merged.

Merging statecharts derived from different SDs is based upon identifying *similar* states in the statecharts. Two nodes of a statechart are *similar* if they have the same state vector and they have at least one incoming transition with the same label. The first condition alone would produce an excessive number of similar nodes since some messages do not change the state vector. The existence of a common incoming transition which we require in addition means that in both cases, an event has occurred which leaves the state variables in an identical assignment. Hence, our definition of similarity takes into account the ordering of the messages and the current state. Figure 6.12 shows how two nodes with identical state vector S and incoming transitions labeled with l can be merged together.

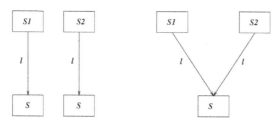

Fig. 6.12. Merging of similar states (before and after the merge).

The process of merging multiple statecharts proceeds as follows: we generate a new statechart and connect its initial node by empty ϵ-transitions with the initial nodes of the individual statecharts derived from each SD. Furthermore, all pairs of nodes which are *similar* to each other are connected by ϵ-transitions. Then we remove ϵ-transitions, and resolve many nondeterministic branches. For this purpose, we use an algorithm which is a variant of the standard algorithm for transforming a nondeterministic finite automaton into a deterministic finite automaton [1]. The output of the algorithm is only deterministic in that there are no ϵ-transitions remaining. There may still be two transitions leaving a state labelled with the same events but different actions. Hence, our algorithm may produce nondeterministic statecharts, which allows a designer to refine the design later.

6.4.4 Step IV: Introducing Hierarchy

So far, we have discussed the generation of flat finite state machines. In practice, however, statechart designs tend to get very large. Thus, the judicious use of hierarchy is crucial to the readability and maintainability of the designs. Highly structured statecharts do not only facilitate clean presentation of complex behavior on the small computer screen, but also emphasize major design decisions. Thus, a clearly structured statechart is easier to understand and refine in an iterative design process. Our approach provides several ways for introducing hierarchy into the generated FSMs. In this chapter, we will discuss methods which use information contained in the state vectors, in associated UML class diagrams, or explicitly given by the user (in the form of preferences and extended sequence diagrams).

The State Vector as a Basis for Hierarchy

State variables usually encode that the system is in a specific mode or state (e.g., agent is the leader or not). Thus, it is natural to partition the statechart into subcharts containing all nodes belonging to a specific mode of the system. More specifically, we recursively partition the set of nodes according to the different values of the variables in the state vectors. In general, however, there are many different ways of partitioning a statechart, not all of them suited for good readability. We therefore introduce additional heuristic constraints (controlled by the user) on the layout of the statechart:

The maximum depth of hierarchy (d_{max})**:** Too many nested levels of compound states limit readability of the generated statechart. On the other hand, a statechart which is too flat will contain very large compound nodes, making reading and maintaining the statechart virtually impossible.

The maximum number of states on a single level ($N_{max}(d)$)**:**   This constraint is somewhat orthogonal to the first one and also aims at generating "handy" statecharts.

The maximum percentage of inter-level transitions: Transitions between different levels of the hierarchy usually limit modularity, but occasionally they can be useful. Thus their relative number should be limited (usually to around 5–10%).

A partial ordering over the state variables ($\prec$)**:** This ordering describes the sequence in which partitions should be attempted. It provides a means to indicate that some state variables may be more "important" than others and thus should be given priority. This ordering encapsulates important design decisions about how the statechart should be split up.

In general, not all of the above constraints can be fulfilled at the same time. Therefore our algorithm has the capability to do a search for an optimal solution. This search is done using backtracking over different variable sequences ordered with respect to $\prec$.

The process of structuring a given subset S of the nodes of a generated FSM is shown in Figure 6.13. Given a subset of variables W of the state vector over which to partition and a (partial) ordering $\prec$, a sequence W' is constructed with respect to the ordering $\prec$. Then the nodes S are partitioned recursively according to the variable sequence W'. Let v_j be the top-level variable (minimal in W') on which to split (line 11). The partition is made up of m equivalence classes corresponding to each possible value of v_j given in the SDs. Before we actually perform the split, we check if the constraints hold (lines 10 and 16). Only then is the set of nodes split and the algorithm descends recursively (line 17). After all node sets have been partitioned, we levelwise assemble all nonempty partitions (line 19). Once this algorithm terminates, we check if it is a "good" hierarchy with respect to our criteria (line 21). Because some of the constraints (e.g., number of interlevel transitions) can only be checked globally, we have to perform these tests after the partitioning.

In case the partition does not meet our design criteria described, a warning will be issued that the given ordering would result in a non-optimal hierarchy and a new ordering of the variables is selected. This selection is done until the criteria are met.

Input. A FSM with nodes N, state vector mapping, μ, ordering $\prec$ over a subset $W \subset V$ of the state variables, and subset of N, $S \subset N$.
Output. A partitioning $\mathcal{P}$ of the FSM

```
 1 W' := ⟨v₁, ..., vₖ⟩ for vᵢ ∈ W and vᵢ ≺ vⱼ, i < j; ok := TRUE;
 2 do
 3     P := PARTITION(S, W', 1);        // partition this set
 4 while ¬ok ∧ ¬OPTIMAL(P) do
 5     ok := TRUE;
 6     W' := select-new-variable-ordering(W);
 7     P := PARTITION(S, W');
 8 done
 9 where PARTITION(S, W', d)
10     if(d > dₘₐₓ ∧ | S |< Nₘᵢₙ(d)) ok := FALSE;
11     vⱼ := first(W');               // split on first var. in W'
12     Dₛ(vⱼ) := ⋃ {μ(s)[j]};
                 s∈S
13     m :=| Dₛ(vⱼ) |;                // m is number of partitions
14     for 1 ≤ i ≤ m do              // on the current level
15        Sᵢ := {s ∈ S | μ(s)[j] = ith(Dₛ(vⱼ))};
16        if(| Sᵢ |> Nₘₐₓ(d)) ok := FALSE;
17        Pᵢ := PARTITION(Sᵢ, rest(W'));// call the partitioning
18     done                          // recursively
19     P := ⟨Pᵢ | Pᵢ ≠ ⟨⟩ ⟩          // assemble result
20 where OPTIMAL(P)
21     check P according to our design criteria
```

Fig. 6.13. Sketch of algorithm for partitioning over the state vector.

Example 2 *Figure 6.14 gives a partitioned statechart for agent communication generated from SD1, SD2 and SD3. The flat statechart was first split over* coordNum, *followed by* leader *and finally* coordGoal *(i.e.* coordNum ≺ leader ≺ coordGoal*).*

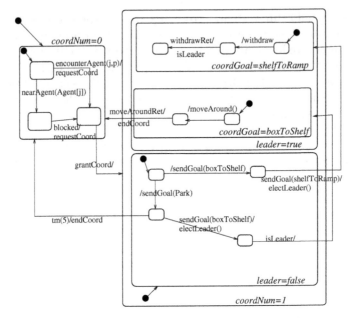

Fig. 6.14. Hierarchical statechart for Agent::coordinate.

Extended Sequence Diagrams

Other authors [7, 14] have already noted that the utility of sequence diagrams to describe system behavior could be vastly increased by extending the notation. A basic SD supports the description of *exemplary* behavior — one concrete interaction — but when used in requirements engineering, a *generative* style is more appropriate, in which each SD represents a collection of interactions. Extensions that have been suggested include the ability to allow `case` statements, loops and sub-SDs. We go further than this and advocate the use of language constructs that allow behavior to be generalized. Example constructs we have devised so far include:

- *any_order*$(m_1, \ldots, m_n)$: specify that a group of messages may occur in any order;
- *or*$(m_1, \ldots, m_n)$: a message may be any one of a group of messages;
- *generalize*$(m, SubSD)$: a message gives the same behavior when sent/received at any point in the sub-sequence diagram;
- *allInstances*(m, I): send a message to all instances in I;

These constructs also suggest ways of introducing structure into the generated statecharts. As an example, *any_order*$(m_1, \ldots, m_n)$ can be implemented by n concurrent statecharts (see Figure 6.15), connected by the UML synchronization operator (the black bar) which waits until all its source states are entered before its transition is taken. This is particularly useful if $m_1, \ldots, m_n$ are not individual messages, but sub-sequence diagrams. Figure 6.15 also shows how the other constructs mentioned above can be implemented as statecharts. *allInstances* is implemented by a local variable that iterates through each instance, and sends the message to that instance.

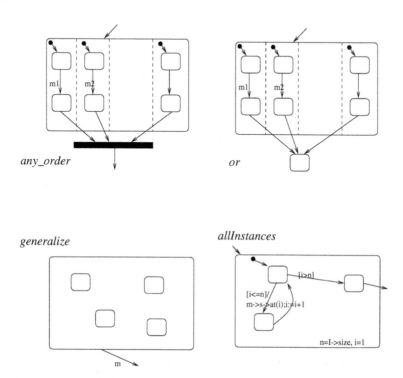

Fig. 6.15. Hierarchy by macro commands.

Example 3 *These extensions of the SDs are convenient if, for example, our agent design requires an emergency shutdown. When activated, it sends the message emergency to each agent. This can be expressed as* allInstances(emergency,Agent::coordinate). *If an agent is coordinating with other agents (regardless if it is the leader or not), a fail-safe state needs to be entered. Such a behavior is shown in Figure 6.16 and has been expressed conveniently as* generalize(emergency, ⟨SD-describing-the-coordinated-behavior⟩). *This specification makes a number of sequence diagrams superfluous in which the emergency message is received in different situations.*

Similarly, in situations where several parts of an interagent communication require no specific order, a compact way of specification can be used, for example, any_order(inquire_box_color, inquire_box_size).

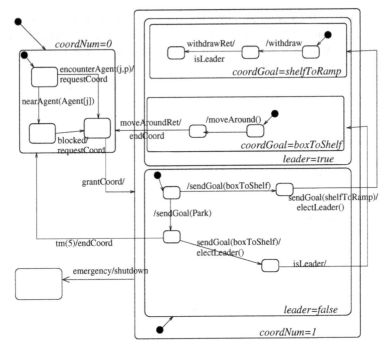

Fig. 6.16. Hierarchical statechart for Agent::coordinate with emergency handling (extension of Figure 6.14).

Class Diagrams

During the synthesis process, it is also important to incorporate other design decisions made by the developer. Within the UML framework, a natural place for high-level design decisions is the *class diagram*. It describes the types of the objects in the system and the static relationships among them.

A hierarchical structure of a generated statechart can easily be obtained from the class diagram: the outermost superstate (surmounting the entire statechart) corresponds to the class node of the corresponding object. Aggregation results in a grouping of nodes. If a class contains several subclasses, the statecharts corresponding to the subclasses are subnodes of the current node.

This way of introducing structure is somewhat higher-level than the first two. Typically, the class diagram can be used to obtain a very abstract structure and the method described above (using state variables) can be used to introduce further structure within each subchart.

6.4.5 Statechart Layout and Hierarchy

For practical usability and readability of the synthesized statechart, a good layout is extremely important. Only then can automatic generation of agent designs and skeletons be accepted by the practitioner. Our current prototype system does not provide sophisticated layout Generation.[3] There is a substantial body of work on automatic layout of graphs (e.g., [3]). In particular, [9] has developed algorithms for automatic positioning of the elements of a hierarchical statechart on the canvas.

Generation of a graph layout is subject to a number of constraints. The most important constraints concern spacing of the graph nodes (how much space does each element require?), routing of the transitions and labeling. A good layout prescribes that the arrows, representing transitions don't cross nodes and other transitions too often. On the other hand, transitions which are too long (e.g., moving around several nodes) reduce readability. Furthermore, the layout algorithm has to take into account that labels on the transitions must be placed carefully such that they do not overlap. For our tool, we are investigating algorithms like [9, 10], techniques coming from VLSI design [4] and layout/labeling of topographical maps.

6.4.6 Multi-View Design

The automatic introduction of hierarchy provides another benefit: multiple views on the design. Since all important information is already contained in the flat statechart, changing hierarchy and layout does not affect the behavior of the system. Therefore, the user can, as described above, set individual preferences on how to structure and display the design. This feature opens up the possibility to keep multiple different hierarchies of the same design within the system at the same time. So, for example, different software engineers, working on different aspects of the agent could work with different hierarchies. Each designer would select a hierarchy which displays his/her focus of interest in a compact way (e.g., on top of the hierarchy in a single supernode). Also, during different stages of the software cycle, different hierarchies can be suitable, e.g., for design, for generation of test cases (e.g., involving the specific values of the state variables), or for debugging [26]. This multi-hierarchy approach exhibits some similarities to defining views in a relational database or individual formatting options within a word-processor.

---

[3] For visualization of the synthesized statechart we are using the tools Dot [18] and daVinci [13].

6.5 Discussion: Reverse Engineering of Agent Communication Protocols

Section 6.4 described the use of scenarios in forward engineering agent-based systems. As described in the Introduction, however, scenarios can also be utilized in reverse engineering. In practical software engineering, legacy code often exists which has to be integrated into a new system. However, in many cases, the code is poorly documented. Before modification or integration of the code can be attempted, reverse engineering needs to be performed, in order to understand how that piece of code works—a time-consuming task. In particular, for agent-based systems, understanding the operation of distributed pieces of software is particularly troublesome.

In the framework of transforming requirements into designs presented in this chapter, reverse engineering is also supported. Given a software artifact that can be executed, the code is run on a number of relevant test cases. In general, such test cases give only the input/output behavior of the code and not the internal execution steps. By instrumenting the code to output internal information (e.g., messages between objects or communication acts between agents), each test case can be associated with an execution trace which is written to a log file. These execution traces are scenarios of the internal behavior of the software, and, as such, they can be used as input to the synthesis algorithm described in Section 6.4. The result is a hierarchical statechart model representing some part of the internal behavior of the code. This model can be used in code understanding or in exploring design extensions. Note that the model obtained depends entirely on the set of test cases that are run. In this way, the user can selectively choose to extract a slice of the overall system model depending on which aspect of the system is of most interest. This technique of using scenarios in reverse engineering can also be used when the source code is not available. It depends only on the capability to execute the code. Figure 6.17 summarizes this procedure.

For this approach to work in practice, a number of important issues need to be addressed. In what follows, $\mathcal{P}$ will abbreviate the existing software artifact and $\mathcal{T}$ will stand for the set of execution traces produced by the instrumented code.

- $\mathcal{P}$ must be instrumented so that the appropriate scenarios can be collected from the executions of each test case. In initial experiments, existing Java code is being reverse engineered. Whilst, in general, code that needs to be reverse engineered is probably legacy code from decades ago (e.g., written in COBOL), it is likely that code in agent-based systems will often be written in Java. The need to re-engineer such Java code may arise from the need to observe an agent-based system in operation or to integrate an agent component that has been

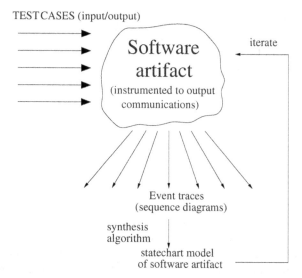

Fig. 6.17. Extracting behavioral models of agent systems using scenarios.

obtained from a possibly unreliable source (e.g., the Internet). Java object code can be instrumented easily using the Jtrek tool [12] which does not require the source code to be available.

- The approach is likely to succeed when re-engineering object-oriented code because it is then straightforward to set up the classes appropriately in the sequence diagrams (execution traces). This class structure will not be available in non-object-oriented code, however, so a substantial amount of manual work would have to be done in order to obtain reasonable traces.
- The traces T are obtained by running the instrumented code on various sequences of input. It is only these test inputs that are represented in the behavioral model generated. On the positive side, this gives the user an easy way of extracting from the code only the information in which (s)he is interested. On the negative side, the model generated will be incomplete. By using traditional techniques to generate test cases with a certain coverage, however, the model can be shown also to possess a certain coverage.
- A realistic system might produce a huge amount of different traces. These, however, might represent small variants of a few traces. Therefore, traces need to be abstracted before they can be used for synthesizing a new statechart. As an example, in the loading dock domain, an agent may rotate by n degrees. For the purposes of modeling, however, only the principal directions e, w, n and s are relevant and so the execution traces must be abstracted in order to avoid overly detailed models.

- Given the set of traces $\mathcal{T}$, for maximum effectiveness, OCL constraints should be set up. This is most likely a manual activity, although it may be possible to partially automate the selection of state variables by instrumenting the code appropriately.

Our work on the reverse engineering aspect is at an early stage. Initial results, however, have shown that there is a great deal of potential in this technique.

6.6 Conclusions

This chapter has presented an algorithm for automatically synthesizing UML statecharts from a set of sequence diagrams. For the development of large-scale agent-based systems, sequence diagrams can be a valuable means to describe inter-agent communication. Sequence diagrams can be extended with additional language constructs to enable generalizations and can be augmented with communication pre- and post-conditions in OCL. This enables the automatic detection and reporting of conflicts and inconsistencies between different sequence diagrams with respect to the pre/post-condition constraints. These annotations are furthermore used in the synthesis algorithm to correctly identify similar states and to merge a number of sequence diagrams into a single statechart. In order to make the algorithm practical, techniques for introducing hierarchy automatically into the generated statechart are employed.

A prototype of this algorithm has been implemented in Java and so far used for several smaller case-studies in the area of agent-based systems, classical object-oriented design [34], and human-computer interaction. In order to be practical for applications on a larger scale, the algorithm is being integrated into state-of-the-art UML-based design tools by way of an XMI interface.

This chapter has also discussed a novel application of the synthesis algorithm in the reverse engineering of existing systems. By simulating an agent-based system on a number of test cases, and instrumenting the code to output appropriate execution traces, these traces can be used as input to the synthesis algorithm and a behavioral model of the software can be extracted. This technique could have applications in understanding existing systems for which documentation no longer exists or which have been obtained by a possibly unreliable means (e.g., the Internet).

The synthesis algorithm presented in this chapter only describes the forward or synthesis part of the design cycle: given a set of sequence diagrams, we generate a set of statecharts. For full support of our methodology, research and development in two directions are of major importance: conflicts detected by the algorithm must not only be reported in an appropriate way to the designer but also should provide explanation on what went wrong and what could be done to avoid this conflict. We will use techniques of model-generation, abduction, and deduction-based explanation generation to provide this kind of feedback.

The other major strand for providing feedback is required when the user, after synthesizing the statechart, refines it or makes changes to the statechart. In that case, it must be checked if the current statechart still reflects the requirements (i.e., the sequence diagrams), and in case it does, must update the sequence diagrams (e.g., by adding new communication acts).

The question of whether UML (or AUML) is an appropriate methodology for the design of large-scale agent-based systems must still be answered. A part of the answer lies in the availability of powerful tools which support the development of agents during all phases of the iterative life-cycle. We are confident that our approach to close the gap between requirements modeling using sequence diagrams and design with statecharts will increase acceptability of UML methods and tools for the design of agent-based systems.

References

1. Aho, A., Sethi, R. and Ullman, J. *Compilers: Principles, Techniques, and Tools.* Addison-Wesley series in Computer Science, Addison-Wesley. 1986.
2. AUML Agent UML. 2001. http://www.auml.org.
3. Battista, G. D., Eades, P., Tamassia, R. and Tollis, I. *Graph Drawing: Algorithms for the Visualization of Graphs.* Prentice Hall. 1999.
4. Bhatt, S. N. and Leighton, F. T. A Framework for Solving VLSI Graph Layout Problems. *J. Comp. Syst. Sci.*, **28**:300–343, 1984.
5. Biermann, A. and Krishnaswamy, R. Constructing Programs from Example Computations. *IEEE Transactions on Software Engineering*, **SE-2**(3):141–153, 1976.
6. Bradshaw, J. *Software Agents.* American Association for Artificial Intelligence / MIT Press. 1997.
7. Breu, R., Grosu, R., Hofmann, C., Huber, F., Krüger, I., Rumpe, B., Schmidt, M. and Schwerin, W. Exemplary and Complete Object Interaction Descriptions. In *Computer Standards and Interfaces*, volume 19, 1998, pp 335–345.
8. Caire, G., Leal, F., Chainho, P., Evans, R., Garijo, F., Gomez, J., Pavon, J., Kearney, P., Stark, J. and Massonet, P. Agent oriented analysis using MESSAGE/UML. In *Agent Oriented Software Engineering*, P. Ciancarini and M. Wooldridge, editors. Springer-Verlag, Berlin. 2001, pp 101–108.
9. Castellø, R., Mili, R. and Tollis, I. G. An algorithmic framework for visualizing statecharts. In *Graph Drawing, (LNCS 1984)*, J. Marks, editor. Springer-Verlag. 2000a, pp 139–149.
10. Castellø, R., Mili, R., Tollis, I. G. and Benson, V. On the automatic visualization of statecharts: The vista tool. In *Formal Methods Tools 2000.* 2000b.
11. Coleman, D., Arnold, P., Bodoff, S., Dollin, C., Gilchrist, H., Hayes, F. and Jeremaes, P. *Object-Oriented Development: the FUSION Method.* Prentice Hall International. 1994.

12. Compaq. Jtrek. 2001 http://www.compaq.com/java/download/jtrek.
13. Fröhlich, M. and Werner, M. (1994). Demonstration of the interactive graph-visualization system davinci. In *Graph Drawing, (LNCS 894)*, R. Tamassia and I. G. Tollis, editors. DIMACS, Springer-Verlag. 1994, pp 266–269.
14. Gehrke, T. and Firley, T. Generative sequence diagrams with textual annotations. In *Formale Beschreibungstechniken für verteilte Systeme (FBT99) (Formal Description Techniques for Distributed Systems)*, Spies and Schätz, editors. München. 1999, pp 65–72.
15. Glinz, M. An integrated formal model of scenarios based on statecharts. In *5th European Software Engineering Conference (ESEC), (LNCS 989)*, Springer-Verlag, 1995, pp 254–271.
16. Harel, D. Statecharts: A visual formalism for complex systems. *Science of Computer Programming*, 8:231–274, 1987.
17. Khriss, I., Elkoutbi, M. and Keller, R. Automating the synthesis of UML statechart diagrams from multiple collaboration diagrams. In *UML98: Beyond the Notation, (LNCS 1618)*, J. Bezivin and P. Muller, editors. Springer-Verlag. 1999, pp 139–149.
18. Koutsofios, E. and North, S. Drawing graphs with *dot*. Technical report, AT&T Bell Laboratories, Murray Hill, NJ, USA, 1996.
19. Leue, S., Mehrmann, L. and Rezai, M. Synthesizing software architecture descriptions from Message Sequence Chart specifications. In *Proc. Thirteenth International Conference on Automated Software Engineering*, IEEE Press, 1998, pp 192–195.
20. Männistö, T., Systä, T. and Tuomi, J. SCED report and user manual. Report A-1994-5, Dept of Computer Science, University of Tampere, 1994. ATM example available with the SCED tool from http://www.cs.tut.fi/~tsysta/sced/.
21. Müller, J. *The Design of Intelligent Agents, (LNAI 1177)*, Springer-Verlag. 1996.
22. Odell, J., Van Dyke Parunak, H. and Bauer, B. Representing Agent Interaction Protocols in UML. In *Agent Oriented Software Engineering, (LNCS 1957)*, P. Ciancarini and M. Wooldridge, editors. Springer-Verlag. 2001, pp 121–140.
23. OMG Unified Modeling Language specification version 1.4, 2001. Available from The Object Management Group (http://www.omg.org).
24. Rao, A. S. and Georgeff, M. P. BDI Agents: From Theory to Practice. In *Proceedings of the First International Conference on Multi-Agent Systems (IC-MAS'95)*, V. Lesser, editor. The MIT Press, 1995, pp 312–319.
25. Rosenberg, D. and Scott, K. *Use Case Driven Object Modeling with UML*. Object Technology Series, Addison Wesley. 1999.
26. Schumann, J. Automatic debugging support for uml designs. In *Proceedings of the Fourth International Workshop on Automated Debugging*, M. Ducasse, editor. 2000. http://xxx.lanl.gov/abs/cs.SE/0011017
27. Singh, M. A customizable coordination service for autonomous agents. In *Intelligent Agents IV: 4th International Workshop on Agent Theories, Architectures, and Languages*, 1998a.
28. Singh, M. Developing formal specifications to coordinate heterogeneous autonomous agents. In *International Conference on Multi Agent Systems*, 1998b, pp 261–268.

29. Somé, S. and Dssouli, R. From scenarios to timed automata: building specifications from users requirements. In *Asia Pacific Software Engineering Conference*, 1995, pp 48–57.
30. Systä, T. Incremental construction of dynamic models for object oriented software systems. *Journal of Object Oriented Programming*, **13**(5):18–27, 2000.
31. Systä, T., Keller, R. K. and Koskimies, K. Summary report of the OOPSLA 2000 workshop on scenario-based round-trip engineering. *ACM SIGSOFT Software Engineering Notes*, **26**(2):24–28, 2001. http://doi.acm.org/10. 1145/505776.505782
32. van Lamsweerde, A. Inferring declarative requirements specifications from operational scenarios. *IEEE Transactions on Software Engineering*, **24**(12):1089–1114, 1998.
33. Warmer, J. and Kleppe, A. *The Object Constraint Language: Precise Modeling with UML*. Addison-Wesley Object Technology Series, Addison-Wesley. 1999.
34. Whittle, J. and Schumann, J. Generating Statechart Designs from Scenarios. In *Proceedings of International Conference on Software Engineeering (ICSE 2000)*, Limerick, Ireland, 2000, pp 314–323.
35. Wooldridge, M. and Ciancarini, P. Agent-oriented software engineering: The state of the art. In *Handbook of Software Engineering and Knowledge Engineering*. World Scientific Publishing Co. 2001.
36. Wooldridge, M. and Jennings, N. Intelligent agents: Theory and practice. *The Knowledge Engineering Review*, **10**(2):115–152, 1995.
37. Wooldridge, M., Jennings, N. and Kinny, D. A methodology for agent-oriented analysis and design. In *Third International Conference on Autonomous Agents (Agents 99)*, Seattle, WA, 1999, pp 69–76.

Part III

Formal Agent Verification and Re-Design

7

Verification Within the KARO Agent Theory

Ullrich Hustadt, Clare Dixon, Renate A. Schmidt, Michael Fisher,
John-Jules Charles Meyer, and Wiebe van der Hoek

7.1 Introduction

The use of *agents* is now seen as an essential tool in representing, understanding and implementing complex software systems. In particular, the
characterization of complex components as *intelligent* or *rational* agents
allows the system designer to analyze applications at a much higher level
of abstraction [13, 45]. In order to describe and reason about such agents,
a number of theories of rational agency have been developed, for example
the BDI [36] and KARO [27] frameworks. Usually, these frameworks are
represented as complex multi-modal logics. These logics, in addition to
their use in agent theories, where the basic representation of agency and
rationality is explored, form the basis for agent-based formal methods. In
both uses, (automated) theorem proving is of vital importance. In agent
theories, automated theorem proving allows us to examine properties of
the overall theory and, in some cases, to characterize computation within
that theory. In agent-based formal methods, theorem proving is clearly
important in developing verification techniques.

The leading agent theories and formal methods in this area all share
similar logical properties. Usually, the agent theories have:

- an *informational* component, being able to represent an agent's beliefs
  (by the modal logic KD45) or knowledge (by the modal logic S5);
- a *dynamic* component, allowing the representation of dynamic activity
  (by temporal or dynamic logic); and
- a *motivational* component, often representing the agent's desires, intentions or goals (by the modal logic KD).

Thus, the predominant approaches use particular combinations of modal
logics. (For definitions of the modal logics mentioned in this chapter we
refer the reader to [4].)

The particular agent theory that we consider here, the KARO framework—KARO is short for Knowledge, Abilities, Results and Opportuni-

ties—combines actions, knowledge, and wishes via propositional dynamic logic PDL, $S5_{(m)}$, and $KD_{(m)}$, respectively [31].

While proof methods have been developed for other agent theories like the BDI framework [37], no such methods exist for the KARO framework. Thus, our aim in this chapter is to examine possible approaches to the development of automated proof methods for the KARO framework. We study two approaches to the problem of proof in this complex system:

- proof methods for the fusion of PDL and $S5_{(m)}$ based upon translation to classical logic and first-order resolution; and
- representation of KARO in terms of the fusion of CTL and $S5_{(m)}$ and proof methods by direct clausal resolution on this combined logic.

These approaches both show how we can verify properties of agent-based systems represented in the KARO theory of rational agents, but there are fundamental differences in the techniques used. The first approach involves translating all modal and dynamic logic aspects into classical logic and then carrying out proof by defining specific orderings on classical resolution. The second approach retains the nonclassical structure and develops appropriate resolution rules for the combined logic. In addition, branching time temporal logic, rather than propositional dynamic logic, is used to represent the agent's dynamic behavior.

7.2 Basic KARO Elements

The KARO logic [27, 31] is a formal system that may be used to *specify*, *analyze* and *reason about* the behaviour of rational agents. Concerning the informational attitudes of agents, in the basic framework [27], it can be expressed that agent i *knows* a fact φ (written as $\mathbf{K}_i\varphi$). The modality $\mathbf{K}_i$ is a standard S5 modality. Consequently, the informational component of KARO is a multi-modal $S5_{(m)}$ logic. In the full system we also consider beliefs; these epistemic and doxastic attitudes were extensively studied in [30]. On an equal footing with these informational attitudes, the language encompasses a *dynamic* component. Starting with some atomic actions Ac_{at}, KARO allows for composite actions such as sequential composition ($\alpha ; \beta$), testing $\varphi!$, conditionals (if φ then α else β), repetition (while φ do α). We also investigated several notions of choice ($\alpha + \beta$) in [21]. The framework is especially fit to reason about the preconditions for such actions: one can express whether agent i is *able* to perform action α ($\mathbf{A}_i\alpha$) or has the *opportunity* to do α ($\mathbf{O}_i\alpha$), and also that φ is a *result* of doing α ($[\mathrm{do}_i(\alpha)]\varphi$). In addition, we can talk about an agent i being able to implement, that is, to bring about a property φ, using the implementability operator $\Diamond_i\varphi$. In this chapter, we concentrate on one particular variant of the KARO framework and define a core subsystem for which we are able to provide sound, complete, and terminating inference systems.

Formally, the logic we consider is an extended modal logic given by the fusion of a PDL-like logic and multi-modal S5 and KD. Given two (or more) modal logics L_1 and L_2 formulated in languages $\mathcal{L}_1$ and $\mathcal{L}_2$ with disjoint sets of modal operators, but the same non-modal base language, the *fusion* $L_1 \oplus L_2$ of L_1 and L_2 is the smallest modal logic L containing $L_1 \cup L_2$. In other words, if L_1 is axiomatized by a set of axioms Ax_1 and L_2 is axiomatized by Ax_2, then $L_1 \oplus L_2$ is axiomatised by the union $Ax_1 \cup Ax_2$. This means, in particular, that the modal operators in L_1 and L_2 do not interact.

The base language of the KARO framework is defined over three primitive types:

- a countably infinite set P of *propositional variables*,
- a set Ag of *agent names* (a finite subset of the positive integers), and
- a countably infinite set Ac_{at} of *atomic actions*.

Formulae are defined inductively as follows:

- $\top$ is an atomic propositional formula;
- $(\varphi \lor \psi)$ and $\neg\varphi$ are propositional formulae provided φ and ψ are propositional formulae;
- $\mathbf{K}_i\varphi$ (knowledge), $[\mathrm{do}_i(\alpha)]\varphi$ (achievement of results by actions), $\mathbf{A}_i\alpha$ (ability), $\mathbf{O}_i\alpha$ (opportunity), $\mathbf{W}_i^s\varphi$ (selected wish), and $\Diamond_i\varphi$ (implementability) are propositional formulae, provided i is an agent name, α is an action formula and φ is a propositional formula;
- id (skip) is an atomic action formula; and
- $(\alpha \lor \beta)$ (nondeterministic choice), $(\alpha\,;\,\beta)$ (sequencing), $\varphi!$ (confirmation or test), $\alpha^{(n)}$ (bounded repetition), and α^* (unbounded repetition) are action formulae, provided α and β are action formulae, φ is a propositional formula, and n is a natural number (in unary coding).

Implicit connectives include the usual connectives such as $\bot$, $\land$, $\rightarrow$, ... for propositional formulae, the duals of $\mathbf{K}_i$, $\mathbf{O}_i$ and $[\mathrm{do}_i(\alpha)]$ (denoted by $\langle\mathrm{do}_i(\alpha)\rangle$), as well as

$$\mathbf{PracPoss}_i(\alpha, \varphi) = \langle\mathrm{do}_i(\alpha)\rangle\varphi \land \mathbf{A}_i\alpha$$
$$\mathbf{Can}_i(\alpha, \varphi) = \mathbf{K}_i\mathbf{PracPoss}_i(\alpha, \varphi)$$
$$\mathbf{Cannot}_i(\alpha, \varphi) = \mathbf{K}_i\neg\mathbf{PracPoss}_i(\alpha, \varphi)$$
$$\mathbf{Goal}_i\varphi = \neg\varphi \land \mathbf{W}_i^s\varphi \land \Diamond_i\varphi$$
$$\mathbf{Intend}_i(\alpha, \varphi) = \mathbf{Can}_i(\alpha, \varphi) \land \mathbf{K}_i\mathbf{Goal}_i\varphi$$

We use the following notational convention in this chapter: We denote atomic actions, as well as first-order constants, by a, b, c, (non-) atomic actions by α, β, agents by i, j, propositional variables by p, q, formulae by φ, ϕ, ψ, ϑ, first-order variables by x, y, z, terms by s, t, u, functions by f,

Table 7.1. The relations $r^*_{(i,\alpha)}$ and sets $c^*_{(i,\alpha)}$.

Let u, w be worlds, i an agent, a an atomic action formula, α, β action formulae, and n a natural number, then

$$r^*_{(i,a)} = \{(u,w) \mid (u,w) \in r_{(i,a)}\}$$
$$r^*_{(i,\mathrm{id})} = \{(u,w) \mid u = w\}$$
$$r^*_{(i,\alpha\,;\,\beta)} = \{(u,w) \mid \exists v \in W\,((u,v) \in r^*_{(i,\alpha)} \wedge (v,w) \in r^*_{(i,\beta)})\}$$
$$r^*_{(i,\alpha\vee\beta)} = \{(u,w) \mid (u,w) \in r^*_{(i,\alpha)} \vee (u,w) \in r^*_{(i,\beta)}\}$$
$$r^*_{(i,\varphi!)} = \{(u,w) \mid u = w \wedge \mathcal{M},w \models \varphi\}$$
$$r^*_{(i,\alpha^{(0)})} = \{(u,w) \mid (u,w) \in r^*_{(i,\mathrm{id})}\}$$
$$r^*_{(i,\alpha^{(n+1)})} = \{(u,w) \mid (u,w) \in r^*_{(i,\alpha\,;\,\alpha^{(n)})}\}$$
$$r^*_{(i,\alpha^*)} = \{(u,w) \mid \exists n \in \mathbb{N}\,(u,w) \in r^*_{(i,\alpha^{(n)})}\}$$

and

$$c^*_{(i,a)} = c_{(i,a)}$$
$$c^*_{(i,\mathrm{id})} = W$$
$$c^*_{(i,\alpha\,;\,\beta)} = \{w \mid c^*_{(i,\alpha)}(w) \wedge \exists v \in W\,((w,v) \in r^*_{(i,\alpha)} \wedge v \in c^*_{(i,\beta)})\}$$
$$c^*_{(i,\alpha\vee\beta)} = \{w \mid w \in c^*_{(i,\alpha)} \vee w \in c^*_{(i,\beta)}\}$$
$$c^*_{(i,\varphi!)} = \{w \mid \mathcal{M},w \models \varphi\}$$
$$c^*_{(i,\alpha^{(0)})} = \{w \mid w \in c^*_{(i,\mathrm{id})}\}$$
$$c^*_{(i,\alpha^{(n+1)})} = \{w \mid w \in c^*_{(i,\alpha;\,\alpha^{(n)})}\}$$
$$c^*_{(i,\alpha^*)} = \{w \mid \exists n \in \mathbb{N}\,w \in c^*_{(i,\alpha^{(n+1)})}\}$$

---

g, h, predicate symbols by P, Q, R, atoms by A, A_1, A_2, literals by L, and clauses by C, D.

The semantics of KARO logic formulae is based on *interpretations* $\mathcal{M} = (W, V, D, I, M)$, where

- W is a nonempty set of worlds;
- V maps propositional variables to subsets of W;
- for every $i \in \mathrm{Ag}$ and every $a \in \mathrm{Ac_{at}}$, D contains a binary relation $r_{(i,a)}$ on W and a subset $c_{(i,a)}$ of W;
- I contains an equivalence relation K_i on W for each agent $i \in \mathrm{Ag}$; and
- M contains a serial relation relation W_i on W for each agent $i \in \mathrm{Ag}$.

Following the characterisation of agent theories in the introduction, D, I, and M comprise the dynamic, informational, and motivational components in the semantics of KARO logic.

The relations $r_{(i,a)}$ and sets $c_{(i,a)}$ are extended to $\mathrm{Ag} \times \mathrm{Ac}$-sorted relations $r^*_{(i,\alpha)}$ and sets $c^*_{(i,\alpha)}$ in a way standard for dynamic logic (Table 7.1).

The semantics of well-formed formulae of the KARO logic is defined as follows:

$$\mathcal{M}, w \models \top$$
$$\mathcal{M}, w \models p \qquad \text{iff } w \in V(p) \text{ where } p \in \mathsf{P}$$
$$\mathcal{M}, w \models \neg\varphi \qquad \text{iff } \mathcal{M}, w \not\models \varphi$$
$$\mathcal{M}, w \models \varphi \vee \psi \qquad \text{iff } \mathcal{M}, w \models \varphi \text{ or } \mathcal{M}, w \models \psi$$
$$\mathcal{M}, w \models [\mathsf{do}_i(\alpha)]\varphi \text{ iff } \forall v \in W \, ((w, v) \in r^*_{(i,\alpha)} \to \mathcal{M}, v \models \varphi)$$
$$\mathcal{M}, w \models \mathbf{A}_i\alpha \qquad \text{iff } w \in c^*_{(i,\alpha)}$$
$$\mathcal{M}, w \models \mathbf{O}_i\alpha \qquad \text{iff } \mathcal{M}, w \models \langle\mathsf{do}_i(\alpha)\rangle\top$$
$$\mathcal{M}, w \models \mathbf{W}^s_i\varphi \qquad \text{iff } \forall v \in W \, ((w, v) \in W_i \to \mathcal{M}, v \models \varphi)$$

$$\mathcal{M}, w \models \mathbf{K}_i\varphi \qquad \text{iff } \forall v \in W \, ((w, v) \in K_i \to \mathcal{M}, v \models \varphi)$$
$$\mathcal{M}, w \models \Diamond_i\varphi \qquad \text{iff } \exists k \in \mathbb{N} \, \exists a_1, \dots, a_k \in \mathsf{Ac_{at}}.$$
$$\mathcal{M}, w \models \mathbf{PracPoss}_i(a_1; \dots; a_k, \varphi)$$

If $\mathcal{M}, w \models \varphi$ we say φ *holds at* w (in $\mathcal{M}$) or φ is *true in* w. A formula φ is *satisfiable* iff there is an interpretation $\mathcal{M}$ and a world w such that $\mathcal{M}, w \models \varphi$.

Even though the logic defined above does not include all the features of the KARO framework, we refer to it as the *KARO logic*.

In this chapter we make the following simplifying assumptions: (i) we assume $\mathbf{A}_i\alpha = \mathbf{O}_i\alpha = \langle\mathsf{do}_i(\alpha)\rangle\top$, (ii) we exclude the unbounded repetition operator α^*, wishes $\mathbf{W}^s_i\varphi$, and implementability $\Diamond_i\varphi$ from the language, and (iii) there is no interaction between the dynamic and informational component. This fragment of the KARO logic is called the *core KARO logic*. In Section 7.6 we will discuss in how far these simplifying assumptions can be relaxed.

7.3 Proof by Translation

The translation approach to modal reasoning is based on the idea that inference in (combinations of) modal logics can be carried out by translating modal formulae into first-order logic and using conventional first-order theorem proving techniques. Various translation morphisms exist and their properties vary with regards the extent to which they are able to map modal logics into first-order logic, the decidability of the fragments of first-order logic into which modal formulae are translated, and the computational behaviour of first-order theorem provers on these fragments, see, e.g., [8, 22, 24, 39].

In the following we present a decision procedure for the satisfiability problem in the core KARO logic consisting of three components: (i) a normalization function which reduces complex action formulae to atomic action subformulae, (ii) a particular translation of normalized formulae into a fragment of first-order logic, (iii) a particular transformation of this fragment of first-order logic into the clausal class DL*, and (iv) a resolution-based decision procedure for DL*.

Table 7.2. Transformation rules for the core KARO logic.

$\neg\langle\mathrm{do}_i(\alpha)\rangle\psi \Rightarrow [\mathrm{do}_i(\alpha)]\neg\psi$	$\neg[\mathrm{do}_i(\alpha)]\psi \Rightarrow \langle\mathrm{do}_i(\alpha)\rangle\neg\psi$
$\langle\mathrm{do}_i(\alpha \vee \beta)\rangle\psi \Rightarrow \langle\mathrm{do}_i(\alpha)\rangle\psi \vee \langle\mathrm{do}_i(\beta)\rangle\psi$	$[\mathrm{do}_i(\alpha \vee \beta)]\psi \Rightarrow [\mathrm{do}_i(\alpha)]\psi \wedge [\mathrm{do}_i(\beta)]\psi$
$\langle\mathrm{do}_i(\alpha\,;\,\beta)\rangle\psi \Rightarrow \langle\mathrm{do}_i(\alpha)\rangle\langle\mathrm{do}_i(\beta)\rangle\psi$	$[\mathrm{do}_i(\alpha\,;\,\beta)]\psi \Rightarrow [\mathrm{do}_i(\alpha)][\mathrm{do}_i(\beta)]\psi$
$\langle\mathrm{do}_i(\mathrm{id})\rangle\psi \Rightarrow \psi$	$[\mathrm{do}_i(\mathrm{id})]\psi \Rightarrow \psi$
$\langle\mathrm{do}_i(\phi!)\rangle\psi \Rightarrow \phi \wedge \psi$	$[\mathrm{do}_i(\phi!)]\psi \Rightarrow \neg\phi \vee \psi$
$\langle\mathrm{do}_i(\alpha^{(1)})\rangle\psi \Rightarrow \langle\mathrm{do}_i(\alpha)\rangle\psi$	$[\mathrm{do}_i(\alpha^{(1)})]\psi \Rightarrow [\mathrm{do}_i(\alpha)]\psi$
$\langle\mathrm{do}_i(\alpha^{(n+1)})\rangle\psi \Rightarrow \langle\mathrm{do}_i(\alpha)\rangle\langle\mathrm{do}_i(\alpha^{(n)})\rangle\psi$	$[\mathrm{do}_i(\alpha^{(n+1)})]\psi \Rightarrow [\mathrm{do}_i(\alpha)][\mathrm{do}_i(\alpha^{(n)})]\psi$

Table 7.3. Translation morphism π.

$\pi([\mathrm{do}_i(a)]\varphi, x) = \forall y\,(R_{(i,a)}(x,y) \rightarrow \pi(\varphi,y))$	$\pi(\top, x) = \top$
$\pi(\langle\mathrm{do}_i(a)\rangle\varphi, x) = \exists y\,(R_{(i,a)}(x,y) \wedge \pi(\varphi,y))$	$\pi(p, x) = Q_p(x)$
$\pi(\mathbf{O}_i\alpha, x) = \pi(\langle\mathrm{do}_i(\alpha)\rangle\top, x)$	$\pi(\neg\varphi, x) = \neg\pi(\varphi, x)$
$\pi(\mathbf{A}_i\alpha, x) = \pi(\langle\mathrm{do}_i(\alpha)\rangle\top, x)$	$\pi(\varphi \vee \psi, x) = \pi(\varphi, x) \vee \pi(\psi, x)$
$\pi(\mathbf{K}_i\varphi, x) = Q_{\mathbf{K}_i\varphi}(x)$	

where a is an atomic action, p is a propositional variable, Q_p is a unary predicate symbol uniquely associated with p, $Q_{\mathbf{K}_i\varphi}$ is a predicate symbol uniquely associated with $\mathbf{K}_i\varphi$, and $R_{(i,a)}$ is a binary predicate symbol uniquely associated with a and i, which represents the relation $r_{(i,a)}$ in the semantics.

7.3.1 Reduction of Complex Actions

Using the rewrite rules given in Table 7.2 and similar rules for $\mathbf{O}_i\alpha$ and $\mathbf{A}_i\alpha$, the normalization function maps any formula φ of the core KARO logic to a normal form $\varphi\!\downarrow$. It is straightforward to see that the rewrite relation defined by these rules is confluent and terminating. The normal form $\varphi\!\downarrow$ of φ is logically equivalent to φ, it is unique, and in the absence of the unbounded repetition operator, $\varphi\!\downarrow$ contains no nonatomic action formulae.

Lemma 1 *Let φ be a formula in the core KARO logic without occurrences of the unbounded repetition operator. Then $\varphi\!\downarrow$ is logically equivalent to φ, and $\varphi\!\downarrow$ does not contain any non-atomic action formulae.*

7.3.2 Translation to First-Order Logic

The particular translation we use has been proposed in [7] and further developed in [40]; both are special cases of the T-encoding introduced in [34]. It allows for conceptually simple decision procedures for extensions of K4 by ordered resolution. As compared to tableaux-based procedures a feature of this approach is the absence of loop checking mechanisms for transitive modal logics.

Without loss of generality we assume that the modal formulae under consideration are normalized and in negation normal form. We define the translation function π as given in Table 7.3. Let $\Pi(\psi)$ be the formula

$$\exists x\, \pi(\psi, x) \wedge \bigwedge\nolimits_{\mathbf{K}_i\varphi \in \Gamma_{\mathbf{K}}(\psi)} \mathrm{Ax}(\mathbf{K}_i\varphi),$$

where $\Gamma_{\mathbf{K}}(\psi)$ is the set of subformulae of the form $\mathbf{K}_i\varphi$ in ψ, and $\mathrm{Ax}(\mathbf{K}_i\varphi)$ is the formula

$$\forall x\, (Q_{\mathbf{K}_i\varphi}(x) \leftrightarrow \forall y\, (R_{(i,\mathbf{K})}(x,y) \rightarrow \pi(\varphi,y)))$$
$$\wedge\ \forall x, y\, (Q_{\mathbf{K}_i\varphi}(x) \wedge R_{(i,\mathbf{K})}(x,y) \rightarrow Q_{\mathbf{K}_i\varphi}(y))$$
$$\wedge\ \forall x, y\, (Q_{\mathbf{K}_i\varphi}(y) \wedge R_{(i,\mathbf{K})}(x,y) \rightarrow Q_{\mathbf{K}_i\varphi}(x))$$
$$\wedge\ \forall x\, R_{(i,\mathbf{K})}(x,x).$$

Here $R_{(i,\mathbf{K})}$ is a binary predicate symbol uniquely associated with the modal operator $\mathbf{K}_i$. No additional definition of $R_{(i,\mathbf{K})}$ is required, in particular, Π does not state the symmetry or transitivity of $R_{(i,\mathbf{K})}$. Note that the translation Π preserves the structure of the core KARO formula, that is, with every subformula occurrence ψ in a core KARO formula φ we can associate a particular subformula occurrence ϑ in $\Pi(\varphi)$ such that $\vartheta = \pi(\psi)$. Based on the close correspondence between the translation morphism Π and the semantics of the core KARO logic it is possible to prove the following.

Theorem 1. *A formula φ of the core KARO logic is satisfiable iff $\Pi(\varphi)$ is first-order satisfiable.*

Proof Sketch.

The only problem in this theorem is caused by the fact that $\Pi(\psi)$ does not ensure that the relations $R_{(i,\mathbf{K})}$ in a first-order model of $\Pi(\psi)$ are equivalence relations while this is the case for the corresponding relations K_i in the modal model. This problem can be overcome along the lines of [7] or [23].   □

One of the advantages of using the translation morphism proposed by De Nivelle is the fact that for any formula φ of the core KARO logic $\Pi(\varphi)$ can easily be seen to belong to a number of well-known solvable first-order classes, including the two-variable fragment of first-order logic [33], the guarded fragment [1], or the clausal class DL^* [8].

A clause C is a DL^*-*clause* iff (i) all literals are unary, or binary, (ii) there is no nesting of function symbols, (iii) every functional term in C contains all variables of C, and (iv) every binary literal (even if it has no functional terms) contains all variables of C. A set of clauses N belongs to the class DL^* iff all clauses in N are DL^*-clauses.

7.3.3 Transformation into DL*

We will now present a structural transformation of first-order formulae into clausal form which will transform translated formulae of the core KARO logic into sets of first-order clauses belonging to the class DL^*.

Let $\text{Pos}(\varphi)$ be the set of positions of a first-order formula φ. If λ is a position in φ, then $\varphi\mid_\lambda$ denotes the subformula of φ at position λ and $\varphi[\psi\mapsto\lambda]$ is the result of replacing $\varphi\mid_\lambda$ at position λ by ψ. The polarity of (occurrences of) first-order subformulae is defined as usual: Any occurrence of a subformula of an equivalence has *zero polarity*. For occurrences of subformulae not below a '$\leftrightarrow$' symbol, an occurrence of a subformula has *positive polarity* if it is one inside the scope of an even number of (explicit or implicit) negations, and it has *negative polarity* if it is one inside the scope of an odd number of negations.

Structural transformation, also referred to as renaming, associates with each element λ of a set of positions $\Lambda\subseteq\text{Pos}(\varphi)$ a predicate symbol $\boldsymbol{Q}_\lambda$ and a literal $\boldsymbol{Q}_\lambda(x_1,\ldots,x_n)$, where $x_1,\ldots,x_n$ are the free variables of $\varphi\mid_\lambda$, the symbol $\boldsymbol{Q}_\lambda$ does not occur in φ and two symbols $\boldsymbol{Q}_\lambda$ and $\boldsymbol{Q}_{\lambda'}$ are equal only if $\varphi\mid_\lambda$ and $\varphi\mid_{\lambda'}$ are equivalent formulae. Let

$$\text{Def}_\lambda^+(\varphi) = \forall x_1\ldots x_n.\,\boldsymbol{Q}_\lambda(x_1,\ldots,x_n)\to\varphi\mid_\lambda \quad\text{and}$$

$$\text{Def}_\lambda^-(\varphi) = \forall x_1\ldots x_n.\,\varphi\mid_\lambda\to\boldsymbol{Q}_\lambda(x_1,\ldots,x_n).$$

The *definition* of $\boldsymbol{Q}_\lambda$ is the formula

$$\text{Def}_\lambda(\varphi) = \begin{cases} \text{Def}_\lambda^+(\varphi) & \text{if } \varphi\mid_\lambda \text{ has positive polarity} \\ \text{Def}_\lambda^-(\varphi) & \text{if } \varphi\mid_\lambda \text{ has negative polarity} \\ \text{Def}_\lambda^+(\varphi)\wedge\text{Def}_\lambda^-(\varphi) & \text{otherwise.} \end{cases}$$

Based on Def_λ we can inductively define $\text{Def}_\Lambda(\varphi)$, where $\Lambda\subseteq\text{Pos}(\varphi)$, by:

$$\text{Def}_\varnothing(\varphi) = \varphi \quad\text{and}$$

$$\text{Def}_{\Lambda\cup\{\lambda\}}(\varphi) = \text{Def}_\Lambda(\varphi[\boldsymbol{Q}_\lambda(x_1,\ldots,x_n)\mapsto\lambda])\wedge\text{Def}_\lambda(\varphi).$$

Here λ is maximal in $\Lambda\cup\{\lambda\}$ with respect to the prefix ordering on positions. A *definitional form* of φ is $\text{Def}_\Lambda(\varphi)$, where Λ is a subset of all positions of subformulae (usually, nonatomic or nonliteral subformulae).

Theorem 2. *Let φ be a first-order formula.*

1. *φ is satisfiable iff $\text{Def}_\Lambda(\varphi)$ is satisfiable, for any $\Lambda\subseteq\text{Pos}(\varphi)$.*
2. *$\text{Def}_\Lambda(\varphi)$ can be computed in linear time, provided Λ includes all positions of nonliteral subformula occurrences and φ is linearized.*

Recall that with every subformula occurrence ψ in a core KARO formula φ we can associate a particular subformula occurrence ϑ in $\Pi(\varphi)$ such that $\vartheta = \pi(\psi)$. So, for every core KARO formula φ we can define a set of $\Lambda(\varphi)$ of positions in $\Pi(\varphi)$ by

$$\Lambda(\varphi) = \{\lambda \mid \text{ there is a nonliteral subformula } \varphi\mid_{\lambda'} \text{ of } \varphi \text{ and } \Pi(\varphi)\mid_\lambda = \pi(\varphi\mid_{\lambda'})\}.$$

Then we can show the following:

Table 7.4. Expansion and inference rules.

Deduce:
$$\frac{N}{N \cup \{\mathrm{Cond}(C)\}}$$

if C is either a resolvent or a factor of clauses in N, and $\mathrm{Cond}(C)$ is the condensation of C.

Delete:
$$\frac{N \cup \{C\}}{N}$$

if C is a tautology or N contains a clause which is a variant of C.

Split:
$$\frac{N \cup \{C \vee D\}}{N \cup \{C\} \mid N \cup \{D\}}$$

if C and D are variable-disjoint.

Resolvents and factors are derived by the following rules.

Resolution:
$$\frac{C \vee A_1 \quad \neg A_2 \vee D}{(C \vee D)\sigma}$$

where (i) σ is a most general unifier of A_1 and A_2, (ii) no literal in C is selected, and $A_1\sigma$ is strictly *succ*-maximal with respect to $C\sigma$, and (iii) $\neg A_2$ is either selected, or $\neg A_2\sigma$ is maximal with respect to $D\sigma$ and no literal in D is selected.

$C \vee A_1$ is called the *positive premise* and $\neg A_2 \vee D$ the *negative premise*. We implicitly assume that the premises have no common variables.

Factoring:
$$\frac{C \vee A_1 \vee A_2}{(C \vee A_1)\sigma}$$

where (i) σ is a most general unifier of A_1 and A_2, and (ii) no literal in C is selected and $A_1\sigma$ is *succ*-maximal with respect to $C\sigma$.

Lemma 2 *Let φ be a formula of the core KARO logic. Then every clause in the clausal form of* $\mathrm{Def}_{A(\varphi)}(\Pi(\varphi))$ *is a* DL^*-*clause.*

7.3.4 A First-Order Resolution Calculus

For the clausal class DL^* a decision procedure can be formulated in the resolution framework of Bachmair and Ganzinger [2]. In this framework, the resolution calculus is parameterized by two parameters: an admissible ordering *succ* and a selection function S. Essentially, an *admissible ordering* is a total (well-founded) strict ordering on the ground level such that for literals ... *succ* $\neg A_n$ *succ* A_n *succ* ... *succ* $\neg A_1$ *succ* A_1 holds. This is extended to the nonground level in a canonical manner. A *selection function* assigns to each clause a possibly empty set of occurrences of negative literals and no restrictions are imposed on the selection function.

The calculus itself consists of general *expansion rules* of the form:

$$\frac{N}{N_1 \mid \cdots \mid N_n}$$

Each represents a finite derivation of alternatives $N_1, \ldots, N_n$ from N. The rules given in Table 7.4 describe how derivation trees can be expanded at the leaves. A *derivation* from a set of clauses N is a finitely branching, ordered tree T with root N and nodes being sets of clauses. The tree is constructed by applications of the expansion rules to the leaves so that factoring, splitting and resolution are applied in this order. We assume that no resolution or factoring inference is computed twice on the same branch of the derivation. Any path $N(= N_0), N_1, \ldots$ in a derivation T is called a *closed branch* in T iff the clause set $\bigcup_j N_j$ contains the empty clause, otherwise it is called an *open branch*. A derivation T is a *refutation* iff every path $N(= N_0), N_1, \ldots$ in it is a closed branch. A derivation T from N is called *fair* if for any path $N(= N_0), N_1, \ldots$ in T, with *limit* $N_\infty = \bigcup_j \bigcap_{k \geq j} N_k$, it is the case that each clause C that can be deduced from nonredundant premises in N_∞ is contained in some N_j. Note that for a finite path $N(= N_0), N_1, \ldots N_n$, the limit N_∞ is equal to N_n.

The calculus is refutationally complete and compatible with a general notion of *redundancy* for clauses and inferences, with which additional don't-care non-deterministic simplification and deletion rules can be applied [2]. For our purposes it is sufficient that tautological clauses and variant clauses are eliminated from the clause set during a derivation.

Theorem 3 ([3]). *Let T be a fair derivation from a set N of clauses. Then,*

1. *If $N(= N_0), N_1, \ldots$ is a path with limit N_∞, N_∞ is saturated up to redundancy.*
2. *N is satisfiable if and only if there exists a path in T with limit N_∞ such that N_∞ is satisfiable.*
3. *N is unsatisfiable if and only if for every path $N(= N_0), N_1, \ldots$ the clause set $\bigcup_j N_j$ contains the empty clause.*

A Decision Procedure for DL*

A decision procedure for DL* can be obtained using an ordering *succ* defined as follows. Let $>_d$ be an ordering on terms which is defined by $s >_d t$ if s is deeper than t, and every variable that occurs in t, occurs deeper in s. Then define $P(s_1, \ldots, s_n) \, succ_A \, Q(t_1, \ldots, t_n)$ by $\{s_1, \ldots, s_n\} >_d^{mul} \{t_1, \ldots, t_n\}$, where $>_d^{mul}$ is the multiset extension of $>_d$. Finally, for a negative literal $\neg A$ let $ms(A)$ denote the multiset $\{A, A\}$, while for a positive literal A, $ms(A)$ denotes $\{A\}$. We define an ordering *succ* on literals by $L_1 \, succ \, L_2$ iff $ms(L_1) \, succ_A \, ms(L_2)$.

Theorem 4 ([8, Theorem 5.4]). *Let N be a set of* DL**-clauses and succ be the ordering of literals defined above. Then,*

1. *succ is an admissible ordering; and*
2. *any derivation from N based on succ terminates in time double exponential in the size of the signature of N.*

A Decision Procedure for Core KARO Logic

We can now put together the four components of our first decision procedure for core KARO logic. Given a formulae φ in the core KARO logic, we proceed by normalizing φ using the rules in Table 7.2, translating the result to first-order logic using the translation morphism Π, transforming the resulting first-order formula to clausal form using Def_Λ and a standard clause form transformation, and finally applying the resolution calculus with the ordering *succ* specified above to the set of clauses we obtain.

Theorem 5 (Soundness, completeness, and termination). *Let φ be a formula of the core KARO logic and N be the clausal form of* $\mathrm{Def}_{\Lambda(\varphi)}(\Pi(\varphi))$. *Then,*

1. *any derivation from N based on succ terminates in time exponential in the size of the signature of N; and*
2. *φ is unsatisfiable iff all branches in any fair derivation with root N are closed.*

Proof [Sketch]. Termination, soundness, and completeness is a consequence of Lemma 1 and Theorems 1, 2, 3, and 4. Note that Theorem 4 states that any derivation from a set N' in the class DL* terminates in time double exponential in the size of the signature of N'. This is basically due to the fact that there is a double exponential upper bound on the number of clauses derivable from N' and the fact that applications of the inference rules as well as redundancy elimination steps require only polynomial time in the size of the derived clause set. However, for clause sets obtained from the translation of formulae of the core KARO logic it is possible to obtain a single exponential upper bound on the number of derivable clauses. The complexity of the inference steps and redundancy elimination steps remains unchanged, thus providing us with the upper bound stated in our theorem.   □

The computation of $\varphi{\downarrow}$ using the transformation rules given in Table 7.2 may require exponential time and the size of $\varphi{\downarrow}$ can be exponential in the size of φ. The translation of $\varphi{\downarrow}$ to first-order logic and the transformation to clausal form requires only linear time. The size of the signature of the resulting clause set N is linear in the size of $\varphi{\downarrow}$. By Theorem 5 the saturation of N requires exponential time in the size of the signature of

N. Overall this gives a decision procedure which requires time double exponential in the size of φ.

A variation of the approach can be used to show that the satisfiability problem of core KARO logic is actually PSPACE-complete and to obtain a decision procedure for core KARO logic which requires only polynomial space. Basically, two modifications are required. First, we have to ensure applications of the normalization function to formulae of the form $\langle \mathrm{do}_i(\alpha \vee \beta)\rangle\psi$ and $[\mathrm{do}_i(\alpha \vee \beta)]\psi$ do not result in formulae in which the subformula ψ occurs twice. This can be achieved by replacing ψ with a new propositional variable q and adding a definition $\forall(q \leftrightarrow \psi)$ for q to the formula, where $\forall$ is the universal modality (see Section 7.6 for a definition of its semantics). Second, we reduce formulae of $S5_{(m)}$ to $K_{(m)}$. Let φ be the result of the first transformation and let n be the number of subformula occurrences of the form $\mathbf{K}_i\psi$ in φ for arbitrary $i \in$ Ag. Let k be a new atomic action not occurring in φ. For each subformula occurrence $\mathbf{K}_i\psi$ we introduce two new propositional variables q_ψ and $q_{\mathbf{K}_i\psi}$, and we let

$$
\begin{aligned}
\Gamma(\mathbf{K}_i\psi) = \ &\forall(q_\psi \leftrightarrow \psi) \wedge \\
&\forall(q_{\mathbf{K}_i\psi} \leftrightarrow [\mathrm{do}_i(k)]q_\psi) \wedge \\
&(q_{\mathbf{K}_i\psi} \rightarrow (q_{\mathbf{K}_i\psi} \wedge [\mathrm{do}_i(k)]q_{\mathbf{K}_i\psi} \wedge \ldots \wedge [\mathrm{do}_i(k)]^n q_{\mathbf{K}_i\psi})) \wedge \\
&(\neg q_{\mathbf{K}_i\psi} \rightarrow (\neg q_{\mathbf{K}_i\psi} \wedge [\mathrm{do}_i(k)]\neg q_{\mathbf{K}_i\psi} \wedge \ldots \wedge [\mathrm{do}_i(k)]^n \neg q_{\mathbf{K}_i\psi}))
\end{aligned}
$$

where $[\mathrm{do}_i(k)]^n$ is an abbreviation for $[\mathrm{do}_i(k)]$ repeated n times. Then the second transformation consists of a series of rewrite steps

$$
\varphi[\mathbf{K}_i\psi] \Rightarrow \varphi[q_{\mathbf{K}_i\psi}] \wedge \Gamma(\mathbf{K}_i\psi),
$$

where ψ itself does not contain any occurrence of a modal operator $\mathbf{K}_j$, until a normal form has been computed. The result $\varphi_\|$ of the two transformations is satisfiability equivalent to the original formula φ. It can be computed in time polynomial in the size of φ, and is of size quadratic in the size of φ. The target logic of the translation can be seen as a notational variant of $\mathcal{ALC}$ with acyclic TBoxes whose satisfiability problem is PSPACE-complete [28]. Therefore:

Theorem 6. *The satisfiability problem of the core KARO logic is PSPACE-complete.*

A computationally space optimal decision procedure for $\mathcal{ALC}$ with acyclic TBoxes, based on translation and a refinement of the resolution calculus using a particular selection function instead of an ordering refinement, can be developed along the lines of [16]. This alternative decision procedure uses only polynomial space in the worst case.

7.4 Proof by Clausal Temporal Resolution

Here we use the simple observation that the use of PDL in the KARO framework is very similar to the use of branching time temporal logic.

Table 7.5. Semantics of $\text{CTL} \oplus \text{S5}_{(m)}$.

$\mathcal{M}, (t, u)$	$\models \top$	
$\mathcal{M}, (t, u)$	$\models p$	iff $(t, u) \in V(p)$ where $p \in \mathsf{P}$
$\mathcal{M}, (t, u)$	$\models \neg\varphi$	iff $\mathcal{M}, (t, u) \not\models \varphi$
$\mathcal{M}, (t, u)$	$\models \varphi \vee \psi$	iff $\mathcal{M}, (t, u) \models \varphi$ or $\mathcal{M}, (t, u) \models \psi$
$\mathcal{M}, (t, u)$	$\models \mathbf{A}\varphi$	iff $\mathcal{M}, (t', u) \models \varphi$ for all timelines t' extending (t, u)
$\mathcal{M}, (t, u)$	$\models \mathbf{E}\varphi$	iff $\mathcal{M}, (t', u) \models \varphi$ for some timeline t' extending (t, u)
$\mathcal{M}, (t, u)$	$\models \bigcirc\varphi$	iff $\mathcal{M}, (t, u + 1) \models \varphi$
$\mathcal{M}, (t, u)$	$\models \Box\varphi$	iff for all $u' \in \mathbb{N}$ if $(u \leq u')$ then $\mathcal{M}, (t, u') \models \varphi$
$\mathcal{M}, (t, u)$	$\models \Diamond\varphi$	iff there exists $u' \in \mathbb{N}$ such that $(u \leq u')$ and $\mathcal{M}, (t, u') \models \varphi$
$\mathcal{M}, (t, u)$	$\models \varphi\mathcal{U}\psi$	iff there exists $u' \in \mathbb{N}$ such that $(u' \geq u)$ and $\mathcal{M}, (t, u') \models \psi$
		and for all $u'' \in \mathbb{N}$ if $(u \leq u'' < u')$ then $\mathcal{M}, (t, u'') \models \varphi$
$\mathcal{M}, (t, u)$	$\models \varphi\mathcal{W}\psi$	iff $\mathcal{M}, (t, u) \models \varphi\mathcal{U}\psi$ or $\mathcal{M}, (t, u) \models \Box\varphi$
$\mathcal{M}, (t, u)$	$\models \mathbf{K}_i\varphi$	iff for all timelines t' and for all $u' \in \mathbb{N}$ if $((t, u), (t', u')) \in R_i$
		then $\mathcal{M}, (t', u') \models \varphi$

Thus, we attempt to use a simple CTL branching time temporal logic to represent the dynamic component of the core KARO logic, while the epistemic component of core KARO logic remains unchanged. Clausal resolution-based theorem proving is then applied to this branching time temporal logic of knowledge, the fusion of CTL and $\text{S5}_{(m)}$.

In the subsequent pages, we give (i) a translation from the core of KARO to the fusion of CTL and $\text{S5}_{(m)}$, (ii) a translation of formulae in $\text{CTL} \oplus \text{S5}_{(m)}$ into a normal form for this logic, and (iii) a resolution decision procedure for these clauses.

7.4.1 Translation into $\text{CTL} \oplus \text{S5}_{(m)}$

We begin by presenting the syntax and semantics for $\text{CTL} \oplus \text{S5}_{(m)}$. Given a countably infinite set P of *propositional variables* and a set Ag of *agent names*, formulae of $\text{CTL} \oplus \text{S5}_{(m)}$ are defined inductively as follows: $\top$ is a $\text{CTL} \oplus \text{S5}_{(m)}$ formula, every propositional variable in P is a $\text{CTL} \oplus \text{S5}_{(m)}$ formula, if φ and ψ are $\text{CTL} \oplus \text{S5}_{(m)}$ formulae, then $\neg\varphi$, $\varphi \vee \psi$, $\mathbf{A}\Diamond\varphi$, $\mathbf{A}\Box\varphi$, $\mathbf{A}(\varphi\mathcal{U}\psi)$, $\mathbf{A}(\varphi\mathcal{W}\psi)$, $\mathbf{A}\bigcirc\varphi$, $\mathbf{E}\Diamond\varphi$, $\mathbf{E}\Box\varphi$, $\mathbf{E}(\varphi\mathcal{U}\psi)$, $\mathbf{E}(\varphi\mathcal{W}\psi)$, and $\mathbf{E}\bigcirc\varphi$ are $\text{CTL} \oplus \text{S5}_{(m)}$ formulae, if φ is a $\text{CTL} \oplus \text{S5}_{(m)}$ formula and i is an agent name in Ag, then $\mathbf{K}_i\varphi$ is a $\text{CTL} \oplus \text{S5}_{(m)}$ formula.

The semantics of $\text{CTL} \oplus \text{S5}_{(m)}$ formulae is as follows. Let S be a set of *states*. A *tree* is a structure (S, η), where S is the set of states and $\eta \subseteq S \times S$ is a relation between states such that (i) $s_0 \in S$ is a unique root node (i.e. $\neg\exists s_i \in S$ such that $(s_i, s_0) \in \eta$), (ii) for each $s_i \in S$ there exists $s_j \in S$ such that $(s_i, s_j) \in \eta$, and (iii) for all $s_i, s_j, s_k \in S$ if $(s_j, s_i) \in \eta$ and $(s_k, s_i) \in \eta$ then $s_j = s_k$. A *timeline*, t, is an infinitely long, linear, discrete sequence of states, indexed by the natural numbers. Note that timelines correspond to the *runs* of Halpern and Vardi [19, 18]. Given a set of trees T, the set of timelines can be extracted by taking the union of the infinite branches

Table 7.6. Translation morphism τ where a is an atomic action, p is a propositional variable, and $done_i^a$ is a propositional variable uniquely associated with a and i.

$\tau([do_i(a)]\varphi) = \mathbf{A}\bigcirc(done_i^a \rightarrow \tau(\varphi))$	$\tau(\top) = \top$
$\tau(\langle do_i(a)\rangle\varphi) = \mathbf{E}\bigcirc(done_i^a \wedge \tau(\varphi))$	$\tau(p) = p$
$\tau(\mathbf{O}_i\alpha) = \tau(\langle do_i(\alpha)\rangle\top)$	$\tau(\neg\varphi) = \neg\tau(\varphi)$
$\tau(\mathbf{A}_i\alpha) = \tau(\langle do_i(\alpha)\rangle\top)$	$\tau(\varphi \vee \psi) = \tau(\varphi) \vee \tau(\psi)$
$\tau(\mathbf{K}_i\varphi) = \mathbf{K}_i\tau(\varphi)$	

that start at the root node of each tree in T. Let TL_T be the set of all timelines in T. A point, p, is a pair $p = (t, u)$, where $t \in TL_T$ is a timeline and $u \in \mathbb{N}$ is a temporal index into t. Given T, a set of trees, let $TLines$ be the set of timelines constructed from T. Two timelines t and t' *coincide up to point* (t, n) if, and only if, $(t, n') = (t', n')$ for all $n' \leq n$. A timeline t' *extends* (t, n) if, and only if, t and t' coincide up to (t, n). Let P_T be the set of all points.

An *interpretation* $\mathcal{M}$ for $\mathsf{CTL} \oplus \mathsf{S5}_{(m)}$ is a structure $\mathcal{M} = (T, \mathcal{R}, V)$ where (i) T is a set of infinite trees, with a distinguished tree r_0, (ii) for every $i \in \mathsf{Ag}$, $\mathcal{R}$ contains an equivalence relation $R_i \subseteq P_T \times P_T$, and (iii) V maps P to subsets of P_T.

The semantics of $\mathsf{CTL} \oplus \mathsf{S5}_{(m)}$ formula is defined in Table 7.5. For any formula φ, if there is some interpretation $\mathcal{M}$ such that $\mathcal{M}, (t_0, 0) \models \varphi$, for any timeline t_0 extracted from the distinguished tree r_0, then φ is said to be *satisfiable* and $\mathcal{M}$ is a *model of* φ. If $\mathcal{M}, (t_0, 0) \models \varphi$ for all interpretations $\mathcal{M}$, for any timeline t_0 extracted from the distinguished tree r_0, then φ is said to be valid.

We assume that formulae of the core KARO logic are normalized using the rewrite rules of Table 7.2. We define a translation τ from core KARO logic into the fusion of CTL and $\mathsf{S5}_{(m)}$ as given in Table 7.6.

Theorem 7. *Let φ be formula of the core KARO logic. Then φ is satisfiable iff $\tau(\varphi\downarrow)$ is.*

Proof [Sketch]. First, given any satisfiable formula φ of the core KARO logic, we can construct a $\mathsf{CTL} \oplus \mathsf{S5}_{(m)}$ model $\mathcal{M}$ such that $\mathcal{M}, (t_0, 0) \models \tau(\varphi\downarrow)$. As φ is satisfiable there must be a model $\mathcal{M}' = (W', V', D', I', M')$ and a world $w_0 \in W'$ such that $\mathcal{M}', w_0 \models \varphi$. As normalization provides a logically equivalent formula $\mathcal{M}', w_0 \models \varphi\downarrow$.

We define a $\mathsf{CTL} \oplus \mathsf{S5}_{(m)}$ interpretation $\mathcal{M} = (T, \mathcal{R}, V)$ and a relation pt : $W \times P_T$ associating worlds in $\mathcal{M}'$ with points in $\mathcal{M}$ as follows.

- $(w_0, (t_0, 0)) \in$ pt;
- for any $w \in W'$ and any point (t, u), if $(w, (t, u)) \in$ pt, then for all relations $r_{(i,a)} \in D'$ and worlds $v \in W'$, $(w, v) \in r_{(i,a)}$ iff there exists a

point $(t', u + 1)$ such that t' extends (t, u) and $(v, (t', u + 1)) \in$ pt and $(t', u + 1) \in V(done_i^a)$, where t' is a new timeline if v is not related to any element of P_T via pt;

- for any $w \in W'$ and any point (t, u), if $(w, (t, u)) \in$ pt, then for every $(w, v) \in I'$, $(w, v) \in K_i$ iff $((t, u), (t', u')) \in R_i$ and $(v, (t', u')) \in$ pt, where t' is a new timeline if v is not related to any element of P_T via pt; and
- for any proposition p, $w \in V'(p)$ iff $(t, u) \in V(p)$.

For any finite timeline $(t, 0), \ldots, (t, i)$ (i.e. there exists a point (t, i) such that no timeline t' exists such that t' extends (t, i) and $(t', i + 1)$ is in t') construct points $(t, i + j)$, $j \geq 1$ and extend t to be an infinite timeline $(t, 0), \ldots, (t, i), (t, i + 1), (t, i + 2) \ldots$. Let P_{Tnew} be the set of such newly constructed points. For all $(t', i + j) \in P_{Tnew}$ let $(t', i + j) \notin V(done_i^a)$ for every atomic action a and every agent i.

The set of paths constructed from the timelines of $\mathcal{M}$ must be suffix, fusion and limit closed. This follows by a result of Emerson [11] and how we have constructed the timelines ensuring infinite timelines.

Now by induction on the structure of normalized formulae of the core KARO logic we can show that for any $\varphi\downarrow$ satisfied at w in $\mathcal{M}'$ we have $\mathcal{M}, (t_0, 0) \models \tau(\varphi\downarrow)$.

Next we show that given a formula ψ with model $\mathcal{M} = (T, \mathcal{R}, V)$ in the fusion of CTL and S5$_{(m)}$ that is equal to $\tau(\varphi\downarrow)$ for some formula φ of the core KARO logic we can construct a model $\mathcal{M}' = (W', V', D', I', M')$ for φ and a function world : $P_T \rightarrow W$ mapping points in $\mathcal{M}$ and to worlds in $\mathcal{M}'$ which satisfy the following properties:

- world$((t_0, 0)) = w_0$;
- for all points (t, u) and $(t', u + 1)$ such that t and t' coincide up to (t, u), $(t', u + 1) \in V(done_i^a)$ iff there exist worlds $w, v \in W'$ such that world$(t, u) = w$ and world$(t', u + 1) = v$ and $(w, v) \in r_{(i, a)}$;
- for all points (t, u) and (t', u'), $((t, u), (t', u')) \in R_i$ iff there exist worlds $w, v \in W'$ such that world$(t, u) = w$ and world$(t', u + 1) = v$ and $(w, v) \in K_i$; and
- for any proposition $p \in \mathsf{P}$, $(t, u) \in V(p)$ iff $w \in V'(p)$.

We can then show by induction on the structure of a normalized formula φ in the core KARO logic that if $\tau(\varphi)$ is satisfied at point (t, u) in $\mathcal{M}$, that is, $\mathcal{M}, (t, u) \models \tau(\varphi)$ where world$(t, u) = w$ then $\mathcal{M}', w \models \varphi$. $\square$

7.4.2 Transformation to Separated Normal Form (SNF$_{karo}$)

Formulae in the fusion of CTL and S5$_{(m)}$ can be rewritten into a normal form, called SNF$_{karo}$, that separates temporal and modal aspects (as is done in [10]). Formulae in SNF$_{karo}$ are of the general form

$$\mathbf{A}\square^* \bigwedge_i T_i$$

where each T_i is known as a *clause* and must be one of the following forms and $\mathbf{A}\square^*$ is the universal relation (which can be defined in terms of the operators 'everyone knows' and 'common knowledge'). For the purposes of the normal form we introduce a symbol start such that $\langle M, (t_0, 0)\rangle \models$ start for any timeline t_0 extracted from the distinguished tree r_0.

$$\text{start} \rightarrow \bigvee_{k=1}^n L_k \qquad \qquad (\textit{initial} \text{ clauses})$$

$$\bigwedge_{j=1}^m L'_j \rightarrow \mathbf{A}\bigcirc \bigvee_{k=1}^n L_k \qquad \qquad (\textit{allpath step} \text{ clauses})$$

$$\bigwedge_{j=1}^m L'_j \rightarrow \mathbf{E}\bigcirc (\bigvee_{k=1}^n L_k)_{\langle c_i \rangle} \qquad (\textit{somepath step} \text{ clauses})$$

$$\bigwedge_{j=1}^m L'_j \rightarrow \mathbf{A}\Diamond L \qquad \qquad (\textit{allpath sometime} \text{ clauses})$$

$$\bigwedge_{j=1}^m L'_j \rightarrow \mathbf{E}\Diamond L_{\langle c_i \rangle} \qquad \qquad (\textit{somepaths sometime} \text{ clauses})$$

$$\text{true} \rightarrow \bigvee_{k=1}^n M_k^i \qquad \qquad (\mathbf{K}_i \text{ clauses})$$

$$\text{true} \rightarrow \bigvee_{k=1}^n L_k \qquad \qquad (\text{literal clauses})$$

where L'_j, L_k, and L are literals and M_k^i are either literals, or modal literals involving the modal operator $\mathbf{K}_i$. Further, each $\mathbf{K}_i$ clause has at least one disjunct that is a modal literal. $\mathbf{K}_i$ clauses are sometimes known as *knowledge clauses*. Each step and sometime clause that involves the $\mathbf{E}$-operator is labelled by an index of the form $\langle c_i \rangle$ similar to the use of Skolem constants in first-order logic. This index indicates a particular path and arises from the translation of formulae such as $\mathbf{E}(L\mathcal{U}L')$. During the translation to the normal form such formulae are translated into several $\mathbf{E}$ step clauses and an $\mathbf{E}$ sometime clause (which ensures that L' must actually hold). To indicate that all these clauses refer to the same path they are annotated with an index. The outer '$\mathbf{A}\square^*$' operator that surrounds the conjunction of clauses is usually omitted. Similarly, for convenience the conjunction is dropped and we consider just the set of clauses T_i. We denote the transformation of formulae in $\mathsf{CTL} \oplus \mathsf{S5}_{(m)}$ into SNF_{karo} by SNF.

Theorem 8. *Let φ be a formula in $\mathsf{CTL} \oplus \mathsf{S5}_{(m)}$. Then,*

1. φ is satisfiable iff $\mathrm{SNF}(\varphi)$ is satisfiable.
2. $\mathrm{SNF}(\varphi)$ can be computed in polynomial time.

Proof [Sketch]. The proof proceeds along the lines of the corresponding proofs in [10, 15]. Given a formula φ in $\mathsf{CTL} \oplus \mathsf{S5}_{(m)}$ we show that any model M of φ can be transformed into a model M' of $\mathrm{SNF}(\varphi)$ and vice versa. $\square$

7.4.3 A Resolution Calculus for SNF_{karo}

In the following we present a resolution-based calculus for SNF_{karo}. In contrast to the translation approach described in the previous section, this calculus works directly on SNF_{karo} formulae. The inference rules are divided into initial resolution rules, knowledge resolution rules, step resolution rules, and temporal resolution rules, which will be described in the following:

If L is a literal, then $\sim L$ denotes A if $L = \neg A$ and it denotes $\neg L$, otherwise. A literal clause may be resolved with an initial clause (IRES1) or two initial clauses may be resolved together (IRES2) as follows, where C and D are disjunctions of literals.

$$\textbf{IRES1:} \quad \frac{\begin{array}{l}\textbf{true} \rightarrow (C \vee L) \\ \textbf{start} \rightarrow (D \vee \sim L)\end{array}}{\textbf{start} \rightarrow (C \vee D)} \qquad \textbf{IRES2:} \quad \frac{\begin{array}{l}\textbf{start} \rightarrow (C \vee L) \\ \textbf{start} \rightarrow (D \vee \sim L)\end{array}}{\textbf{start} \rightarrow (C \vee D)}$$

During knowledge resolution we apply the following rules which are based on the modal resolution system introduced by Mints [32]. In general we may only apply a (knowledge) resolution rule between two literal clauses, a knowledge and a literal clause, or between two knowledge clauses relating to the same modal operator, e.g., two $\mathbf{K}_1$ clauses.

$$\textbf{KRES1:} \quad \frac{\begin{array}{l}\textbf{true} \rightarrow C \vee M \\ \textbf{true} \rightarrow D \vee \sim M\end{array}}{\textbf{true} \rightarrow C \vee D} \qquad \textbf{KRES2:} \quad \frac{\begin{array}{l}\textbf{true} \rightarrow C \vee \mathbf{K}_i L \\ \textbf{true} \rightarrow D \vee \mathbf{K}_i \sim L\end{array}}{\textbf{true} \rightarrow C \vee D}$$

$$\textbf{KRES3:} \quad \frac{\begin{array}{l}\textbf{true} \rightarrow C \vee \mathbf{K}_i L \\ \textbf{true} \rightarrow D \vee \sim L\end{array}}{\textbf{true} \rightarrow C \vee D} \qquad \textbf{KRES4:} \quad \frac{\begin{array}{l}\textbf{true} \rightarrow C \vee \neg \mathbf{K}_i L \\ \textbf{true} \rightarrow D \vee L\end{array}}{\textbf{true} \rightarrow C \vee \mathrm{mod}(D)}$$

The function $\mathrm{mod}(D)$ used in KRES4 is defined on disjunctions D of literals or modal literals, as follows.

$$\begin{aligned}\mathrm{mod}(A \vee B) &= \mathrm{mod}(A) \vee \mathrm{mod}(B) \\ \mathrm{mod}(\mathbf{K}_i L) &= \mathbf{K}_i L \\ \mathrm{mod}(\neg \mathbf{K}_i L) &= \neg \mathbf{K}_i L \\ \mathrm{mod}(L) &= \neg \mathbf{K}_i \sim L\end{aligned}$$

The last resolution rule requires explanation. Take KRES4 and distribute in the external $\mathbf{K}_i$ operator from the surrounding $\mathrm{A}\square^*$ operator into the second premise obtaining $\textbf{true} \rightarrow \neg \mathbf{K}_i \neg D \vee \mathbf{K}_i L$ where D is a disjunction of literals or modal literals. Since, in S5, from axioms 4, 5 and D we have

$$\begin{aligned}&\vdash \quad \neg \mathbf{K}_i \mathbf{K}_i \varphi \Leftrightarrow \neg \mathbf{K}_i \varphi \\ &\vdash \neg \mathbf{K}_i \neg \mathbf{K}_i \neg \varphi \Leftrightarrow \mathbf{K}_i \neg \varphi.\end{aligned}$$

so we can delete $\neg \mathbf{K}_i \neg$ from any of the disjuncts in D that are modal literals and obtain the required resolvent.

Finally, we require the following rewrite rule to allow us to obtain the most comprehensive set of literal clauses for use during step and temporal resolution

$$\textbf{KRES5:} \quad \frac{\textbf{true} \rightarrow D \vee \mathbf{K}_i L_1 \vee \mathbf{K}_i L_2 \vee \ldots}{\textbf{true} \rightarrow D \vee L_1 \vee L_2 \vee \ldots}$$

where D is a disjunction of literals.

'Step' resolution consists of the application of standard classical resolution to formulae representing constraints at a particular moment in time, together with simplification rules for transferring contradictions within states to constraints on previous states.

Pairs of step clauses may be resolved using the (step resolution) rules SRES1, SRES2, and SRES3.

SRES1:
$$\frac{\begin{array}{l} P \to \mathbf{A}\bigcirc(F \vee L) \\ Q \to \mathbf{A}\bigcirc(G \vee {\sim}L) \end{array}}{(P \wedge Q) \to \mathbf{A}\bigcirc(F \vee G)}$$

SRES2:
$$\frac{\begin{array}{l} P \to \mathbf{E}\bigcirc(F \vee L)_{\langle c_i \rangle} \\ Q \to \mathbf{A}\bigcirc(G \vee {\sim}L) \end{array}}{(P \wedge Q) \to \mathbf{E}\bigcirc(F \vee G)_{\langle c_i \rangle}}$$

SRES3:
$$\frac{\begin{array}{l} P \to \mathbf{E}\bigcirc(F \vee L)_{\langle c_i \rangle} \\ Q \to \mathbf{E}\bigcirc(G \vee {\sim}L)_{\langle c_i \rangle} \end{array}}{(P \wedge Q) \to \mathbf{E}\bigcirc(F \vee G)_{\langle c_i \rangle}}$$

A step clause may be resolved with a literal clause (where G is a disjunction of literals) and any index is carried to the resolvent to give resolution rules SRES4 and SRES5.

SRES4:
$$\frac{\begin{array}{l} P \to \mathbf{A}\bigcirc(F \vee L) \\ \mathbf{true} \to (G \vee {\sim}L) \end{array}}{P \to \mathbf{A}\bigcirc(F \vee G)}$$

SRES5:
$$\frac{\begin{array}{l} P \to \mathbf{E}\bigcirc(F \vee L)_{\langle c_i \rangle} \\ \mathbf{true} \to (G \vee {\sim}L) \end{array}}{P \to \mathbf{E}\bigcirc(F \vee G)_{\langle c_i \rangle}}$$

Once a contradiction within a state is found, the following rule can be used to generate extra global constraints.

SRES6:
$$\frac{Q \to \mathbf{P}\bigcirc\mathbf{false}}{\mathbf{true} \to {\sim}Q}$$

where $\mathbf{P}$ is either path operator. This rule states that if, by satisfying Q in the last moment in time a contradiction is produced, then P must never be satisfied in *any* moment in time. The new constraint therefore represents $\mathbf{A}\square^*{\sim}Q$.

During temporal resolution the aim is to resolve one of the sometime clauses, $Q \Rightarrow \mathbf{P}\Diamond L$, with a set of clauses that together imply $\square{\sim}L$ along the same path, for example a set of clauses that together have the effect of $F \to \bigcirc\square{\sim}L$. However the interaction between the '$\bigcirc$' and '$\square$' operators makes the definition of such a rule non-trivial and further the translation to SNF$_{karo}$ will have removed all but the outer level of $\square$-operators. So, resolution will be between a sometime clause and a *set* of clauses that together imply an $\square$-formula that occurs on the same path, which will contradict the $\Diamond$-clause.

TRES1:
$$\frac{\begin{array}{l} P \to \mathbf{A}\bigcirc\mathbf{A}\square L \\ Q \to \mathbf{A}\Diamond{\sim}L \end{array}}{Q \to \mathbf{A}({\sim}P\mathcal{W}{\sim}L)}$$

TRES2:
$$\frac{\begin{array}{l} P \to \mathbf{A}\bigcirc\mathbf{A}\square L \\ Q \to \mathbf{E}\Diamond{\sim}L_{\langle c_i \rangle} \end{array}}{Q \to \mathbf{E}({\sim}P\mathcal{W}{\sim}L)_{\langle c_i \rangle}}$$

TRES3:
$$\frac{\begin{array}{l} P \to \mathbf{E}\bigcirc\mathbf{E}\square L_{\langle c_i \rangle} \\ Q \to \mathbf{A}\Diamond{\sim}L \end{array}}{Q \to \mathbf{A}({\sim}P\mathcal{W}{\sim}L)}$$

TRES4:
$$\frac{\begin{array}{l} P \to \mathbf{E}\bigcirc\mathbf{E}\square L_{\langle c_i \rangle} \\ Q \to \mathbf{E}\Diamond{\sim}L_{\langle c_i \rangle} \end{array}}{Q \to \mathbf{E}({\sim}P\mathcal{W}{\sim}L)_{\langle c_i \rangle}}$$

In each case, the resolvent ensures that once Q has been satisfied, meaning that the eventuality $\diamond\sim L$ must be satisfied on some or all paths, the conditions for triggering a $\square$-formula are not allowed to occur, that is, P must be false, until the eventuality $(\sim L)$ has been satisfied. It may be surprising that resolving a A-formula with a E-formula in TRES3 results in a A-formula. This is because the eventuality $\sim L$ must appear on *all* paths so similarly the resolvent will also hold on all paths

Given a set N of SNF$_{karo}$ clauses to be tested for satisfiability, the following steps are performed:

1. Perform initial, knowledge and step resolution (including simplification and subsumption) on N until either
   (a) false is derived: Terminate noting that N is unsatisfiable; or
   (b) no new resolvents are generated: Continue to step (2).
2. Select an eventuality from the right-hand side of a sometime clause within N. Search for a set of clauses with which one of the temporal resolution rules can be applied.
3. If the resolvent is new (i.e., is not subsumed by previously detected resolvents) translate into SNF$_{karo}$ and go to step (1). Otherwise if no new resolvents have been found for any eventuality, terminate declaring N satisfiable, else go to step (2).

Simplification and subsumption are also carried out during a derivation.

Theorem 9. *Let N be a set of SNF$_{karo}$ clauses. Then,*

1. any derivation from N terminates; and
2. N is unsatisfiable iff N has a refutation by the temporal resolution procedure described above.

Proof [Sketch]. The proof proceeds along the lines of the corresponding proofs in [10, 9, 15]. A graph is constructed representing the set of SNF$_{karo}$ clauses. Deletions of portions of the graph from which models cannot be constructed are shown to correspond to resolution rules. An empty graph is obtained if and only if the set of clauses is unsatisfiable. $\square$

7.4.4 A Decision Procedure for Core KARO Logic

We can now put the four components of our second decision procedure for core KARO logic together. Given a formulae φ in the core KARO logic, we proceed by normalizing φ using the rules in Table 7.2, translate the result into the fusion of CTL and S5$_{(m)}$, transforming the resulting formula to SNF$_{karo}$, and finally applying the temporal resolution procedure for SNF$_{karo}$ to the set of SNF$_{karo}$ clauses we obtain.

Theorem 10 (Soundness, completeness, and termination). *Let φ be a formula of the core KARO logic and let $N = \mathrm{SNF}(\tau(\varphi\downarrow))$. Then,*

1. any derivation from N terminates; and

2. φ is unsatisfiable iff N has a refutation by the temporal resolution procedure described above.

*Proof F.*ollows from Lemma 1 and Theorems 7, 8, and 9.   □

7.5 Eve in a Blocks World

In this section, we look at a small example. We specify a blocks world problem in KARO logic and show how the two approaches described in Sections 7.3 and 7.4 can be used to solve the problem. To make the example more interesting, the specification makes use of the implementability operator which has been excluded from the core KARO logic. To deal with implementability in the translation approach, we extend the translation morphism π by $\pi(\Diamond_i\varphi, x) = \exists y . \pi(\varphi, y)$, while in the SNF approach we extend the translation morphism τ by $\tau(\Diamond_i\varphi) = \mathbf{E}\Diamond\tau(\varphi)$. We will discuss the appropriateness of both definitions in the following section.

Consider two agents, Adam and Eve, living in a blocks world containing four blocks a, b, c, and d. We use is_on(X,Y), is_clear(X), on_floor(X) to describe that a block Y is on top of a block X, that no block is on top of X, and that X is on the floor, respectively. We allow only one atomic action: put(X,Y), which has the effect of Y being placed on X. Eve has the ability of performing a put(X,Y) action if and only if X and Y are clear, Y is not identical to X, and Y is not equal to c (axiom (A_1)). The axiom (E_1) describes the effects of performing a put action: After any action put(X,Y) the block Y is on X and X is no longer clear. The axioms (N_1) to (N_4) describe properties of the blocks world which remain unchanged by performing an action. For example, if block Z is clear and not equal to some block X, then putting some arbitrary block Y (possibly identical to Z) on X leaves Z clear (axiom (N_1)). Additionally, the axioms themselves remain true irrespective of the actions which are performed.

(A_1) $\mathbf{A}_E$put$(X,Y) \equiv ($is_clear$(X) \wedge$ is_clear$(Y) \wedge X \neq Y \wedge Y \neq c)$

(E_1) $[$do$_i($put$(X,Y))]($is_on$(X,Y) \wedge \neg$is_clear$(X))$

(N_1) $($is_clear$(Z) \wedge Z \neq X) \rightarrow [do_i(put(X,Y))](is_clear(Z))$

(N_2) $($is_on$(V,Z) \wedge Z \neq Y) \rightarrow [do_i(put(X,Y)))](is_on(V,Z))$

(N_3) $(X = Y) \wedge (U \neq V) \rightarrow [do_i(\alpha)](X = Y \wedge U \neq V)$

(N_4) $($on_floor$(Z) \wedge Z \neq Y) \rightarrow [do_i(put(X,Y))]on_floor(Z)$

In the axioms above i is an element of $\{A, E\}$ where A and E denote Adam and Eve. Recall that in the core KARO logic we identify $\mathbf{A}_i\alpha$ with $\langle$do$_i(\alpha)\rangle\top$. Consequently, the axiom (A_1) becomes

(A_1') $\langle$do$_E($put$(X,Y))\rangle\top \equiv (is_clear(X) \wedge$ is_clear$(Y) \wedge X \neq Y \wedge Y \neq c)$

A tower is defined as follows:

(C_1) $\text{tower}(X_1, X_2, X_3, X_4) \equiv \bigwedge_{i \neq j}(X_i \neq X_j) \wedge \text{on\_floor}(X_1)$
$\wedge \text{ is\_on}(X_1, X_2) \wedge \text{is\_on}(X_2, X_3)$
$\wedge \text{ is\_on}(X_3, X_4) \wedge \text{is\_clear}(X_4)$

We are given the initial conditions

(I) $\mathbf{K}_E \text{is\_on}(a, b) \wedge \mathbf{K}_E \text{is\_clear}(b) \wedge \mathbf{K}_E \text{is\_clear}(c)$
$\wedge \mathbf{K}_E \text{is\_clear}(d) \wedge \mathbf{K}_E \text{on\_floor}(a)$

In the following we will prove that the axioms (A_1) to (C_1) together with (I) imply that if Eve knows that Adam puts block c on block b, then she knows that she can implement the tower (a, b, c, d), that is, we show that the assumption

(K_1) $\mathbf{K}_E \langle \text{do}_A(\text{put}(b, c)) \rangle \top \wedge \neg \mathbf{K}_E \Diamond_E \text{tower}(a, b, c, d)$

leads to a contradiction.

Although the problem is presented in a first order setting, as we have a finite domain we can easily form all ground instances of the axioms in our specification. Thus, in the following, an expression 'is_on(a, b)' denotes a propositional variable uniquely associated with the atom is_on(a, b) in our specification. Due to axiom (N_3) which states that equality and inequality of blocks remains unaffected by Eve's actions, we can eliminate all equations from the instantiated axioms.

7.5.1 Solving the Eve Example by Translation

We will first show how we obtain a refutation for the specification of Eve's blocks world using the translation approach. Let ψ be the conjunction of the axioms (A_1) to (C_1), (I), and (K_1). Then $\text{CL}_{\text{DL}^*}(\Pi(\psi))$ contains amongst others the following clauses which will be used in our refutation. The axioms from which a particular clause originates are indicated in square brackets to the left of the clause. Recall that $\pi(p, x) = Q_p(x)$ where Q_p is a unary predicate symbol uniquely associated with the propositional variable p. To simplify our notation we will write 'is_on(a, b, x)' instead of '$Q_{\text{is\_on}(a,b)}(x)$'. Note that the translation of the axiom (A'_1) and the left conjunction of (K_1) contain existential quantifiers which lead to the introduction of Skolem functions during the transformation to clausal normal form. Consequently, the clauses (1) and (17) contain unary Skolem functions g_b^c and g_c^d, respectively. These Skolem functions are associated with particular actions, namely, put(b, c) and put(c, d), respectively. In addition, the Skolem constant ϵ is introduced by Π itself.

$[A_1']$	(1)	$\neg\text{is\_clear}(c,y) \vee \neg\text{is\_clear}(d,y) \vee R_{(E,\text{put}(c,d))}(x,g_c^d(x))_*$
$[E_1]$	(2)	$\neg R_{(A,\text{put}(b,c))}(x,y)_* \vee \text{is\_on}(b,c,y)$
$[E_1]$	(3)	$\neg R_{(E,\text{put}(c,d))}(x,y)_* \vee \text{is\_on}(c,d,y)$
$[N_1]$	(4)	$\neg\text{is\_clear}(c,x) \vee \neg R_{(A,\text{put}(b,c))}(x,y)_* \vee \text{is\_clear}(c,y)$
$[N_1]$	(5)	$\neg\text{is\_clear}(d,x) \vee \neg R_{(A,\text{put}(b,c))}(x,y)_* \vee \text{is\_clear}(d,y)$
$[N_1]$	(6)	$\neg\text{is\_clear}(d,x) \vee \neg R_{(E,\text{put}(c,d))}(x,y)_* \vee \text{is\_clear}(d,y)$
$[N_2]$	(7)	$\neg\text{is\_on}(a,b,x) \vee \neg R_{(A,\text{put}(b,c))}(x,y)_* \vee \text{is\_on}(a,b,y)$
$[N_2]$	(8)	$\neg\text{is\_on}(a,b,x) \vee \neg R_{(E,\text{put}(c,d))}(x,y)_* \vee \text{is\_on}(a,b,y)$
$[N_2]$	(9)	$\neg\text{is\_on}(b,c,x) \vee \neg R_{(E,\text{put}(c,d))}(x,y)_* \vee \text{is\_on}(b,c,y)$
$[N_4]$	(10)	$\neg\text{on\_floor}(a,x) \vee \neg R_{(A,\text{put}(b,c))}(x,y)_* \vee \text{on\_floor}(a,y)$
$[N_4]$	(11)	$\neg\text{on\_floor}(a,x) \vee \neg R_{(E,\text{put}(c,d))}(x,y)_* \vee \text{on\_floor}(a,y)$
$[C_1]$	(12)	$\neg\text{on\_floor}(a,y) \vee \neg\text{is\_on}(a,b,y) \vee \neg\text{is\_on}(b,c,y)$
		$\vee \neg\text{is\_on}(c,d,y) \vee \neg\text{is\_clear}(d,y) \vee \text{tower}(a,b,c,d,y)_*$
$[K_1]$	(13)	$Q_{\mathbf{K}_E\langle\text{do}_E(\text{put}(b,c))\rangle\top}(\epsilon)$
$[K_1]$	(14)	$\neg Q_{\mathbf{K}_E\text{tower}(a,b,c,d)}(\epsilon)$
$[K_1]$	(15)	$Q_{\mathbf{K}_E\text{tower}(a,b,c,d)}(x) \vee R_{(E,\mathbf{K})}(x,h_{\mathbf{K}_E}(x))_*$
$[K_1]$	(16)	$Q_{\mathbf{K}_E\text{tower}(a,b,c,d)}(x) \vee \neg\text{tower}(a,b,c,d,y)_*$
$[\text{Ax}]$	(17)	$\neg Q_{\mathbf{K}_E\langle\text{do}_E(\text{put}(b,c))\rangle\top}(x) \vee \neg R_{(E,\mathbf{K})}(x,y)_* \vee Q_{\langle\text{do}_E(\text{put}(b,c))\rangle\top}(y)$
$[\text{Ax}]$	(18)	$\neg Q_{\langle\text{do}_E(\text{put}(b,c))\rangle\top}(x) \vee R_{(A,\text{put}(b,c))}(x,g_b^c(x))_*$
$[\text{Ax}]$	(19)	$\neg Q_{\mathbf{K}_E\text{is\_on}(a,b)}(x) \vee \neg R_{(E,\mathbf{K})}(x,y)_* \vee \text{is\_on}(a,b,y)$
$[\text{Ax}]$	(20)	$\neg Q_{\mathbf{K}_E\text{is\_clear}(b)}(x) \vee \neg R_{(E,\mathbf{K})}(x,y)_* \vee \text{is\_clear}(b,y)$
$[\text{Ax}]$	(21)	$\neg Q_{\mathbf{K}_E\text{is\_clear}(c)}(x) \vee \neg R_{(E,\mathbf{K})}(x,y)_* \vee \text{is\_clear}(c,y)$
$[\text{Ax}]$	(22)	$\neg Q_{\mathbf{K}_E\text{is\_clear}(d)}(x) \vee \neg R_{(E,\mathbf{K})}(x,y)_* \vee \text{is\_clear}(d,y)$
$[\text{Ax}]$	(23)	$\neg Q_{\mathbf{K}_E\text{on\_floor}(a)}(x) \vee \neg R_{(E,\mathbf{K})}(x,y)_* \vee \text{on\_floor}(a,y)$
$[I]$	(24)	$Q_{\mathbf{K}_E\text{is\_on}(a,b)}(\epsilon)$
$[I]$	(25)	$Q_{\mathbf{K}_E\text{is\_clear}(b)}(\epsilon)$
$[I]$	(26)	$Q_{\mathbf{K}_E\text{is\_clear}(c)}(\epsilon)$
$[I]$	(27)	$Q_{\mathbf{K}_E\text{is\_clear}(d)}(\epsilon)$
$[I]$	(28)	$Q_{\mathbf{K}_E\text{on\_floor}(a)}(\epsilon)$

We have obtained the refutation of $\text{CL}_{\text{DL}^*}(\Pi(\psi))$ by using the first-order theorem prover SPASS 1.0.0 [44] which implements the resolution framework of [2]. As an ordering we used a recursive path ordering. Since any recursive path ordering is compatible with the strict subterm ordering, SPASS is a decision procedure by Theorem 5. In every nonunit clause we marked the maximal literal of the clause by an index $\cdot_*$. Thus, inference steps are restricted to these literals. Finding the refutation takes SPASS less than 0.01 seconds.

We observe that clause (16) consists of two variable-disjoint sub-clauses. This clause will be subject to splitting which introduces two branches into our search space: One on which $Q_{\mathbf{K}_E\text{tower}(a,b,c,d)}(x)$ is an element of the clause set and one on which $\neg\text{tower}(a,b,c,d,y)$ is an element of the clause set instead. For the first set of clauses we directly obtain a contradiction using clause (14). For the second set of clauses

$[16.2]$	(29)	$\neg\text{tower}(a,b,c,d,y)_*$

replaces clause (16). We see that among the clause (1) to (16), only (1), (12), (18), and (15) contain a positive literal which is maximal and can thus serve as positive premises in resolution steps. We can derive among others the following clauses:

[18.2, 2.1] (30) $\neg Q_{\langle do_E(put(b,c))\rangle\top}(x) \vee$ is_on$(b,c,g_b^c(x))_*$

[18.2, 4.2] (31) $\neg$is_clear$(c,x) \vee \neg Q_{\langle do_E(put(b,c))\rangle\top}(x) \vee$ is_clear$(c,g_b^c(x))_*$

[18.2, 5.2] (32) $\neg$is_clear$(d,x) \vee \neg Q_{\langle do_E(put(b,c))\rangle\top}(x) \vee$ is_clear$(d,g_b^c(x))_*$

[18.2, 7.2] (33) $\neg$is_on$(a,b,x) \vee \neg Q_{\langle do_E(put(b,c))\rangle\top}(x) \vee$ is_on$(a,b,g_b^c(x))_*$

[18.2,10.2] (34) $\neg$on_floor$(a,x) \vee \neg Q_{\langle do_E(put(b,c))\rangle\top}(x) \vee$ on_floor$(a,g_b^c(x))_*$

[1.3, 3.1] (35) $\neg$is_clear$(c,x) \vee \neg$is_clear$(d,x) \vee$ is_on$(c,d,g_c^d(x))_*$

[1.3, 6.2] (36) $\neg$is_clear$(c,x) \vee \neg$is_clear$(d,x) \vee$ is_clear$(d,g_c^d(x))_*$

[1.3, 8.2] (37) $\neg$is_clear$(c,x) \vee \neg$is_clear(d,x)
$\vee \neg$is_on$(a,b,x) \vee$ is_on$(a,b,g_c^d(x))_*$

[1.3, 9.2] (38) $\neg$is_clear$(c,x) \vee \neg$is_clear(d,x)
$\vee \neg$is_on$(b,c,x) \vee$ is_on$(b,c,g_c^d(x))_*$

[1.3,11.2] (39) $\neg$is_clear$(c,x) \vee \neg$is_clear$(d,x) \vee \neg$on_floor(a,x)
$\vee$ on_floor$(a,g_c^d(x))_*$

[12.6,29.1] (40) $\neg$on_floor$(a,x) \vee \neg$is_clear$(d,x) \vee \neg$is_on(b,c,x)
$\vee \neg$is_on$(c,d,x) \vee \neg$is_on$(a,b,x)_*$

Intuitively, clause (40) says that there is no situation x in which the blocks a, b, c, and d form a tower. The remainder of the derivation shows that this assumption leads to a contradiction. We choose clause (37) to derive the following clause:

[37.4,40.2] (41) $\neg$is_clear$(d,x) \vee \neg$is_clear$(c,x) \vee \neg$is_on(a,b,x)
$\vee \neg$is_clear$(d,g_c^d(x)) \vee \neg$on_floor$(a,g_c^d(x))$
$\vee \neg$is_on$(c,d,g_c^d(x)) \vee \neg$is_on$(b,c,g_c^d(x))_*$

Note that in clause (41) all literals containing a Skolem term originate from the negative premise (40) while all the remaining literals originate from the positive premise (37). Intuitively, literals containing the Skolem term $g_c^d(x)$ impose constraints on the situation we are in after performing a put(c,d) action in a situation x, while the remaining literals which have x as their final argument impose constraints on situation x itself.

Since literals containing a Skolem term are deeper than the remaining literals, the ordering restrictions on the resolution inference rule restrict applications of resolution to these literals. In the following part of the derivation we consecutively eliminate these literals by resolution inferences with the clauses (35), (36), (38), and (39) and obtain

(42) $\neg$is_clear$(d,x) \vee \neg$is_clear$(c,x) \vee \neg$is_on$(a,b,x)_*$
$\vee \neg$on_floor$(a,x) \vee \neg$is_on(b,c,x)

Here again the literal $\neg$is_on(a,b,x) is maximal. This time we choose clause (33) which is related to a put(b,c) action as positive premise.

[33.4,42.3] (43) $\neg Q_{\langle do_E(put(b,c))\rangle\top}(x) \vee \neg$is_on$(a,b,x)$
$\vee \neg$is_clear$(d,g_b^c(x)) \vee \neg$is_clear$(c,g_b^c(x))$
$\vee \neg$on_floor$(a,g_b^c(x)) \vee \neg$is_on$(b,c,g_b^c(x))_*$

By inference steps with the clauses (30), (31), (32), and (34) we eliminate all literals containing Skolem terms and obtain

$$(44) \quad \neg Q_{\langle do_E(put(b,c))\rangle \top}(x) \vee \neg is\_on(a,b,x)_* \vee \neg is\_clear(d,x)$$
$$\vee \neg is\_clear(c,x) \vee \neg on\_floor(a,x)$$

Intuitively, this part of the derivation has established that in any situation x where clause (42) is false, it is possible to perform a $put(b,c)$ action which results in a situation x' where $is\_on(b,c,x')$ is true.

Using clause (15) we can derive the following clauses from (17), (19), (21), (22) and (23)

$$[15.2,17.2] \quad (45) \quad Q_{\mathbf{K}_E tower(a,b,c,d)}(x) \vee \neg Q_{\mathbf{K}_E \langle do_E(put(b,c))\rangle \top}(x)$$
$$\vee Q_{\langle do_E(put(b,c))\rangle \top}(h_{\mathbf{K}_E}(x))_*$$

$$[15.2,19.2] \quad (46) \quad Q_{\mathbf{K}_E tower(a,b,c,d)}(x) \vee \neg Q_{\mathbf{K}_E is\_on(a,b)}(x) \vee is\_on(a,b,h_{\mathbf{K}_E}(x))_*$$

$$[15.2,21.2] \quad (47) \quad Q_{\mathbf{K}_E tower(a,b,c,d)}(x) \vee \neg Q_{\mathbf{K}_E is\_clear(c)}(x) \vee is\_clear(c,h_{\mathbf{K}_E}(x))_*$$

$$[15.2,22.2] \quad (48) \quad Q_{\mathbf{K}_E tower(a,b,c,d)}(x) \vee \neg Q_{\mathbf{K}_E is\_clear(d)}(x) \vee is\_clear(d,h_{\mathbf{K}_E}(x))_*$$

$$[15.2,23.2] \quad (49) \quad Q_{\mathbf{K}_E tower(a,b,c,d)}(x) \vee \neg Q_{\mathbf{K}_E on\_floor(a)}(x) \vee on\_floor(a,h_{\mathbf{K}_E}(x))_*$$

which are then used to derive

$$(50) \quad \neg Q_{\mathbf{K}_E \langle do_E(put(b,c))\rangle \top}(x) \vee \neg Q_{\mathbf{K}_E is\_on(a,b)}(x) \vee \neg Q_{\mathbf{K}_E is\_clear(d)}(x)$$
$$\vee \neg Q_{\mathbf{K}_E is\_clear(c)}(x) \vee \neg Q_{\mathbf{K}_E on\_floor(a)}(x) \vee Q_{\mathbf{K}_E tower(a,b,c,d)}(x)$$

from clause (44). Using clauses (13) and (24) to (28) we derive from (50):

$$(51) \quad Q_{\mathbf{K}_E tower(a,b,c,d)}(\epsilon)$$

which contradicts clause (14). Thus, with a final inference step we derive the empty clause:

$$[14.1,51.1] \quad (52) \quad \square$$

7.5.2 Solving the Eve Example by Temporal Resolution

The specification of the problem can be written as formulae in the normal form as follows. For example (E_1) instantiated where $X = a$ and $Y = b$ can be written as the following two rules:

$$\mathbf{true} \rightarrow \mathbf{A}\bigcirc(\neg done_E^{put(a,b)} \vee is\_on(a,b))$$
$$\mathbf{true} \rightarrow \mathbf{A}\bigcirc(\neg done_E^{put(a,b)} \vee \neg is\_clear(a))$$

The conjunction of initial conditions is rewritten by a new proposition v and each conjunct, e.g. $\mathbf{K}_E is\_on(a,b)$ can be can be written as follows:

(I_0) $\qquad\qquad\qquad\qquad$ **start** $\rightarrow v$

(I_1) $\qquad\qquad\qquad\qquad$ **true** $\rightarrow \neg v \vee \mathbf{K}_E is\_on(a,b)$

and similarly with the conjuncts $\mathbf{K}_E is\_clear(b)$, $\mathbf{K}_E is\_clear(c)$, $\mathbf{K}_E is\_clear(d)$ and $\mathbf{K}_E on\_floor(a)$ (giving I_0–I_5). We try to prove

$$\mathbf{K}_E \langle \mathrm{do}_A(\mathrm{put}(b,c)) \rangle \top \rightarrow \mathbf{K}_E \Diamond_E \mathrm{tower}(a,b,c,d)$$

First, we translate as follows:

$$\mathbf{K}_E \mathbf{E} \bigcirc (\mathrm{done}_A^{\mathrm{put}(b,c)}) \rightarrow \mathbf{K}_E \mathbf{E} \Diamond \mathrm{tower}(a,b,c,d)$$

Next we must negate and look for a contradiction with the specification above, i.e.,

$$\mathbf{K}_E \mathbf{E} \bigcirc (\mathrm{done}_A^{\mathrm{put}(b,c)}) \wedge \neg \mathbf{K}_E \mathbf{E} \Diamond \mathrm{tower}(a,b,c,d).$$

Next we rewrite into the normal form introducing new variables w, x, y, z and replacing $\mathrm{tower}(a,b,c,d)$ with its definition.

(G_1)	$\mathbf{start} \rightarrow w$	
(G_2)	$\mathbf{true} \rightarrow \neg w \vee \mathbf{K}_E y$	
(G_3)	$y \rightarrow \mathbf{E} \bigcirc (\mathrm{done}_A^{\mathrm{put}(b,c)})$	
(G_4)	$\mathbf{true} \rightarrow \neg w \vee \neg \mathbf{K}_E \neg z$	
(G_5)	$\mathbf{true} \rightarrow \neg z \vee x$	
(G_6)	$x \rightarrow \mathbf{A} \bigcirc x$	
(G_7)	$\mathbf{true} \rightarrow \neg x \vee \neg \mathrm{on\_floor}(a) \vee \neg \mathrm{is\_on}(a,b) \vee \neg \mathrm{is\_on}(b,c)$	
	$\vee \neg \mathrm{is\_on}(c,d) \vee \neg \mathrm{is\_clear}(d)$	

First, we apply the rules SRES1, SRES2 and SRES4 to (G_6), (G_7), and the instantiations of (N_1), (N_2), (N_4), (E_1), and (A_1) given below

(N_1)	$\mathrm{is\_clear}(d) \rightarrow \mathbf{A} \bigcirc (\neg \mathrm{done}_E^{\mathrm{put}(c,d)} \vee \mathrm{is\_clear}(d))$
(N_2)	$\mathrm{is\_on}(a,b) \rightarrow \mathbf{A} \bigcirc (\neg \mathrm{done}_E^{\mathrm{put}(c,d)} \vee \mathrm{is\_on}(a,b))$
(N_2)	$\mathrm{is\_on}(b,c) \rightarrow \mathbf{A} \bigcirc (\neg \mathrm{done}_E^{\mathrm{put}(c,d)} \vee \mathrm{is\_on}(b,c))$
(N_4)	$\mathrm{on\_floor}(a) \rightarrow \mathbf{A} \bigcirc (\neg \mathrm{done}_E^{\mathrm{put}(c,d)} \vee \mathrm{on\_floor}(a))$
(E_1)	$\mathbf{true} \rightarrow \mathbf{A} \bigcirc (\neg \mathrm{done}_E^{\mathrm{put}(c,d)} \vee \mathrm{is\_on}(c,d))$
(A_1)	$\mathrm{is\_clear}(c) \wedge \mathrm{is\_clear}(d) \rightarrow \mathbf{E} \bigcirc \mathrm{done}_E^{\mathrm{put}(c,d)}{}_{\langle c_1 \rangle}$

obtaining

$$x \wedge \mathrm{is\_clear}(d) \wedge \mathrm{is\_on}(a,b) \wedge \mathrm{is\_on}(b,c) \wedge \mathrm{on\_floor}(a) \wedge \mathrm{is\_clear}(c)$$
$$\rightarrow \mathbf{E} \bigcirc \mathbf{false}_{\langle c_1 \rangle}.$$

An application of SRES6 to this step clause results in

(G_8)	$\mathbf{true} \rightarrow \neg x \vee \neg \mathrm{is\_clear}(d) \vee \neg \mathrm{is\_on}(a,b) \vee \neg \mathrm{is\_on}(b,c)$
	$\vee \neg \mathrm{on\_floor}(a) \vee \neg \mathrm{is\_clear}(c)$

Next we again apply the rules SRES1, SRES2, and SRES4 to (G_6), (G_8), and instantiations of (N_1), (N_2), (N_4), (E_1), and (G_3) obtaining the following

$$\mathrm{is\_clear}(c) \wedge \mathrm{is\_clear}(d) \wedge \mathrm{is\_on}(a,b) \wedge \mathrm{on\_floor}(a) \wedge x \wedge y \rightarrow \mathbf{E} \bigcirc \mathbf{false}_{\langle c_2 \rangle}.$$

With an application of SRES6 to this clause we obtain

(G_9) **true** $\rightarrow \neg x \lor \neg y \lor \neg \text{is\_clear}(c) \lor \neg \text{is\_clear}(d)$
$$\lor \neg \text{is\_on}(a,b) \lor \neg \text{on\_floor}(a)$$

Resolving (G_9) with (G_5) using KRES1 and then with (G_4) using KRES4 we obtain

(G_{10}) **true** $\rightarrow \neg z \lor \neg \mathbf{K}_E y \lor \neg \mathbf{K}_E \text{is\_clear}(c) \lor \neg \mathbf{K}_E \text{is\_clear}(d)$
$$\lor \neg \mathbf{K}_E \text{is\_on}(a,b) \lor \neg \mathbf{K}_E \text{on\_floor}(a)$$

which can be resolved with the initial conditions (I_1), (I_3), (I_4), (I_5), and (G_2) using KRES1 to obtain

(G_{11}) **true** $\rightarrow \neg w \lor \neg v.$

Finally resolving (G_{11}) with (I_0) and (G_1) using IRES1 and IRES2 the contradiction

$$\text{start} \rightarrow \textbf{false}$$

is obtained.

7.6 Beyond the Core KARO Logic

In Sections 7.3 and 7.4, we have presented two methods for modal reasoning in a restricted core of the KARO logic. We will now consider whether and how each method can be extended to cover a larger fragment of the KARO logic, and then indicate how KARO can be put to work in more complex environments than the blocks world.

In the full framework, $\mathbf{O}_i \alpha$ and $\mathbf{A}_i \alpha$ are not the same. There $\mathbf{O}_i \alpha = \langle \text{do}_i(\alpha) \rangle \top$, and $\mathbf{A}_i \alpha$ is defined as in Section 7.2. Consequently, we can extend the normalization function defined by the rewrite rules in Table 7.2 to reduce any formula φ with occurrences of $\mathbf{O}_i \alpha$, $\mathbf{A}_i \alpha$, or $[\text{do}_i(\alpha)]\psi$ where α is a nonatomic action formula to a formula $\varphi \!\downarrow$ which is logically equivalent to φ and in the absence of the unbounded repetition operator $\varphi \!\downarrow$ contains no nonatomic action formulae.

In the translation approach, the translation function π has to be modified such that $\pi(\mathbf{A}_i a, x) = c_i^a(x)$ where a is an atomic action, and c_i^a represents the relation $c_{(i,a)}$ in our semantics. In the clausal temporal resolution approach $\mathbf{A}_i \alpha$ is simply represented by propositional variables c_i^α uniquely associated with i and α. It seems an alternative for both approaches that would incorporate also a commitment operator could exploit the ideas of [41, 42].

We have also excluded wishes in our presentation. In the full KARO framework, $\mathbf{W}_i^s$ is a KD modality. The incorporation of wishes into the translation approach presents no difficulties. The translation function π is extended by $\pi(\mathbf{W}_i^s \varphi, x) = \forall y . R_{(i,\mathbf{W})}(x,y) \rightarrow \pi(\varphi, y)$, where $R_{(i,\mathbf{W})}$ is a binary predicate symbol uniquely associated with the modal operator $\mathbf{W}_i^s$, and $\Pi(\psi)$ contains additional conjuncts $\forall x \, \exists y \, R_{(i,\mathbf{W})}(x,y)$ for every agent i, ensuring that the binary relations $R_{(i,\mathbf{W})}$ are serial. For the clausal temporal resolution approach the addition of wishes to the core of KARO requires (i) an extension of the normal form which allows for clauses for the wishes of each agent, and (ii) additional sound and complete resolution rules for the KD modalities $\mathbf{W}_i^s$.

The implementability operator $\Diamond_i$ excluded from core KARO logic is one of the most interesting operators of KARO logic. Recall that the semantics of $\Diamond_i$ is defined by

$$\mathcal{M}, w \models \Diamond_i \varphi \text{ iff } \exists k \in \mathbb{N} \, \exists a_1, \ldots, a_k \in \mathsf{Ac_{at}}.$$
$$\mathcal{M}, w \models \mathbf{PracPoss}_i(a_1; \ldots; a_k, \varphi)$$

where $\mathbf{PracPoss}_i(\alpha, \varphi)$ is an abbreviation for $\langle \mathrm{do}_i(\alpha) \rangle \varphi \wedge \mathbf{A}_i \alpha$. So, $\Diamond_i \varphi$ holds if we can find atomic actions $a_1, \ldots, a_k$ such that agent i is able to perform the sequence $a_1; \ldots; a_k$ and performing this sequence possibly leads to a situation in which φ is true. Intuitively, proving $\Diamond_i \varphi$ requires that we find a *plan* which might bring about a situation in which φ is true. In other words, the intention for including the implementability operator into KARO logic is to internalize the *planning problem* in the logic.

However, it turns out that this intuition is slightly misleading. To give a precise analysis of the implementability operator, let us add modal operators $\forall$ and $\exists$ to our language with the following semantics.

$$\mathcal{M}, w \models \forall \varphi \text{ iff } \forall v \in W. \, \mathcal{M}, v \models \varphi$$
$$\mathcal{M}, w \models \exists \varphi \text{ iff } \exists v \in W. \, \mathcal{M}, v \models \varphi$$

The modal operator $\forall$ is the *universal modality* while $\exists$ is the *dual universal modality*.

Furthermore, if $\varphi[\psi_1]$ is a formula containing a subformula occurrences of ψ_1, then by $\varphi[\psi_1']$ we denote the formula obtained by replacing in φ the subformula occurrences of ψ_1 by the formulae ψ_1'.

Lemma 3 *1. Let $\varphi[\Diamond_i \psi]$ be a formula of KARO logic with a positive subformula occurrence of $\Diamond_i \psi$ and no negative subformula occurrences of the form $\Diamond_j \vartheta$. Then $\varphi[\Diamond_i \psi]$ is satisfiable iff $\varphi[\exists \psi]$ is satisfiable.*
2. Let $\varphi[\Diamond_i \vartheta]$ be a formula of KARO logic with a negative subformula occurrence of $\Diamond_i \vartheta$. Then the unsatisfiability of $\varphi[\Diamond_i \vartheta]$ implies the unsatisfiability of $\varphi[\exists \vartheta]$, but not vice versa.

Proof [Sketch]. This lemma follows from the fact that the existential quantification over atomic actions in the semantical definition of $\Diamond_i$ is not restricted to atomic actions occurring in φ. Instead it refers to the infinite supply of atomic actions in $\mathsf{Ac_{at}}$. $\qquad\qquad\square$

Thus, positive occurrences of $\Diamond_i$ give little indication of the existence of a plan. The mapping of $\Diamond_i \varphi$ to $\exists y \, \pi(\varphi, y)$ by the translation morphism π as defined in Section 7.5 is only correct for positive occurrences of $\Diamond_i \varphi$, but not for negative occurrences. There is no straightforward way to translate negative occurrences of $\Diamond_i$ that correctly reflects its semantics.

Although the language of SNF_{karo} contains with $\mathbf{A}\square^*$ a combination of operators corresponding to the master modality, $\mathbf{A}\square^*$ can only occur at one particular position, that is, surrounding a conjunction of clauses. For positive occurrences of $\Diamond_i$ we can show that $\mathbf{E}\Diamond\tau(\varphi)$ is a correct translation of $\Diamond_i\varphi$ by extending the model transformation sketched in the proof of Theorem 7. Again, there is no straightforward way to translate negative occurrences of $\Diamond_i$.

However, it is clear that the current semantical definition of $\Diamond_i$ fails to correspond to our intuitive understanding of implementability.

A more accurate semantical definition restricts the choice of atomic actions $a_1, \ldots, a_k$, which an agent i performs to bring about a situation where φ holds, to a particular finite set of actions, for example, the set of atomic actions occurring in the formula under consideration. So, if $\text{Ac}_{at}\psi$ denotes the finite set of atomic actions occurring in a formula ψ, then the modified semantical definition could be as follows,

$$\mathcal{M}, w \models \Diamond_i\varphi \text{ iff } \exists k \in \mathbb{N}\ \exists a_1, \ldots, a_k \in \text{Ac}_{at}\psi.$$
$$\mathcal{M}, w \models \mathbf{PracPoss}_i(a_1;\ \ldots;\ a_k, \varphi)$$

where ψ is a specific KARO formula. In this case the existential quantifier in the definition of $\Diamond_i\varphi$ can be replaced by a disjunction over all actions in $\text{Ac}_{at}\psi$. Then $\Diamond_i\varphi$ can be embedded into CTL^* as $\varphi \vee \mathbf{E}(\bigvee_{a \in \text{Ac}_{at}\psi}(c_i^a \wedge \bigcirc done_i^a)))\mathcal{U}\varphi)$. Although this formula is not in CTL, it can be rewritten into a satisfiability equivalent set of SNF_{karo} clauses making use of the additional expressiveness of SNF_{karo} clauses due to the index labels we can attach to step clauses.

Also the use of the unbounded repetition operation on actions is excluded from the core KARO logic we have considered. This operation is not first-order definable and there can be no translation into first-order logic based solely on the semantics of the unbounded repetition operation. Unbounded repetition also presents problems for the clausal temporal resolution approach as we require that only atomic actions a occur in $[\text{do}_i(a)]\varphi$ and $\mathbf{A}_i a$. In the presence of unbounded repetition we are not able to remove occurrences of α^* or nonatomic action below unbounded repetition using the rules of Table 7.2 or similar rewrite rules. However, one possibility which may be fruitful is to translate formulae such as $\langle \text{do}_i(a^*)\rangle\varphi$, where a is an atomic action, directly into CTL as $\varphi \vee \mathbf{E}\bigcirc(\mathbf{E}(done_i^a\mathcal{U}(\varphi \wedge done_i^a)))$. This could be further rewritten into the normal form SNF_{karo}.

It is important to note that embeddings of the extension of core KARO logic by unbounded repetition into first-order logic and $\text{CTL} \oplus \text{S5}_{(m)}$ do exist. There are polynomial time computable, satisfiability equivalence preserving embeddings of $\text{S5}_{(m)}$ into Converse PDL [43] and of Converse PDL into PDL [6]. The combination of these two embeddings allows us to reduce the satisfiability problem of the extension of core KARO logic by unbounded repetition to the satisfiability problem of PDL. The satisfiability problem of PDL is EXPTIME-complete [14, 35] and so are the satisfiability problem of the guarded fragment with relations of bounded arity GF_k [17] and CTL [12]. Thus, there are again polynomial time computable embeddings τ_{GF_k} and τ_{PDL} mapping formulae of PDL to satisfiability equivalent formulae in GF_k and CTL, respectively. However, these embeddings are based on the fact that any polynomial space alternating Turing machine T and its input I can be embedded into GF_k and PDL in such a way that the resulting formula $\varphi_{(T,I)}$ is satisfiable iff the original Turing machine T halts on I in an accepting state. Then, given a decision procedure for PDL as a polynomial space alternating Turing machine M_{PDL}, τ_{GF_k} and τ_{PDL} can be used to translate M_{PDL} together with a PDL formula ψ into a formula $\varphi_{(M_{PDL},\psi)}$ of the target logic which satisfies the property stated above. Thus, these embeddings together with the appropriate decision procedures for the target logics provide us with decision procedures for the extension of core KARO logic by unbounded repetition.

While this approach is an appropriate way to establish the complexity of a class of problems, it is doubtful whether it can be used to obtain practical proof methods. The embeddings τ_{GF_k} and τ_{PDL} induce mappings from computations of a decision procedure M_{PDL} for the source logic PDL to interpretations of the target logic. So, we can only expect to be as efficient as the decision procedure M_{PDL}. In contrast, the embeddings Π and τ described in Sections 7.3 and 7.4, respectively, constitute mappings from interpretations of the source logic to interpretations of the target logic. The embeddings do not impose any constraints on the way we solve the satisfiability problem in the target logic. This means, we can take advantage of the sophisticated techniques available for the target logics.

In the full KARO framework, interaction between the dynamic logic and epistemic logic components of KARO logic is allowed and various additional properties of the modal operators have been investigated [27]. Of particular interest is *accordance*, formalized by the axiom schema $\mathbf{K}_i[do_i(\alpha)]\varphi \rightarrow [do_i(\alpha)]\mathbf{K}_i\varphi$. This is similar to the interaction axiom between linear time temporal logic and $S5_{(m)}$, $\mathbf{K}_i\bigcirc\varphi \rightarrow \bigcirc\mathbf{K}_i\varphi$, given in [13], known as synchrony and perfect recall and is known to make the validity problem much more complex. For example in the single agent case allowing this interaction between propositional linear time temporal logic and S5 turns the satisfiability problem from a PSPACE-complete problem into a double exponential time complete problem [18]. However, in many cases the addition of such interactions even leads to undecidability [18] so care is needed here.

Furthermore it is interesting to consider what fragment of the fusion of CTL and $S5_{(m)}$ we obtain when translating from KARO specifications in this way. For example is it ever possible to obtain $A\diamond L$ from translating from the core of KARO? Our conjecture is it is not possible and therefore we do not require the temporal resolution rules TRES1 and TRES3.

Although the blocks world is a well accepted test-bed for planning and AI, we are also aiming at applying KARO in other areas. Breunesse [5] used a subset of KARO to reason about soccer players in the simulation league of RoboCup [38], where, as in the blocks world, the number of atomic actions is limited, but, unlike the blocks world, the result of these actions is not precise. Thus, in [5], besides knowledge, probabilities are added to the framework. His work shows that to overcome the accumulating uncertainties after a sequence of actions, there is a need to incorporate some notion of *sensing* to KARO, which, together with the notions of updating one's belief in a KARO setting, gives the agents a richer and dynamic epistemic attitude.

Another KARO issue still in research is the question how to *realise* agents that are specified in KARO. A first step towards this end was taken in [29], where we try to link KARO to agent programming languages. In essence, an agent programming language enables the programmer to program (the dynamics of) mental states. Thus, the semantics of such a program can be conceived of as 'mental state transformers'. KARO should be a suitable verification language for such a programming language. In [29], we analyzed the language 3APL [20] of which the semantics is given in terms of goal-base (KARO: commitments) and a belief-base (KARO: knowledge) of the agent, and were able to identify a number of 3APL-specific properties about them. In particular, we gave a number of properties that the practical reasoning rule of 3APL satisfies. Explaining this in detail would require too much additional definitions here. For further details the reader is referred to [29].

7.7 Conclusion

Although there exist a number of theories of rational agency which are formulated in the framework of combinations of modal logics, the work on practical proof methods for the expressive logics involved in these theories has been sparse. Examples are the tableaux-based proof methods developed by Rao and Georgeff for propositional BDI logics [37], and the resolution-based proof methods developed by Dixon, Fisher, and Wooldridge for temporal logics of knowledge [10]. In this chapter, we presented the current state of our attempt to provide proof methods for the logics of the KARO framework, whose expressiveness exceeds those of previous theories of rational agency.

The presentation of the proof methods in Sections 7.3 and 7.4, and the discussion in Section 7.6, shows that although our proof methods already cover an interesting core fragment of the KARO framework, there are still essential gaps. We believe that this is not a sign that our approach is insufficient, but due to the fact that combinations of interacting logic inherently pose difficult proof theoretical problems, which have not received the necessary attention. Recent experiments support the view that even for rather simple classes of temporal and dynamic logic formulae the performance of various theorem provers varies greatly [25, 26]. This indicates that the theoretical and practical problems of theorem proving in temporal and dynamic logic, and their extensions, is not yet well investigated.

One of the motivations for pursuing two different approaches at the same time is the fact that the strength of the approaches lies within different areas of the KARO framework. The translation approach allows a quite elegant treatment of the informational component of KARO. On the other hand, the clausal temporal resolution approach has a better potential to provide a complete calculus for the dynamic component of KARO, in particular, in the presence of unbounded repetition.

A promising approach is the possibility of combining both proof methods. In [23] we present a combination of clausal temporal resolution (restricted to a linear time temporal logic) and the translation approach plus first-order resolution (restricted to extension of the multi-modal logic $\mathsf{K}_{(m)}$), and we were able to show soundness, completeness, and termination of this combination of logics.

References

1. Andréka, H., van Benthem, J. and Németi, I. Modal languages and bounded fragments of predicate logic. *J. Philos. Logic*, **27**(3):217–274, 1998.
2. Bachmair, L. and Ganzinger, H. Resolution theorem proving. In *Handbook of Automated Reasoning*, A. Robinson and A. Voronkov, editors. Elsevier. 2001, chapter 2, pp 19–99.
3. Bachmair, L., Ganzinger, H. and Waldmann, U. Superposition with simplification as a decision procedure for the monadic class with equality. In *Proc. KGC'93, (LNCS 713)*, Springer, 1993, pp 83–96.
4. Blackburn, P., de Rijke, M. and Venema, V. *Modal Logic*. Cambridge University Press. 2001.
5. Breunesse, C. B. *The logic of soccer*. Master's thesis, ICS, University of Utrecht, The Netherlands, 2000.
6. De Giacomo, G. Eliminating "converse" from converse PDL. *J. Logic, Language and Inform.*, **5**(2):193–208, 1996.
7. De Nivelle, H. Translation of S4 into GF and 2VAR. Unpublished manuscript, 1999.
8. De Nivelle, H., Schmidt, R. A. and Hustadt, U. Resolution-based methods for modal logics. *Logic J. IGPL*, **8**(3):265–292, 2000.
9. Dixon, C., Fisher, M. and Bolotov, A. Clausal resolution in a logic of rational agency. *Artificial Intelligence*, **139**(1):47–89.
10. Dixon, C., Fisher, M. and Wooldridge, M. Resolution for temporal logics of knowledge. *J. Logic Computat.*, **8**(3):345–372, 1998.

11. Emerson, E. A. Alternative semantics for temporal logics. In *Theoret. Computer Sci.*. 1983, pp 121–130.
12. Emerson, E. A. Temporal and modal logic. In *Handbook of Theoretical Computer Science*, J. van Leeuwen, editor. Elsevier. 1990, pp 997–1072.
13. Fagin, R., Halpern, J. Y., Moses, Y. and Vardi, M. Y. *Reasoning About Knowledge*. MIT Press. 1996.
14. Fischer, M. J. and Ladner, R. Propositional dynamic logic of regular programs. *J. Computer and System Sci.*, **18**:194–211, 1979.
15. Fisher, M., Dixon, C. and Peim, M. Clausal temporal resolution. *ACM Trans. Computational Logic*, **2**(1):12–56, 2001.
16. Georgieva, L., Hustadt, U. and Schmidt, R. A. Computational space efficiency and minimal model generation for guarded formulae. In *Proc. LPAR'01, (LNAI 2250)*, Springer, 2001, pp 85–99.
17. Grädel, E. On the restraining power of guards. *J. Symbolic Logic*, **64**:1719–1742, 1999.
18. Halpern, J. Y. and Vardi, M. Y. The complexity of reasoning about knowledge and time. I Lower bounds. *J. Computer and System Sci.*, **38**:195–237, 1989.
19. Halpern, J. Y. and Vardi, M. Y. The complexity of reasoning about knowledge and time: Extended abstract. In *Proc. STOC'86*, 1986, pp 304–315.
20. Hindriks, K. V., de Boer, F. S., van der Hoek, W. and Meyer, J-J. Ch. Agent programming in 3APL. *Internat. J. Autonomous Agents and MultiAgent Systems*, **2**(3):357–401, 1999.
21. van der Hoek, W., van Linder, B. and Meyer, J-J. Ch. On agents that have the ability to choose. *Studia Logica*, **65**:79–119, 2000.
22. Hustadt, U. *Resolution-based decision procedures for subclasses of first-order logic*. PhD thesis, Saarland University, Saarbrücken, Germany, 1999.
23. Hustadt, U., Dixon, C., Schmidt, R. A. and Fisher, M. Normal forms and proofs in combined modal and temporal logics. In *Proc. FroCoS 2000, (LNAI 1794)*, Springer, 2000, pp 73–87.
24. Hustadt, U. and Schmidt, R. A. Using resolution for testing modal satisfiability and building models. In *SAT2000: Highlights of Satisfiability Research in the Year 2000*, I. Gent, H. van Maaren and T. Walsh, editors. IOS Press. 2000, pp 459–483.
25. Hustadt, U. and Schmidt, R. A. Formulae which highlight differences between temporal logic and dynamic logic provers. In *Issues in the Design and Experimental Evaluation of Systems for Modal and Temporal Logics*. Technical Report DII 14/01, Department of Informatics, University of Siena, 2001, pp 68–76.
26. Hustadt, U. and Schmidt, R. A. Scientific benchmarking with temporal logic decision procedures. In *Proc. KR2002*, Morgan Kaufmann, 2002, pp 533–544.
27. van Linder, B., van der Hoek, W. and Meyer, J-J. Ch. Formalizing abilities and opportunities of agents. *Fundamenta Informaticae*, **34**(1,2):53–101, 1998.
28. Lutz, C. Complexity of terminological reasoning revisited. In *Proc. LPAR'99, (LNAI 1705)*, Springer, 1999, pp 181–200.
29. Meyer, J-J. Ch., de Boer, F., van Eijk, R., Hindriks, K. and van der Hoek, W. *On programming KARO agents*. Logic Journal of the IGPL, **9**(2):245–256, 2001.
30. Meyer, J-J. Ch. and van der Hoek, W. *Epistemic Logic for AI and Computer Science*. Cambridge University Press. 1995.

31. Meyer, J-J. Ch., van der Hoek, W. and van Linder, B. A logical approach to the dynamics of commitments. *Artificial Intelligence*, **113**(1–2):1–40, 1999.
32. Mints, G. Gentzen-type systems and resolution rules. Part I: Propositional logic. In *Proc. COLOG-88, (LNCS 417)*, Springer, 1990, pp 198–231.
33. Mortimer, M. On languages with two variables. *Z. Math. Logik Grundlagen Math.*, **21**:135–140, 1975.
34. Ohlbach, H. J. Combining Hilbert style and semantic reasoning in a resolution framework. In *Proc. CADE-15, (LNAI 1421)*, Springer, 1998, pp 205–219.
35. Pratt, V. R. Models of program logics. In *Proc. 20th Symp. Found. Comput. Sci.*, IEEE Computer Society Press, 1979, pp 115–122.
36. Rao, A. S. and Georgeff, M. P. Modeling agents within a BDI-architecture. In *Proc. KR-91*, Morgan Kaufmann, 1991, pp 473–484.
37. Rao, A. S. and Georgeff, M. P. Decision procedures for BDI logics. *J. Logic Computat.*, **8**(3):293–343, 1998.
38. RoboCup. Robocup web site. http://www.robocup.org, (1998–2001).
39. Schmidt, R. A. Decidability by resolution for propositional modal logics. *J. Automated Reasoning*, **22**(4):379–396, 1999.
40. Schmidt, R. A. and Hustadt, U. A Principle for Incorporating Axioms into the First-Order Translation. In *Proc. CADE-19, (LNAI 2741)*, Springer, 2003, pp 412–426.
41. Schmidt, R. A. and Tishkovsky, D. On calculi and Kripke semantics for multi-agent systems within the KARO framework. In *IJCAR 2001: Short Papers*, Department of Informatics, University of Siena, 2001, pp 150–159.
42. Schmidt, R. A., Tishkovsky, D. and Hustadt, U. Interactions between knowledge, action and commitment within agent dynamic logic. *Studia Logica*. To appear.
43. Tuominen, H. Dynamic logic as a uniform framework for theorem proving in intentional logic. In *Proc. CADE-10, (LNAI 449)*, Springer, 1990, pp 514–527.
44. Weidenbach, Ch. et al. System description: SPASS version 1.0.0. In *Proc. CADE-16, (LNAI 1632)*, Springer, 1999, pp 378–382.
45. Wooldridge, M. *Reasoning about Rational Agents*. MIT Press. 2000.

8

Assuring the Behavior of Adaptive Agents

Diana F. Spears

8.1 Introduction

Agents are becoming increasingly prevalent and effective. Robots and softbots, working individually or in concert, can relieve people of a great deal of labor-intensive tedium. Designers can furnish agents with plans to perform desired tasks. Nevertheless, a designer cannot possibly foresee all circumstances that will be encountered by the agent. Therefore, in addition to supplying an agent with a plan, it is essential to also enable the agent to learn and modify its plan to adapt to unforeseen circumstances. The introduction of learning, however, often makes the agent's behavior significantly harder to predict.[1] The goal of this research is to verify the behavior of adaptive agents. In particular, our objective is to develop efficient methods for determining whether the behavior of learning agents remains within the bounds of prespecified constraints (called "properties") after learning. This includes verifying that properties are preserved for single adaptive agents as well as verifying that global properties are preserved for multi-agent systems in which one or more agents may adapt.

An example of a property is Asimov's First Law [2]. This law, which has also been studied by Weld and Etzioni [34], states that an agent may not harm a human or allow a human to come to harm. The main contribution of Weld and Etzioni is a "call to arms: before we release autonomous agents into real-world environments, we need some credible and computationally tractable means of making them obey Asimov's First Law ... how do we stop our artifacts from causing us harm in the process of obeying our orders?" Of course, this law is too general for direct implementation and needs to be operationalized into specific properties

---

[1] Even adding a simple, elegant learning mechanism such as chunking in Soar can substantially reduce system predictability (Soar project members, personal communication).

testable on a system, such as "Never delete a user's file." This chapter addresses Weld and Etzioni's call to arms in the context of adaptive agents. To respond to this call, we are developing APT agents, which are agents that are **a**daptive, **p**redictable, and **t**imely. Adaptation is achieved by learning/evolving agent plans, predictability by formal verification, and timeliness by streamlining reverification using the knowledge of what learning was done.

Rapid reverification after learning is a key to achieving timely agent responses. Our results include proofs that certain useful learning operators are *a priori* guaranteed to be "safe" with respect to important classes of properties, i.e., if the property holds for the agent's plan prior to learning, then it is guaranteed to still hold after learning. If an agent uses these "safe" learning operators, it will be guaranteed to preserve the properties with *no re*verification required. This is the best one could hope for in an online situation where rapid response time is critical. For other learning operators and property classes our a priori results are negative. However, for these cases we have developed *incremental* reverification algorithms that can save time over total reverification from scratch.

The novelty of our approach is not in machine learning or verification per se, but rather the synthesis of the two. There are numerous important potential applications of our approach. For example, if antiviruses evolve more effective behaviors to combat viruses, we need to ensure that they do not evolve undesirable virus-like behavior. Another example is data mining agents that can flexibly adapt their plans to dynamic computing environments but whose behavior is adequately constrained for operation within secure or proprietary domains. A third example is planetary rovers that adapt to unforeseen conditions while remaining within critical mission parameters.

The last important application that we will mention is in the domain of power grid and telecommunications networks. The following is an event that occurred (*The New York Times*, September 21, 1991, Business Section). In 1991 in New York, local electric utilities had a demand overload. In attempting to assist in solving the regional shortfall, AT&T put its own generators on the local power grid. This was a manual adaptation, but such adaptations are expected to become increasingly automated in the future. As a result of AT&T's actions, there was a local power overload and AT&T lost its own power, which resulted in a breakdown of the AT&T regional communications network. The regional network breakdown propagated to create a national breakdown in communications systems. This breakdown also triggered failures of many other control networks across the country, such as the air traffic control network. Air travel nationwide was shut down. In the future, it is reasonable to expect that such network controllers will be implemented using multiple, distributed cooperating software agents [15], because global control tends to be too computationally expensive and risky. This example dramatically illustrates the potential vulnerability of our national resources unless these agents satisfy *all* of the following criteria: continuous execution, flexible adaptation to failures, safety, reliability, and timely responses. Our approach ensures that agents satisfy all of these.

8.2 Agent Learning

The ability to adapt is key to survival in dynamic environments. The study of adaptation (learning) in agents is as old as the field of AI. More recently [27], it has blossomed into a field of its own. When agents are adaptive, the following questions need to be addressed:

1. Is learning applied to one or more agents?
2. If multiple agents, are they competing or cooperating?
3. What element(s) of the agent(s) get adapted?
4. What technique(s) are used to adapt?

The answers to questions 1 and 2 are quite variable among published papers. This chapter assumes that learning is applied to one agent at a time, and that the agents cooperate. Regarding question 3, typically it is an agent's plan (strategy) that undergoes adaptation. In other words, learning changes a plan. Example plan representations include action sequences such as in the Procedural Reasoning System (PRS) [10], rule sets [14], finite-state automata [9], or neural networks [21]. Here, we assume finite-state automaton (FSA) plans that map perceptions to actions. Unlike PRS plans, beliefs, goals, and intentions are implicitly embedded in an FSA. FSA plans are stimulus-response, like neural networks or rule-based plans.

Learning alters some component of a plan, for example, it may change the choice of action to take in response to a stimulus. Learning may be motivated by observation, it could be initiated in response to success/failure, or it could be prompted by a general need for performance improvement [13]. The motivation influences the choice of learning technique. Regarding question 4, nearly every learning technique has been used for agents, including analogy, induction, rote, clustering, reinforcement learning (RL), evolutionary algorithms (EAs), backpropagation, and Bayesian updating. The two most prevalent agent learning techniques are RL (e.g., [17, 35]) and EAs (e.g., [1, 24]). A very popular form of RL is Q-learning [33], where agents update their probabilities of taking actions in a given situation based on penalty/reward. This chapter assumes EA learning, as described below. The reason for choosing EA learning is that this is one of the most effective methods known for developing FSA strategies for agents, e.g., see [9]. Unlike RL, EAs can learn the FSA topology.

We assume that learning occurs in two phases: an offline and an online phase. During the offline phase, each agent starts with a randomly

```
Procedure EA
t = 0; /* initial generation */
initialize_population(t);
evaluate_fitness(t);
until termination-criterion do
    t = t + 1; /* next generation */
    select_parents(t);
    perturb(t);
    evaluate_fitness(t);
end until
end procedure
```

Fig. 8.1. The outline of an evolutionary algorithm (EA).

initialized population of candidate FSA plans. This population is evolved using the evolutionary algorithm outlined in Figure 8.1. The main loop of this algorithm consists of selecting parent plans from the population, applying perturbation (evolutionary learning) operators to the parents to produce offspring, evaluating the fitness of the offspring, and then returning the offspring to the population if they are sufficiently fit.

At the start of the online phase, each agent selects one "best" (according to its "fitness function") plan from its population for execution. The agents are then fielded and plan execution is interleaved with learning. The purpose of learning during the online phase is to fine-tune the plan and adapt it to keep pace with a shifting environment. The evolutionary algorithm of Figure 8.1 is also used during this phase, but the assumption is a population of size one and incremental learning (i.e., one learning operator applied per plan per generation, which is a reasonable rate for EAs [3]). This is practical for situations in which the environment changes gradually, rather than radically.

8.3 APT Agents Paradigm

This section presents a general APT framework, which assumes cooperating agents. This framework is then illustrated with a detailed example.

8.3.1 General Framework

In the APT agents framework (see Figure 8.2), there are one or more agents with "anytime" plans, i.e., plans that are continually executed in response to internal and external environmental conditions. Let us begin with step (1) in Figure 8.2. There are at least a couple of ways that plans could be formed initially. For one, a human plan designer could engineer the initial plans. This may require considerable effort and knowledge. An appealing alternative is to use machine learning or evolutionary algorithms to develop initial plans.

OFFLINE:

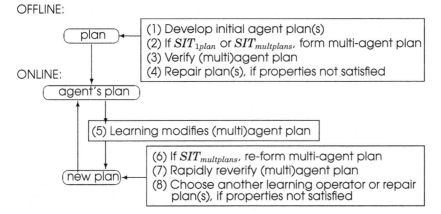

Fig. 8.2. The APT agents framework.

Human plan engineers or learning can develop plans that satisfy agents' goals to a high degree, but to provide strict behavioral (especially global) guarantees, formal verification is also required. Therefore, we assume that prior to fielding the agents, the (multi)agent plan has been verified offline to determine whether it satisfies critical properties, such as safety properties (steps (2) and (3)). If a property fails to be satisfied, the plan is repaired (step (4)). Steps (2) through (4) require some clarification. If there is a single agent, then it has one plan and that is all that is verified and repaired, if needed. We call this SIT_{1agent}. If there are multiple agents that cooperate, we consider two possibilities. In SIT_{1plan}, every agent uses the same multi-agent plan that is the composition of the individual agent plans. This multi-agent plan is formed and verified to see if it satisfies global multi-agent coordination properties. The multi-agent plan is repaired if verification identifies any errors, i.e., failure of the plan to satisfy a property. In $SIT_{multplans}$, each agent independently uses its own individual plan. To verify global properties, one of the agents, which acts as the verification and validation (V&V) agent, takes the composition of these individual plans to form a multi-agent plan. This multi-agent plan is what is verified. For $SIT_{multplans}$, one or more individual plans are repaired if the property is not satisfied.

After the initial plan(s) have been verified and repaired, the agents are fielded (online) and they apply learning to their plan(s) as needed (step (5)). Learning (e.g., with evolutionary operators) may be required in order to adapt the plan to handle unexpected situations or to fine-tune the plan. If SIT_{1agent} or SIT_{1plan}, the single (multi)agent plan is adapted. If $SIT_{multplans}$, each agent adapts its own plan, after which the composition is formed. For all situations, one agent then rapidly *re*verifies the new (multi)agent plan to ensure it still satisfies the required properties (steps (6) and (7)). Whenever (re)verification fails, it produces a counterexample that is used to guide the choice of an alternative learning operator or other plan repair as needed (step (8)). This process of executing, adapting, and reverifying plans cycles indefinitely as needed. The main focus of this chapter is steps (6) and (7). Kiriakidis and Gordon [18] address the issue of repairing plans (steps (4) and (8)) when (re)verification errors are found.

We have just presented a general framework. It could be instantiated with a variety of plan representations, learning methods, and verification techniques. To make this framework concrete, this chapter assumes particular choices for these elements of the framework. In particular, we assume that plans are in the form of finite-state automata, plan learning is accomplished with evolutionary algorithms, the method of verification is model checking [7], and properties are implemented in FSA form, i.e., automata-theoretic (AT) model checking [8] is performed. Model checking consists of building a finite model of a system and checking whether a desired property holds in that model. In the context of this chapter, model checking determines whether $S \models P$ for plan S and property P, i.e., whether plan S "models" (satisfies) property P. The output is either "yes" or "no" and, if "no," one or more counterexamples are provided. Before beginning with the formalisms for these elements, we illustrate them with an example.

8.3.2 Illustrative Example

This subsection presents a multi-agent example for SIT_{1plan} and $SIT_{multplans}$ that is used throughout this chapter to illustrate the definitions and ideas. The section starts by addressing $SIT_{multplans}$, where multiple agents have their own independent plans. Later in the section we address SIT_{1plan}, where each agent uses a joint multi-agent plan.

Imagine a scenario where a vehicle has landed on a planet for the purpose of exploration and sample collection, for example, as in the Pathfinder mission to Mars. Like the Pathfinder, there is a lander (called agent "L") from which a mobile rover emerges. However, in this case there are two rovers: the far ("F") rover for distant exploration, and the intermediary ("I") rover for transferring data and samples from F to L.

We assume an agent designer has developed the initial plans for F, I, and L, shown in Figures 8.3 and 8.4. These are simplified, rather than realistic, plans – for the purpose of illustration. Basically, rover F is either collecting samples/data (in state COLLECTING) or it is delivering them to rover I (when F is in its state DELIVERING). Rover I can either be receiving samples/data from rover F (when I is in its RECEIVING state) or it can deliver them to lander L (when it is in its DELIVERING state). If

L is in its RECEIVING state, then it can receive the samples/data from I. Otherwise, L could be busy transmitting data to Earth (in state TRANS-MITTING) or pausing between actions (in state PAUSING).

As mentioned above, plans are represented using FSAs. Each FSA has a finite set of states (i.e., the vertices) and allowable state-to-state transitions (i.e., the directed edges between vertices). The purpose of having states is to divide the agent's overall task into subtasks. A state with an incoming arrow not from any other state is an *initial state*. Plan execution begins in an initial state.

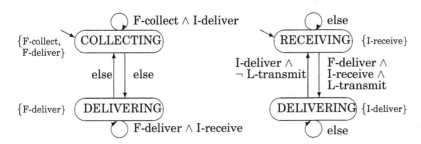

Fig. 8.3. Plans for rovers F (left) and I (right).

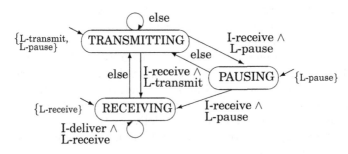

Fig. 8.4. Plan for the lander L.

Plan execution occurs as the agent takes actions, such as agent F taking action F-collect or F-deliver. Each agent has a repertoire of possible actions, a subset of which may be taken from each of its states. A plan designer can specify this subset for each state. The choice of a particular action from this subset is modeled as nondeterministic. It is assumed that further criteria, not specified here, are used to make the final runtime choice of a single action from a state.

Let us specify the set of actions for each of the agents (F, I, L) in our example of Figures 8.3 and 8.4. F has two possible actions: F-collect and F-deliver. The first action means that F collects samples and/or data, and the second action means that it delivers these items to I. Rover I also has two actions: I-receive and I-deliver. The first action means I receives samples/data from F, and the second means that it delivers these items to L. L has three actions: L-transmit, L-pause, and L-receive. The first action means L transmits data to Earth, the second that it pauses between operations, and the third that it receives samples/data from I. For each FSA, the set of allowable actions from each state is specified in Figures 8.3 and 8.4 in small font within curly brackets next to the state. For example, rover F can only take action F-deliver from its DELIVERING state.

The *transition conditions* (i.e., the logical expressions labeling the edges) in an FSA plan describe the set of (multi-agent) actions that enable a state-to-state transition to occur. The operator $\land$ means "AND," $\lor$ means "OR," and $\neg$ means "NOT." The condition "else" will be defined shortly. The transition conditions of one agent can refer to the actions of one or more other agents. This is because each agent is assumed to be reactive to what it has observed other agents doing. If not visible, agents communicate their action choice.

Once an agent's action repertoire and its allowable actions from each state have been defined, "else" can be defined. The transition condition "else" labeling an outgoing edge from a state is an abbreviation denoting the set of all remaining actions that may be taken from the state that are not already covered by other transition conditions. For example, in Figure 8.4, L's three transition conditions from state TRANSMITTING are (I-receive $\land$ L-transmit), (I-receive $\land$ L-pause), and "else." L can only take the action L-transmit or L-pause from this state. However, rover I could take I-deliver instead of I-receive. Therefore, in this case "else" is equivalent to ((I-deliver $\land$ L-transmit) $\lor$ (I-deliver $\land$ L-pause)).

Each FSA plan represents a set of allowable action sequences. In particular, a plan is the set of all action sequences that begin in an initial state and obey the transition conditions. An example action sequence allowed by F's plan is $\langle$(F-collect $\land$ I-deliver), (F-collect $\land$ I-receive), (F-deliver $\land$ I-receive), ...$\rangle$ where F takes its actions and observes I's actions at each step in the sequence.

At run-time, these FSA plans are interpreted in the following manner. At every discrete time step, every agent (F, I, L) is at one of the states in its plan, and it selects the next action to take. Agents choose their actions independently. They do not need to synchronize on action choice. The choice of action might be based, for example, on sensory inputs from the environment. Although a complete plan would include the basis for action choice, as mentioned above, here we leave it unspecified in the FSA plans. Our rationale for doing this is that the focus of this chapter is on the verification of properties about correct action sequences. The basis for action choice is irrelevant to these properties.

Once each agent has chosen an action, all agents are assumed to observe the actions of the other agents that are mentioned in its FSA transition conditions. For example, F's transition conditions mention I's actions, so F needs to observe what I did. Based on its own action and those of the other relevant agent(s), an agent knows the next state to which it will transition. There is only one possible next state because the FSAs are assumed to be deterministic. The process of being in a state, choosing an action, observing the actions of other agents, then moving to a next state, is repeated indefinitely.

So far, we have been assuming $SIT_{multplans}$ where each agent has its own individual plan. If we assume SIT_{1plan}, then each agent uses the same multi-agent plan to decide its actions. A multi-agent plan is formed by taking a "product" (composition) of the plans for F, I, and L. This product models the synchronous behavior of the agents, where "synchronous" means that at each time step every agent takes an action, observes actions of other agents, and then transitions to a next state.[2] Multi-agent actions enable state-to-state transitions in the product plan. For example, if the agents jointly take the actions F-deliver and I-receive and L-transmit, then all agents will transition from the joint state (COLLECTING, RECEIVING, TRANSMITTING) to the joint state (DELIVERING, DELIVERING, RECEIVING) represented by triples of states in the FSAs for F, I, and L. A multi-agent plan consists of the set of all action sequences that begin in a joint initial state of the product plan and obey the transition conditions.

Regardless of whether the situation is $SIT_{multplans}$ or SIT_{1plan}, a multi-agent plan needs to be formed to verify global multi-agent coordination properties (see step 2 of Figure 8.2). Verification of global properties consists of asking whether *all* of the action sequences allowed by the product plan satisfy a property.

One class of (global) properties of particular importance, which is addressed here, is that of forbidden multi-agent actions that we want our agents to always avoid, called *Invariance* properties. An example is property P1: ¬(I-deliver ∧ L-transmit), which states that it should always be the case that I does not deliver at the same time that L is transmitting. This property prevents problems that may arise from the lander simultaneously receiving new data from I while transmitting older data to Earth. The second important class addressed here is *Response* properties. These properties state that if a particular multi-agent action (the "trigger") has occurred, then eventually another multi-agent action (the necessary "response") will occur. An example is property P2: If F-deliver has occurred, then eventually L will execute L-receive.

If the plans in Figures 8.3 and 8.4 are combined into a multi-agent plan, will this multi-agent plan satisfy properties P1 and P2? Answering this question is probably difficult or impossible for most readers if the determination is based on visual inspection of the FSAs. Yet there

---

[2] The case of an agent not taking an action is represented as action "pause."

are only a couple of very small, simple FSAs in this example! This illustrates how even a few simple agents, when interacting, can exhibit complex global behaviors, thereby making global agent behavior difficult to predict. Clearly there is a need for rigorous behavioral guarantees, especially as the number and complexity of agents increases. Model checking fully automates this process. According to our model checker, the product plan for F, I, and L satisfies properties P1 and P2.

Rigorous guarantees are also needed after learning. Suppose lander L's transmitter gets damaged. Then one learning operator that could be applied is to delete L's action L-transmit, which thereafter prevents this action from being taken from state TRANSMITTING. After applying a learning operator, reverification may be required.

In a multi-agent situation, what gets modified by learning? Who forms and verifies the product FSA? And who performs repairs if verification fails, and what is repaired? The answers to these questions depend on whether it is SIT_{1plan} or $SIT_{multplans}$. If SIT_{1plan}, the agent with the greatest computational power, e.g., lander L in our example, maintains the product plan by applying learning to it, verifying it, repairing it as needed, and then sending a copy of it to all of the agents to use. If $SIT_{multplans}$, an agent applies learning to its own individual plan. The individual plans are then sent to the computationally powerful agent, who forms the product and verifies that properties are satisfied. If repairs are needed, one or more agents are instructed to repair their own individual plans.

It is assumed here that machine learning operators are applied one-at-a-time per agent rather than in batch and, if $SIT_{multplans}$, the agents co-evolve plans by taking turns learning [24]. Beyond these assumptions, this chapter does not focus on the learning operators per se (other than to define them). It focuses instead on the outcome resulting from the application of a learning operator. In particular, we address the reverification issue.

8.4 Background

This section gives useful background definitions needed for understanding reverification. We discuss plans, learning, and verification.

8.4.1 Agent Plans

Each agent's plan is assumed to be in the form of a finite-state automaton (FSA). FSAs have been shown to be effective representations of reactive agent plans/strategies (e.g., [6, 9, 16]). A particular advantage of the FSA plan representation is that it can be verified with popular verification methods. Example FSAs are shown in Figures 8.3 and 8.4. When using an

FSA plan, an agent may be in one of a finite number of states, and actions enable it to transition from state to state. Action begins in an initial (i.e., marked by an incoming arrow from nowhere) state. The transition conditions (Boolean algebra expressions labeling FSA edges) in an FSA plan succinctly describe the set of actions that enable a state-to-state transition to occur. We use $V(S)$, $I(S)$, $E(S)$, and $M(v_i, v_j)$ to denote the sets of vertices (states), initial states, edges, and the transition condition from state v_i to state v_j for FSA S, respectively. $\mathcal{L}(S)$ denotes the language of S, i.e., the set of all action sequences that begin in an initial state and satisfy S's transition conditions. These are the action sequences (called *strings*) allowed by the plan. The FSAs are assumed to be deterministic and complete, i.e., for every allowable action there is a unique next state.

In SIT_{1plan} or $SIT_{multplans}$, there are multiple agents. Prior to initial verification (and in $SIT_{multplans}$ this is also needed prior to subsequent verification), the synchronous multi-agent product FSA is formed. This is done by taking the Cartesian product of the states and the intersection of the transition conditions. Model checking then consists of verifying that all sequences of multi-agent actions allowed by the product plan satisfy a property.

Each multi-agent action is an *atom* of the Boolean algebra used in the product FSA transition conditions. To help in understanding the discussions below, we briefly define a Boolean algebra atom. In a Boolean algebra $\mathcal{K}$, there is a partial order among the elements, $\preceq$, which is defined as $x \preceq y$ if and only if $x \wedge y = x$. The distinguished elements 0 and 1 are defined as $\forall x \in \mathcal{K}$, $0 \preceq x \preceq 1$. The atoms of $\mathcal{K}$, $\Gamma(\mathcal{K})$, are the nonzero elements of $\mathcal{K}$ minimal with respect to $\preceq$. For example, suppose there are two agents, A and B. A has two possible actions, A-receive or A-pause, and B has two possible actions, B-receive or B-deliver. Then (A-pause $\wedge$ B-receive) is an atom, or multi-agent action. On the other hand (B-receive) is not an atom because it is equivalent to ((A-receive $\wedge$ B-receive) $\vee$ (A-pause $\wedge$ B-receive)). An atom is interpreted as follows. If the agents take multi-agent action (atom) x, then each agent will transition from its state v_1 to state v_2 whenever $x \preceq M(v_1, v_2)$.

Now we can formalize $\mathcal{L}(S)$. A string (action sequence) $\mathbf{x}$ is an infinite-dimensional vector, $(x_0, ...) \in \Gamma(\mathcal{K})^\omega$. A *run* $\mathbf{v}$ *of string* $\mathbf{x}$ is a sequence $(v_0, ...)$ of vertices such that $\forall i$, $x_i \preceq M(v_i, v_{i+1})$. In other words, a run of a string is the sequence of vertices visited in an FSA when the string satisfies the transition conditions along the edges. Then $\mathcal{L}(S) = \{\mathbf{x} \in \Gamma(\mathcal{K})^\omega \mid \mathbf{x}$ has a run $\mathbf{v} = (v_0, ...)$ in S with $v_0 \in I(S)\}$. Such a run is called an *accepting run*, and S is said to *accept* string $\mathbf{x}$.

8.4.2 Adaptive Agents: The Learning Operators

Adaptation is accomplished by evolving the FSAs (see Figure 8.1). In this subsection we define the evolutionary perturbation operators, also called "machine learning operators." A machine learning operator $o : S \rightarrow S'$ changes a (product or individual) FSA S to post-learning FSA S'. For a complete taxonomy of our learning operators, see [11]. Here we do not address learning that changes the set of FSA states, nor do we address learning that alters the Boolean algebra used in the transition conditions, e.g., via abstraction. Results on abstraction may be found in [12]. Instead, we focus here on edge operators.

Let us begin with our most general learning operator, which we call o_{change}. It is defined as follows. Suppose $z \preceq M(v_1, v_2)$, $z \neq 0$, for $(v_1, v_2) \in E(S)$ and $z \not\preceq M(v_1, v_3)$ for $(v_1, v_3) \in E(S)$. Then $o_{change}(M(v_1, v_2)) = M(v_1, v_2) \wedge \neg z$ (step 1) and/or $o_{change}(M(v_1, v_3)) = M(v_1, v_3) \vee z$ (step 2). In other words, o_{change} may consist of two steps – the first to remove condition z from edge (v_1, v_2) and the second to add the same condition z to edge (v_1, v_3). Alternatively, o_{change} may consist of only one of these two steps. Sometimes for simplicity we assume that z is a single atom, in which case o_{change} simply changes the next state after taking action z from v_2 to v_3. A particular *instance* of this operator is the result of choosing v_1, v_2, v_3 and z.

Four one-step operators that are special cases of o_{change} are: o_{add} and o_{delete} to add and delete FSA edges (if a transition condition becomes 0, the edge is considered to be deleted), and o_{gen} and o_{spec} to generalize and specialize the transition conditions along an edge. Generalization adds actions to a transition condition (with $\vee$), whereas specialization removes actions from a transition condition (with $\wedge$). An example of generalization is the change of the transition condition (B-deliver $\wedge$ A-receive) to ((B-deliver $\wedge$ A-receive) $\vee$ (B-receive $\wedge$ A-receive)). An example of specialization would be to change the transition condition (B-deliver) to (B-deliver $\wedge$ A-receive).

Two-step operators that are special cases of o_{change} are: $o_{delete+gen}$, $o_{spec+gen}$, $o_{delete+add}$, and $o_{spec+add}$. These operators move an edge or part of a transition condition from one outgoing edge of vertex v_1 to another outgoing edge of vertex v_1. An example of $o_{delete+gen}$ using the FSA for rover I (Figure 8.3, rightmost FSA) might be to delete the edge (DELIVERING, DELIVERING) and add its transition condition via generalization to (DELIVERING, RECEIVING). Then the latter edge transition condition would become 1. The two-step operators are particularly useful because they preserve FSA determinism and completeness. One-step operators must be paired with another one-step operator to preserve these constraints.

Gordon [11] defines how each of these learning operators translates from a single agent FSA to a multi-agent product FSA. This extra translation process is required for $SIT_{multplans}$. The only translation that we need to be concerned with here is that o_{gen} applied to a single FSA may translate to o_{add} in the product FSA. We will see the implications of this in Section 8.6 on incremental reverification.

8.4.3 Two Characterizations of the Learning Operators

To understand some of the a priori theorems about property-preserving operators that are presented in Section 8.5, it is necessary to characterize the learning operators according to the effect that they can have on accessibility. We begin with two basic definitions of accessibility [11]:

Definition 1 *Vertex v_n is accessible from vertex v_0 if and only if there exists a path (i.e., a sequence of edges) from v_0 to v_n.*

Definition 2 *Atom (action) $a_{n-1} \in \Gamma(\mathcal{K})$ is accessible from vertex v_0 if and only if there exists a path from v_0 to v_n and $a_{n-1} \preceq M(v_{n-1}, v_n)$.*

Accessibility from initial states is central to model checking, and therefore changes in accessibility introduced by learning should be considered. There are two fundamental ways that our learning operators may affect accessibility: *locally* (abbreviated "L"), i.e., by directly altering the accessibility of atoms or states that are part of the learning operator definition; *globally* (abbreviated "G"), i.e., by altering the accessibility of any states or atoms that are not part of the learning operator definition. For example, any change in accessibility of v_1, v_2, v_3, or atoms in $M(v_1, v_2)$ or $M(v_1, v_3)$ in the definition of o_{change} is considered local; other changes are global.

The symbol ↑ denotes "can increase" accessibility, and ⤯ denotes "cannot increase" accessibility. We use these symbols with G and L, e.g., ↑ G means that a learning operator can (but does not necessarily) increase global accessibility. The following results characterize the learning operators based on their effect on accessibility:

- o_{delete}, o_{spec}, $o_{delete+gen}$, $o_{spec+gen}$: ⤯ G ⤯ L
- o_{add}: ↑ G ↑ L
- o_{gen}: ⤯ G ↑ L
- $o_{delete+add}$, $o_{spec+add}$, o_{change}: ↑ G

These results are useful for Sections 8.5 and 8.6, which present theorems and algorithms for efficient reverification.

Finally, consider a different characterization (partition) of the learning operators, which is necessary for understanding some of the results about preservation of Response properties in Section 8.5. For this partition, we distinguish those operators that can introduce at least one new string (action sequence) with an infinitely repeating substring (e.g., (a,b,c,d,e,d,e,d,e,...) where the ellipsis represents infinite repetition of d followed by e) into the FSA language versus those that cannot. The only operators belonging to the second ("cannot") class are o_{delete} and o_{spec}.

8.4.4 Predictable Agents: Formal Verification

The verification method assumed here, model checking, consists of building a finite model of a system and checking whether the desired property holds in that model. In other words, model checking determines whether $S \models P$ for plan S and property P, i.e., whether P holds for *every* string (action sequence) in $\mathcal{L}(S)$.

This chapter focuses primarily on Response properties. For results on Invariance properties, and examples of FSA representations of properties, see [11]. Although our implementation uses FSAs for properties, for the sake of succinctness this chapter describes properties with linear temporal logic (LTL) [20]. The general LTL form for Invariance properties is ($\square \neg p$, i.e., "always not p"). The general LTL form for Response properties is ($\square(p \rightarrow \Diamond q)$ i.e., "always if trigger p occurs then eventually response q will occur").

8.5 APT Agents: A Priori Results

Total reverification from scratch is time-consuming; it has time complexity exponential in the number of agents. Thus, our objective is to lower the time complexity of reverification. The ideal solution is to identify *"safe" machine learning operators* (SMLOs), i.e., machine learning operators that are a priori guaranteed to preserve properties and require no run-time reverification cost. For a plan S and property P, suppose verification has succeeded prior to learning, i.e., $S \models P$. Then a machine learning operator $o(S)$ is a SMLO if and only if verification is guaranteed to succeed after learning, i.e., if $S' = o(S)$, then $S \models P$ implies $S' \models P$.

We next present theoretical results, from [11]. Proofs for all theorems may be found in [11]. Our two initial theorems, Theorems 1 and 2, which are designed to address the one-step operators, may not be immediately intuitive. For example, it seems reasonable to suspect that if an edge is deleted somewhere along the path from a trigger to a response, then this could cause failure of a Response property to hold – because the response is no longer accessible. In fact, this is not true. What actually happens is that deletions reduce the number of strings in the language. Therefore, if the original language satisfies the property then so does the smaller language. Theorem 1 formalizes this (in the reverse direction). The corollaries follow immediately from the theorems.

Theorem 1 *Let S and S' be FSAs, where S' is identical to S, but with additional edges. We define $o : S \rightarrow S'$ as $o : E(S) \rightarrow E(S')$, where $E(S) \subseteq E(S')$. Then $\mathcal{L}(S) \subseteq \mathcal{L}(S')$.*

Corollary 1 *o_{delete} is a SMLO for any FSA property (which includes Invariance and Response properties).*

Corollary 2 o_{add} *is not necessarily a SMLO for any FSA property.*

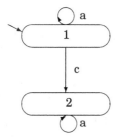

Fig. 8.5. An example to illustrate Corollaries 1 and 2.

Because the intuitions for these corollaries may not be apparent, let us consider an example. Suppose that the following properties must hold for the FSA plan of Figure 8.5:

Invariance: $\Box(\neg b)$
Response: $\Box(c \rightarrow \Diamond a)$

If we delete the lowest edge labeled "a," then both properties still hold. The Response property still holds because a string is an *infinite* sequence of atoms; thus, the only string remaining in the language is an infinite sequence of a's. If we replace the deleted edge by adding a new edge labeled "b," then the Invariance and Response properties are both violated.

Theorem 2 *For FSAs S and S' let* $o : S \rightarrow S'$ *be defined as* $o : M(S) \rightarrow M(S')$ *where* $\exists z \in \mathcal{K}$ *(the Boolean algebra),* $z \neq 0$, $(v_1, v_2) \in E(S)$, *such that* $o(M(v_1, v_2)) = M(v_1, v_2) \vee z$. *Then* $\mathcal{L}(S) \subseteq \mathcal{L}(S')$.

Corollary 3 o_{spec} *is a SMLO for any FSA property.*

Corollary 4 o_{gen} *is not necessarily a SMLO for any FSA property.*

The intuitions for these corollaries are similar to those for Corollaries 1 and 2.

The above theorems and corollaries cover the one-step operators. We next consider theorems that are needed to address the two-step operators. Although we found results for the one-step operators that were general enough to address *any* FSA property, we were unable to do likewise for the two-step operators. Our results for the two-step operators determine whether these operators are necessarily SMLOs for Invariance or Response properties in particular. These results are quite intuitive. Theorem 3 distinguishes those learning operators that will satisfy Invariance properties from those that will not:

Theorem 3 *A machine learning operator is guaranteed to be a SMLO with respect to any Invariance property P if and only if $\gamma\,G$ and $\gamma\,L$ are both true.*

Corollary 5 *Operators $o_{delete+gen}$ and $o_{spec+gen}$ are guaranteed to be SMLOs with respect to any Invariance property.*

Corollary 6 *Operators $o_{delete+add}$, $o_{spec+add}$, o_{change} are not necessarily SMLOs with respect to Invariance properties.*

In other words, increasing local and global accessibility can lead to violation of Invariance properties. Any two-step operator that has "add" as its second step is therefore not necessarily a SMLO.

Theorem 4 characterizes those learning operators that cannot be guaranteed to be SMLOs with respect to Response properties:

Theorem 4 *Any machine learning operator that can introduce a new string with an infinitely repeating substring into the FSA language cannot be guaranteed to be a SMLO for Response properties.*

Corollary 7 *None of the two-step learning operators is guaranteed to be a SMLO with respect to Response properties.*

The problem arises because the infinitely repeating substring can occur between the trigger and the required response.

Operators o_{delete} and o_{spec} are SMLOs, and $o_{delete+gen}$ and $o_{spec+gen}$ are SMLOs for Invariance properties. However, most of these results are negative, where a result is considered to be "negative" if the operator is not a SMLO. In addition to the results here, we have additional results to cover the case where agents learn independently in a multi-agent situation $(SIT_{multplans})$ [11]. However, unfortunately the majority of these results are negative as well. In general, we have found it to be very difficult to find general, positive a priori results. To avoid resorting to the full cost of total reverification, we have explored an alternative solution. In particular, for those operators that do not have positive a priori results, we can still save time over total reverification by using incremental reverification algorithms, which are described in the next section.

8.6 APT Agents: Incremental Reverification

We just learned that operators o_{spec} and o_{delete} are "safe" learning operators (SMLOs), whereas o_{gen} and o_{add} are not. It is also the case that o_{gen} and o_{add} can cause problems (e.g., for Response properties) when they are part of a two-step operator. Therefore, we have developed incremental reverification algorithms for these two operators.

Recall that there are two ways that operators can alter accessibility: globally (G) or locally (L). Furthermore, recall that o_{add} can increase accessibility either way ($\uparrow$ G $\uparrow$ L), whereas o_{gen} can only increase accessibility locally ($\not{\uparrow}$ G $\uparrow$ L). We say that o_{gen} has only a "localized" effect on accessibility, whereas the effects of o_{add} may ripple through many parts of the FSA. The implication is that we can have very efficient incremental methods for reverification tailored for o_{gen}, whereas we cannot do likewise for o_{add}. This is also true for both two-step operators that have o_{gen} as their second step, i.e., $o_{delete+gen}$ and $o_{spec+gen}$. Because no computational advantage is gained by considering o_{add} per se, we develop incremental reverification algorithms for the most general operator o_{change}. These algorithms apply to all of our operators.

Prior to reverification, the product FSA must be re-formed (step (2) of Figure 8.2). Subsection 6.2 presents one incremental algorithm for reforming a product FSA. It also presents two incremental reverification algorithms—the first is for execution after any instance of o_{change}, and the second is only for execution after instances of o_{gen} (or $o_{delete+gen}$ or $o_{spec+gen}$). Both algorithms are sound (i.e., whenever they conclude that reverification succeeds, it is in fact true that $S' \models P$) for Invariance and Response properties. Both are complete for Invariance properties (i.e., whenever they conclude that reverification fails, there is indeed at least one error). However, they are not complete for Response properties, i.e., they may find false errors (property violations). See [11] for proofs regarding soundness and completeness.

Prior to describing the incremental algorithms, we first present the nonincremental (total) versions. These algorithms do not assume that learning has occurred, and they apply to all situations. They are more general (not tailored for learning), but less efficient, than our incremental algorithms.

For implementation efficiency, all of our algorithms assume that FSAs are represented using a table of the transition function $\delta(v_1, a) = v_2$, which means that for state v_1, taking action a leads to next state v_2, as shown in Table 8.1. Rows correspond to states and columns correspond to multi-agent actions. This representation is equivalent to the more visually intuitive representation of Figures 8.3 and 8.4. In particular, Table 8.1 is equivalent to the FSA in Figure 8.4 for the lander agent L. In Table 8.1, states are abbreviated by their first letter, and the multi-agent actions are abbreviated by their first letters. For example, "crt" means agent F takes action (F-collect), I takes (I-receive), and L takes (L-transmit). The table consists of entries for the next state, i.e., it corresponds to the transition function. A "0" in the table means that there is no transition for this state-action pair. With this tabular representation, o_{change} is implemented as a perturbation (mutation) operator that changes any table entry to another randomly chosen value for the next state. Operator o_{gen} is a perturbation operator that changes a 0 entry to a next state already appearing in that row. For example, "R" is in row "T" of Table 8.1, so o_{gen} could change "0" to "R" in row "T," column "crr."

Table 8.1. The transition function for agent L's FSA plan: The rows correspond to states and the columns correspond to multi-agent actions.

	crt	crr	crp	cdt	cdr	cdp	drt	drr	drp	ddt	ddr	ddp
T	R	0	P	T	0	T	R	0	P	T	0	T
R	0	T	0	0	R	0	0	T	0	0	R	0
P	0	0	R	0	0	T	0	0	R	0	0	T

8.6.1 Total Algorithms

The algorithms described in this subsection make no assumption about learning having occurred, i.e., they are general-purpose verification methods. The particular automata theoretic (AT) verification algorithm we have chosen is from Courcoubetis et al. [8]. This algorithm, called $Total_{AT}$, does depth-first search through the FSA starting at initial states and visiting all reachable states – in order to look for all verification errors, i.e., failures to satisfy the property. The algorithm assumes properties are represented as Büchi FSAs [5]. [3]

Suppose there are n agents, and $1 \leq j_k \leq$ the number of states in the FSA for agent k. Then the algorithm forms all product states $v = (v_{j_1}, .., v_{j_n})$ and specifies their transitions:

```
Procedure product
for each product state v = (v_{j_1}, .., v_{j_n}) do
        if all v_{j_k}, 1 ≤ k ≤ n, are initial states, then v is a product initial state
        endif
        for each multi-agent action a_i do
                if (δ(v_{j_k}, a_i) == 0) for some k, 1 ≤ k ≤ n, then δ(v, a_i) = 0
                else δ(v, a_i) = (δ(v_{j_1}, a_i),...., δ(v_{j_n}, a_i)); endif
        endfor
endfor
end procedure
```

Fig. 8.6. $Total_{prod}$ product algorithm.

---

[3] Because the negation of a Response property cannot be expressed as a Büchi FSA, we use a First-Response property approximation. This suffices for our experiments [11].

```
Procedure verify
    for each state v ∈ V(S ⊗ ¬P) do
        visited(v) = 0
    endfor
    for each initial state v ∈ I(S ⊗ ¬P) do
        if (visited(v) == 0) then dfs(v); endif
    endfor
end procedure
Procedure dfs(v)
    visited(v) = 1;
    if v ∈ B(S ⊗ ¬P) then
        seed = v;
        for each state v ∈ V(S ⊗ ¬P) do
            visited2(v) = 0
        endfor
        ndfs(v)
    endif
    for each successor (i.e., next state) w of v do
        if (visited(w) == 0) then dfs(w); endif
    endfor
end procedure
Procedure ndfs(v) /* the nested search */
    visited2(v) = 1;
    for each successor (i.e., next state) w of v do
        if (w == seed) then print "Bad cycle. Verification error";
        break
        else if (visited2(w) == 0) then ndfs(w); endif
        endif
    endfor
end procedure
```

Fig. 8.7. $Total_{AT}$ verification algorithm.

In AT model checking, asking whether $S \models P$ is equivalent to asking whether $\mathcal{L}(S) \subseteq \mathcal{L}(P)$ for property P. This is equivalent to $\mathcal{L}(S) \cap \overline{\mathcal{L}(P)}$ = ∅, which is algorithmically tested by first taking the product (⊗) of the plan FSA S and an FSA corresponding to $\neg P$, i.e., $S \otimes \neg P$. The FSA corresponding to $\neg P$ accepts $\overline{\mathcal{L}(P)}$. The product implements language intersection. The algorithm then determines whether $\mathcal{L}(S \otimes \neg P) \neq \varnothing$, which implies $\mathcal{L}(S) \cap \overline{\mathcal{L}(P)} \neq \varnothing$ $(S \not\models P)$.

To implement AT verification, we first need to form the product FSA $S \otimes \neg P$, which equals $S_1 \otimes \ldots \otimes S_n$, where $S_1, \ldots, S_{n-1}$ are the agents' plans and S_n equals $\neg P$. The algorithm for doing this, $Total_{prod}$ shown in Figure 8.6, forms product states and then specifies the transition function for these states.

Once the product FSA has been formed, it can be verified. Figure 8.7 shows the algorithm from Courcoubetis et al. [8] that we use. We call this algorithm $Total_{AT}$ because it is total automata-theoretic verification. Algorithm $Total_{AT}$ checks whether $S \not\models P$ for any property P, i.e., whether $\mathcal{L}(S \otimes \neg P) \neq \varnothing$. This is true if there is some "bad" state in a special set of states $B(S \otimes \neg P)$ that is reachable from an initial state and reachable from itself, i.e., part of an accessible cycle and therefore visited infinitely often. The algorithm of Figure 8.7 performs this check using a nested depth-first search on the product $S \otimes \neg P$. The first depth-first search begins at initial states and visits all accessible states. Whenever a state $s \in B(S \otimes \neg P)$ is discovered, it is called a "seed," and a nested search begins to look for a cycle that returns to the seed. If there is a cycle, this implies the $B(S \otimes \neg P)$ (seed) state can be visited infinitely often, and therefore the language is nonempty (i.e., there is some action sequence in the plan that does not satisfy the property) and verification fails.

8.6.2 Incremental Algorithms

Algorithm $Total_{AT}$ can be streamlined if it is known that learning occurred. The incremental reverification algorithms make the assumption that $S \models P$ prior to learning, i.e., any errors found from previous verification have already been fixed. Then learning occurs, i.e., $o(S) = S'$, followed by product re-formation, then incremental reverification (see Figure 8.2).

```
Procedure product
I(S) = ∅;
for each product state v = (v_{j_1}, ..., v_i, ..., v_{j_n}) formed from state v_i do
    if visited(v) then I(S) = I(S) ∪ {v}; endif
    if (δ(v_{j_k}, a_adapt) == 0) for some k, 1 ≤ k ≤ n, then δ(v, a_adapt) = 0
    else δ(v, a_adapt) = (δ(v_{j_1}, a_adapt),..., w_i',..., δ(v_{j_n}, a_adapt)); endif
endfor
end procedure
```

Fig. 8.8. Inc_{prod} product algorithm.

The first algorithm is an incremental version of $Total_{prod}$, called Inc_{prod}, shown in Figure 8.8, which is tailored for re-forming the product FSA (step (6) of Figure 8.2) after o_{change}. For simplicity, all of our algorithms assume o_{change} is applied to a single atom, which we assume is a multi-agent action. Since we use the tabular representation, this translates to changing one table entry. Recall that in $SIT_{multiplans}$ learning is applied to an individual agent FSA, then the product is re-formed. In all situations, the product must be re-formed with the negated property FSA after learning

```
Procedure verify
    for each state v ∈ V(S ⊗ ¬P) do
        visited(v) = 0
    endfor
    for each new initial state v ∈ I(S ⊗ ¬P) do
        if (visited(v) == 0) then dfs(v); endif
    endfor
end procedure
Procedure dfs(v)
    visited(v) = 1;
    if v ∈ B(S ⊗ ¬P) then
        seed = v;
        for each state v ∈ V(S ⊗ ¬P) do
            visited2(v) = 0
        endfor
        ndfs(v)
    endif
    if v ∈ I(S ⊗ ¬P) and w ≠ 0 and (visited(w) == 0),
    where w = δ(v, a_adapt), then dfs(w)
    else
        for each successor (i.e., next state) w of v do
            if (visited(w) == 0) then dfs(w); endif
        endfor
    endif
end procedure
```

Fig. 8.9. Procedures verify and dfs of the Inc_{AT} reverification algorithm. Procedure ndfs is the same as in Figure 8.7.

if the type of reverification to be used is AT. Algorithm Inc_{prod} assumes the product was formed originally using $Total_{prod}$. Inc_{prod} capitalizes on the knowledge of which (multi)agent state, v_1, and multi-agent action, a, have their next state altered by operator o_{change}. Since the previously generated product is stored, the only product FSA states whose next state is modified are those states that include v_1 and transition on a.

After o_{change} has been applied, followed by Inc_{prod}, incremental model checking is performed. Our incremental model checking algorithm, Inc_{AT} shown in Figure 8.9, changes the set of initial states (*only* during model checking) in the product FSA to be the set of all product states formed from state v_1 (whose next state was affected by o_{change}). Reverification begins at these new initial states, rather than the actual initial FSA states. This algorithm also includes another form of streamlining. The only transition taken by the model checker from the new initial states is on action a. This is the transition that was modified by o_{change}. Thereafter, Inc_{AT} proceeds exactly like $Total_{AT}$.

We next present an incremental reverification algorithm that is extremely time-efficient. It gains efficiency by being tailored for specific situations (i.e., only in SIT_{1agent} or SIT_{1plan} when there is one FSA to reverify), a specific learning operator (o_{gen}), and a specific class of properties (Response). A similar algorithm for Invariance properties may be found in [12].

```
Procedure check-response-property
    if y ⊨ q then
        if (z ⊨ q and z ⊨ ¬p) then output "S' ⊨ P"
        else output "Avoid this instance of o_gen"; endif
    else
        if (z ⊨ ¬p) then output "S' ⊨ P"
        else output "Avoid this instance of o_gen"; endif
    endif
end procedure
```

Fig. 8.10. Inc_{gen-R} reverification algorithm.

The algorithm, called Inc_{gen-R}, is in Figure 8.10. This algorithm is applicable for operator o_{gen}. However note that it is also applicable for $o_{delete+gen}$ and $o_{spec+gen}$, because according to the a priori results of Section 8.5 the first step in these operators is either o_{delete} or o_{spec} which are known to be SMLOs.

Assume the Response property is $P = \Box(p \rightarrow \Diamond q)$ where p is the trigger and q is the response. Suppose property P holds for plan S prior to learning, i.e., $S \models P$. Now we generalize $M(v_1, v_3) = y$ to form S' via o_{gen} $(M(v_1, v_3)) = y \vee z$, where $y \wedge z = 0$ and $y, z \neq 0$. We need to verify that $S' \models P$.

The algorithm first checks whether a response could be required of the new transition condition $M(v_1, v_3)$. We define a response to be required if for at least one string in $\mathcal{L}(S)$ whose run includes (v_1, v_3), the prefix of this string before visiting vertex v_1 includes the trigger p not followed by response q, and the string suffix after v_3 does not include the response q either. Such a string satisfies the property if and only if $y \models q$ (i.e., for every atom $a \preceq y$, $a \preceq q$). Thus if $y \models q$ and the property is true prior to learning (i.e., for S), then it is possible that a response is required and thus it must be the case that for the newly added z, $z \models q$ to ensure $S' \models P$. For example, suppose a, b, c, and d are atoms, the transition condition y between STATE4 and STATE5 equals d, and $S \models P$, where $P = \Box (a \rightarrow \Diamond d)$. Let $\mathbf{x} = (a, b, b, d, ...)$ be an accepting string of S ($\in \mathcal{L}(S)$) that includes STATE4 and STATE5 as the fourth and fifth vertices in its accepting run. $P = \Box (a \rightarrow \Diamond d)$, and therefore $y \models q$ (because $y = q = d$). Suppose o_{gen} generalizes M(STATE4, STATE5) from d to (d $\vee$ c), where z

is c, which adds the string $\mathbf{x}' = (a, b, b, c, ...)$ to $\mathcal{L}(S')$. Then $z \not\models q$. If the string suffix after (a, b, b, c) does not include d, then there is now a string which includes the trigger but does not include the response, i.e., $S' \not\models P$. Finally, if $y \models q$ and $z \models q$, an extra check is made to be sure $z \models \neg p$ because an atom could be both a response and a trigger. New triggers are thus avoided. The second part of the algorithm states that if $y \not\models q$ and no new triggers are introduced by generalization, then the operator is "safe" to do. It is guaranteed to be safe ($S' \models P$) in this case because a response is not required.

Inc_{gen-R} is a powerful algorithm in terms of its execution speed, but it is based upon the assumption that the learning operator's effect on accessibility is localized, i.e., that it is o_{gen} with SIT_{1agent} or SIT_{1plan} but not $SIT_{multplans}$. (Recall from Subsection 4.2 on the learning operators that single agent o_{gen} may translate to multi-agent o_{add} in the product FSA.) An important advantage of this algorithm is that it never requires forming a product FSA, even with the property. A disadvantage is that it may find false errors. Another disadvantage of Inc_{gen-R} is that it does not allow generalizations that add triggers. If it is desirable to add new triggers during generalization, then one needs to modify Inc_{gen-R} to call Inc_{AT} when reverification with Inc_{gen-R} fails – instead of outputting "Avoid this instance of o_{gen}." This modification also fixes the false error problem, *and* preserves the enormous time savings (see next section) when reverification succeeds.

Finally, we also have two incremental algorithms, Inc_I and Inc_{gen-I}, described in Gordon [11]. These algorithms do model checking that is not automata-theoretic, but is instead streamlined specifically for Invariance properties.

8.6.3 Time Complexity Evaluation

Theoretical worst-case time complexity comparisons, as well as the complete set of experiments, are in [11]. Here we present a subset of the results, using Response properties. Before describing the experimental results, let us consider the experimental design. [4] The underlying assumption of the design was that these algorithms would be used in the context of evolutionary learning, and therefore the experimental conditions closely mimic those that would be used in this context. In keeping with this design assumption, FSAs were randomly initialized, subject to a restriction – because the incremental algorithms assume $S \models P$ prior to learning, we restrict the FSAs to comply with this. Another experimental design decision was to show scaleup in the size of the FSAs.[5] Throughout

---

[4] All code was written in C and run on a Sun Ultra 10 workstation.

[5] Our first objective was to see how the reverification performs on FSAs large enough to handle real-world applications. Future experiments will focus on scaling up the number of agents.

the experiments there were assumed to be three agents, with each agent's plan using the same 12 multi-agent actions. Each individual agent FSA had 25 or 45 states. A suite of five Response properties was used (see [11]). The learning operator was o_{change} or o_{gen}. Although the two-step $o_{delete+gen}$ and $o_{spec+gen}$ are more useful than o_{gen}, only the generalization step can generate verification errors. Thus we use the simpler o_{gen} in the experiments. Every algorithm was tested with 30 runs – six independent runs for each of five Response properties. For every one of these runs, a different random seed was used for generating the three FSAs and for generating a new instance of the learning operator. However, it is important to point out that on each run all algorithms being compared with each other used the *same* FSAs, which were modified by the *same* learning operator instance.

Let us consider Tables 8.2 and 8.3 of results. Table entries give average (arithmetic mean) cpu times in seconds. Table 8.2 compares the performance of total reverification with the incremental algorithms that were designed for o_{change}. The situation assumed for these experiments was $SIT_{multplans}$. Three FSAs were initialized, then the product was formed. Operator o_{change}, which consisted of a random choice of next state, was then applied to one of the FSAs. Finally, the product FSA was re-formed and reverification done.

The method for generating Table 8.3 was similar to that for Table 8.2, except that o_{gen} was the learning operator and the situation was assumed to be SIT_{1plan}. Operator o_{gen} consisted of a random generalization to the product FSA.

The algorithms (rows) are in triples "p," "v" and "b" or else as a single item "v=b." A "p" next to an algorithm name implies it is a product algorithm, a "v" that it is a verification algorithm, and a "b" implies that the entry is the sum of the "p" and "v" entries, i.e., the time for *both* reforming the product and reverifying. If no product needs to be formed, then the "b" version of the algorithm is identical to the "v" version, in which case there is only one row labeled "v=b."

Table 8.2. Average cpu time (in seconds) over 30 runs (5 Response properties, 6 runs each) with operator o_{change}.

	25-state FSAs	45-state FSAs
Inc_{prod} **p**	.000574	.001786
$Total_{prod}$ **p**	.097262	.587496
Inc_{AT} **v**	.009011	.090824
$Total_{AT}$ **v**	.024062	.183409
Inc_{AT} **b**	.009585	.092824
$Total_{AT}$ **b**	.121324	.770905

Table 8.3. Average cpu time (in seconds) over 30 runs (5 Response properties, 6 runs each) with operator o_{gen}.

	25-state FSAs	45-state FSAs
Inc_{prod} **p**	.000006	.000006
$Total_{prod}$ **p**	.114825	.704934
Inc_{AT} **v**	94.660700	2423.550000
$Total_{AT}$ **v**	96.495400	2870.080000
Inc_{AT} **b**	94.660706	2423.550006
$Total_{AT}$ **b**	96.610225	2870.784934
Inc_{gen-R} **v=b**	.000007	.000006

Before we present and address the experimental hypothesis, let us first address why Table 8.3 has higher cpu times for Inc_{AT} and $Total_{AT}$ than Table 8.2. This disparity is caused by a difference in the number of verification errors (property violations). In particular, no errors occurred after o_{change}, but errors did occur after o_{gen}. The lack or presence of errors in these experiments is a by-product of the particular random FSA that happened to be generated, as well as the choice of learning operator. In the future, we plan to analyze *why* certain operators tend to generate more errors than others for particular classes of properties.

Now let us present and address the experimental hypothesis. We tested the hypothesis that the *incremental* algorithms are faster than the *total* algorithms – for both product and reverification. As shown in the tables, this hypothesis is confirmed in all cases. All differences are statistically significant ($p < .01$, using a Wilcoxon rank-sum test) except those between Inc_{AT} and $Total_{AT}$ in Table 8.3. In fact, according to a theoretical worst-case complexity analysis [11], in the worst case Inc_{AT} will take as much time as $Total_{AT}$. Nevertheless we have found in practice, for our applications, that it usually provides a reasonable time savings.

What about Inc_{gen-R}, which is even more specifically tailored? First, recall that Inc_{gen-R} can produce false errors.[6] For the results in Table 8.3, 33% of Inc_{gen-R}'s predictions were wrong (i.e., false errors) for the size 25 FSAs and 50% were wrong for the size 45 FSAs. On the other hand, consider the maximum observable speedup in Tables 8.2 and 8.3. By far the best results are with Inc_{gen-R}, which shows a $\frac{1}{2}$-*billion-fold speedup* over $Total_{AT}$ on size 45 FSA problems! This alleviates the concern about Inc_{gen-R}'s false error rate – after all, one can afford a 50% false error rate given the speed of trying another learning operator instance and reverifying.

It is possible to infer the performance of the incremental algorithms for the two-step operators based on their performance with the one-step operators. For example, we know that o_{delete} is a SMLO. We also know

---

[6] False errors are not a problem for Inc_{AT} in these experiments [11].

Table 8.4. Learning operators with the fastest reverification method.

	$SIT_{1agent/1plan}$ and Invariance	$SIT_{1agent/1plan}$ and Response	$SIT_{multplans}$ and Invariance	$SIT_{multplans}$ and Response
o_{change}	Inc_I	Inc_{AT}	Inc_I	Inc_{AT}
$o_{delete+add}$	Inc_I	Inc_{AT}	Inc_I	Inc_{AT}
$o_{spec+add}$	Inc_I	Inc_{AT}	Inc_I	Inc_{AT}
$o_{delete+gen}$	$None$	Inc_{gen-R}	Inc_I	Inc_{AT}
$o_{spec+gen}$	$None$	Inc_{gen-R}	Inc_I	Inc_{AT}

that the most efficient reverification algorithm following o_{gen} for a Response property is Inc_{gen-R}. Combining these two results, we can conclude that Inc_{gen-R} will also be the most efficient reverification algorithm to use for $o_{delete+gen}$. We conclude this section by summarizing, in Table 8.4, the fastest algorithm (based on our results) for every two-step operator (since they tend to be more useful than one-step operators), situation, and property type. Results for Inc_I are discussed in [11]. In Table 8.4, "None" means no reverification is required, i.e., the learning operator is a priori guaranteed to be a SMLO for this situation and property class.

8.7 Applications

To test our overall framework, we have implemented a simple example of cooperating planetary rovers that have to coordinate their plans. They are modeled as co-evolving agents assuming $SIT_{multplans}$. By using the a priori results and incremental algorithms, we have seen considerable speedup.

We are also developing another implementation that uses reverification during evolution [30]. Two agents compete in a board game, and one of the agents evolves its plan to improve it. The key lesson that has been learned from this implementation is that although the types of FSAs and learning operators are slightly different from those studied previously, and the property is quite different (it's a check for a certain type of cyclic behavior on the board), initial experiments show that the methodology and basic results here could potentially be easily extended to a variety of multi-agent applications.

8.8 Related Research

The FAABS'00 proceedings [26] provides an excellent sample of current research on predictable agents—including examples of significant applications, e.g., see Pecheur and Simmons [23]. For related work on predictable agents whose plans are expressed as finite-state automata and verified with model checking, Lee and Durfee [19] is a good example. Nevertheless, almost none of this research addresses adaptive agents.

In fact, even the issue of verifying adaptive *software* has been largely neglected. The research of Sokolsky and Smolka [29] is a notable exception, especially since it presents a method for incremental reverification. However, their research is about reverification of software after user edits rather than adaptive multi-agent systems.

Three papers in the FAABS'00 proceedings consider verifiable adaptive agents. The first, by Zhu [36], assumes that all possible adaptations are known a priori and can be captured in the agent's (verifiable) plan. The second, by Owre et al. [22], considers applicability of the Symbolic Analysis Laboratory (SAL) for reverifying agents' plans after adaptations such as determinization have altered the plans. Efficiency is considered, thus making this an APT agents architecture. The third paper, by Kiriakidis and Gordon [18], describes an APT agents architecture somewhat different from the one in this chapter. To alleviate much of the overhead incurred when repairing plans if reverification fails, Kiriakidis and Gordon formulate their framework within the paradigm of discrete supervisory control [25].

Barley and Guesgen [4] address an interesting issue pertaining to APT agents. They determine whether agents' adaptations preserve completeness (coverage). In particular, they specify conditions under which it is guaranteed that solutions found by an agent's problem solver will remain solutions, in spite of adaptation.

Finally, there are alternative methods for constraining the behavior of agents, which are complementary to reverification and self-repair. Turney [32] mentions a wide variety of possible alternatives. "Laws" can constrain behavior, e.g., Shoham and Tennenholtz [28] design agents that obey *social* laws, and Spears and Gordon [31] design agents that obey *physics* laws. Although laws constrain behavior, a plan designer may not be able to anticipate all needed laws beforehand – especially if the agents have to adapt. Therefore, initial engineering of laws should be coupled with efficient reverification after learning.

8.9 Summary and Open Problems

To handle real-world domains and interactions with people, agents must be adaptive, predictable, *and* rapidly responsive. An approach to resolving these potentially conflicting requirements is presented here. In summary, we have shown that certain machine learning operators are a priori (with no run-time reverification) safe to perform, i.e., they are property preserving. All of the a priori results are independent of the size of the FSA and are therefore applicable to any FSA that has been model checked originally.

We then presented novel incremental reverification algorithms for the cases in which the a priori results are negative. Experimental results are shown which indicate that these algorithms can substantially improve the time complexity of reverification over total reverification from scratch. One of the algorithms showed as much as a $\frac{1}{2}$-billion-fold speedup on average over traditional verification.

The significance of this work is that any early offline assurances about agent behavior risk being rendered obsolete by subsequent adaptation. What has been shown here is that for some adaptations reverification can be localized to just the region of the plan affected by the change, thus making retesting potentially very fast. Furthermore, we have identified property-preserving adaptations that require no reverification, i.e., behavioral assurance is guaranteed to be preserved without the need to retest it. A limitation of this research is that not all properties, plans, and learning methods are amenable to localization. Our results are applicable only when such localization is possible.

A great deal remains to be done on APT agents. A recent RIACS/NASA Ames Workshop on the Verification and Validation of Autonomous and Adaptive Systems (Asilomar, CA; December 2000) raised intriguing questions that could lead to fruitful future research (http://ase.arc.nasa.gov/vv2000/asilomar-report.html).

One important direction for future research would be to explore how to achieve APT agents in the context of a variety of different agent architectures or classes of relevant agent properties/constraints. For example, this chapter assumes that agent plans are represented as deterministic finite-state automata. However there are many other options, such as stochastic finite-state automata or rule sets. The Automated Software Engineering Group at NASA Ames is currently pursuing APT-related research in the context of neural network architectures. Regarding classes of properties, Manna and Pneuli [20] provide a taxonomy of temporal logic properties that could be considered.

Also, recall that one of the agents in a multi-agent situation acts as the V&V agent. Is it possible to distribute the V&V burden among multiple agents? We plan to investigate this question.

Another profitable direction for future research is to explore the wide variety of machine learning methods potentially used by APT agents [27]. The list of possible learning techniques is broad and includes statistical learning, case-based inference, reinforcement learning, Bayesian updating, evolutionary learning, inductive inference, speedup learning, and theory refinement. These learning methods enable adaptation to changing environmental conditions, and they can also increase the efficiency and/or effectiveness of plans used by agents.

Finally, deeper analyses of *why* certain learning techniques are better/worse (in terms of the number of verification errors they cause) for particular classes of properties could be quite beneficial. Such analyses

could inspire new a priori results, new incremental reverification algorithms, as well as new "safe" learning algorithms.

References

1. Arora, N. and Sen, S. Resolving social dilemmas using genetic algorithms. In *Proceedings of the AAAI Symposium on Adaptation, Coevolution and Learning in Multiagent Systems*, AAAI Press, Stanford, CA, 1996, pp 1–5.
2. Asimov, I. *I, Robot*. Fawcett Publications, Inc., Greenwich, CT. 1950.
3. Bäck, T. and Schwefel, H. P. An overview of evolutionary algorithms for parameter optimization. *Evolutionary Computation*, 1(1):1–24, MIT Press, 1993.
4. Barley, M. and Guesgen, H. *Towards safe learning agents*. Technical Report, University of Auckland, 2001.
5. Büchi, J. On a decision method in restricted second-order arithmetic. In *Methodology and Philosophy of Science, Proceedings of the Stanford International Congress*, Stanford University Press, Stanford, CA, 1962, pp 1–11.
6. Burkhard, H. Liveness and fairness properties in multiagent systems. In *Proceedings of the 13th International Joint Conference on Artificial Intelligence (IJCAI'93)*, Morgan-Kaufmann, Chambéry, France, 1993, pp 325–330.
7. Clarke, E. and Wing, J. Formal methods: State of the art and future directions. *ACM Computing Surveys*, 28(4):626–643, Association for Computing Machinery Publishers, 1997.
8. Courcoubetis, C., Vardi, M., Wolper, M. and Yannakakis, M. Memory-efficient algorithms for the verification of temporal properties. *Formal Methods in Systems Design*, 1:257–288, Kluwer, 1992.
9. Fogel, D. On the relationship between duration of an encounter and the evolution of cooperation in the iterated Prisoner's Dilemma. *Evolutionary Computation*, 3(3):349–363, MIT Press, 1996.
10. Georgeoff, M. and Lansky, A. Reactive reasoning and planning. In *Proceedings of the Sixth National Conference on Artificial Intelligence (AAAI'87)*, Seattle, WA, Morgan-Kaufmann, 1987, pp 677–682.
11. Gordon, D. Asimovian adaptive agents. *Journal of Artificial Intelligence Research*, 13:95–153, Morgan-Kauffman, 2000.
12. Gordon, D. Well-behaved Borgs, Bolos, and Berserkers. In *Proceedings of the 15th International Conference on Machine Learning (ICML'98)*, Madison, WI, Morgan-Kaufmann, 1998, pp 224–232.
13. Grecu, D. and Brown, D. Dimensions of learning in agent-based design. In *Proceedings of the 4th International Conference on AI in Design – Workshop on "Machine Learning in Design"*, Stanford, CA, AAAI Press, 1996, pp 21–26.
14. Grefenstette, J., Ramsey, C. and Schultz, A. Learning sequential decision rules using simulation models and competition. *Machine Learning*, 5(4):355–382, Kluwer, 1990.
15. Jennings, R., Mamdani, E., Corera, J., Laresgoiti, I., Perriolat, F., Skarek, P. and Varga, L. Using ARCHON to develop real-world DAI applications. *IEEE Expert*, 11(6):64–70, IEEE Computer Society Publishers, 1996.
16. Kabanza, F. Synchronizing multiagent plans using temporal logic specifications. In *Proceedings of the First International Conference on MultiAgent Systems (ICMAS'95)*, San Francisco, CA, MIT Press, 1995, pp 217–224.

17. Kaelbling, L, Littman, M. and Moore, A. Reinforcement learning: A survey. *Journal of Artificial Intelligence Research*, **4**:237–285, Morgan-Kauffman, 1996.
18. Kiriakidis, K. and Gordon, D. Adaptive supervisory control of multiagent systems. In *Formal Approaches to Agent-Based Systems (FAABS'00), (LNAI 1871)*, Greenbelt, MD, Springer-Verlag, 2001, pp 304–305.
19. Lee, J. and Durfee, E. On explicit plan languages for coordinating multiagent plan execution. In *Proceedings of the 4th Workshop on Agent Theories, Architectures, and Languages (ATAL'97), (LNAI 1365)*, Providence, RI, Springer-Verlag, 1997, pp 113–126.
20. Manna, Z. and Pnueli, A. The anchored version of the temporal framework. *Lecture Notes in Computer Science*, **345**:201–284, Springer-Verlag, 1989.
21. Miller, W., Sutton, R. and Werbos, P. (editors). *Neural Networks for Control.* MIT Press, Cambridge, MA. 1992.
22. Owre, S., Ruess, H., Rushby, J. and Shankar, N. Formal approaches to agent-based systems with SAL. In *Formal Approaches to Agent-Based Systems (FAABS'00) Abstracts*, Greenbelt, MD, 2001.
23. Pecheur, C. and Simmons, R. From Livingstone to SMV: Formal verification for autonomous spacecrafts. In *Formal Approaches to Agent-Based Systems (FAABS'00), (LNAI 1871)*, Greenbelt, MD, Springer-Verlag, 2001, pp 103–113.
24. Potter, M., Meeden, L. and Schultz, A. Heterogeneity in the coevolved behaviors of mobile robots: The emergence of specialists. In *Proceedings of the 17th International Conference on Artificial Intelligence (IJCAI'01)*, Seattle, WA, Morgan-Kaufmann, 2001, pp 1337–1343.
25. Ramadge, P. and Wonham, W. Supervisory control of a class of discrete event processes. *SIAM Journal of Control and Optimization*, **25**(1):206–230, Globe Publishers, 1987.
26. Rash, J, Rouff, C., Truszkowski, W., Gordon D. and Hinchey, M. (editors). In *Formal Approaches to Agent-Based Systems (FAABS'00), (LNAI 1871)*, Greenbelt, MD, Springer-Verlag, 2001.
27. Sen, S. (editor). In *Proceedings of the AAAI Symposium on Adaptation, Co-evolution and Learning in Multiagent Systems*, AAAI Spring Symposium, Stanford, CA, AAAI Press, 1996.
28. Shoham, Y. and Tennenholtz, M. Social laws for artificial agent societies: Offline design. *Artificial Intelligence*, **73**(1-2):231–252, Elsevier Science Publishers, 1995.
29. Sokolsky, O. and Smolka, S. Incremental model checking in the modal mu-calculus. In *Proceedings of the Sixth Conference on Computer-Aided Verification (CAV'94), (LNCS 818)*, Stanford, CA, Springer-Verlag, 1994, pp 351–363.
30. Spears, W. and Gordon, D. Evolving finite-state machine strategies for protecting resources. In *Proceedings of the Foundations of Intelligent Systems (ISMIS'00), (LNAI 1932)*, Charlotte, NC, Springer-Verlag, 2000, pp 166–175.
31. Spears, W. and Gordon, D. Using artificial physics to control agents. In *Proceedings of the IEEE International Conference on Information, Intelligence and Systems (ICIIS'99)*, Bethesda, MD, IEEE Computer Society Publishers, 1999, pp 281–288.
32. Turney, P. Controlling super-intelligent machines. *Canadian Artificial Intelligence*, **27**:3–35, Canadian Society for Computational Studies of Intelligence Publishers, 1991.

33. Watkins, C. *Learning from delayed rewards*. Doctoral dissertation, Cambridge University, Cambridge, England, 1989.
34. Weld, D. and Etzioni, O. The first law of robotics. In *Proceedings of the Twelfth National Conference on Artificial Intelligence*, Seattle, WA, MIT Press, 1994, pp 1042–1047.
35. Wolpert, D., Wheeler, K. and Tumer, K. General principles of learning-based multiagent systems. In *Proceedings of the Third International Conference on Autonomous Agents*, Seattle, WA, Association for Computing Machinery Publishers, 1999, pp 77–83.
36. Zhu, H. Formal specification of agent behaviors through environment scenarios. In *Formal Approaches to Agent-Based Systems (FAABS'00), (LNAI 1871)*, Greenbelt, MD, Springer-Verlag, 2001, pp 263–277.

9

Agents in a Wild World

Tim Menzies and Ying Hu

9.1 Introduction

A Turing machine is a lonely machine. It talks to no one and no outsider talks to it. Within its walls, nothing happens unless its read-write device changes an entry on a Turing tape. No external force ever stops the tape rolling backwards and forwards, searching for its solitary conclusions.

An agent machine is a social machine. Situated within some environment, the agent busily attempts to achieve goals while being buffeted by *wild forces* outside of its control. Beliefs that seemed reasonable only an hour ago may become obsolete. It is as if the Turing tape of our agent machine can be *wildly scribbled on* by the environment, without the agent noticing.[1]

To assess the impacts of wild interaction, this chapter will consider an agent dealing with devices of the form of Figure 9.1. Such devices contain *hidden* variables, *inputs* variables and *observable* variables. For the purposes of this analysis, it is irrelevant if the devices are subroutines within the agent or sensors and actuators attached to the environment. In either case, our agent can change only the *controllable* inputs. The other inputs are *wild* and are set by forces outside of the control of the agent; e.g. the environment, or the actions of other agents. We will assume no knowledge of the wild inputs. In this model, nondeterminism is modeled as wild variables that control choice operators at all nondeterministic choice points within the hidden variables.

We will assume that some of the observables are *assessable* by some oracle. This oracle generates a small number of *scored classes* that offer a coarse-grain assessment of the behavior of a system; e.g. "very good," "good," "fair," "poor," "very poor." For example, if the device can achieve N

---

[1] We owe this image to the keynote address of Dr. James Hendler at the first NASA Goddard Workshop on Formal Approaches to Agent-Based Systems, April 5–7, 2000.

output goals, then the oracle could output "good" if more than (say) 80% of those goals are reached.

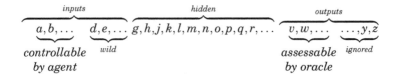

Fig. 9.1. An agent with wild inputs.

A *treatment* is some setting to the controllable inputs. The task of our agent is to *minimize* the *cost* of both *finding* and *applying* its treatments while *maximizing* the *score* of the classes generated by the oracle. We will assume that it *costs* some effort to adjust the control inputs. The rest of this article assumes all controls cost "1" unit of effort (and this could be simply adjusted if required).

The challenge facing our agent is that much of the device is *hidden* or *wild*. Any treatments must be effective over the range of possible behaviors that result from the *wild* inputs impacting the *hidden* variables. Hence, we say that the range of possible outputs from the device represents a space of what-if scenarios and a treatment *restricts* the space of possible what-ifs by restricting the space of settings to the control variables.

This chapter argues that:

CLAIM1: In the average case, it is possible to learn effective and cheap treatments, despite the wild variables.

CLAIM2: It is possible to redesign particular devices in order to *increase* their immunity to wild variables.

CLAIM1 will be defended using an average case analysis, some experimentation, and a literature review. Such an average case analysis may not apply to particular systems. Hence **CLAIM2** is required in order to increase the chances that a particular system exhibits our desired average case behavior.

To demonstrate these claims, we need:

1. A formal model of the hidden variables. We will assume that the hidden variables form a *negation-free horn clause theory*. We will further assume that some *nogood* predicate can report pairs of incompatible variables. A sample negation-free horn clause theory and a *nogood* predicate are shown in Figure 9.2.
2. A definition of the execution method of that theory. We will assume that execution means the construction of consistent proof trees across

```
% rules
happy            if tranquility(hi) or rich and healthy.
healthy          if diet(light).
satiated         if diet(fatty).
tranquility(hi)  if satiated or conscience(clear)

% facts
diet(fatty).
diet(light).

% contradiction knowledge, e.g. diet(fatty) and diet(light)
% are nogood.
nogood(X,Y)  :-
    X =.. [F|A1],
    Y =.. [F|A2],
    A1 \= A2.
```

Fig. 9.2. A theory.

the horn clauses, where *consistent* is defined with respect to the *nogood* predicates.

3. A theoretical sensitivity result that shows that adequate treatments can be developed for our device *across the entire range of possible wild inputs*. We will show that the entire range of possible wild inputs will, in the average case, result in a limited number of settings to the assessable outputs.

This demonstration will be made in three parts. Section 9.3 offers a theoretical argument for CLAIM1. Section 9.4 discusses empirical results that support our theory. Section 9.5 argues for **CLAIM2**. Related work is discussed throughout this chapter. This work extends earlier studies on testing nondeterministic systems [19, 21, 18]. Also, before beginning, we offer some notes on how this work connects with the standard agent literature (see Section 9.2).

Note that this analysis will only be an *average case analysis*. Such an argument for *average case* success says little about our ability to handle *uncommon, critical cases*. Hence, our analysis must be used with care if applied to safety-critical software. On the other hand, many applications are not safety-critical since such software costs in excess of one million dollars per thousand lines of code [32, p276]; i.e., safety-critical applications are cost-justified in only a minority of cases.

9.2 A Quick Overview of Agents

This chapter applies concepts from the truth maintenance literature [7] to engineering controllers for agents. Hence, it is somewhat distant from the rest of the papers in this volume. To bridge the gap, this section offers some notes on the standard agent literature.

A spectrum of agents types is offered by Wooldridge and Jennings [35]. *Weak agents* are:

Autonomous: Agents act without intervention by a human operator.
Socialable: Agents interact extensively with other agents.
Reactive: Agents must react to changing circumstances.
Pro-active: Agents can take the initiative within a simulation.

This chapter is an exploration of the mathematics of the above features of weak agency. Before we can trust agents to work correctly and autonomously, we need to certify that they will behave correctly, even in wild domains. Before agents can learn to trust each other during social action, they must assess another agent, even if much of that agent is wild. Further, reactions and proactions are futile in unless we can certify that those actions are effective, even in wild domains.

Wooldridge and Jennings distinguish *weak agency* from *strong agents*. Strong agents possess mentalistic attitudes or can be emotional or animated. A commonly used framework for strange agents is the beliefs, desires and intentions (BDI) paradigm of [30] and (partially) implemented within the dMARS system [6]:

Beliefs: the current state of entities and environment as perceived by the agent (abstract labels or percepts)
Desires: future states an agent would like to be in (a.k.a. goals)
Intentions: commitment of an agent to achieve a goal by progressing along a particular future path that leads to the goal (a.k.a. a plan).

In this BDI paradigm, deliberation is done through the selection of a goal, selection of a plan that will be used to form an intention, selection of an intention, and execution of the selected intention. All these decisions are based on the beliefs the agent has about the current state of the environment. In wild environments, plan generation is futile unless we can first assert that the wild influences do not destroy the plan.

Wooldridge and Jennings make no comments beyond strong agency. However, other researchers have explored further extensions: Pearce and Heinze added another layer on top of dMARS to process the patterns of standard agent usage seen in simulations [29]. Their *command agents* divide reasoning into the following tasks:

Situation awareness: Extracting the essential features from the environment.
Assessment: Ranking the extracted features.
Tactic selection: Exploring the space of options.
Selection of operational procedure: Mapping the preferred option onto the available resources.

In repeated applications of this framework, Pearce and Heinze report that the command agents framework offers a significant productivity increase over standard dMARS. However, these researchers don't know how to validate their agent systems (pers. communication). One of the original motivations of this work was the need to certify command agents in particular and other agent systems in general.

For other interesting applications of agent technology, see [13, 9, 1, 27, 28] and the other chapters in this volume.

9.3 Usual Case Analysis of Wild Influences

In this section, we begin our case for **CLAIM1**; i.e. in the average case, it is possible to learn effective and cheap treatments, despite the wild variables. Wild variables inject a degree of randomness into how a device will operate. We show here that such a random search within a device containing *nogoods* can be controlled by a small number of key *funnel variables* (defined below). It will be argued that:

1. The range of behaviors within a device containing *nogoods* is small if there are few possible *worlds of belief* (defined below).
2. The total number of possible *worlds of belief* is small if the *funnel size* is small.
3. In the average case, the funnel size is indeed quite small.

These three points are necessary, but not sufficient preconditions for **CLAIM1**. The next section (2) will show that the small number of key variables within the funnel can be controlled using just the available controllable inputs.

9.3.1 Worlds of Belief

A theorem prover exploring a device containing *nogood* variables often reaches incompatible options; e.g. pairs of variables depreciated by the *nogood* predicate. For example, in Figure 9.2, two such incompatible beliefs are diet(light) and diet(fatty).

When such incompatible pairs are reached, the theorem prover must choose which variable to believe. As the reasoning progresses, this continual choice of what to believe leads to a particular *world of belief*.

Given a model such as Figure 9.2 and a goal such as happy, then worlds of belief can be generated as follows.

- The individual pathways to the goals are collected. Figure 9.3 shows the possible pathways are $Path_1 \ldots Path_3$, shown in Figure 9.3.
- Anything that has not been asserted as a fact is an *assumption*. If we have asserted happy, then $Path_2$ contains the assumptions tranquility(hi) and satiated and diet(fatty).

$Path_1$ happy $\leftarrow$ tranquility(hi) $\leftarrow$ conscience(clear)
$Path_2$: happy $\leftarrow$ tranquility(hi) $\leftarrow$ satiated $\leftarrow$ diet(fatty)
$Path_3$: happy $\leftarrow$ and1 $\begin{cases} \leftarrow \text{rich} \\ \leftarrow \text{healthy} \leftarrow \text{diet(light)} \end{cases}$

Fig. 9.3. Three pathways to happy generated across Figure 9.4 (which is a graphical form of Figure 9.2).

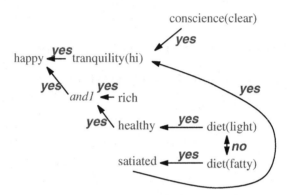

Fig. 9.4. The rules of Figure 9.2 converted to an and-or graph. All nodes here are or-nodes except *and1*. All parents of an and-node must be believed if we are to believe and-node. In this graph *no-edges* represent illegal pairs of inferences; i.e., things we can't believe at the same time such as diet(light) and diet(fatty). All other edges are *yes-edges* which represent legal inferences.

- No path can contain mutually exclusive assumptions or contradict the goal; i.e., assuming ¬happy is illegal since, in this example, we already believe happy.
- The generated pathways should be grouped together into maximal consistent subsets. Each such subset is a world of belief. Our example generates two worlds: $World_1 = \{Path_1, Path_3\}$ and $World_2 = \{Path_1, Path_2\}$.
- A world contains what we can conclude from and-or graphs. A goal is proved if it can be found in a world.

Worlds are generated when inconsistencies are detected. There are at least three methods to control such generation:

Method A- Full worlds search: Method A is to generate a world for every possible resolution. Method A takes a long time[2] and pragmatic agents should avoid it.

Method B- Random worlds search: Method B is to generate a world for one on resolution, picked at random, then continue on. Method B is often combined with a "rest-retry" mechanism. That is, method B is applied X times, with the system reset between each application.

Method C- Use of domain knowledge: Method C is to carefully select one resolution, based on domain knowledge. This chapter is focused on the effects of the unknown knowledge (the wild variables) rather than the effects of known knowledge; i.e. Method C is not of interest here.

Random worlds search (method B) best simulates the impact of wild inputs. Such a partial random search will find only some subset of the possible paths, particularly if it is run for a heuristically selected time interval. That is, random worlds searching may not reliably infer that, e.g., healthy is an uncertain conclusion. Depending on how the conflict between diet(light) and diet(happy) is resolved at runtime, this system will sometimes nondeterministically conclude healthy and sometimes it won't.

CLAIM1 can be formally expressed as follows: the wild inputs do not greatly influence what worlds are explored. Traditional complexity results are pessimistic about such a claim. If a graph lacks *nogoods*, then it can be searched very fast. (see the linear-time and-or graph traversal algorithm in the appendix). However, the presence of *nogoods* changes all that. Gabow et al. [8] showed that building pathways across programs with impossible pairs (e.g. variables marked by a *nogood* predicate) is NP-complete for all but the simplest programs (a program is very simple if it is very small, or it is a simple tree, or it has a dependency networks with out degree ≤ 1). The traditional view is that NP-complete tasks are only practical when incomplete domain-specific heuristics are applied to constrain the task. The application of such heuristics to all possible inputs cannot be proven. Hence, in the traditional view, using such heuristics can produce *wildly* differing results when:

I. *Not enough worlds are generated to cover the range of possible conclusions.* This first case could arise from heuristics pruning possible inferences at runtime. Random worlds search can suffer from this problem.

---

[2] Method A is a synonym for "explore every option in the program." Experience suggests that this is often an intractable process; e.g., the state-space explosion problem of model checkers [11]; or the intractable branching problem of qualitative reasoning [2].

II. *Too many worlds are generated and we are swamped with possibilities.*
This second case arises when heuristics fail to prune the search space.
Full worlds search can suffer from this problem.

Both problems are removed if *the total number of possible worlds is
small*. If so, then:

- Problem I disappears if all the possible conclusions can be reached by
  sampling just a few worlds.
- Problem II disappears if a large number of worlds is not possible.

9.3.2 Funnels Control Worlds

This section argues that the number of worlds is small if the *funnel* size
is small. Before describing the funnel, we first categorize assumptions
into three important groups: the dependent, the noncontroversial, and
the remaining variables that lie in the *funnel*. Only this third group of
funnel variables will determine how many worlds are generated.

Some assumptions are *dependent* on other assumptions. For example,
in *Path*$_2$, the tranquility(hi) assumption depends fully on satiated
which, in turn, fully depends on diet(fatty). In terms of exploring all
the effects of different assumptions, we can ignore the dependent assumptions.

Another important category of assumptions are the assumptions that
contradict no other assumptions. These *noncontroversial* assumptions are
never at odds with other assumptions and so do not effect the number of
worlds generated. In our example, the noncontroversial assumptions are
everything except diet(light) and diet(healthy). Hence, like the
dependent assumptions, we will ignore these noncontroversial assumptions.

The remaining assumptions are the *controversial, nondependent* assumptions or the *funnel* assumptions. These funnel assumptions control
how all the other assumptions are grouped into worlds of belief. DeKleer's
key insight in the ATMS research was that a multi-world reasoning device need only focus on the funnel [5].[3] When switching between worlds,
all we need to resolve is which funnel assumptions we endorse. Continuing our example, if we endorse diet(light) then all the conclusions in
World$_2$ follow and if we endorse diet(healthy) then all the conclusions
in *World*$_1$ follow.

Paths meet and clash in the funnel. If the size of the funnel is very
small, then the number of possible clashes is very small and the number

---

[3] DeKleer called the funnel assumptions the *minimal environments* We do not
adopt that terminology here since DeKleer used consistency-based abduction
while we are exploring set-covering abduction here. For an excellent discussion
that defines and distinguishes set-covering from consistency-based methods,
see [3].

of possible resolutions to those clashes is also very small. When the number of possible resolutions is very small, the number of possible worlds is very small and random search can quickly probe the different worlds of beliefs (since there are so few of them). Hence, if we can show that the average size of the funnel is small, then **CLAIM1** is supported.

9.3.3 Average Funnel Size

Suppose some goal can be reached by a narrow funnel M or a wide funnel N as follows:

$$
\left.
\begin{array}{l}
\xrightarrow{a_1} M_1 \\
\xrightarrow{a_2} M_2 \\
\cdots \\
\xrightarrow{a_m} M_m
\end{array}
\right\}
\xrightarrow{c} goal_i \xleftarrow{d}
\left\{
\begin{array}{l}
N_1 \xleftarrow{b_1} \\
N_2 \xleftarrow{b_2} \\
N_3 \xleftarrow{b_2} \\
N_4 \xleftarrow{b_2} \\
\cdots \\
N_n \xleftarrow{b_n}
\end{array}
\right.
$$

We say that the probability of reaching the goal is the value *reached*.

Under what circumstances will the narrow funnel be favored over the wide funnel? More precisely, when are the odds of reaching $goal_i$ via the narrow funnel much greater than the odds of reaching $goal_i$ via the wide funnel? The following analysis is taken from [20] which is a simplification of [25].

To find the average funnel size, we begin with the following definitions. Let the M funnel use m variables and the N funnel use n variables. For comparison purposes, we express the size of the wider funnel as a ratio α of the narrower funnel; i.e.,

$$(9.1) \qquad\qquad n = \alpha m$$

Each member of M is reached via a path with probability a_i while each member of N is reached via a path with probability b_i. Two paths exist from the funnels to this goal: one from the narrow neck with probability c and one from the wide neck with probability d. The probability of reaching the goal via the narrow pathway is

$$(9.2) \qquad\qquad narrow = c \times_{i=1}^{m} a_i$$

while the probability of reaching the goal via the wide pathway is

$$(9.3) \qquad\qquad wide = d \times_{i=1}^{n} b_i$$

Let $P(narrow \mid reached)$ and $P(wide \mid reached)$ denote the conditional probabilities of using one of the funnels, given that the goal is reached. The ratio R of these conditional probabilities informs us when the narrow funnel is favored over the wider funnel.

(9.4) $$R = \frac{P(narrow \mid reached)}{P(wide \mid reached)} = \frac{\left(\frac{narrow}{reached}\right)}{\left(\frac{wide}{reached}\right)} = \frac{narrow}{wide}$$

Narrow funnels are more likely than wider funnels when

(9.5) $$R \gg 1$$

To compute the frequency of Equation 9.5, we have to make some assumptions about the probability distributions of *narrow* and *reached*. [25] showed that if a_i and b_i come from uniform probability distributions, then narrow funnels are more likely than wide funnels. In the case of such uniform distributions,

(9.6) $$\sum_{i=1}^{m} a_i = 1 \therefore a_i = \frac{1}{m} \therefore narrow = c \left(\frac{1}{m}\right)^m$$

Similarly, under the same assumptions,

(9.7) $$wide = d \left(\frac{1}{n}\right)^n$$

Under this assumption of uniformity, $R > 1$ when

(9.8) $$\frac{narrow}{wide} = \frac{c \left(\frac{1}{m}\right)^m}{d \left(\frac{1}{n}\right)^n}$$

Recalling that $n = \alpha m$, this expression becomes

(9.9) $$(\alpha m)^{\alpha m} m^{-m} > \frac{d}{c}$$

Consider the case of two funnels, one twice as big as the other; i.e. $\alpha = 2$. This expression can then be rearranged to show that $\frac{narrow}{wide} > 1$ is true when

(9.10) $$(4m)^m > \frac{d}{c}$$

At $m = 2$, Equation 9.10 becomes $d < 64c$. That is, to access $goal_i$ from the wider funnel, the pathway d must be 64 times more likely than the pathway c. This is not highly likely and this becomes less likely as the narrower funnel grows. By the same reasoning, at $m = 3$, to access $goal_i$ from the wider funnel, the pathway d must be 1728 times more likely than the narrower pathway c. That is, under the assumptions of this uniform case, as the wide funnel gets wider, it becomes less and less likely that it will be used.

To explore the case where $\sum_{i=1}^{m} a_i \neq 1$ and $\sum_{i=1}^{m} b_i \neq 1$ (i.e. the non-uniform probability distribution case), we created and executed a small simulator many times. In this simulator, we found the frequency at which $R > t$ where t was some threshold value.

To execute the simulator, we required some knowledge of the distributions of *narrow* and *wide* when they are computed by a nondeterministic search. Those distributions were taken from an average case analysis of reachability across graphs such as Figure 9.4. This reachability analysis is discussed below.

A Reachability Model

Menzies, Cukic, Singh and Powell [21] computed the odds of reaching some random part of a space of nondeterminate choices from random inputs. The analysis assumed that software had been transformed into a possibly cyclic directed graph containing and-nodes and or-nodes; e.g. Figure 9.2 has been converted to Figure 9.4. A simplified description of their analysis is presented here. For example, in the full model, all variables are really random gamma or beta distribution variables specified by a *mean* and a *skew* parameter; see [21] for details.

Assume that "*in*" number of inputs have been presented to a graph containing V nodes. From these inputs, we grow a tree of pathways down to some random node within the graph. The odds of reaching a node straight away from the inputs is

$$(9.11) \qquad\qquad x_0 = \frac{in}{V}$$

The probability of reaching an and-node with *andp* parents is the probability of reaching all its parents; i.e.,

$$(9.12) \qquad\qquad x_{and} = x_i^{andp}$$

where x_i is the probability we computed in the prior step of the simulation (and x_0 being the base case). The probability of reaching an or-node with *orp* parents is the probability of not missing any of its parents; i.e.,

$$(9.13) \qquad\qquad x_{or} = 1 - (1 - x_i)^{orp}$$

If the ratio of and-nodes in a network is *andf*, then the ratio of or-nodes in the same network is $1 - andf$. The odds of reaching some random node x_j is the weighted sum of the probabilities of reaching and-nodes or-nodes; i.e.,

$$(9.14) \qquad\qquad x_j = andf * x_{and} + orf * x'_{or}$$
$$(9.15) \qquad\qquad x'_{or} = x_{or} * x_{no\,loop} * x_{no\,clash}$$

X'_{or} is similar to the original x_{or}, but it is modified by Equation 9.15, for the following reasons. Recall from Figure 9.2 that some nodes are *nogood* with other nodes and the average size of the *nogood* set for each variable is *no*. The probability $x_{no\ clash}$ is that a new node can be added to the tree of pathways of size $size_j$ at level j is the probability that this new node will not contradict any of the or-nodes in the current path:

$$(9.16) \qquad x_{no\ clash} = \left(1 - \frac{no}{V}\right)^{size_j * orf}$$

Not only must a new node not contradict with other nodes in the tree of pathways, it must also not introduce a loop into the tree, since loops do not contribute to revealing unseen nodes.

$$(9.17) \qquad x_{no\ loop} = \left(1 - \frac{1}{V}\right)^{size_j * orf}$$

Observe the use of $size_j * orf$ in Equation 9.16 and Equation 9.17. And-nodes contradict no other nodes; hence we only need to consider contradictions for *orf* of the system. Also, since every and-node has an or-node as a parent, then we need only check for loops amongst the or-nodes.

Having calculated x_j, we can convert it to the number of tests N required to be 99% sure of finding a fault with probability x_j as follows. Equation 9.13 is really the sampling-with-replacement equation where *orp* is the number of trials N. We can use sampling-with-replacement to find the certainty of finding some event after N trials. If we demand a 99% certainty of reaching a node at step j (i.e., $y = 0.99$), then we can re-arrange Equation 9.13 to

$$(9.18) \qquad N(x_j) = \frac{log(1 - 0.99)}{log(1 - x_j)}$$

After 150,000 simulations of this model, some best and worst cases were identified. These are shown in Figure 9.5 labeled *pessimistic* and *optimistic* respectively. In the pessimistic case, we restricted the depth of our search to some trivial size: $j < 10$. In this pessimistic case, more than 10,000 random inputs are required to reach half the nodes in the graphs we simulated. In the optimistic case, we gave the search engine greater freedom to explore: $j < 100$. In this optimistic case, less than 100 random inputs would reach over half the nodes in the graphs we simulated.

Simulating Funnels

Having some knowledge of the distributions, we can now compute the frequency of Equation 9.5 (i.e., $R \gg 1$) for nonuniform distributions. For one run of the Equation 9.4 simulator, m and α were picked at random from the ranges:

$$m \in \{1, 2, \ldots 10\}; \alpha \in \{1, 1.25, 1.5, \ldots 10\}$$

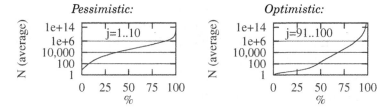

Fig. 9.5. 150,000 runs of the simulator generated x_j figures which were converted into number of tests N required using Equation 9.18. X-axis shows the percentile distribution of the output of the runs.

The a_i, b_i, c, d needed for Equations 9.2 and 9.3 were taken from one of three distributions: the pessimistic and optimistic curves shown in Figure 9.5, plus a log-normal curve (just for comparison purposes). For the log-normal curve, mean μ and standard deviation σ^2 of the logarithm of the variables were picked at random from the following ranges:

$$\mu \in \{1, 2, \ldots 10\}; \; spread \in \{0.05, 0.1, 0.2, 0.4, 0.8\}$$

μ and *spread* where then converted into probability as follows:

$$\sigma^2 = spread * \mu; \; probability = 10^{-1 * normDist(\mu, \sigma^2)}$$

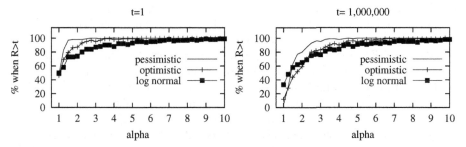

Fig. 9.6. 10000 runs of the funnel simulator: Y-axis shows what percentage of the runs satisfies $R > t$.

R was then calculated and the number of times R exceeded different values for t is shown in Figure 9.6. As might be expected, at $t = 1, \alpha = 1$ the funnels are the same size and the odds of using one of them is 50%. As α increases, then increasingly $R > t$ is satisfied and the narrower funnel is preferred to the wider funnel. The effect is quite pronounced. For example, for all the studied distributions, if the wider funnel is 2.25 times bigger than the narrow funnel, random search will be 1,000,000 times as likely as to use the narrow funnel (see the lower graph of Figure 9.6).

Interestingly, as reachability drops, the odds of using the narrow funnel increase (see the *pessimistic curves* in Figure 9.6). That is, the harder the search, the less likely the search will suffer from the problem of nondeterminate search under-sampling the space.

9.3.4 Exploiting the Funnel via Random Search

Prior research is pessimistic about finding the funnels in tractable time. Assumption-based truth maintenance systems incrementally build and update the *minimal environments* (a.k.a. funnels) that control the total assumption space [5]. In practice, finding the minimal environments takes time exponential on theory size [17].

However, such pessimism may be misplaced. There is no need to *find* the funnel in order to *exploit* it since *any* pathway from inputs to goals must pass through the funnel (by definition). Repeated application of some random search technique will stumble across the funnel variables, providing that search technique reaches the goals. Further, assuming small funnels, such a random search would not have to run for very long to sample all the possible worlds.

There is some evidence in the literature for this optimistic view that random search can quickly sample the behavior of a wild system:

- For CNF representations, it is well established that random search with retries can demonstrate satisfiability in theories too large for full search [15].
- Williams and Nayak found that a random worlds search algorithm performed as well as the best available assumption-based truth maintenance system (which conducts a full worlds search) [34].
- Menzies, Easterbrook et al. report experiments comparing random world search with full world search for requirements engineering. After millions of runs, they concluded that randomized world search found almost as many goals in less time as full worlds search [22].
- In other work, Menzies and Michael compared a full worlds search with a random worlds search. As expected, the full worlds search ran slow ($O(2^N)$) while the random worlds search ran much faster ($O(N^2)$); see Figure 9.7. What is more interesting is that, for problems where both search methods terminated, the random worlds search found 98% of the goals found by the full worlds search [24].

9.4 Controlling the Funnel

The previous section argued that (i) funnel variables control a device; (ii) the number of funnel variables is small; and (iii) this small funnel can be found quickly via randomized search. This is not enough to prove

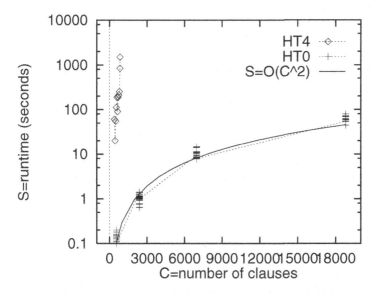

Fig. 9.7. HT4: full worlds search- fork one world for each consistent possibility reached from inputs. HT0: Random worlds search- when contradictions are found, pick one resolution at random, then continue. In the zone where both algorithms terminated, HT0's random world search found 98% of the goals found by HT4's full worlds search [24].

CLAIM1. It remains to be shown that the funnel variables can be controlled using just the available controllable inputs. This section uses experiments with *treatment learners* to argue that the funnel can be influenced by the controllers.

9.4.1 Treatment Learners: An Overview

Treatment learners input a sample of a device's behavior that has been classified by the oracle in Figure 9.1. These learners output a conjunction that is a constraint on future control inputs of the device. This conjunction, called the *treatment*, is a control strategy that "nudges" the device away from "bad" behavior towards "good" behavior (where "good" and "bad" is defined by the oracle).

The learnt treatments must be carefully assessed. Ideally, the treatments can be applied to the device that generated the data. However, commonly, this is not practical and the learnt treatments should be studied using an N-way cross-validation study on the training data (i.e., N times, learn on $\frac{N-1}{N}$ of the data then test on the remaining $\frac{1}{N}$-th of the data).

As we shall see, treatment learners are very simple and can only work if there exist a small number of funnel attributes that control the behavior of the systems. **CLAIM1** holds in domains where treatment learners can return adequate treatments.

The TAR2 [23, 12] treatment learner used in these experiments is an optimization and generalization of the TAR1 system [26]. The following experiments use examples presented in this text, data generated by [23], and examples from the UC Irvine machine learning database (http://www.ics.uci.edu/~mlearn/). In keeping with the abstract model of Figure 9.1, examples were selected with many uncertain variables. For example, the CAR data was generated from some model of car assessment, the details of which are unavailable to us. Also, the CMM2 and REACH examples were generated from models where key control values were picked at random for each different run. In all these cases, treatment learners were able to build adequate controllers.

The following brief sketch of TAR2 skips over numerous details. For example, TAR2 generates treatments in increasing size order. That is, smaller and cheaper treatments are generated before larger and more expensive treatments. Also, when not all attributes in the input data set are controllable, TAR2 has a facility for focusing the treatments only on the controllable inputs. Further, sometimes treatments can be too restrictive. This can happen when the proposed treatment contains many conjunctions and little of the input data falls within that restriction. In such a case, the treatment must be relaxed, lest TAR2 over-fits on the theory. For more on these and other details, see [12].

9.4.2 Treatment Learning: The Details

TAR2 input classified examples like those in Figure 9.8 and output a *treatment*; i.e., a conjunction of control attribute values. To find the treatments, TAR2 accesses a *score* for each classification. For a golfer, the classes in Figure 9.8 could be scored as *none=0* (i.e., worst), *some=1*, *lots=2* (i.e., best). TAR2 then seeks attribute ranges that occur more frequently in the highly scored classes than in the lower scored classes. Let $a = r$ be some attribute range (e.g., *outlook=overcast*) and $X(a = r)$ be the number of occurrences of that attribute range in class X (e.g., *lots(outlook=overcast)=4*). If *best* is the highest scoring class (e.g., *best = lots*) and *others* are the non-best class (e.g. *others = {none, some}*), then $\Delta_{a=r}$ is a measure of the worth of $a = r$ to improve the frequency of the *best* class. $\Delta_{a=r}$ is calculated as follows:

$$\Delta_{a=r} = \sum_{X \in others} \left(\frac{(score(best) - score(x)) * (best(a=r) - X(a=r))}{|examples|} \right)$$

where $|$ *examples* $|$ is the number of categorized examples; e.g. Figure 9.8 has $|$ *examples* $| = 14$ entries.

#	outlook	temperature (°F)	humidity	windy?	time on course
1	sunny	85	86	false	none
2	sunny	80	90	true	none
3	sunny	72	95	false	none
4	rain	65	70	true	none
5	rain	71	96	true	none
6	rain	70	96	false	some
7	rain	68	80	false	some
8	rain	75	80	false	some
9	sunny	69	70	false	lots
10	sunny	75	70	true	lots
11	overcast	83	88	false	lots
12	overcast	64	65	true	lots
13	overcast	72	90	true	lots
14	overcast	81	75	false	lots

Fig. 9.8. A log of some golf-playing behavior.

The attribute ranges in our golf example generate the Δ histogram shown in Figure 9.9.i. A *treatment* is a subset of the attribute ranges with an *outstanding* $\Delta_{a=r}$ value. For our golf example, such attributes can be seen in Figure 9.9.i: they are the outliers with outstandingly large Δs on the right-hand-side.

To *apply* a treatment, TAR2 rejects all example entries that contradict the conjunction of the attribute rages in the treatment. The ratio of classes in the remaining examples is compared to the ratio of classes in the original example set. For example Figure 9.10 shows the frequency of classes in the untreated classes and after two different treatments. The *best treatment* is the one that most increases the relative percentage of preferred classes. In Figure 9.10, the best treatment is *outlook=overcast*; i.e., if we bribe disc jockeys to always forecast overcast weather, then in 100% of the cases, we should be playing lots of golf.

9.4.3 On the Generality of Treatment Learners

Figure 9.9 shows the Δ distribution generated by TAR2 in several domains. Figure 9.9 lends support to **CLAIM1**: in nearly all the distributions there exist outstanding outliers for Δ (denoted by a black bar in Figure 9.9). The *worst* Δ distribution we have seen is the CAR distribution of Figure 9.9.ii where the maximum Δ seen is -7. But even in this worst case, something like **CLAIM1** still holds. By flipping the scoring measure used on the classes, we can coerce TAR2 into finding treatments that drive the system into a worse situation; see Figure 9.11. So even when we can't advise our agents how to improve a system, we can still

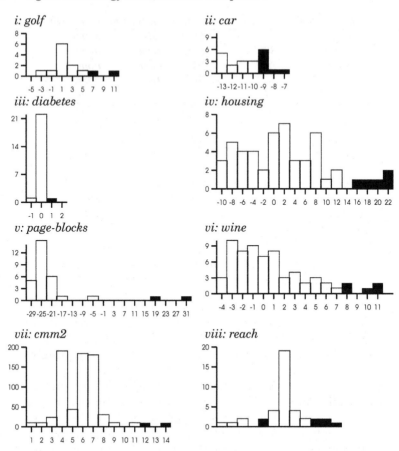

Fig. 9.9. Δ distribution seen in eight data sets. Outstandingly high *deltaf* values shown in black. Y-axis is the number of times a particular Δ was seen. Figures ii,iii,iv,v,vi come from datasets taken from the UC Irvine machine learning database at http://www.ics.uci.edu/~mlearn/. Figures i,ii,viii are discussed in this text. Figure vii comes from data generated in [23].

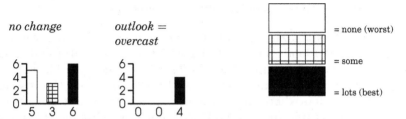

Fig. 9.10. Finding treatments that can improve golf playing behavior. With no treatments, we only play golf lots of times in $\frac{6}{5+3+6} = 57\%$ of cases. With the restriction that *outlook=overcast*, then we play golf lots of times in 100% of cases.

advise what *not* to do. In the case of CAR domain, this advise would be "don't buy two seater cars".

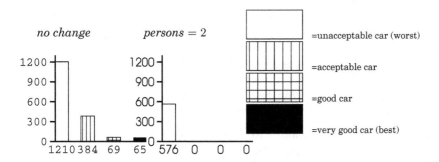

Fig. 9.11. Finding treatments that can degrade cars. By reversing its scoring function, TAR2 can be made to output treatments that favor *bad* classifications. For example, in the CAR dataset from the UC Irvine machine learning database (http://www.ics.uci.edu/~mlearn/), $\frac{1210}{384+69+65+1210}$ = 70% of cars are unacceptable. However, with the restriction of *person=2*, then 100% of all cars are unacceptable.

There is much evidence that many domains contain a small number of variables that are crucial in determining the behavior of the whole system. This phenomenon has been called various names including *small funnels* (as above), *master-variables* in scheduling [4]; *prime-implicants* in model-based diagnosis [31]; *backbones* in satisfiability [33]; *dominance filtering* in design [14]; and *minimal environments* in the ATMS [5]. These experimental results suggest that treatment learning in particular and **CLAIM1** in general should be widely applicable.

Note that if the outstanding Δs are all from wild variables, then TAR2 will fail. We have not seen this case in practice. In all the domains studied so far, a subset of the total domain variables were used as inputs. Usually, these variables were selected on some idiosyncratic or pragmatic grounds, e.g., these were variables for which data had already been collected. Despite idiosyncratic nature of their collection method, these attributes were sufficient to learn effective treatments.

9.5 Sensitivity

Optimistic conclusions derived from an average case analysis (such as shown above) may not apply to particular systems. Hence, this chapter now turns to **CLAIM2**; i.e., it is possible to redesign particular devices in order to *increase* their immunity to wild variables.

To show **CLAIM2**, we need to first describe the use of TAR2 for sensitivity analysis. As we shall see, this kind of analysis can be used to find design options that *increase* or *decrease* the likelihood that **CLAIM1** will hold for a particular device.

Suppose a designer has access to several alternate versions of some device. The alternate versions may come from a range of possible design choices. Suppose further that these devices have been implemented, executed, and their output classified by some oracle. If TAR2 is applied to this output, it will generate numerous treatments, sorted by their impact on the class distribution. Our designer can study this range of treatments to answer three interesting questions:

Q1:What is the *best* variation? This best variation would be scored highest by TAR2; e.g., see Figure 9.10.

Q2:What is the *worst* variation? This worst variation can be found using the techniques described above around Figure 9.11.

Q3:How *important* is variation X? Between the *best* and *worst* treatment are a range of alternative treatments. To assess the significance of some design option, the analyst only needs to see where this option appears within this range.

To determine what features of a device influence reachability, we only need to apply TAR2 to the outputs above from Equation 9.14. We will classify each run as one of $\{0, 10, 20, ..., 90\}$. A run is classified, e.g., 90 if 90% to 100% of its goals are reached. The rationale for this classification scheme is as follows:

- Wild variables increase the variability in the behavior of a device.
- One measure of such variability is *reachability*; i.e. how many *randomly selected inputs probes* are required to reach *all the possible behaviors* of a system.
- We say that the *reachability is high* if the number of such probes is *small*. If the reachability is, e.g., *impossibly* high, then an agent must conduct an impractically large number of experiments on a device (more than 10^6) in order to design control strategies.

TAR2 generated Figure 9.12. Figure 9.12, left can be read as follows:

If: The and-nodes are not common (*andf* < 25% of all nodes) and if or-nodes have far more parents than and-nodes ...
Then: In the majority of cases, the reachability will be 70% or more.

Figure 9.12, middle, can be read as follows:

If: The and-nodes are very common (*andf* > 75%), then for certain values of *V* and *in* ...
Then: In the overwhelming majority of cases, the reachability will be very low (0% to 10%)

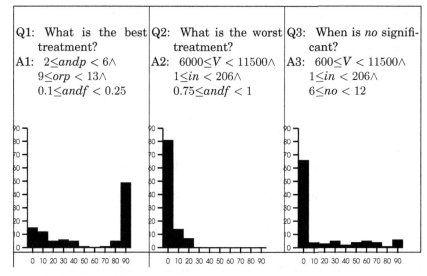

Q1: What is the best treatment?	Q2: What is the worst treatment?	Q3: When is *no* significant?
A1: $2 \leq andp < 6 \wedge$ $9 \leq orp < 13 \wedge$ $0.1 \leq andf < 0.25$	A2: $6000 \leq V < 11500 \wedge$ $1 \leq in < 206 \wedge$ $0.75 \leq andf < 1$	A3: $600 \leq V < 11500 \wedge$ $1 \leq in < 206 \wedge$ $6 \leq no < 12$

Fig. 9.12. Studying the impacts of design options on reachability. Y-axis shows percentage of runs falling into each X-axis bucket. X-axis shows the percentage of the runs falling into a 10% bucket; e.g., 50% of the left-hand-side runs fell into the 90% to 100% reachable bucket.

These two conclusions do support **CLAIM2**. That is, using TAR2, it is possible to assess features of a device according to how those features change our ability to quickly understand that device.

More interesting than Figure 9.12, left, and Figure 9.12, middle, is Figure 9.12, right, which explores the relative impact of nondeterminacy on reachability. Nondeterministic devices contain *nogood*s that define sets of nodes which can't be believed at the same time. The *no* variable is the average number of *nogood*s associated with a node. If $no = 0$, then the same search can take linear time using, e.g., the `walk` algorithm shown in the appendix. If $no > 0$ then the graph contains incompatible pairs and the results of [8] discussed near the end of 9.3.1 apply; i.e., a search can take exponential time to execute, in the worse case. Such an exponential time search would imply a very poor reachability. In order to avoid such worst case behavior, many researchers reject nondeterminism. For example, Nancy Leveson comments that "nondeterminacy is the enemy of reliability" [16].

Contrary to the pessimism of, e.g., Leveson, Figure 9.12, right, suggests that even when $no > 0$, then only certain ranges of *no* result in reachability problems. Figure 9.12, right, was the *worst* effect ever seen in the TAR2 treatments that mentioned the *no* variable. Clearly, some ranges of *no* have a disastrous effect on reachability. In the case of $6 \leq no \leq 12$, then for certain other parameter values, the reachability will be poor. However, while *no* can determine reachability, other attributes can dominate the *no* effect. Recall that Figure 9.12, middle, showed treatments that have a *worse* impact than in Figure 9.12, right, *without* mentioning the *no* variable.

This kind of sensitivity analysis can be finely tuned to a particular device:

1. The parameters required for the reachability model are set using an analysis of the code in that particular project.
2. When uncertainty exists over those parameters, plausible minimum and maximum bounds for those parameters are determined.
3. Equation 9.14 is executed using random inputs picked from the preceding two points.
4. TAR2 learns treatment on the data collected from the preceding run.

9.6 Discussion

Can we trust agents to work adequately autonomously in wild environments? The uncertainty of such environments might make agent coordination, reaction and pro-action ineffectual.

To answer this question we have explored an alternative to classical formal analysis. Traditional formal analysis makes a *deterministic assumption* where all computation is controlled. However, agents working in dynamic environments cannot access all knowledge in that domain. Nor can they stop the environment, or other agents, changing beliefs without informing our agent. Hence, this deterministic assumption may not be valid for agents working in highly dynamic environments.

We have presented here a nonstandard formal analysis that makes a *nondeterministic assumption*. At issue was our ability to control a device, despite random perturbations to that device from the environment (or from other agents). Assuming that the device is of the form of Figure 9.2 (i.e. negation-free horn clauses plus some *nogood* predicates), then there will exist a *funnel* within the theory. This funnel contains the key variables that control the rest of the system. Theoretically, it has been shown that, on average, the size of the funnel is small. Hence, only a small number of different behaviors are possible, despite the inputs from the wild inputs. Also, using some experiments with the TAR2 treatment learner, it was argued that these funnel variables can be controlled from the inputs.

All the above was an average case analysis. By applying TAR2 to our theoretical model, it is possible to theoretically assess alternate designs according to how well they "nudge" a system into this desired average case behavior. Several "nudges" were discussed above include the effects of nondeterminism within a system. Compared to other factors, nondeterminism was not the most significant problem associated with search a device.

Our current research direction is to test our theory on real models reduced to our negation-free horn clauses. To this end, we are building translators from SCR state charts [10] to our and-or graphs. Once built, we will test if:

- The range of actual behaviors within these state charts are as small as predicted by funnel theory.
- The theoretical assessments of alternate designs seen in Section 9.5 will let us find new designs that are less influenced by the wild inputs.

References

1. Clancey, W., Sachs, P., Sierhuis, M. and van Hoof, R. Brahms: Simulating practice for work systems design. In *Proceedings PKAW '96: Pacific Knowledge Acquisition Workshop*, P. Compton, R. Mizoguchi, H. Motoda and T. Menzies, editors. Department of Artificial Intelligence, 1996.
2. Clancy, D. and Kuipers, B. Model decomposition and simulation: A component based qualitative simulation algorithm. In *AAAI-97*, 1997.
3. Console, L. and Torasso, P. A spectrum of definitions of model-based diagnosis. *Computational Intelligence*, 7:133–141, 1991.
4. Crawford, J. and Baker, A. Experimental results on the application of satisfiability algorithms to scheduling problems. In *AAAI '94*, 1994.
5. DeKleer, J. An Assumption-Based TMS. *Artificial Intelligence*, **28**:163–196, 1986.
6. d'Inverno, M. and Wooldridge, M. A formal specification of dMARS. In *Intelligent Agents IV: Proc. of the Fourth International Workshop on Agent Theories. Architectures and Languages*, A. Singh and M. Wooldridge, editors. Springer Verlag, 1998.
7. Doyle, J. A truth maintenance system. *Artificial Intelligence*, **12**:231–272, 1979.
8. Gabow, H., Maheshwari, S. and Osterweil, L. On two problems in the generation of program test paths. *IEEE Transactions on Software Engineering*, **SE-2**:227–231, 1976.
9. Han, K. and Veloso, M. Automated robot behaviour recognition applied to robot soccer. In *Proceedings of the Sixteenth Interntional Joint Conference on Artificial Intelligence. Workshop on Team Behaviour and Plan Recognition*, 1999, pp 47–52.
10. Heitmeyer, C. L., Jeffords, R. D. and Labaw, B. G. Automated consistency checking of requirements specifications. *ACM Transactions on Software Engineering and Methodology*, **5**(3):231–261, 1996.
11. Holzmann, G. The model checker SPIN. *IEEE Transactions on Software Engineering*, **23**(5):279–295, 1997.
12. Hu, Y. *Treatment learning*. Masters thesis, University of British Columbia, Department of Electrical and Computer Engineering. In preparation, 2002.
13. Jones, R. M., Laird, J. E., Nielsen, P. E., Coulter, K. J., Kenny, P. G. and Koss, F. V. Automated intelligent pilots for combat flight simulation. *AI Magazine*, **20**(1):27–41, 1999.

14. Josephson, J., Chandrasekaran, B., Carroll, M., Iyer, N., Wasacz, B. and Rizzoni, G. Exploration of large design spaces: an architecture and preliminary results. In *AAAI '98*, 1998.

15. Kautz, H. and Selman, B. Pushing the envelope: Planning, propositional logic and stochastic search. In *Proceedings of the Thirteenth National Conference on Artificial Intelligence and the Eighth Innovative Applications of Artificial Intelligence Conference*, Menlo Park, AAAI Press / MIT Press, 1996, pp 1194–1201.

16. Leveson, N. *Safeware System Safety and Computers*. Addison-Wesley. 1995.

17. Menzies, T. and Compton, P. Applications of abduction: Hypothesis testing of neuroendocrinological qualitative compartmental models. *Artificial Intelligence in Medicine*, **10**:145–175, 1997.

18. Menzies, T. and Cukic, B. Adequacy of limited testing for knowledge based systems. *International Journal on Artificial Intelligence Tools (IJAIT)*, June 2000a.

19. Menzies, T. and Cukic, B. When to test less. *IEEE Software*, **17**(5):107–112, 2000b.

20. Menzies, T. and Cukic, B. Average case coverage for validation of AI systems. In *AAAI Stanford Spring Symposium on Model-based Validation of AI Systems*, 2001.

21. Menzies, T., Cukic, B., Singh, H. and Powell, J. Testing nondeterminate systems. In *ISSRE 2000*, 2000.

22. Menzies, T., Easterbrook, S., Nuseibeh, B. and Waugh, S. An empirical investigation of multiple viewpoint reasoning in requirements engineering. In *RE '99*, 1999.

23. Menzies, T. and Kiper, J. Better reasoning about software engineering activities. In *ASE-2001*, 2001.

24. Menzies, T. and Michael, C. Fewer slices of pie: Optimising mutation testing via abduction. In *SEKE '99*, Kaiserslautern, Germany, 17-19 June, 1999.

25. Menzies, T. and Singh, H. Many maybes mean (mostly) the same thing. In *2nd International Workshop on Soft Computing applied to Software Engineering*, Netherlands, February, 2001.

26. Menzies, T. and Sinsel, E. Practical large scale what-if queries: Case studies with software risk assessment. In *Proceedings ASE 2000*, 2000.

27. Muscettola, N., Nayak, P. P., Pell, B. and Williams, B. Remote agent: To boldly go where no AI system has gone before. *Artificial Intelligence*, **103**(1-2):5–48, 1998.

28. Nayak, P. P. and Williams B. C. Fast context switching in real-time propositional reasoning. In *Proceedings of AAAI-97*, 1997.

29. Pearce, A., Heinz, C. and Goss, S. Meeting plan recognition requirements for real-time air-mission simulations, 2000.

30. Roa, A. and Georgeff, M. BDI agents: From theory to practice. In *Proceedings of the First International Conference on Multi-Agent Systems*, San Francisco, CA, June 1995.

31. Rymon, R. An se-tree-based prime implicant generation algorithm. In *Annals of Math. and A.I., special issue on Model-Based Diagnosis*, volume 11, 1994.

32. Schooff, R. and Haimes, Y. Dynamic multistage software estimation. *IEEE Transactions on Systems, Man, and Cybernetics*, **29**(2):272–284, 1999.

33. Singer, J., Gent, I. P. and Smaill, A. Backbone fragility and the local search cost peak. *Journal of Artificial Intelligence Research*, **12**:235–270, 2000.
34. Williams, B. and Nayak, P. A model-based approach to reactive self-configuring systems. In *Proceedings AAAI '96*, 1996, pp 971–978.
35. Wooldridge, M. and Jennings, N. Intelligent agents: Theory and practice. *The Knowledge Engineering Review*, **10**(2):115–152, 1995.

Part IV

Significant Applications

Formal Methods at NASA Goddard Space Flight Center

Christopher A. Rouff, James L. Rash, Michael G. Hinchey, and Walter F. Truszkowski

10.1 Introduction

Research into agent-based systems began at NASA Goddard Space Flight Center (GSFC) in the mid-1990s. Up until that time, space missions had been primarily operated manually from ground control centers. The high cost of unautomated operations prompted NASA and others operating space missions to seriously look into automating as many functions as possible. The agent researchers at GSFC recognized that giving ground systems and satellites greater autonomy would significantly reduce the cost of operations, and that agent technology was an excellent candidate as a means to enable this to be accomplished.

It was also recognized that introducing new and revolutionary technology into a space mission is often met with resistance. From the viewpoints of the mission Principal Investigator (PI) and the Mission Operations Manager, new technology adds risk to an already risky endeavor. A proven success record for a technology is usually mandated. Agent technology and intelligent software, like other new and emerging technologies, would have an uphill battle for acceptance in operational space missions due to the perceived risks of using any new technology. To lower the risk of using agent technology in space missions, we began investigating techniques for assuring the correctness of agent software.

To accomplish its cost reduction objectives, NASA has set far-reaching autonomy goals for ground-based and space-based systems. More reliance on intelligent systems and less on human intervention characterizes its autonomy goals. These goals of cost reduction have been further complicated by NASA's plans to use constellations of nanosatellites for future science data-gathering, which NASA has little experience operating even manually, much less with autonomous systems.

The Advanced Architectures and Automation Branch at Goddard Space Flight Center (GSFC) has a leading role in the development of agent-based approaches to realize NASA's autonomy goals. Two major successes of the branch were the development of the Lights-Out Ground Operations System (LOGOS) [4][16] and the Agent Concept Testbed (ACT) [17].

LOGOS was the first multi-agent system developed in the Branch and provided an initial insight into the power of agent communities. The agents in LOGOS acted as surrogate controllers and interfaced with the legacy software that controllers normally used.

Based on the success of this first prototype, development was done on ACT, an environment in which richer agent and agent-community concepts were developed through detailed prototypes and operational ground-based and space-based scenarios. ACT has given GSFC more experience in architecting and developing communities of agents as well as the tradeoffs and complications that accompany such systems.

The goal of our work is to transition proven agent technology into operational NASA systems. The implementation of the multi-agent systems mentioned above provided an opportunity to exercise and evaluate the capabilities supported by the agent architectures and refine the architectures as required. It also provided an opportunity for space mission designers and developers to see agent technology in action. This experience has enabled them to make a better determination of the role that agent technology could play in their missions.

There have been many definitions of agents [2][19]. For the purpose of this chapter we will define an agent as a software system that is autonomous and has the ability to perceive and affect its environment and communicate with other agents. A multi-agent system, or community of agents, is simply a collection of agents that cooperate to accomplish a common goal. LOGOS and ACT are each multi-agent systems. The remainder of this chapter describes a formal specification of LOGOS and errors found during the specification.

10.2 LOGOS Overview

The Lights Out Ground Operations System (LOGOS) is a prototype multi-agent system for automating satellite ground operations systems. It uses a community of software agents that work cooperatively to perform ground system operations normally done by human operators using traditional ground system software tools such as orbit generators, schedulers, and command sequence planners.

During the implementation of LOGOS, several errors occurred that involved race conditions. Due to the parallel nature of the asynchronous communications as well as the internal parallelism of the agents themselves, finding the race conditions using normal debugging techniques proved extremely difficult.

Following the development of LOGOS, the development team decided to use formal methods to check for additional inter-agent race conditions and omissions using formal specification techniques. The resulting specification revealed several omissions as well as race conditions. Our experience to date has shown that even at the level of requirements, formalization can help to highlight undesirable behavior and equally importantly can help to find errors of omission.

10.2.1 LOGOS Architecture

An architecture of LOGOS is shown in Figure 10.1. LOGOS was made up of ten agents, some that interfaced with legacy software, some that performed services for the other agents in the community, and others that interfaced with an analyst or operator. All agents had the ability to communicate with all other agents in the community, though not all agents actually needed this capability.

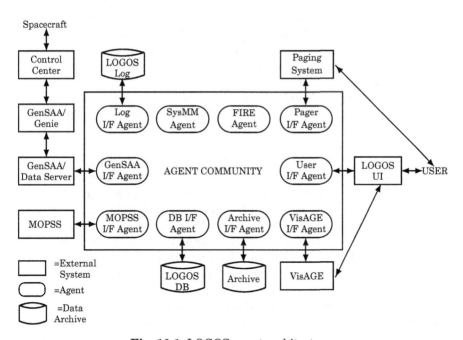

Fig. 10.1. LOGOS agent architecture.

The System Monitoring and Management Agent (SysMMA), kept track of all agents in the community and provided addresses of agents for other agents requesting services. Each agent when started had to register its capabilities with SysMMA and obtain addresses of other agents whose services they would need.

The Fault Isolation and Resolution Expert (FIRE) agent resolved satellite anomalies. FIRE was notified of anomalies during a satellite pass. FIRE contained a knowledge base of potential anomalies and a set of possible fixes for each. If it did not recognize an anomaly or was unable to resolve it, it sent the anomaly to UIFA to be forwarded to a human analyst for resolution.

The User Interface Agent (UIFA) was the interface between the agent community and the graphical user interface that the analyst or operator used to interact with the LOGOS agent community. UIFA received notification of anomalies from the FIRE agent, handled the logon of users to the system, kept the user informed with reports, routed commands to be sent to the satellite, and performed other maintenance functions. If the attention of an analyst was needed but none was logged on, UIFA would send a request to the PAGER agent to page the required analyst.

The VisAGE Interface Agent (VIFA) interfaced with the VisAGE 2000 data visualization system. VisAGE provided the capability to display spacecraft telemetry and agent log information. Real-time telemetry information was displayed by VisAGE as it was downloaded during a pass. VIFA requested the data from the GIFA and AIFA agents (see below). An analyst could also use VisAGE to visualize historical information to help monitor spacecraft health or to determine solutions to anomalies or other potential spacecraft problems.

The Pager Interface Agent (PAGER) was the agent community interface to the analyst's pager system. If an anomaly occurred or other situation arose that needed an analyst's attention, a request was sent to the PAGER agent, which then sent a page to the analyst.

The Database Interface Agent (DBIFA) and the Archive Interface Agent (AIFA) stored short term and long term data, respectively, and the Log agent (LOG) stored agent logging data for debugging, illustration and monitoring purposes. The DBIFA stored such information as the valid users and their passwords, and the AIFA stored telemetry data.

The GenSAA/Genie Interface Agent (GIFA) interfaced with the GenSAA/Genie ground station software, which handled communications with the spacecraft. GenSAA/Genie provided the ability to download telemetry data, maintain scheduling information, and upload commands to the spacecraft. As anomalies and other data were downloaded from the spacecraft, GIFA routed the data to other agents based on their requests for information.

The MOPSS (Mission Operations Planning and Scheduling System) Interface Agent (MIFA) interfaced with the MOPSS ground station planning and scheduling software. MOPSS kept track of the satellite's orbit and the time of the next pass and how long it would last. It also sent out updates to the satellite's schedule to requesting agents when the schedule changed.

10.2.2 Operational Scenario

An example scenario of how the agents in LOGOS would communicate and cooperate would start with MIFA receiving data from the MOPSS scheduling software that the spacecraft would be in contact position in two minutes. MIFA would then send a message to the other agents to let them know of the upcoming event in case they needed to do some preprocessing before the contact. When GIFA received the message from MIFA, it sent a message to the GenSSA Data Server to start receiving transmissions from the control center.

After receiving data, the GenSSA Data Server sent the satellite data to GIFA, which had rules indicating what data to send to which agents. As well as sending data to other agents, GIFA also sent engineering data to the archive agent (AIFA) for storage and trend information to the visualization agent (VIFA). Updated schedule information was sent to the scheduling agent (MIFA), and a report was sent to the user interface agent (UIFA) to send on to an analyst for monitoring purposes. If there were any anomalies, anomaly reports were sent to the FIRE agent for resolution.

If there was an anomaly, the FIRE agent would try to fix it automatically by using a knowledge base containing possible anomalies and a set of possible resolutions for each anomaly. To fix an anomaly, FIRE would send a spacecraft command to GIFA to be forwarded on to the spacecraft. After exhausting its knowledge base, if FIRE was not able to fix the anomaly, then FIRE forwarded the anomaly to the user interface agent, which then paged an analyst and displayed it on his/her computer for action. The analyst would then formulate a set of commands to send to the spacecraft to resolve the situation. The commands would then be sent to the FIRE agent (so it could add the new resolution to its knowledge base for future reference and to validate the commands) and then sent to the GIFA agent, which would send it to the GenSAA/Genie system for forwarding on to the spacecraft.

There were many other interactions going on between the agents and the legacy software that were not covered above. Examples include the DBIFA requesting user logon information from the database, the AIFA requesting archived telemetry information from the archive database to be sent to the visualization agent, and the pager agent sending paging information to the paging system to alert an analyst of an anomaly needing his or her attention.

10.3 Selecting a Formal Method for LOGOS

During the implementation of the LOGOS agent community, several errors occurred that involved race conditions:

- an agent would run correctly on one computer, but when run from another computer would miss a message or work incorrectly;
- adding additional unrelated agents to the community would cause an agent to crash, miss messages, or hang;
- errors would occur that could not consistently be repeated; and
- buffers would overflow on an inconsistent basis.

Due to the parallel nature of the asynchronous communications, as well as the internal parallelism of the agents themselves, finding the race conditions using normal debugging techniques proved extremely difficult, if not impossible. In most cases, the development team performed a thorough review of the code to manually check for possible problems. Once race conditions were found to be the problem with a few errors, the team began checking each new error with an eye towards a possible race condition. The team also identified code with the potential for race conditions and restructured or rewrote it to reduce the possibility. The usual approach to do this was to remove unnecessary processes or make unnecessary parallel tasks sequential.

Following the implementation of LOGOS, the development team wanted to check for additional undiscovered errors and explore methods and techniques for checking the correctness of future agent software. The fact that several errors occurred during implementation meant that there might be several more unknown to us. We also knew that the appearance of these errors could be dependent on such nonrepeatable conditions as network congestion.

After looking at several possibilities for finding errors in highly parallel software, the development team decided to use formal methods to see if additional inter-agent race conditions and omissions could be found. Several formal specification languages where investigated and Communicating Sequential Processes (CSP) [9] [6] was chosen due to its ability for modeling communicating processes and the availability of local expertise.

The CSP specification of LOGOS brought to light several omissions and race conditions [14] that were not discovered during normal testing. We found that CSP offered additional advantages for LOGOS specification: its simple structure and the degree to which it naturally lends itself to modeling parallel processes, of which LOGOS has many.

10.4 Sample LOGOS Formal Specification

The CSP specification of LOGOS was based on the agent design documents and, when necessary, on inspection of the LOGOS Java code. LOGOS is a proof-of-concept system, so there were several parts that were specified and designed but not implemented. The CSP specification reflects what was actually implemented or would be implemented in the near term. A more in-depth discussion of this specification can be found in [7].

In the CSP specification, LOGOS is defined as a process with agents running in parallel as independent processes communicating through an in-house developed software bus, Workplace, that provides the messaging mechanism between the agents. The high-level definition of LOGOS is given by:

$$LOGOS = AIFA \| DBIFA \| FIRE \| LOG \| MIFA \| PAGER$$
$$\| SysMMA \| UIFA \| VIFA \| Workplace$$

The above states that each of the agents runs in parallel with the other agents and with the *WorkPlace* communications software. Each agent is able to communication with any other agent, but not all agents actually need to communicate with other agents.

The agents affect their environment and other agents by sending messages over communication channels. Channels connect to other agents or to the outside environment; the agents do not communicate by direct function call. Channels connect to either an effector/perceptor component of the agent or the inter-agent communication component. The effector/perceptor channels provide the function of connecting an agent to its environment.

For channels that communicate with the environment, the channel names start with the letter "E". A channel has the name *Eout* if it sends data to the environment and *Ein* if it receives data from the environment. In the LOGOS context, the environment would consist of the User Interface for the UIFA, the pager system for the PAGER agent, MOPSS for the MIFA, VisAGE for VIFA, the databases for the DBIFA and AIFA, and GenSAA/Genie for GIFA.

For communications with other agents, the agents use the inter-agent communications component and the channels start with the letter "I". Agents communicate with each other via message passing based on KQML [10]. Each message has a unique message ID and, when appropriate, an in-reply-to ID that references the original message to which an agent may be replying.

The Iin channel is used to receive messages from other agents and the Iout channel is used to send messages to other agents. Each message is formatted with the name of the agent to which the message is to be sent, the sending agent, a performative, and parameters/parameter values based on the performative.

The WorkPlace software backplane is used to route the messages to the correct agent on the correct system. For specification purposes, we describe the communications taking place over channels. When a message is broadcast on an agent's Iout channel, Workplace will deliver it to the appropriate agent's Iin channel.

From the above, an agent is defined as:

$$Agent_i \hat{=} Bus_i \| Env_i$$

where each agent has a uniquely defined *BUS* and *ENV* process. The *BUS* process defines the inter-agent communication, and the *ENV* process defines how the agent communicates with entities in the outside environment (such as pagers, databases, and the user interface).

The following sections give three sample specifications from the pager interface agent, the database interface agent, and the user interface agent. Also provided is an example of a race condition that was found.

10.4.1 Pager Agent

The following is the specification of the pager agent. The pager agent sends pages to an engineer or controller when there is a spacecraft anomaly that the FIRE agent cannot solve and there is no one logged on to notify. The pager agent receives requests from the user interface agent (UIFA), gets paging information from the database agent, and, when instructed by the UIFA, stops paging. The pager agent is defined as:

$$PAGER \hat{=} PAGER\_BUS_{\{\}\{\}} \| PAGER\_ENV$$

As discussed above, the pager agent is defined as a process, *PAGER*, that is also defined as two processes running in parallel: a *BUS* process and an *ENV* process. The first empty set in the parameter list for *PAGER_BUS* represents the list of requests made to the database agent for paging information on a particular specialist. The second empty set represents the list of specialists that are currently being paged. The paged parameter is a set and not a bag, because even though someone can be paged multiple times, a stop page command only has to be sent one time, not the number of times the specialist was paged (a set does not allow duplicate elements while a bag does). It is assumed a specialist has only one pager. Since the pager agent initially starts out with no requests for pages, these sets are initialized to empty.

The above bus and environment processes for an agent are defined in terms of their input events. The *BUS* process is defined as:

$PAGER\_BUS_{db\_waiting,\ paged} = pager.In?Msg \rightarrow$
    case

        $GET\_USER\_INFO_{db\_waiting,\ paged,\ pagee,\ text}$
           if $msg = (START\_PAGING,\ specialist,\ text)$

        $BEGIN\_PAGING_{db\_waiting,\ paged,\ in\_reply\_to\_in(msg),\ pager\_num}$
           if $msg = (RETURN\_DATA,\ pager\_num)$

        $STOP\_CONTACT_{db\_waiting,\ paged,\ pagee}$
           if $msg = (STOP\_PAGING,\ pagee)$

        $pager.Iout!(head(msg),\ UNRECOGNIZED)$
           $\rightarrow PAGER\_BUS_{db\_waiting,\ paged}$
        otherwise

The above specification states that the process *PAGER_BUS* receives
a message on its *Iin* channel (the pager's in channel from *WorkPlace*) and
stores it in a variable called *msg*. Depending on the contents of the message, one of four different processes is executed.

If the message has a *START_PAGING* performative, then the
GET_USER_INFO process is called with parameters of the type of specialist to page (*pagee*) and the text to send the *pagee*. If the message has
a *RETURN_DATA* performative with a *pagee*'s pager number, then the
database has returned a pager number and the *BEGIN_PAGING* process
is executed with a parameter containing the original message id (used as
a key to the *db_waiting* set) and the passed pager number.

The third type of message that the pager agent might receive is one
with a *STOP_PAGING* performative. This message contains a request to
stop paging a particular specialist (stored in the *pagee* parameter). When
this message is received, the *STOP_PAGING* process is executed with
the parameter of the specialist type. If the pager agent receives any other
message than the above three messages, an error message is returned to
the sender of the message (which is the first item of the list) stating that
the message is *UNRECOGNIZED*. After this, the *PAGER_BUS* process
is again executed.

The following are the definitions of the three processes referenced
above.

$GET\_USER\_INFO_{db\_waiting,\ paged,\ pagee,\ text} =$
$\quad pager.Iout!(DBIFA,\ Id = msgId(),\ RETURN\_DATA,\ pagee)$
$\quad \rightarrow PAGER\_BUS_{db\_waiting \cup \{(Id,\ pagee,\ text)\},\ paged}$

$BEGIN\_PAGING_{db\_waiting,\ paged,\ MsgId,\ pager\_num} =$
$\quad pager.Eout!(pagee, pager\_num,\ text,\ START)\ |$
$\quad\quad (\exists!(MsgId,\ x,\ t) \in db\_waiting\ |\ pagee = x \wedge text = t)$
$\quad \rightarrow PAGER\_BUS_{db\_waiting/\{(MsgId,\ pagee,\ text)\},}$
$\quad\quad\quad\quad\quad\quad\quad\quad_{paged \cup \{(pagee,\ pager\_num)\}}$

$STOP\_CONTACT_{db\_waiting,\ paged,\ pagee} =$
$\quad pager.Eout!(pagee,\ pager\_num,\ STOP)\ |$
$\quad\quad (\exists!(pagee,\ y) \in paged\ |\ pager\_num = y)$
$\quad \rightarrow PAGER\_BUS_{db\_waiting,\ paged/\{(pagee,\ pager\_num)\}}$

The *GET_USER_INFO* process sends a message to the database agent over the pager's *Iout* channel requesting the *pagee*'s pager number. After the message is sent, the *PAGER_BUS* process is called with the tuple *(message ID, pagee, text)* unioned with the set *db_waiting* containing the set of messages waiting for a response from the database. Not waiting for the database to return the pager number allows the *PAGER_BUS* process to receive and process other messages while it is waiting for the database to answer. There is also the chance that more than one page request will come in before the first one is answered. A set is used to hold all of the pending requests from the database because a set does not contain duplicate elements. Also, since message ids are always unique, the message id is used as the key to the tuple.

BEGIN_PAGING sends the type of specialist to be paged, the pager number, and related text over the environment channel to the actual paging system. After this message is sent, the *PAGER_BUS* process is executed with the *pagee*'s tuple deleted from the *db_waiting* set and the tuple *(pagee, pager_number)* added to the set of specialists currently being paged (the set *paged*).

The *STOP_CONTACT* process extracts from the set paged the tuple that contains the pager number for the *pagee* and sends a message to the paging system with the specialist type, the number of the pager, and a command to stop the page. Next, the process calls the pager's BUS process with the tuple *(pagee, pager_number)* removed from the *paged* set.

One thing to note is that if a specialist is paged once, then paged a second time, this information is lost, since the element *(pagee, pager_number)* overwrites the previous element in the set. If in the future this becomes unacceptable, then a bag will need to be used instead of a set and an additional value added to the tuple to distinguish multiple pages to the same specialist (perhaps using the time of a page as a key).

Since the pager agent does not receive any messages from the paging system, the *PAGER_ENV* process does not need to be defined, and is therefore left undefined.

10.4.2 Database Agent

The database interface agent (DBIFA) provides access to a database management system. It stores text on the status and operation of the spacecraft and retrieves information on users. Its definition is:

$DBIFA \hat{=} DBIFA\_BUS \| DBIFA\_ENV$

which states that the database agent consists of two processes, the BUS process that communicates with other agents and the *ENV* process that communicates with the database.

The *BUS* process for the DBIFA is defined as:

$DBIFA\_BUS = dbifa.Iin?msg \rightarrow$
  $case$
    $dbifa.Eout!anomaly \rightarrow dbifa.Ein?result$
      $\rightarrow DBIFA\_BUS$
    $if\ msg = (REQUEST,\ LOG,\ anomaly)$

    $dbifa.Eout!telemetry \rightarrow dbifa.Ein?result$
      $\rightarrow DBIFA\_BUS$
    $if\ msg = (REQUEST,\ LOG,\ telemetry)$

    $dbifa.Eout!sc\_cmd\_sent \rightarrow dbifa.Ein?result$
      $\rightarrow DBIFA\_BUS$
    $if\ msg = (REQUEST,\ LOG,\ sc\_cmd\_sent)$

    $dbifa.Eout!sc\_cmd\_executed \rightarrow dbifa.Ein?resut$
      $\rightarrow DBIFA\_BUS$
    $if\ msg = (REQUEST,\ LOG,\ sc\_cmd\_executed)$

    $dbifa.Eout!request\_human \rightarrow dbifa.Ein?result$
      $\rightarrow DBIFA\_BUS$
    $if\ msg = (REQUEST,\ LOG,\ request\_human)$

$$RETURN\_USER\_SPECIALTY_{requesting\_agent(msg),\ anomally,\ msg\_id(msg)}$$
$$if\ msg = (REQUEST,\ RETURN\_DATA,\ anomaly)$$

$$RETURN\_USER\_PASSWORD_{requesting\_agent(msg),\ username,\ msg\_id(msg)}$$
$$if\ msg = (REQUEST,\ RETURN\_DATA,\ username)$$

$$RETURN\_REPORT_{requesting\_agent(msg),\ report\_type,\ msg\_id(msg)}$$
$$if\ msg = (REQUEST,\ RETURN\_DATA,\ report\_type)$$

$$dbifa.Iout!(head(msg), UNRECOGNIZED)$$
$$\rightarrow DBIFA\_BUS$$
$$otherwise$$

The above definition states that the *DBIFA_BUS* process reads messages from the *dbifa.Iin* channel and depending on the content of the message executes a particular process. The DBIFA receives several messages from the FIRE agent to log anomalies, telemetry information, commands sent to the spacecraft, commands executed by the spacecraft, and the times when it requests intervention from a user to handle an anomaly. Other messages received by the database agent are requests from the pager agent for pager numbers and from the user interface agent for a user with a particular specialty (to handle an anomaly or other problem), a user's password, and a report on the current state of the spacecraft.

If a message is a request to store data in the database, the process sends the data to the database on the *dbifa.Eout* channel, then waits for a response on the *dbifa.Ein* channel and gives control back to the *DBIFA_BUS*. It does not send a confirmation to the requesting agent. Waiting for the database to return comfirmation before continuing is a potential source of deadlock. Also, if there is any error from the database, the process does not pass the error back to the requesting agent. This was due to the prototype nature of LOGOS and should be corrected in future versions.

The first five processes in the above case statement are all requests from agents to store data in the database. The first one is a request to log an anomaly, the second is a request to log a telemetry value, the third is a request to log that the spacecraft was sent a command, the fourth is a request to log that a spacecraft command was executed, and the fifth is a request to log that human intervention was requested to solve an anomaly. The last process in the case statement is for the case when an agent receives a malformed message. In this case, the receiving process returns the message to the sender with a performative of *UNRECOG-NIZED*.

The remaining three processes are requests for information from other agents and call other processes to handle the requests. The following process definitions for the DBIFA define the responses to the above messages.

$RETURN\_USER\_SPECIALTY_{agent,\ anomaly,\ msg\_id}$ =
    $dbifa.Eout!(specialist,\ anomaly)$
    $\rightarrow dbifa.Ein?specialist\_name$
    $\rightarrow dbifa.Iout!(agent,\ msg\_id,\ specialist\_name)$
    $\rightarrow DBIFA\_BUS$

$RETURN\_PAGER\_NUMBER_{agent,\ specialist,\ msg\_id}$ =
    $dbifa.Eout!(specialist,\ PAGER)$
    $\rightarrow dbifa.Ein?pager\_number$
    $\rightarrow dbifa.Iout!(agent,\ msg\_id,\ pager\_number)$
    $\rightarrow DBIFA\_BUS$

$RETURN\_USER\_PASSWORD_{agent,\ username,\ msg\_id}$ =
    $dbifa.Eout!username$
    $\rightarrow dbifa.Ein?(username, password)$
    $\rightarrow dbifa.Iout!(agent,\ msg\_id,\ username,\ password)$
    $\rightarrow DBIFA\_BUS$

$RETURN\_REPORT_{agent,\ report\_type,\ msg\_id}$ =
    $dbifa.Eout!report\_type$
    $\rightarrow dbifa.Ein?(report\_type, report)$
    $\rightarrow dbifa.Iout!(agent,\ msg\_id,\ report\_type,\ report)$
    $\rightarrow DBIFA\_BUS$

The processes *RETURN_USER_SPECIALTY*, *RETURN_USER_PASS-WORD*, and *RETURN_REPORT* all represent requests to retrieve data from the database. After requesting data from the database, they all wait for the data to be returned before continuing. This is a situation that can lead to a deadlock state since there is no timeout mechanism. Once DB-IFA receives the response from the database over the *dbifa.Ein* channel, it sends the data back to the requesting agent over the dbifa.Iout channel along with the original message id.

Since the database agent does not receive any unsolicited messages from the database system (all messages between the database and DBIFA are synchronized), the *DBIFA_ENV* process does not need to be defined, and is therefore left undefined.

10.4.3 User Interface Agent

The user interface agent (UIFA) provides a connection between the user interface and the LOGOS agent community. The UIFA receives commands from the user interface and passes those commands to the appropriate agent and also receives data from other agents and sends that information to the user interface.

Like the other agents, the UIFA specification consists of a *BUS* and *ENV* process:

$$UIFA \triangleq UIFA\_BUS_{[], [], \{\}} \| UIFA\_ENV$$

The first bag parameter represents user password requests that have been made to the database agent, and the second bag holds the names of the users that have logged on. They are bags instead of sets because a single user can be logged on multiple times simultaneously and a bag allows duplicate elements while a set does not. The third parameter is the set of anomalies that are waiting to be sent to the user interface when there are no users logged on. It is a set because duplicate anomalies are only reported once. The three bags/sets are initialized to empty because, when LOGOS starts up, no users should be logged in and no anomalies have been recorded.

The specification of the UIFA_BUS process is:

$$UIFA\_BUS_{db\_waiting,\ logged\_in,\ anomomalies} =$$
$$UIFA\_INTERNAL_{db\_waiting,\ logged\_in,\ anomalies} \|$$
$$UIFA\_AGENT_{db\_waiting,\ logged\_in,\ anomalies}$$

The above states that the *UIFA_BUS* process can either be the *UIFA-_AGENT* process or the *UIFA_INTERNAL* process. The *UIFA_AGENT* process defines the response UIFA makes to messages received from other agents over the *uifa.Iin* channel. These messages are requests from other agents to send the user interface data or are responses to requests that the UIFA made earlier to another agent. The *UIFA_INTERNAL* process transfers password-related data from the *UIFA_ENV* process to the *UIFA_BUS*.

The definition for the *UIFA_INTERNAL* process is rather simple and is solely for transferring password information received from the user in the *UIFA_ENV* process to the database agent for validation. It also needs to store the password information in the *db_waiting* parameter for future retrieval by the *UIFA_BUS* process when the database agent returns the password validation information (as will be seen below). The *UIFA_INTERNAL* process is defined as:

$$UIFA\_INTERNAL_{db\_waiting,\ logged\_in,\ anomalies} =$$
$$uifa.pass?(user\_name,\ password)$$
$$\rightarrow uifa.Iout!(DBIFA, RETURN\_DATA, user\_name, password)$$
$$\rightarrow UIFA\_BUS_{db\_waiting \cup (user\_name,\ password),\ logged\_in,\ anomalies}$$

which states that when *UIFA_ENV* sends a user name/password tuple over the *uifa.pass* channel, this process sends the tuple to the database agent for validation and then calls the *UIFA_BUS* process again with the *(user_name, password)* tuple added to the *db_waiting* bag. Later, when the database agent returns with its stored password for this user, it will be compared with the user name and password received from the user interface and removed from *db_waiting*.

The following gives a partial specification of the *UIFA_AGENT* process and how it handles messages received from other agents:

$$UIFA\_AGENT_{db\_waiting,\ logged\_in,\ anomalies} = uifa.In?msg \rightarrow$$

$\quad case$

$\quad\quad RESOLVE\_ANOMALY_{db\_waiting,\ logged\_in,\ anomalies,\ new\_anomaly}$

$\quad\quad\quad if\ msg = (REQUEST,\ RESOLVE,\ new\_anomaly)$

$\quad\quad RECEIVED\_SPECIALIST_{db\_waiting,\ logged\_in,\ anomalies,\ new\_anomaly,\ specialist}$

$\quad\quad\quad if\ msg = (RETURN\_DATA,\ specialist)$

$\quad\quad RECEIVED\_PASSWORD_{db\_waiting,\ logged\_in,\ anomalies,\ user\_name,\ db\_password}$

$\quad\quad\quad if\ msg = (RETURN\_DATA,\ user\_name,\ db\_password)$

$\quad\quad uifa.Eout!(REFERRED,\ referred\_anomalies)$

$\quad\quad\quad \rightarrow UIFA\_BUS_{db\_waiting,\ logged\_in,\ anomalies}$

$\quad\quad\quad if\ msg = (RETURN\_DATA,\ referred\_anomalies)$

$\quad\quad\quad\quad \wedge\ logged\_in \neq []$

$\quad\quad uifa.Eout!(user\_name,\ INVALID)$

$\quad\quad\quad \rightarrow UIFA\_BUS_{db\_waiting/(user\_name,\ y)\bullet(\exists!(user\_name,\ y)\in\ db\_waiting),logged\_in,\ anomalies}$

$\quad\quad\quad if\ msg = (USER\_EXCEPTION,\ user\_name,\ exception)$

$\quad\quad\quad\quad \wedge logged\_in \neq []$

$\quad\quad uifa.Iout!(head(msg),\ UNRECOGNIZED)$

$\quad\quad\quad \rightarrow UIFA\_BUS_{db\_waiting,\ logged\_in,\ anomalies}$

$\quad\quad otherwise$

The first element of the above case statement is a request for the user to solve an anomaly, which is processed by *UIFA_RESOLVE_ANOMALY* (described below). The *REFERRED* command sends the user interface a list of anomalies the FIRE agent has sent the user interface that have not yet been fixed. The *USER_EXCEPTION message* indicates that the user name does not exist and sends an invalid log-in message to the user interface. The processes named *RESOLVE_ANOMALY, RECEIVED-*

SPECIALIST, and _RECEIVED_PASSWORD_ need to test state information before passing data on to the user interface. _RESOLVE_ANOMALY_ checks whether a user is logged on before passing the anomaly to the user interface. If a user is logged on, the process sends the anomaly to the user interface. If a user is not logged on, then the process pages a user who has the required subsystem specialty. The paging works as follows:

1. Request the specialist type needed for this type of anomaly from the database.
2. Once the data is received from the database, sending the pager the specialist type to page.
3. Waiting for the user to log in.

When a user logs in and the password is received from the database and validated, the process checks whether any anomalies have occurred since the last log in. If anomalies exist, the process sends them to the user interface after informing the user interface that the user's name and password have been validated.

The following is the specification of what the UIFA does when it receives a request to send the user interface an anomaly.

$$RESOLVE\_ANOMALY_{db\_waiting,\ logged\_in,\ anomalies,\ new\_anomaly} =$$
$$uifa.Eout!new\_anomaly \rightarrow UIFA\_BUS_{db\_waiting,logged\_in,anomalies}$$
$$\quad if\ logged\_in \neq []$$
$$else$$
$$uifa.Iout(DBIFA,\ REQUEST,\ SPECIALIST,\ new\_anomaly)$$
$$\quad \rightarrow UIFA\_BUS_{db\_waiting,\ logged\_in,\ anomalies\ \cup\ new\_anomaly}$$

_RESOLVE_ANOMALY_ states that when the UIFA receives an anomaly it first checks whether a user is logged on by checking the list of users in the bag _logged_in_. If a user is logged on, then UIFA sends the anomaly to the user interface over the environment channel _uifa.Eout_. If a user is not logged on, then UIFA sends a message to the database asking it for a specialist who can handle the given anomaly (the returned information will later be sent to the pager).

The following is the specification as to what happens when the specialist type is received from the database agent:

$$RECEIVED\_SPECIALIST_{db\_waiting,\ logged\_in,\ anomalies,}^{\qquad\qquad\qquad new\_anomaly,\ specialist} =$$
$$\rightarrow uifa.Iout!(PAGER,\ new\_anomaly)$$
$$\quad if\ logged\_in = []$$
$$\rightarrow UIFA\_BUS_{db\_waiting,\ logged\_in,\ anomalies}$$

_RECEIVED_SPECIALIST_ states that when the name of the specialist is received from the database, the process sends to the pager agent the type of specialist to page. If someone has logged on since the request to the database was made, then the process does not send this information to the pager and nothing further is done (the anomaly was sent to the logged-on user).

The following specifies what happens when a password is received from the user interface:

$$RECEIVED\_PASSWORD_{db\_waiting,\ logged\_in,\ anomalies,\ user,\ db\_password} =$$
$$uifa.Eout!(user,\ VALID)$$
$$\rightarrow CHECK\_ANOMALIES_{db\_waiting/(user,\ db\_password),\ logged\_in\cup(user),\ anomalies}$$
$$if\ (user,\ db\_password) \in db\_waiting$$
$$else$$
$$\rightarrow uifa.Eout!(user, INVALID)$$
$$\rightarrow UIFA\_BUS_{db\_waiting/(user,\ y)\bullet(\exists!(user,\ y)\in db\_waiting),\ logged\_in,\ anomalies}$$

The above password validation process, *RECEIVED_PASSWORD*, is executed when the database agent returns the password requested by *UIFA_ENV* as described below. The process that is executed after *RECEIVED_PASSWORD* is dependent on whether the password is valid or not. The *RECEIVED_PASSWORD* process validates the password by checking whether the tuple *(user name, password)* received from the database is in the bag *db_waiting*. If it is, *RECEIVED_PASSWORD* sends a *VALID* message to the user interface and calls the *CHECK_ANOMALIES* process with the *(user name, password)* tuple removed from the *db_waiting* bag and the user name added to the *logged_in* bag. If the *(user name,password)* tuple is not in *db_waiting*, *RECEIVED_PASSWORD* sends an *INVALID* message to the user interface and calls the *UIFA_BUS* process with the *(user name, password)* tuple removed from *db_waiting*.

The following are the processes executed when the user name and password are validated:

$$CHECK\_ANOMALIES_{db\_waiting,\ logged\_in,\ anomalies} =$$
$$uifa.Iout(PAGER,\ STOP\_PAGING)$$
$$\rightarrow SEND\_ANOMALIES_{db\_waiting,\ logged\_in,\ anomalies}$$
$$if\ anomalies \neq \{\}$$
$$else$$
$$\rightarrow UIFA\_BUS_{db\_waiting,\ logged\_in,\ anomalies}$$

$$SEND\_ANOMALIES_{db\_waiting,\ logged\_in,\ a\cup A} =$$
$$uifa.Eout!a \rightarrow SEND\_ANOMALIES_{db\_waiting,\ logged\_in,\ A}$$

$SEND\_ANOMALIES_{db\_waiting,\ logged\_in,\ a\cup\{\}} =$
    $uifa.Eout!a \rightarrow UIFA\_BUS_{db\_waiting,\ logged\_in,\ \{\}}$

In this process, the *anomalies* set is checked to see whether it is non-empty, and if it is, then the process *SEND_ANOMALIES* executes. If the *anomalies* set is empty, then the *UIFA_BUS* process executes. The *SEND_ANOMALIES* process sends each of the anomalies in the *anomalies* set to the user interface one at a time and then deletes each from the set. When the *anomalies* set is empty, the *UIFA_BUS* process is called again.

The *ENV process* for the UIFA reads messages from the user interface and processes them or passes them on to other agents as needed. The *ENV* definition is:

$UIFA\_ENV = uifa.Ein?msg \rightarrow$
    case
        $uifa.pass!(user\_name,\ password) \rightarrow UIFA\_ENV$
            $if\ msg = (LOGIN,\ user\_name,\ password)$

        $uifa.Iout!(MIFA,\ REQUEST,\ SCHEDULE) \rightarrow UIFA\_ENV$
            $if\ msg = (GET\_SCHEDULE)$

        $uifa.Iout!(DBIFA,\ REQUEST,\ REPORT) \rightarrow UIFA\_ENV$
            $if\ msg = (GET\_CURRENT\_REPORT)$

        $uifa.Iout!(FIRE,\ SC\_COMMAND,\ command) \rightarrow UIFA\_ENV$
            $if\ msg = (SC\_COMMAND,\ command)$

The above definition for the *UIFA_ENV* process states that it reads a message off of the environment channel *uifa.Ein* (from the user interface) and stores it in the *msg* variable. The process that executes next is dependent on the content of the message from the user interface. If it is a user name and password, then *UIFA_ENV* sends it over the *uifa.pass* channel to the *UIFA_BUS* process, which then sends the user name and password to the database agent (see above).

The other three possibilities in the case statement are requests from the user for the current schedule, a report, or a command to send to the spacecraft. In each of these three cases, *UIFA_ENV* sends the message to the indicated agent over the *uifa.Iout* channel with the request.

10.5 Benefits of Using Formal Methods on Agent-Based Systems

The following describes some of the benefits we found while using formal methods on LOGOS. These include finding race conditions, omissions in the requirements and design, and a more thorough understanding of a system designed and developed by about a dozen people.

10.5.1 Detecting Race Conditions

While specifying the user interface agent, we discovered that a race condition exists between the *RESOLVE_ANOMALY* process and the *RECEIVED_PASSWORD* process. The race condition can occur if an anomaly occurs at about the same time a user logs in, but before the user is completely logged in. The race condition can occur in several ways. The following scenario illustrates one of them:

1. A user logs in.
2. The user interface passes the user name and password to the user interface agent (UIFA).
3. UIFA sends the database agent (DBIFA) the user name, requesting a return of the password.
4. While UIFA is waiting for the DBIFA to send the password back, the FIRE agent sends UIFA an anomaly to send to the user.
5. A process in UIFA checks to see whether the user is logged on, which is not the case, but, before it can set the variable to indicate an anomaly is waiting, the process blocks.
6. At this point, the password is received from the database, and this UIFA process determines that the password is valid and checks to see whether there are any anomalies waiting, which is not the case (because the process in #5 is blocked and has not set the variable yet), and then sends a valid login message to the user interface.
7. At this point, the process in #5 above becomes unblocked and continues; it then finishes setting the variable indicating that an anomaly is waiting, has the user paged, and then blocks waiting for a new user to log in.

Although the above situation is by no means fatal since in the end a user is paged, nevertheless, a user is paged even though one who could handle the anomaly immediately is already logged on. In addition, if the anomaly needed an immediate response, time would be wasted while the second user responded to the page.

From the above, it is evident that this is an invariant condition for UIFA. The invariant is that the *anomaly-waiting* variable and the *user-logged-in variable* should never be set to true at the same time. If this invariant is violated, then the condition exists that a user is logged in and the anomaly process has unnecessarily paged a user and is waiting for that user to login instead of sending the anomaly to the current user.

This condition can be fixed fairly easily. In each agent, there is a process that executes regularly to do any needed housekeeping functions. Some code could be added that checks whether the anomaly-waiting variable is set at the same time the user-logged-in variable is set and then calls the appropriate routine to send the anomaly to the user and unset the anomaly-waiting variable.

Another potential race condition occurs when a user logs in and enters an incorrect password. When the database returns the correct password to the UIFA, the UIFA has in its bag the name of the user and the entered password. If this password is incorrect, it normally can be easily deleted, because the element in the bag can be indexed by the user name. A problem can arise if the password is incorrect and if, before the database has a chance to reply, the same user logs in again with a different password. In this case, when the database returns the correct password from the first occurrence, it will not know which *(username, password)* tuple to delete.

The solution to this problem is also straight forward. The message id of the request to the database should be used as the key and not the username, since the message id is unique. The database will also return the message id in the "in-reply-to" field of its message. So instead of storing the couple *(username, password)* in *db_waiting*, the triple *(message id, username, password)* should be used.

10.5.2 Omissions

Due to the prototype nature of LOGOS, many omissions existed. The omissions were usually one of two types:

- What should an agent do when another agent never responds to a request?
- How long should an agent wait for another agent to respond to a request?

The following are some samples of omissions from the pager agent:

- Should the pager agent automatically resubmit a page if there has been no response within a specified amount of time, or should this command come from the user interface agent?
- Should the pager agent change whom they are paging after an elapsed period of time, and what should that time interval be? Or, again, should that information come from the UIFA?
- What happens when the pager agent receives a request to page someone already paged (i.e., the pager has not yet received a request to stop paging the party that the pager is being requested to page)? In

this situation, the pager agent can either re-page the party or ignore the request. In addition, if a party can be paged multiple times, does the software have to keep track of the number of times the party was paged or other relevant information?

• Should the pager agent cache specialist pager numbers and information for a specific amount of time, or should they always be requested from the database (even if there is an active, unanswered page for a specialist)?

• There is nothing specified as to what should be done if the requested pagee does not exist.

10.5.3 Better Understanding of the System

The development team concurs with the conclusion reached by others that a formal specification process supports team communications at a rigorous and precise level that is difficult to reach with other approaches. Code walk-throughs can provide a means for precise communications within a team, but it does not provide a way to communicate at a high level of abstraction as does a formal specification language like CSP, nor can it be expected to provide the general possibility of mathematical proof of properties of the system described by the code. Further, CSP enables accurate communications between the developers and the customer at any abstraction level that is appropriate, whether early or late in the development process. When the customer has a more accurate understanding of the system, the developer is better enabled to obtain from the customer an accurate understanding of the customer's actual requirements and demonstrate this understanding to the customer. Thus, better mutual understanding of the system under development is supported by the use of formal specifications.

10.6 Conclusion

Our experience to has shown that even at the level of requirements, formalization in CSP can help to highlight undesirable behavior and errors of omission. We are currently working on using formal and semi-formal techniques for specifying our next generation multi-agent system to check for possible error conditions (including deadlock) between components of the agents and between the agents themselves.

We have found that the results that formal specifications can provide are extremely helpful, but developing them is very time intensive, and the results may not be available until after the project has been completed (as in this case). We have found that tools are essential to speeding up this process. It is well recognized in the formal methods community that a significant advance in the usability of formal methods would require the availability of certain tools. The authors' experience supports the call for development of intelligent editing, animation, and test-case generation tools. The perceived and actual overhead of using formal methods could be reduced with the availability of such tools, and the accessibility of formal methods could be increased.

To further enhance the efficacy of formal methods in practice, we would also call for the creation of more integrated sets of such tools. Then to include in the tool set automated theorem proving capabilities with respect to the specifications of produced systems would surely bring about a revolution in the field of systems development. We are currently experimenting with model checkers such as Spin [8] and in the future the Java PathFinder [5] for checking existing Java code for errors. We are also actively researching the development of other tools that can speed the process of developing formal specifications and checking these specifications for errors.

As programming languages such as Java make it easier to develop concurrent systems, the need to find race conditions and other concurrency related errors will become even more important. The only cost-effective way that has been described for doing this with any assurance requires the use of formal methods. We believe that the development of tools will ease the process of learning and using formal methods.

References

1. d'Inverno M. and Luck, M. *Understanding Agent Systems*. Springer-Verlag. 2001.
2. Ferber, J. *Multi-Agent Systems, An Introduction to Distributed Artificial Intelligence*. Addision-Wesley. 1999.
3. *Foundation for Intelligent Agents*, Geneva, Switzerland, November 28, 1997.
4. Hallock, L., Truszkowski, W., Rouff, C. and Karlin, J. Agent-Based Spacecraft Autonomy. In *Proceedings of Institute for Operations Research and the Management Sciences (INFORMS)*, 1999.
5. Havelund, K. Model Checking Java Programs using Java PathFinder. *International Journal on Software Tools for Technology Transfer*, 1999.
6. Hinchey, M. G. and Jarvis, S. A. *Concurrent Systems: Formal Development in CSP*. McGraw-Hill International Series in Software Engineering, London and New York. 1995.
7. Hinchey, M., Rash, J. and Rouff, C. Verification and Validation of Autonomous Systems. In *Proceedings of 2001 IEEE/NASA Software Engineering Workshop*, 27-29 November, 2001.
8. Holzmann, H. J. *Design and Validation of Computer Protocols*. Prentice Hall Software Series, Englewood Cliffs, NJ. 1991.
9. Hoare, C. A. R. *Communicating Sequential Processes*. Prentice Hall International Series in Computer Science, Hemel Hempstead. 1985.

10. Labrou, Y. and Finin, T. *A Proposal for a new KQML Specification*. Technical Report TR CS-97-03, Computer Science and Electrical Engineering Department, University of Maryland Baltimore County, Baltimore, MD 21250, 1997.
11. LOGOS Overview, Design and Specification Documents. http://agents. gsfc.nasa.gov/products.html
12. LOGOS System Overview Document. http://agents.gsfc.nasa.gov/ documents/code588/LOGOS.stuff/logosoverview.pdf
13. Rash, J., Rouff, C., Truszkowski, W., Gordon-Spears, D. and Hinchey, M. (Editors). *First NASA Workshop on Formal Approaches to Agent-Based Systems, (LNAI 1871)*, Springer-Verlag, 2001.
14. Rouff, C., Rash, J. and Hinchey, M. Experience Using Formal Methods for Specifying a Multi-Agent System. In *Proceedings of the Sixth IEEE International Conference on Engineering of Complex Computer Systems (ICECCS 2000)*, 2000.
15. Rouff, C. and Truszkowski, W. A Process for Introducing Agent Technology into Space Missions. *IEEE Aerospace Conference*, 11-16 March, 2001.
16. Truszkowski, W. and Hallock, H. Agent Technology from a NASA Perspective. In *CIA-99, Third International Workshop on Cooperative Information Agents*, Uppsala, Sweden, 31 July - 2 August, Springer-Verlag, 1999.
17. Truszkowski, W. and Rouff, C. An Overview of the NASA LOGOS and ACT Agent Communities. *World Multiconference on Systemics, Cybernetics and Informatics*, Orlando, Florida, 22-25 July, 2001.
18. *VisAGE 3.0 User's Manual*. NASA Goddard Space Flight Center, Code 588.0, 2000. http://tidalwave.gsfc.nasa.gov/avatar/
19. Wooldridge, M. Intelligent Agents. In *Multiagent Systems*. G. Weiss, editor. MIT Press. 1999.

11

Formal Verification of Autonomy Models

Charles Pecheur, Reid Simmons, and Peter Engrand

11.1 Introduction

As NASA's missions continue to explore Mars and beyond, the great distances from Earth will require that they be able to perform many of their tasks with an increasing amount of autonomy, including navigation, self-diagnosis, and on-board science. For example, the Autonomous Controller for the In-Situ Propellant Production facility, designed to produce spacecraft fuel on Mars, must operate with infrequent and severely limited human intervention to control complex, real-time, and mission-critical processes over many months in poorly understood environments [9].

While autonomy offers promises of improved capabilities at a reduced operational cost, there are concerns about being able to design, implement and verify such autonomous systems in a reliable and cost-effective manner. Traditional scenario-based testing methods fall short of providing the desired confidence level, because of the combinatorial explosion of possible situations to be analyzed.

Often, formal verification techniques based on model checking[1] are able to efficiently check all possible execution traces of a system in a fully automatic way. However, the system typically has to be manually converted beforehand into the syntax accepted by the model checker. This is a tedious and complex process, that requires a good knowledge of the model checker, and is therefore usually carried externally by a formal methods expert, rather than by the system designer himself.

This chapter presents the application of formal verification techniques in the development of autonomous controllers based on Livingstone, a model-based health management and control system that helps to achieve this autonomy by detecting and diagnosing anomalies and suggesting possible recovery actions. We describe a translator that converts

---

[1] As opposed to those based on proof systems, which can provide even more general results but require an even more involved and skilled guidance.

the models used by Livingstone into specifications that can be verified with the SMV model checker from Carnegie Mellon University. The translator converts both the Livingstone model and the specification to be verified from Livingstone to SMV, and then converts any diagnostic trace from SMV back to Livingstone. It thereby shields the Livingstone application designer from the technicalities of the SMV model checker.

Section 11.2 presents the Livingstone health management system and its modeling language. Section 11.3 introduces symbolic model checking and the SMV tool. Section 11.4 introduces our translator and describes the different translations that it performs. Section 11.5 presents its use in different NASA applications, and lessons learned from those experiences. Section 11.6 discusses other possible approaches to verification of model-based autonomy, Section 11.7 presents some comparable work, and finally Section 11.8 draws final conclusions.

11.2 Livingstone

11.2.1 Overview

Livingstone is a model-based health monitoring system developed at NASA Ames [21]. It uses a symbolic, qualitative model of a physical system, such as a spacecraft, to infer its state and diagnose faults. Livingstone is one of the three parts of the Remote Agent (RA), an autonomous spacecraft controller developed by NASA Ames Research Center jointly with the Jet Propulsion Laboratory. The two other components are the Planner/Scheduler [14], which generates flexible sequences of tasks for achieving mission-level goals, and the Smart Executive [17], which commands spacecraft systems to achieve those tasks. Remote Agent was demonstrated in flight on the Deep Space One mission (DS-1) in May 1999, marking the first control of an operational spacecraft by AI software [15]. Livingstone is also used in other applications such as the control of a propellant production plant for Mars missions [5], the monitoring of a mobile robot [19], and intelligent vehicle health management (IVHM) for the X-37 experimental space transportation vehicle.

The functioning of Livingstone is depicted in Figure 11.1. The *Mode Identification* module (MI) estimates the current state of the system by tracking the commands issued to the device. It then compares the predicted state of the device against observations received from the actual sensors. If a discrepancy is noticed, Livingstone performs a diagnosis by searching for the most likely configuration of component states that are consistent with the observations. Using this diagnosis, the *Mode Recovery* module (MR) can suggest an action to recover to a given goal configuration.

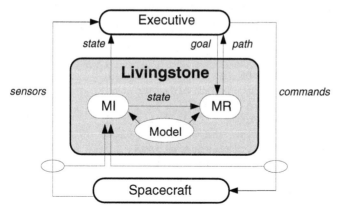

Fig. 11.1. Livingstone mode identification (MI) and mode recovery (MR).

This work is based on the original Livingstone 1 program that flew on DS-1 as part of the Remote Agent. Livingstone 1 is a Lisp program and uses a Lisp-style language called MPL (Model Programming Language) to describe the models. Livingstone has since then been rewritten from the ground up in C++ to address flight software requirements. The new Livingstone 2 also sports a new Java-like modeling language called JMPL.

11.2.2 The MPL Language

The model used by Livingstone describes the normal and abnormal functional modes of each component in the system, using a declarative formalism called MPL. The model is composed from a hierarchy of elementary *components*, assembled into compound *modules*. Each component definition may have parameters and describes the *attributes* and *modes* of the component. Attributes are the state variables of the component, ranging over qualitative, discrete values: continuous physical domains have to be abstracted into discrete intervals such as {low, nominal, high} or {neg, zero, pos}. Modes identify both nominal and fault modes of the component. Each mode specifies constraints on the values that variables may take when the component is in that mode, and how the component can transition to other modes (by definition, spontaneous transitions to any fault mode can happen from any mode). The Livingstone model thus represents a combination of concurrent finite-state transition systems. For example, Figure 11.2 sketches a simple MPL model for a valve, with a parameter ?name used for naming purposes. It has two attributes, flow and cmd, whose discrete types have been defined beforehand in the two (defvalues ...) declarations. It has two nominal modes, open and closed, and two fault modes, stuck-open and stuck-closed. Its initial mode is closed. The closed mode enforces flow=off and allows a transition do-open to the open mode, triggered when the cmd variable has value open.

```
(defvalues flow (off low nominal high))
(defvalues valve-cmd (open close no-cmd))
(defcomponent valve (?name)
  (:inputs ((cmd ?name) :type valve-cmd))
  (:attributes ((flow ?name) :type flow) ...)
  (:background :initial-mode closed)
  (closed :type ok-mode :model (off (flow ?name))
    :transitions ((do-open :when (open (cmd ?name))
      :next open) ...))
  (open :type ok-mode ...)
  (stuck-closed :type fault-mode ...)
  (stuck-open :type fault-mode ...))
```

Fig. 11.2. A simple MPL Model of a valve.

Components are combined in module declarations, with constraints expressing their interconnections. For example, the declaration in Figure 11.3 models two valves A and B connected in series.

```
(defmodule valve-pair (?name)
  (:structure (valve (A ?name))
              (valve (B ?name)))
  (:facts (flow-equal (flow (A ?name))
                      (flow (B ?name))))))
```

Fig. 11.3. An MPL Model for two valves connected in series.

11.2.3 Semantics of Livingstone Models

For our purpose, an MPL model reduces to a set of variables and three sets of conditions over the values of those variables, respectively defining the initial states, the static constraints and the transition relation.

Formally, an MPL model defines a finite set X of *state variables* such that each variable $x \in X$ has an associated finite domain D_x. A *state* s assigns to each variable $x \in X$ a value $s(x) \in D_x$. We write S_X for the set of all such states.

The atomic propositions on which all logical conditions are built are variable *assignments* $x = v$, where $x \in X$ and $v \in D_x$. We write Σ_X for the set of all such assignments. A *state formula* is a boolean formula over assignments. State formulae apply to states in the natural way: a state s satisfies $x = e$ iff $s(x) = e$. We write $s \models \phi$ for "s satisfies ϕ" [2], and $[\![\phi]\!]$ for the set of states $\{s \mid s \models \phi\}$.

A *transition rule* is the form $\phi \Rightarrow$ id $next\,\psi$, where ϕ and ψ are state formulae. A *transition formula* is a boolean combination of transition rules. Transition rules and formulae serve to define admissible transitions between pairs of states: given states s, s', we say that $(s, s') \models \phi \Rightarrow$ id $next\,\psi$ if and only if, if $s \models \phi$, then $s' \models \psi$.

We can now map an MPL model to an *abstract specification* structure $\langle X, I, C, T \rangle$ where:

- X is the set of *state variables*;
- I is the *initial conditions*, expressed as a set of state formulae;
- C is the *state conditions*, also expressed as a set of state formulae; and
- T is the *transition conditions*, expressed as a set of transition formulae.

The sets I, C and T represent conjunctions; for example, we can write $s \models I$ for $s \models \bigwedge_{\phi \in I} \phi$. Abstract specifications are defined compositionally, following the component hierarchy. For each elementary component c, X contains the declared attributes, plus a *mode variable* m_c ranging over the modes of the component. I contains the initial conditions and C contains component constraints and conditional mode-specific constraints of the form $(m_c = m) \Rightarrow \phi$. T contains a single condition of the form

$$(\rho_1 \wedge \ldots \wedge \rho_n) \vee \rho'_1 \vee \ldots \vee \rho'_m$$

with one rule ρ_i of the form $(m_c = m) \wedge \phi \Rightarrow$ id $next\,\psi$ for each transition declared in the component, and one rule ρ'_j of the form **True** $\Rightarrow$ id $next\,(m_c = m')$ for each fault mode m'. Intuitively, this formula represents, for each component, the choice between a nominal transition satisfying the transition declarations in the model, and a fault transition to any of the fault modes.

For compound modules, variables and conditions are the union of the respective variables and conditions of their submodules, augmented with any additional attributes and state conditions from the module itself.

We then formalize the semantics of an MPL model in terms of a *transition system*[3] $\langle S, S_0, R, L \rangle$ where

- S is a set of states;

---

[2] We omit the obvious natural extension of satisfiability from propositions to formulae. The same remarks holds for transition formulae in the next paragraph.

[3] This kind of transition system is known as a *Kripke structure*, and is the one commonly used in temporal logic theory (see e.g. [6]). In [21], the semantics of Livingstone models are formalized using a slightly different but equivalent structure.

- $S_0 \subseteq S$ is the set of initial states;
- $R \subseteq S \times S$ is the transition relation, saying which states can follow each other as time progresses; and
- $L : S \to \Sigma_X$ is the labeling function, saying which propositions are true in each state.

Given an abstract specification $\langle X, I, C, T \rangle$ for an MPL model, the transition system $\langle S, S_0, R, L \rangle$ for that model is given by

$$S = S_X$$
$$S_0 = \{s \in S_X \mid s \models I \wedge s \models C\}$$
$$R = \{(s, s') \in S_X \times S_X \mid (s, s') \models T \wedge s' \models C\}$$
$$L(s) = \{x = v \mid s(x) = v\}$$

As we shall see in Section 11.4.2, our purpose is to translate MPL models into SMV models in a way that preserves this semantics.

For diagnosis purposes, Livingstone needs two subsets of X to be identified, corresponding respectively to the *commands* (inputs) and *observables* (outputs) of the system. A probability is also associated with each fault mode. In a nutshell, the *mode identification* (MI) problem consists in incrementally generating a (most likely) set of trajectories consistent with known initial conditions and the sequence of command and observable values so far. The *mode recovery* (MR) problem is to find command values that will achieve a given constraint in the next state, given a set of possible current states. A detailed description of how these problems are solved in Livingstone is beyond our scope, see [21] for details.

11.3 Symbolic Model Checking and SMV

11.3.1 Introduction

Model checking is a verification technology based on the exhaustive exploration of a system's achievable states. Given a model of a concurrent system and an expected property of that system, a model checker will run through all possible executions of that system, including all possible interleavings of concurrent threads, and report any execution that leads to a property violation. We refer the reader to [6] and [1] for a general introduction to the theory and practice of model checking.

Classical, explicit-state model checkers such as SPIN [12] do this by generating and exploring every single state. In contrast, symbolic model checking manipulates whole sets of states at once, implicitly represented as the logical conditions that those states satisfy. These conditions are encoded into data structures called *(Ordered) Binary Decision Diagrams* (BDDs) [2] that provide a compact representation and support very efficient manipulations.

Symbolic model checking can often address much larger systems than explicit state model checkers. It has traditionally been applied to hardware systems, and is increasingly being used to verify software systems as well. It does not work well for all kinds of models, however: the complexity of the BDDs can outweigh the benefits of symbolic computations, and BDDs are still exponential in the size of the system in the worst case.

11.3.2 Symbolic Model Checking

We will only sketch the intuition behind BDDs and their use for model checking here. The reader is referred to the literature for a deeper and more formal discussion. [6] has an excellent introductory presentation in chapters 5 and 6.

Binary Decision Diagrams

A BDD is a graph structure used to represent a *boolean function*, that is, a function f over boolean variables $b_1, \ldots, b_n$ with boolean result $f(b_1, \ldots, b_n)$. Each node of the graph carries a variable b_i and has two outgoing edges. It can be read as an *if-then-else* branching on that variable, with the edges corresponding to the *if* and *else* part. The leaves of the BDD are logical values 0 and 1 (i.e. *false* and *true*). For example, a BDD for $f(a, b, c) = a \vee (b \wedge c)$ is shown in Figure 11.4.

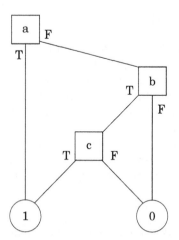

Fig. 11.4. BDD for $a \vee (b \wedge c)$.

By fixing the order of variables in the graph, merging identical subgraphs and removing nodes with identical children, any boolean function over a given set of variables can be represented as a unique BDD. Furthermore, all needed operations can be efficiently computed over BDDs.[4] For a given boolean function, the size of the BDDs and thus the computation costs are highly dependent on the selected ordering among variables. Finding an optimal ordering is computationally infeasible, and some functions have an exponential BDD size for any ordering. Finding a good reordering becomes a critical and tricky issue for large systems.

If the variables $\bar{b} = (b_1, \ldots, b_n)$ represent the state of some system,[5] then a set of states S can be represented as the condition $S(\bar{b})$ that those states satisfy, which can be encoded as a BDD. Similarly, a transition relation T over states can be encoded as a BDD $T(\bar{b}, \bar{b}')$ over two generations of the state variables $\bar{b}$ and $\bar{b}'$.

These elements provide the basis for symbolic model checking. For example, given the BDDs $S(\bar{b})$ and $T(\bar{b}, \bar{b}')$, we can compute the BDD id $next(S)$ of the *successors* of S, that is, all states reachable from S through T, as

$$\text{id}\,next(S)(\bar{b}) = \exists \bar{b}'.S(\bar{b}') \wedge T(\bar{b}', \bar{b})$$

By iterating this computation from a given set of initial states until we reach a fixed point, we can compute the reachable state space of the system as a BDD. We can just as easily go backwards and compute the BDD id $pred(S)$ of the *predecessors* of S (from which S is reachable) by using $T(\bar{b}, \bar{b}')$ instead of $T(\bar{b}', \bar{b})$ above. That is the basis for checking CTL temporal logic formulae, as we will see shortly.

Temporal Logic and CTL

Typically, the property to be verified is provided to the model checker as a formula in *temporal logic*. As opposed to propositional or first-order logic, which reasons about a given state of the world, temporal logic allows us to reason about how different states follow each other over time. In temporal logic, we can say things like "the engine will never overheat" or "all faults will eventually be detected."

In our case, we focus on the SMV tool that uses *Computation Tree Logic* (CTL). CTL is a branching-time temporal logic, which means that it supports reasoning over both the breadth and the depth of the tree of possible executions. In CTL, temporal operators always associate a branching quantifier E or A to a path quantifier X, U, F or G.[6] CTL operators

---

[4] Needed operations are boolean operations, restrictions of variables and quantification. Good performance is achieved by caching the result of each subcomputation in a hash table.

[5] Note that other finite types, such as enumerations or (small) integer ranges, can be encoded into boolean variables.

[6] Note that F and G can be derived from U, as F ϕ = id *true* U ϕ and G ϕ = ¬F ¬ϕ

are summarized in Table 11.1; their meaning is illustrated in Figure 11.5 (black and gray circles are states where p and q hold, respectively).

Table 11.1. Summary of CTL operators.

Syntax	Reads as...	ϕ holds in s if...
$E\pi$	exists π	π holds on some path from s
$A\pi$	always π	π holds on all paths from s

a. State formulae ϕ

Syntax	Reads as ...	π holds on $(s_0, s_1, \dots)$ if...
$X\,\phi$	next ϕ	ϕ holds in s_1
$G\,\phi$	globally ϕ	ϕ holds in s_n for all n
$F\,\phi$	finally ϕ	ϕ holds in s_n for some n
$\phi\,U\,\phi'$	ϕ until ϕ'	ϕ' holds in s_n for some n, and ϕ holds in s_k for all $k < n$

b. Path formulae π

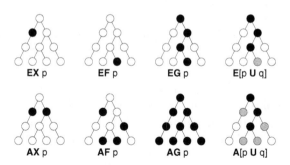

Fig. 11.5. CTL operators.

For example, the CTL formula

$$AG\ (\text{request} \Rightarrow AF\ \text{response})$$

states that from any state (**A**lways **G**lobally) where there is a request, one has to reach (**A**lways **F**inally) a state where there is a response.

BDD-Based Model Checking

CTL operators can be characterized recursively; this provides the basis for symbolic model checking of CTL. For example, EG ϕ can be defined as the (greatest) solution for Z in the following equation:

$$Z = \phi \wedge \mathsf{EX}\, Z$$

Noticing that $\mathsf{EX}\, Z$ is nothing else than $\mathrm{id}\, pred(Z)$, we can compute the BDD for $\mathsf{EG}\, \phi$ from the BDD for ϕ as follows: starting from $Z^0 = \textbf{True}$, we repeatedly compute $Z^{n+1} = \phi \wedge \mathrm{id}\, pred(Z^n)$ until we reach a fixed point. That fixed point is the set of states that satisfy $\mathsf{EG}\, \phi$.

11.3.3 SMV

To analyze Livingstone models, we use the *Symbolic Model Verifier* (SMV), from Carnegie Mellon University (CMU) [3]. SMV was the first and is still one of the most widely used symbolic model checkers. The SMV software takes as input a model to be verified, written in a custom modeling language. This model also contains the properties to be verified, written as CTL formulas. Upon completion, SMV reports a true/false answer for each specified property, along with an execution trace witnessing the property violation, in case of a false answer. Internally, SMV uses BDD-based symbolic model checking as described in the previous section. SMV does not reorder variables by default, but provides options to apply reordering and to export and import variable orderings in text files that can be modified by the user.

An SMV model is organized as a hierarchy of MODULE declarations. A module has a name and optional parameters, and contains a sequence of declarations. There are various types of declarations, among which we list only the ones that we use here[7]:

- VAR var_1 : $type_1$; ...; var_n : $type_n$;
  declares each var_i as either a state variable with a finite type (either boolean, an enumeration $\{val_1, \ldots, val_m\}$, or an integer range), or a submodule, where $type_i$ is a module name and parameters.
- DEFINE id_1 := $expr_1$; ...; id_n := $expr_n$;
  defines each id_i as a shorthand for $expr_i$. This is a macro mechanism: each $expr_i$ is substituted wherever id_i appears; no new BDD variable is created for id_i.
- INIT *form*
  declares a constraint on initial states. *form* is a boolean expression over state variables.
- TRANS *tranform*
  declares a constraint on transitions. *tranform* is a formula over variables before and after a transition, denoted var and next(var), respectively.

---

[7] We use *constraint-style* definitions based on the INIT/TRANS/INVAR declarations. SMV also allows *assignment-style* definitions, based on assigning initial and next values to each variable. Assignment-style is the most common and preferred way, but constraint-style is more flexible and adapted when translating from Livingstone models.

- INVAR *form*
  declares a constraint on all states.
- SPEC *ctlform*
  declares a property to be verified, as a CTL formula.

The SMV program has to have a module called main that is the top level of the hierarchy. The different INIT, TRANS and INVAR constraints combine together across the module hierarchy exactly as in MPL models in Section 11.2.3, forming three resulting conditions $I(s)$, $T(s, s')$ and $C(s)$. Concretely, SMV computes the BDDs for those three conditions, and then uses them to verify that each SPEC declaration is satisfied in all initial states of the model.

11.4 Verification of Livingstone Models

11.4.1 Introduction

Livingstone involves the interaction between various components: the reasoning engine that performs the diagnosis, the model that provides application-specific knowledge to it, the physical system being diagnosed, the executive that drives it and acts upon diagnosis results. There are many ways that one could attempt to provide better verification tools for all or parts of such a system, borrowing from various existing techniques, from improved testing up to computer-supported mathematical proofs. The focus of the work presented here is on the verification of the Livingstone model, by turning this model into a representation suitable for model checking. We defer the discussion of other potential approaches to Section 11.6. For now, let us point out that since the model is specific to the application that it is used for, it is indeed where the correctness issues are most likely to occur during the development of a given application.

In many previous experiences in model checking of software, the system to be verified has been translated by hand from its original design to the custom input syntax of the target verification tool. This translation is by far the most complex and time-consuming part, typically taking weeks or months, whereas the running of the verification is a matter of minutes or hours thanks to the processing power of today's computers. The net result is that software model checking has been so far mostly performed off-track by formal methods experts, rather than by field engineers as part of the development process. This gap between verification and software development formalisms and tools is recognized as one of the main obstacles to the widespread adoption of formal verification by the software industry.

Our goal is to allow Livingstone application developers to use model checking to assist them in designing and correcting their models, as part of their usual development environment. To achieve that, we have developed a translator to automate the conversion between MPL and SMV. To completely isolate the Livingstone developer from the syntax and technical details of the SMV version of his model, we need to address three kinds of translation, as shown in Figure 11.6:

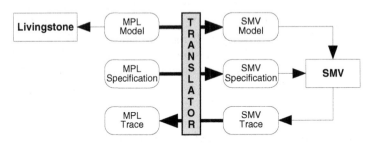

Fig. 11.6. Translation between MPL and SMV.

- The MPL model needs to be translated into an SMV model amenable to model checking.
- The specifications to be verified against this model need to be expressible in terms of the MPL model and similarly translated.
- Finally, the diagnostic traces produced by SMV need to be converted back in terms of the MPL model.

These three aspects are covered by our translator and are detailed in the following subsections. The translator program has been written in Lisp[8] and is about 4000 lines long.

11.4.2 Translation of Models

The translation of MPL models to SMV is facilitated by the strong similarities between the underlying semantic frameworks of Livingstone and SMV. As can be seen by comparing the models in Sections 11.2.3 and 11.3.3, both boil down to a synchronous transition system, defined through propositional logic constraints I on initial states, C on all states and T on transitions. Based on this, there is a straightforward mapping from MPL to SMV language elements, summarized in Table 11.2.

Translation of transition relations has to allow for fault transitions too. For each component, a DEFINE declaration is produced that defines a symbol faults as the set of its fault modes. Then each MPL transition from a mode M to a mode M' with condition P is translated into the following SMV declaration:

---

[8] Lisp was a natural choice considering the Lisp-style syntax of the MPL language.

Table 11.2. Mapping of MPL to SMV elements.

MPL description	MPL syntax	SMV syntax
attribute type	(defvalues T (V ...))	V, ...
elementary component	(defcomponent C ...)	MODULE C ...
compound module	(defmodule M ...)	MODULE M ...
component attributes	(:attributes (A :type T) ...)	VAR A : V, ...; ...
subcomponents	(:structure M ...)	VAR X : M; ...
mode transitions	:transitions ...	TRANS ...
mode constraints	:model ...	INVAR ...
component constraints	:facts ...	INVAR ...
initial conditions	:initial-mode ...	INIT ...

```
TRANS (mode=M & P) -> (next(mode)=M' |
    next(mode) in faults)
```

If we compare this to the MPL transition formula

$$(\rho_1 \wedge \ldots \wedge \rho_n) \vee \rho_1' \vee \ldots \vee \rho_m'$$

of Section 11.2.3, each ρ_i corresponds to the nominal part

```
(mode=M & P) -> next(mode)=M'
```

while the fault part

```
next(mode) in faults
```

corresponds to the whole disjunction $\rho_1' \vee \ldots \vee \rho_m'$. On this basis, one can easily see that the conjunction of all TRANS declarations of a component is indeed equivalent to the transition formula above.

As an example, Figure 11.7 sketches the SMV translation of the MPL model in Figure 11.2.

```
MODULE valve
VAR     mode: {open,closed,stuck-open,stuck-closed};
        cmd: {open,close,no-cmd};
        flow: {off,low,nominal,high};
        ...
DEFINE faults:={stuck-open,stuck-closed};
INIT mode=closed
INVAR mode=closed -> flow=off
...
TRANS (mode=closed & cmd=open) ->
        (next(mode)=open | next(mode) in faults)
...
```

Fig. 11.7. SMV Model of a valve.

The main difficulty in performing the translation comes from discrepancies in variable naming rules between the flat name space of Livingstone and the hierarchical name space of SMV. Each MPL variable reference, such as (flow valve-1), needs to be converted into a SMV qualified variable reference w.r.t. the module hierarchy, e.g. ispp.inlet. valve-1.flow. Furthermore, MPL models have loose scoping rules: any attribute can be referred to from any other component or module. In contrast, SMV enforces conventional lexical scoping, so attributes that are used out of their scope must be detected and passed along explicitly as parameters of the SMV modules that need them.[9] To optimize this process, the translator builds a lexicon of all variables declared in the MPL model with their SMV counterpart, and then uses it in all three parts of the translation.

11.4.3 Translation of Specifications

The specifications to be verified with SMV are added to the MPL model using a new defverify declaration[10]. The defverify declaration also defines the top-level module to be verified. The properties to be verified are expressed in a Lisp-like syntax that extends the existing MPL syntax for logic expressions. For example, the declaration in Figure 11.8 specifies a CTL property to be verified with ispp as the top-level module. Informally, the specification says that, from any non-fault state, a high flow in valve 1 can eventually be reached. Figure 11.9 shows the top-level SMV module that is produced from that declaration, including the conversion of the CTL operators from MPL's Lisp style (always (globally ...)) into SMV's conventional style AG ....

```
(defverify
  (:structure (ispp))
  (:specification
    (always (globally (impliesn
      (not (broken))
      (exists (eventually (high (flow valve-1)))))))))
```

Fig. 11.8. A sample specification in MPL.

CTL is very expressive but requires a lot of caution and expertise to be used correctly. To alleviate this problem, the translator provides different features for expressing model properties.

---

[9] This is appropriate, as SMV passes parameters by reference.

[10] This is specific to the translator and rejected by Livingstone; an added empty Lisp macro definition easily fixes this problem.

```
MODULE main
  VAR ispp : ispp;
  SPEC AG ((!broken) ->
    EF (ispp.inlet.valve-1.flow = high))
```

Fig. 11.9. Translation of a sample specification in SMV.

Plain CTL

CTL operators are supported in MPL's Lisp-like syntax, as illustrated above.

Specification Patterns

The translator provides predefined specification templates for some common classes of properties that are generally useful to check, independently of any given application. The user can refer to them by their meaningful name, and the translator automatically produces the corresponding CTL specifications. The following templates are currently supported:

- (:specification :inconsistency)
  Verifies the global consistency of the model. This generates SPEC 0 (i.e., the always false specification). This specification can only be (vacuously) valid if the model is empty, i.e., if no consistent initial state exists. If the model is consistent, the specification will be false.[11]
- (:specification :reachability)
  Verifies that all modes of all components are reachable (a variant only checks selected components).
- (:specification :path-reachability S0 S1 S2 ...)
  Whenever S0 is reached, checks the existence of a path reaching S1, then S2, etc. A variant restricts the path to fault-free states.
- (:specification :completeness)
  Verifies whether there is *at least one* enabled transition in any mode of any component, by taking the disjunction of the conditions of all transitions of each mode.
- (:specification :disjointness)
  Verifies whether there is *at most one* enabled transition in any mode of any component[12] by considering pairwise conjunctions of the conditions of all transitions of each mode. Completeness and disjointness are complementary, together they ensure that the transition clauses are well-formed.

---

[11] Note that there is no way to have a *consistency* specification that would fail on inconsistent models, since any specification is vacuously valid on such models.

[12] Note that according to the semantics of MPL models, several enabled transitions would have to be *simultaneously* followed, likely resulting in an inconsistent next state.

Note that all but the first template are more than syntactic macros, they depend on structural information, such as modes and transition conditions, being extracted from the model.

Auxiliary Functions

The translator supports some auxiliary functions that can be used in CTL formulas to concisely capture Livingstone concepts such as occurrence of faults, activation of commands or probability of faults. Table 11.3 gives a representative sample. Some functions are translated solely in terms of existing variables using DEFINE declarations, while others, such as failed, require the introduction of new variables[13].

Table 11.3. Some auxiliary functions for MPL model specifications.

(broken heater) = Heater is in a failed state.
(multibroken 2) = At least two components are failed.
(failed heater) = On last transition, heater failed.
(multicommand 2) = At least two commands are activated.
(brokenproba 3) = Combined probability of currently failed components is at least of order 3.

The probability analysis opens an interesting perspective. Fault probabilities are mapped to small integers, based on their order of magnitude (rounded if necessary). For example, $p = 10^{-3}$ maps to 3. We then compute the combined order of magnitude for multiple faults by integer addition,[14] which SMV can do using BDDs. This is definitely an approximate method, that is no substitute for a precise approach such as Markov chain analysis. It does however provide a convenient way to separate between more and less likely fault scenarios.

Specification Variables

Verification variables can be introduced as attribute declarations in the (defverify ...) statement. These attributes work as universally quantified variables in the specifications. This is achieved in SMV with an undetermined constant variable, using the constraint TRANS x = next(x) but no INIT constraint. The universal quantification then comes as a by-product of the verification for all possible initial states.

Such variables are useful for relating values at different points within a CTL formula. For example, the formula

---

[13] The latter are omitted by default, since the new variables can cause a big penalty on the performance of SMV.

[14] Since $10^{-a} \cdot 10^{-b} = 10^{-(a+b)}$, assuming independence of faults.

$$\forall m.\mathsf{AG}\,(\mathrm{id}\,send = m \Rightarrow \mathsf{AF}\,\mathrm{id}\,rcv = m)$$

expresses that any message sent is eventually received. Section 11.5.1 describes in more details the verification of functional dependency properties, which are based on such verification variables.

Model Restrictions

An additional state or transition constraint can be added as a (:model ...) clause in the (defverify ..) statement. The constraint is simply added to the model. This is convenient for restricting the verification to particular conditions, in particular, using the auxiliary functions above. One can, for example, limit the number of simultaneous commands or prune out combined faults below some probability threshold.

Observers

The translator allows the definition of *observer automata*, which are cross-breeds between modules (in that they can refer to other components or modules) and components (in that they can have modes). An observer, however, can have no internal variables, other than keeping track of mode. Observers are useful in some situations where the CTL specification language is inadequate for representing the specifications that one wants to verify.

11.4.4 Backward Translation of Traces

When a violated specification is found, SMV reports a diagnostic trace, consisting of a sequence of states leading to the violation. This trace is essential for diagnosing the nature of the violation. The states in the trace, however, show variables by their SMV names. To make sense to the Livingstone developer, it has to be translated back in terms of the variables of the original MPL model. This can done using the lexicon generated for the model translation in the reverse direction.[15]

A more arduous difficulty is that the diagnostic trace merely indicates the states that led to the violation but gives no indication of what, within those states, is really responsible. Two approaches to this diagnosis problem are currently being investigated. One is based on using visualization tools to expose the trace, the other one uses a truth maintenance system to produce causal explanations [20].

---

[15] As of this writing, translation of traces is still to be implemented in our translator. It poses no fundamental technical difficulty but requires some effort in parsing SMV's output trace.

11.5 Applications

This section gives a fairly detailed account of the use of our verification tools by Livingstone application engineers in the In-Situ Propellant Production (ISPP) project at NASA Kennedy Space Center (KSC). It summarizes a more detailed presentation in [8]. The purpose of this experience was not only to experiment with the translator and SMV, but also to study the potentials and challenges of putting such a tool in the hands of application practitioners. Another application, focusing on the Deep Space One spacecraft, is also briefly described. We conclude with some comments on the nature of the verification problem for autonomy models, and a short discussion of alternative model checking tools that have been or could be used.

11.5.1 In-Situ Propellant Production

Since 1998, the NASA Kennedy Space Center (KSC) has been working with the Livingstone developers at NASA Ames to apply Livingstone to the In-Situ Propellant Production (ISPP) plant, a system intended to produce spacecraft propellant using the atmosphere of Mars [5]. This plant, built in KSC's Applied Chemistry Laboratory, is capable of producing a large amount of oxygen with a small quantity of seed hydrogen, based on the Reverse Water Gas Shift reaction (RWGS) (Figure 11.10). In a human Mars mission, this plant would be required to operate for 500 or more days without human intervention. The Livingstone monitoring and diagnosis software provides built-in autonomy capabilities for ISPP.

Verification Methodology

One of the fundamental issues for the effective verification of models deals with the construction of meaningful specifications that validate the model (where a rough-and-ready definition of "meaningful" is a temporal form which captures some global system behavior, such as something stated as a high level design specification).

Our effort focused on the observation of modeling error "phenomena" (i.e., observable effects of those errors) and then the investigation of the underlying causes of the error's phenomena so that specification properties could be inferred and could lead to future re-usable specification patterns. These observations consisted of two modeling errors which had been previously encountered and diagnosed by the modelers. Nevertheless, it should be stressed that as a result of the investigation of the second error, two additional modeling errors were detected which had gone unnoticed during the normal testing of the model by the developers.

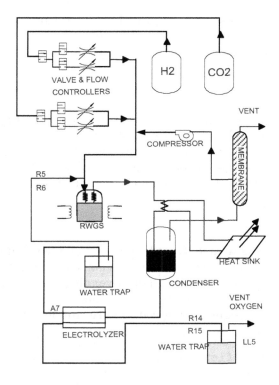

Fig. 11.10. RWGS process for ISPP.

First Error

The first error to be investigated dealt with a mis-modeled fluid flow behavior.[16] The model involves a component called a *sorption pump*, which absorbs the carbon dioxide (CO_2) from the atmosphere, and a complex set of flow branches through which the CO_2 is then sent for chemical transformation. For each branch, the model defines its admittance[17] and the flow that traverses it, both in terms of qualitative values {off, low, high}. Model constraints capture the relations between the different flows and admittances.

The modeling error occurred when the developers omitted the constraint that ties the global flow to the global admittance and the CO_2 pressure in the sorption pump. This omission led to the model manifesting flow through a flow branch with a zero admittance (e.g. with a closed valve on the path).

---

[16] This experiment was performed on the model of an earlier version of the ISPP system, based on the so-called Sabatier-Electrolysis chemical process.

[17] Admittance is a measure of fluid impedance of pipes and orifices.

In order to exhibit this error, we stated in CTL the property that *if the outlet valve of the sorption pump is blocking, then there is no flow through the branch*. In the MPL model, this was expressed as:

```
(all (globally (impliesn (off (admittance outlet))
                         (off (flow z-flow-module))))))
```

When the model and specification were translated and processed by SMV, a counter-example was returned, showing a violating state where `(flow z-flow-module)` was `high` although `(admittance outlet)` was `off`. The model developers acknowledged that that information would have likely allowed them to isolate their error much more quickly.

Second Error

The second error was related to modeling flows and flow differences in a component called `rwgs`. A set of constraints aims at defining an attribute `(relative-flow rwgs)` as the (qualitative) difference between the incoming and outgoing flows `(flow-in rwgs)` and `(flow-out rwgs)`. As the result of an oversight during code re-use, the following constraint fragment was used

```
(when (on (flow-in O2))
      (high-in (relative-flow rwgs)))
```

where `O2` should have been replaced by `rwgs`. The result found by the developers during their normal testing was an anomalous behavior of the model, where `rwgs` was filling up while the `O2` component connected to it was also filling up. Though the error seems obvious, this "mis-naming" proved to be difficult to detect using both testing by the developer and model checking with SMV.

Functional Dependency

We used this second error as an opportunity to study and demonstrate the verification of *functional dependency* properties using SMV. We say that a variable y functionally depends on variables $x_1, \ldots, x_n$ if and only if any given values for $x_1, \ldots, x_n$ uniquely determine the value of y. In practice, y could in this case be defined as a function of $x_1, \ldots, x_n$, but Livingstone provides no way to do this. Instead, the dependency has to be expressed as general propositional constraints, a potentially error-prone task.

We can express functional dependency of y w.r.t. $x_1, \ldots, x_n$ using CTL with universally quantified variables as

$$\forall v_1, \ldots, v_n, v. \ (\text{EF}\, x_1 = v_1 \wedge \ldots \wedge x_n = v_n \wedge y = v) \Rightarrow$$
$$(\text{AG}\, x_1 = v_1 \wedge \ldots \wedge x_n = v_n \Rightarrow y = v)$$

In other words, if for some values v_i for each x_i you get some value v for y, then for the same v_i you always get the same v.

In the case of the second error above, (relative-flow rwgs) was meant as a function of (flow-in rwgs) and (flow-out rwgs), so we added verification variables some-flow-in, some-flow-out and some-relative-flow and checked the property

```
(impliesn
  (exists (finally
    (and (= (flow-in rwgs_trap) some-flow-in)
         (= (flow-out rwgs_trap) some-flow-in)
         (= (relative-flow rwgs) some-relative
                                      -flow)))))
  (always (globally
    (impliesn
      (and (= (flow-in rwgs_trap) some-flow-in)
           (= (flow-out rwgs_trap) some-flow-in))
      (= (relative-flow rwgs) some-relative
                                    -flow)))))
```

SMV reported this property as false, as expected, but some further steps were needed to get a meaningful diagnosis. Indeed, the property amounts to a disjunction,[18] so a complete counter-example has two sides, one for each half of the property, giving the two different values of (relative-flow rwgs) for the same (flow-in rwgs) and (flow-out rwgs). However, by design SMV only gives a single counter-example trace, corresponding to the first half, in this case:

```
(off (flow-in rwgs_trap))
(off (flow-out rwgs_trap))
(equal (relative-flow rwgs))
```

To obtain the second half of the counter-example, the second half of the property was instantiated as a separate specification using the values from the first counter-example:

```
(always (globally
  (impliesn
    (and (off (flow-in rwgs_trap))
         (off (flow-out rwgs_trap)))
    (equal (relative-flow rwgs)))))
```

Verification of this new specification generated the second counter-example pinpointing the problem exposed above:

---

[18] As $(EF\ \phi) \Rightarrow (AG\ \psi)$ is equivalent to $(AG\ \neg\phi) \vee (AG\ \psi)$.

```
(off (flow-in rwgs_trap))
(off (flow-out rwgs_trap))
(high-in (relative-flow rwgs))
```

Although we finally achieved our goal of detecting and identifying a functional dependency violation, the method to follow is fairly involved and cumbersome. Functional dependency properties are prime candidates for better automated support in the translator. Complete support will require more than specification patterns, though, as results have to be extracted from the first SMV run to prepare for the second one.

Experimental Notes

The size of the RWGS Model used which contained the second error is 10^{17} States. Although this is a relatively large state space, SMV needed less than a minute to return a result. The size of the latest RWGS Model is on the order of 10^{55} states, and can still be processed in a matter of minutes using an enhanced version of SMV [22]. The Livingstone model of ISPP features a huge state space but little depth (all states can be reached within at most three transitions), for which the symbolic processing of SMV is very appropriate.

The experience has also been a steep learning curve for the application developer in charge of the formal verification experiment at KSC. This adds further evidence that writing a correct temporal specification can be a subtle error prone task, part of which consists in verifying the specification itself in order to check that it truly conveys the property that one wants to check.

11.5.2 Deep Space One

Livingstone was originally developed to provide model-based diagnosis and recovery for the Remote Agent architecture on the DS1 spacecraft. It is also in this context that the translator to SMV was originally developed. The full Livingstone model for the spacecraft runs to several thousand lines of MPL code. Using the translator, we have automatically constructed SMV models and verified several important properties, including consistency and completeness of the mode transition relations, and reachability of each mode. Using the translator, we were able to identify several (minor) bugs in the DS1 models (this was after the models had been extensively tested by more traditional means) [16].

11.5.3 Lessons Learned

Concrete applications have shown that the nature of the verification problem for Livingstone models is quite distinct from the verification of a more conventional concurrent application. A typical concurrent system is a collection of active entities, each following a well-scoped algorithm. In contrast, a typical Livingstone module describes a passive component such as a tank, valve or sensor; it states how this component reacts to external commands but hardly ever imposes any kind of order of operations in the component itself. On top of that, faults amount to unrestricted spontaneous transitions in every component that allows them.

This results in state spaces that have a very peculiar shape: a huge branching factor, due to all the command variables that can be set and all the faults that can occur at any given step, but a very low depth, due to the very little inherent sequential constraints in the model. In other words, a typical reachability tree for an MPL model is very broad but very shallow, with every state reachable from the initial one within a few transitions.

Because Livingstone models are so loosely constrained, they are also hit head-on by the combinatorial state space explosion, as the multiple configurations of each component essentially multiply with each other. This leads to huge state spaces (10^{55} for the latest ISPP model), that preclude any explicit state enumeration approach. For BDD-based symbolic processing, though, the complexity is rather related to the logical complexity of the model, and the ones we have seen so far fit (sometimes barely) within reach of the available tools. In particular, SMV needs only a few fixpoint iterations for each property because the models are so shallow.

This also affects the kind of properties that are useful to verify. Looking for deadlocks makes no sense in the presence of spontaneous fault transitions, though more focused reachability properties can reveal inconsistencies in the model. More typically, though, one is interested in consistency and completeness properties, because the declarative nature of MPL makes it very easy to come up with an over- or under-constrained model.

11.5.4 Alternative Model Checkers

Most of the experiments with the translator presented here have used the SMV package from Carnegie Mellon to perform the verification itself. However, SMV has reached the limits of available memory (256Mb in most experiments) with larger models, which has forced us to consider and try different improvements and alternatives. We list the most significant ones here.

Reordering Variables

As explained in Section 11.3.3, BDD size depends critically on a fixed ordering among model variables, and SMV provides options to optimize that ordering. We had to use this technique on a first-generation model of ISPP with 10^{50} states. After some trial and error, we captured an optimized ordering that lead to successful verification of that model.

New SMV Versions

A new, upward-compatible version of SMV, called *NuSMV* [4], has been recently re-built from scratch at IRST (Trento, Italy), in collaboration with CMU. NuSMV features much improved performance, and a cleaner, well-documented and modular source code amenable to customization. A couple quick tests with NuSMV confirmed a significant speedup but did not improve the memory performance, which has been the limiting factor in our applications.

Elimination of Variables

Certainly the most successful action towards scaling up to more complex models has been the adoption of an enhanced version of SMV developed by Bwolen Yang [22]. This version performs an analysis of the state constraints in the model to detect variables that can be expressed in terms of others, in the same sense as the functional dependency in Section 11.5.1. When such a variable is found, it is replaced by the corresponding expression and removed from the model, resulting in a reduction of the BDDs. This works out particularly well on Livingstone models, which are rich in state constraints expressing functional dependencies. On the latest model, this simplification reduced the BDD depth by more than a third, from 588 down to 379 binary variables. As a result, reachability of all modes, which exhausted memory with the standard SMV, completed in 29 seconds with the enhanced version.

Bounded Model Checking

The symbolic model checking community has shown a recent interest in *bounded model checking* using SAT solvers[19] instead of BDDs, such as the BMC (Bounded Model Checker) tool from Carnegie Mellon. BMC performs only an approximate verification, as the model is explored only down to a given depth, but never suffers from exponential space blow up, finds the shortest counter-examples and is quite fast in practice (though NP-complete in theory). While we have not had the opportunity to try BMC on Livingstone models, this seems a promising approach: as the models are expected to be shallow, the limitation of depth should not be too penalizing. Indeed, an important part of an average Livingstone

---

[19] SAT solvers implement decision procedures for propositional logic.

model resides in the static state constraints, and many interesting properties, such as functional dependencies, could be analyzed statically on those constraints using standard SAT techniques.

11.6 Comparison of Verification Approaches

The functionality of Livingstone results from the interaction between multiple parts of a quite different nature:

- The *Livingstone engine* that performs model-based reasoning for diagnosis purposes.
- The *Livingstone model* that provides domain-specific knowledge to the engine.
- The *plant* or physical system that is being diagnosed, including the system software layer that provides the abstraction used by Livingstone.
- The rest of the controller, including the *executive* that drives the plant and interprets diagnoses, and the human or automated environment (such as a planner/scheduler) that feeds commands to the executive.

It is clear that verifying the proper operation of Livingstone in such a context is a complex task that will require more than one method. In this section, we want to discuss the merits and limits of different methods.

Verification of Models

In Section 11.4, we have seen that Livingstone models lend themselves quite nicely to formal, exhaustive analysis using symbolic model checking. In doing so we should not lose sight, however, that we are not verifying a diagnosis engine but a general dynamic model of the plant. We can check whether that model has some desirable structural properties and matches our characterization of its physical counterpart, but not, in general, whether its faults will be properly diagnosed. Yet, some necessary conditions for diagnosis can be verified on the model, such as whether different faults are always differentiable based on a given set of observables.

Ideally, model-based reasoning would always infer the right diagnosis from a correct model, but in practice, performance tradeoffs may preclude that, or there could not be enough information to discriminate between different diagnoses. Thus, model-based verification does not alleviate the need for testing the model within the actual Livingstone algorithm.

Verification of the Engine

The engine is a relatively compact piece of software performing complex artificial intelligence algorithms. It is a sequential, deterministic program but it manipulates large and dynamic data structures. Doing model checking on the engine alone would make little sense, as it has a huge but mostly data-related state space; some form of formal proof of its constituting algorithms would make more sense. Nevertheless, the engine is also the more stable and better understood part, built around well-documented algorithms. Since it remains basically unchanged between applications, the verification of its correctness can be done once and for all by its designers. From the point of view of its users, Livingstone should be viewed as a stable, trustable part, just as C programmers trust their C compiler.

Verification of the Application

As explained above, we still want to verify a Livingstone application as a whole, including the engine, the model and its environment (controller and plant), or at least some abstract simulation of its relevant parts.

We could, in principle, model all that for the purpose of model checking. It would have to include a specification of the Livingstone engine algorithms and its data structures. In particular, the Livingstone model itself would appear not as a transition system but as a huge data structure used by the engine. Producing such a specification would be an arduous and error-prone task. Furthermore, the size of the data structures involved would likely render the model hopelessly intractable.

An alternative solution, that we are currently investigating, is to perform a controlled execution of Livingstone within a testbed, both instrumented to allow backtracking and state comparisons. Using this technique, a wide range of behaviors can be automatically and efficiently explored, using the same kind of state space exploration algorithm as used in explicit state model checkers.

11.7 Related Work

Initial experiments in applying model checking to autonomy models were performed by Penix, Pecheur and Havelund in 1998 [18] and focused on the HSTS model-based planner/scheduler [14]. HSTS models are composed of a large number of tightly coupled declarative real-time constraints whose combined effects are difficult to apprehend. The experiments were done on a small sample model of an autonomous robot. A useful subset of the planner modeling language, omitting the real-time aspects but covering the robot example, was translated into the input syntax of three mainstream model checkers: SMV [3], Spin [12] and Murphi [7]. No translation tool was built, but the translations were done by hand in a systematic way amenable to automation. The analysis identified several flaws in the model that were not identified during testing. Out of the three model checkers used, SMV allowed the most direct translation and was by far the fastest: 0.05 seconds vs. approx. 30 seconds for Spin or Murphi. The good performance of SMV can be attributed to similar factors as for Livingstone models: easy translation of declarative constraints and large loosely coupled models. Planner models also contain timing information that was ignored here since untimed model checkers were used.

In a continuing effort, Khatib [10, 11] is exploring the translation of HSTS models to UPPAAL [13]. UPPAAL is a real-time model checker, and is therefore able to deal with the timing aspects of HSTS models. UPPAAL has been used successfully to verify properties on a timed version of the same robot model as used in the earlier experiments.

11.8 Conclusions

Our MPL to SMV translator will allow Livingstone-based application developers to take their MPL model, specify desired properties in a natural extension of their familiar MPL syntax, use SMV to check them and get the results in terms of their MPL model, without reading or writing a single line of SMV code. This kind of separation is an important step towards a wider adoption of verification methods and tools by the software design community.

SMV seems to be very appropriate for certifying Livingstone models for several reasons. First of all, the Livingstone and SMV execution models have a lot in common; they are both based on conditions on finite-range variables and synchronous transitions. Second, the BDD-based symbolic model checking is very efficient for such synchronous systems and appears to fit well to the loosely constrained behaviors captured by Livingstone models. Due to this good match and to the high level of abstraction already achieved by the Livingstone models themselves, it is possible to perform an exhaustive analysis of a direct translation of those models, even for fairly complex models. Although SMV has been pushed to its limits a couple of times, recent improvements such as variable elimination, or new avenues such as SAT-based model checking, will allow us to push those limits even further. In contrast, more conventional software model checking applications almost always require some abstraction and simplification stage to make the model amenable to model checking.

This work shows that verification of Livingstone models can be a useful tool for improving the development of Livingstone-based applications.

It is, however, only one piece in the larger problem of building and validating autonomous applications. It cannot establish that the Livingstone mode identification will properly identify a situation (though it can establish that there is not enough information to do it). Neither does it address the interaction of Livingstone with other parts of the system, including real hardware with hard timing issues. Other complementary approaches are needed. In this line of work, we are currently prototyping an analytic testing approach based on a controlled execution of an instrumented version of the real Livingstone program in a simulated environment.

References

1. Berard, B., Bidoit, M., Finkel, A., Laroussinie, F., Petit, A., Petrucci, L. and Schnoebelen, Ph. *Systems and Software Verification: Model-Checking Techniques and Tools*, Springer. 2001.
2. Bryant, R. E. Graph-based algorithms for boolean function manipulation. *IEEE Transactions on Computers*, **C-35**(8), 1986.
3. Burch, J. R., Clarke, E. M., McMillan, K. L., Dill, D. L. and Hwang, J. Symbolic model checking: 10^{20} states and beyond. *Information and Computation*, **98**(2):142-170, June 1992.
4. Cimatti, A., Clarke, E., Giunchiglia, F. and Roveri, M. NuSMV: a new symbolic model verifier. In *Proceedings of International Conference on Computer-Aided Verification*, 1999.
5. Clancy, D., Larson, W., Pecheur, C., Engrand, P. and Goodrich, C. *Autonomous Control of an In-Situ Propellant Production Plant*. Technology 2009 Conference, Miami, November 1999.
6. Clarke, E. M., Grumberg, O. and Peled, D. *Model Checking*, MIT Press. 1999.
7. Dill, D. L., Drexler, A. J., Hu, A. J. and Yang, C. H. Protocol Verification as a Hardware Design Aid. In *1992 IEEE International Conference on Computer Design: VLSI in Computers and Processors*, IEEE Computer Society, 1992, pp 522-525.
8. Engrand, P. Model checking autonomy models for a martian propellant production plan. In *Proceedings of the AAAI Symposium on Model-Based Validation of Intelligence*, March 2001.
9. Gross, A. R., Sridhar, K. R., Larson, W. E., Clancy, D. J., Pecheur, C. and Briggs, G. A. Information Technology and Control Needs for In-Situ Resource Utilization. In *Proceedings of the 50th IAF Congress*, Amsterdam, Holland, October 1999.
10. Khatib, L., Muscettola, N. and Havelund, K. Verification of plan models using UPPAAL. In *Proceedings of First Goddard Workshop on Formal Approaches to Agent-Based Systems, (LNAI 1871)*, Springer-Verlag, April 2000.
11. Khatib, L., Muscettola, N. and Havelund, K. Mapping temporal planning constraints into timed automata. In *Eighth International Symposium on Temporal Representation and Reasoning, TIME-01*, IEEE Computer Society, June 2001.
12. Holzmann, G. J. The Model Checker SPIN. *IEEE Transactions on Software Engineering*, **23**(5), May 1997.

13. Larsen, K. G., Pettersson, P. and Yi, W. UPPAAL in a Nutshell. In *Springer International Journal of Software Tools for Technology Transfer 1(1+2)*, 1997.
14. Muscettola, N. HSTS: Integrating planning and scheduling. In *Intelligent Scheduling*, M. Fox and M. Zweben, editors. Morgan Kaufmann. 1994.
15. Muscettola, N., Nayak, P. P., Pell, B. and Williams, B. Remote Agent: To Boldly Go Where No AI System Has Gone Before. *Artificial Intelligence*, **103**(1-2):5-48, August 1998.
16. Nayak, P. P. et al. Validating the DS1 Remote Agent Experiment. In *Proceedings of the 5th International Symposium on Artificial Intelligence, Robotics and Automation in Space (iSAIRAS-99)*, ESTEC, Noordwijk, 1999.
17. Pell, B., Bernard, D. E., Chien, S. A., Gat, E., Muscettola, N., Nayak, P. P., Wagner, M. and Williams, B. C. An Autonomous Spacecraft Agent Prototype. *Autonomous Robots*, **5**(1), March 1998.
18. Penix, J., Pecheur, C., Havelund, K. Using Model Checking to Validate AI Planner Domain Models. In *Proceedings of the 23rd Annual Software Engineering Workshop*, NASA Goddard, December 1998.
19. Simmons, R. G., Goodwin, R., Haigh, K. Z., Koenig, S., O'Sullivan, J. and Veloso, M. M. Xavier: Experience with a layered robot architecture. *Intelligence*, 2001.
20. Simmons, R. and Pecheur, C. Automating Model Checking for Autonomous Systems. *AAAI Spring Symposium on Real-Time Autonomous Systems*, March 2000.
21. Williams, B. C. and Nayak, P. P. A Model-Based Approach to Reactive Self-Configuring Systems. In *Proceedings of AAAI-96*, 1996.
22. Yang, B., Simmons, R., Bryant, R. and O'Hallaron, D. Optimizing symbolic model checking for invariant-rich models. In *Proceedings of International Conference on Computer-Aided Verification*, 1999.

A

Walking And-Or Graphs in Linear Time

Tim Menzies and Ying Hu

The function walk shown below returns a list of nodes reachable across some and-or graph g from supplied inputs ins. Walk assumes that the graph does not contain *nogoods*.

```
STRUCT node {
     type      : one OF {and,or}
     parents   : list OF node
     kids      : list OF node
     waiting   : integer
}

FUNCTION walk(g: list of node, ins: list of node):
                list OF node {
     LOCAL v,k: node,
           out,todo: list OF node;
     FOR v ∈ g {v.waiting ← {IF v.type=="and" THEN |v.parents|
                ELSE 1 }}
     out ← ins
     todo ← ins
     WHILE (v ← pop(todo)) {
          out ← push(out,v)
          FOR k ∈ v.kids {
               k.waiting--
               IF k.waiting==0 THEN {todo ← push(todo,k)}
          }
     }
     RETURN out
}
```

On each visit to a node k, a waiting counter is decremented. When that counter goes to zero, then the algorithm has visited enough parents v to permit a visit to the child. That child node is then added to a todo stack so that its children can be explored at subsequent iteration.

Note that *all* the parents of an and-node must be visited before visiting the and-node while only *one* parent of and or-node need be visited before we can visit and or-node. To implement this, and-nodes have their waiting initialized to the number of parents while or-nodes have their waiting set to one.

Each node k is visited, at maximum, once for each parent of that node v. Hence, the algorithm's time complexity is $O(N)$ where N is the number of nodes in the graph.

Index